Atheism's New Clothes is a unique introduction t‹ ... Glass insightfully presents a wide range of cutting-edge tnemes ... New Atheists, and he both carefully analyzes and fairly assesses their arguments. In doing so, he not only draws on the work of leading theistic philosophers of religion, but he builds a solid case for Christian theism as rationally sound, evidentially supportable, explanatorily powerful, and existentially relevant.
Paul Copan, Professor and Pledger Family Chair of Philosophy and Ethics, Palm Beach Atlantic University, West Palm Beach, Florida; author of True for You, But Not for Me *and* Is God a Moral Monster?

This is the essential one-volume rebuttal of the New Atheists. David Glass carefully examines their arguments and offers comprehensive answers. Because it covers so much ground and is written in a clear and accessible style, this book deserves to be read by everyone who has been challenged by Dawkins, Hitchens and the other polemicists against religion.
James Hannam, author of God's Philosophers

The New Atheists assert that belief in God, and particularly in the revealed God of Christianity, is illogical and (unlike science) not based on evidence. In this book, David Glass argues cogently that Christian faith is very much underpinned by sound evidence and it is the New Atheists who display a tendency to ignore evidence, once outside their immediate spheres of expertise. Those who feel threatened by the strident, and at times arrogant, tones of the New Atheists will find much here to support them in giving reasons for the hope that is in them.
Alan Hibbert, Emeritus Professor of Applied Mathematics, Queen's University Belfast

David Glass gives a sustained, measured, and carefully reasoned but ultimately devastating critique of the arguments and rhetoric of the present day cult of new atheism - a real joy to read.
Rodney D. Holder, Course Director, The Faraday Institute, St Edmund's College, Cambridge; author of God, the Multiverse, and Everything

In this lucid and engaging book, David Glass explores the Achilles heel of the arguments of the New Atheists, the supposition that the phenomena of the physical and living world are – at least in principle – explicable in exclusively materialist terms. On the contrary, the most recent developments in our understanding of the cosmos and the workings of the mind would suggest the great metaphysical questions of reason and purpose are as compelling as ever. A timely and fascinating book.
James Le Fanu, historian of science and medicine, social commentator, columnist for the Daily Telegraph; *author of* Why Us?

With consummate analytical skill and scrupulous fairness, David Glass demonstrates that the emperors of the New Atheism have no clothes. This book, which is both scientifically and philosophically informed, is a must-read addition to the growing literature on the science–religion debate and the intellectual defence of Christianity.

John Lennox, Professor of Mathematics, University of Oxford; author of Gunning for God *and* God's Undertaker

The New Atheists are certainly vocal, but are they also reasonable? In this remarkably accessible book, David Glass exposes their frequent failure to understand what they attack, meticulously assesses their arguments, and then goes beyond critique to present a many-sided positive case – scientific, historical, and philosophical – for Christian theism. No other work on this subject combines such wide scope with such consistently high quality.

Timothy McGrew, Professor of Philosophy, Western Michigan University; Director, The Library of Historical Apologetics

For too long, atheists have been trying to claim the intellectual high ground and dismiss the credibility of Christianity. David Glass has provided a comprehensive and coherent rebuttal of the claims of the new breed of atheists. Well-researched and engagingly written, his analysis blends academic rigour with wider accessibility. The pretentious bluster of many of Christianity's critics is exposed for what it is and a thoughtful and clear presentation of the grounds for Christian faith explained. A helpful description of the nature of faith, engaging with some of the great theologians and philosophers, provides a balanced approach to using evidence in religious thought. Glass provides exemplary use of the hard sciences and historical studies to show how faith can integrate evidence in a coherent way. Not only a contribution to academic thought, this is an excellent aide to contemporary apologetics.

Chris Sinkinson, Moorlands College; author of Confident Christianity

This book represents Christian apologetics at its finest. David Glass's grasp of the material is both broad and deep and very impressive; there is no aspect of the New Atheism which is left unexamined. Whilst always fair to his opponents we are treated to a *tour de force* which is second to none. This is a clear, accessible, well-reasoned critique of Dawkins, Hitchens, Dennett, Harris *et al.* and a positive presentation of the credibility of the Christian faith.

Melvin Tinker, Vicar of St John Newland, Hull; author of Reclaiming Genesis

Glass clearly and comprehensively deconstructs the arguments, assertions and attitudes of the New Atheism whilst building a robust positive case for Christian theism.

Peter S. Williams, author of A Sceptic's Guide to Atheism *and* The Case for God

DAVID H. GLASS

ATHEISM'S NEW CLOTHES

EXPLORING AND EXPOSING THE
CLAIMS OF THE NEW ATHEISTS

APOLLOS (an imprint of Inter-Varsity Press)
Norton Street, Nottingham NG7 3HR, England
Email: ivp@ivpbooks.com
Website: www.ivpbooks.com

First published 2012

British Library Cataloguing in Publication Data
A catalogue record for this book is available from the British Library.

ISBN: 978-1-84474-571-5

Set in Monotype Garamond 11/13pt
Typeset in Great Britain by Servis Filmsetting Ltd, Stockport, Cheshire
Printed and bound in Great Britain by the MPG Books Group

Inter-Varsity Press publishes Christian books that are true to the Bible and that communicate the gospel, develop discipleship and strengthen the church for its mission in the world.

Inter-Varsity Press is closely linked with the Universities and Colleges Christian Fellowship, a student movement connecting Christian Unions in universities and colleges throughout Great Britain, and a member movement of the International Fellowship of Evangelical Students. Website: www.uccf.org.uk.

To my parents,
for their love, support and prayers

CONTENTS

PREFACE

The emergence of a new version of atheism in recent years represents a watershed in public discourse about belief in God. With the publication of best-selling books by Richard Dawkins, Daniel Dennett, Sam Harris and Christopher Hitchens in the years 2004 to 2007, the New Atheism was born.[1] Whatever one makes of their views about religious belief, there is no doubt that they have generated enormous interest in the question of God's existence. For many people, belief in God is not a topic for discussion and certainly not for debate; it is simply a matter for the individual conscience. Not so with the New Atheists. For them the question of God's existence is far too important to be ignored.

A central feature of the New Atheism is its uncompromising attitude towards religious belief. According to the New Atheists, belief in God is a delusion because it is based on faith rather than evidence and because science has removed the need for God. They also think it is a dangerous delusion because it is responsible for much of the suffering throughout the world. These characteristics of the New Atheism distinguish it from other forms

---

1. Sadly Christopher Hitchens died on 15 December 2011 while this book was in production. Many will miss him irrespective of whether they agreed with his views or not.

of atheism. There are many atheistic writers who are also concerned to argue against the existence of God, but they do not think that religious believers are necessarily irrational or delusional. Similarly, while other authors draw attention to suffering caused by religion, the New Atheists take these concerns to a new level, envisioning a future where religion has been so marginalized that it no longer has any role to play in public life. Much of their rhetoric and ridicule of religious belief can be seen as a means to achieving that end.

When I first came across the New Atheists, I was bewildered by their portrayal of Christian belief. Of course, legitimate criticisms can and should be made against some of the things done in the name of Christianity, but overall their account of Christianity is completely at odds with my own experience. For example, consider their claim that having faith is incompatible with reason, evidence and science. In my own case nothing could be further from the truth. Had I not thought a lot about evidence and reasons for Christianity and how it relates to science, I'm not sure I would have had any faith at all. Let me try to explain.

I recall starting to question my beliefs as a teenager. How could I know that what I had been taught was true? Could I just take other people's word for it? Or could I somehow work things out for myself? Now, I don't want to give the wrong impression; I wasn't about to become a sceptic and, if truth be told, I was much too interested in sport to worry about these kinds of questions seriously, but they were there in the background. My questions seemed to be particularly relevant in two areas that were of interest to me: Christianity and science. My discovery that a lot had been written about how we acquire knowledge sparked a long-term interest in these issues. Looking back I must admit that some of the views I adopted were quite naive, but hopefully my views have improved over time. Like many people in the modern world, I had a vague sense that science and Christianity were somehow in conflict, but the more I studied, the more I came to the conclusion that just the opposite was true. I found that belief in God provided a foundation for science and science itself provided some of the most striking reasons for believing in God.

One of the things I find particularly disappointing about the New Atheists is their failure to take philosophical arguments about the existence of God seriously. Many of their objections to belief in God are very naive from a philosophical point of view, as many of their fellow atheists are quick to point out. Ironically, not only do the New Atheists fail to engage seriously with the best arguments of theist philosophers, but they even fail to draw upon the best arguments of atheist philosophers. They seem to think they can ignore philosophical issues by appealing to science instead, but this is seriously mistaken. Whether it is acknowledged or not, anyone claiming that science has removed the need for God has moved well beyond the realm of science itself and is doing philosophy.

Interestingly, science itself raises all sorts of philosophical questions. For example, research on the foundations of quantum mechanics raises philosophical as well as scientific issues, and there is no simple way to separate the two. The same applies to research on consciousness, the foundations of probability, and understanding scientific concepts such as explanation, evidence and inference. On a wide range of topics, scientists cannot ignore philosophical questions and philosophers cannot ignore scientific questions. For this reason, most philosophers try to be scientifically informed. A philosopher who tried to explain the nature of space and time without considering Einstein would not be taken seriously. Similarly, many leading figures in science, such as Galileo, Newton, Einstein and Bohr, have been philosophically well informed. Unfortunately, this is not always the case with the New Atheists; their disregard for philosophical issues on the very topic on which they speak with most confidence – the existence of God – is a major shortcoming.

My goal in writing this book is to explore these issues and to explain why I think the New Atheists are mistaken. Many books have been written on this topic, so why another one? Some responses to the New Atheists have been primarily theological in nature; some have focused on just one of the New Atheists; some have focused on the topic of God's existence without defending any kind of revelation from God; and some have offered a negative critique without putting forward a positive case. All of these approaches have their merits, but the approach here will be to address the objections raised by the New Atheists and also to present a positive case for Christian theism by drawing on recent work by philosophers of religion. In presenting a positive case, one limitation is that it will not be possible to address objections raised by prominent atheist philosophers. The focus here is on the New Atheism, not atheism in general, and so the positive arguments offered are not intended to provide an exhaustive treatment, but to show that there is a serious case to be made.

The structure of the rest of the book is as follows. Chapter 1 provides an overview of the New Atheism and draws attention to some of the criticisms of it. Chapter 2 deals with the New Atheists' view of faith, which arguably shapes their views on all the other topics considered. Chapter 3 investigates whether there really is a conflict between science and belief in God as the New Atheists maintain. Chapters 4 and 5 challenge the view that there is no rational basis for belief in God by presenting several arguments for the existence of God. Chapter 6 demonstrates what is wrong with

Dawkins's argument that God almost certainly does not exist. This chapter is based on a paper of mine which is used by kind permission from Springer Science+Business Media: *Sophia*, 'Darwin, Design and Dawkins' Dilemma', vol. 51, 2012, pp. 31–57, David Glass, © Springer Science+Business Media B.V. 2011. The same chapter also draws on material from a book chapter of mine which is used by permission of Oxford University Press: 'Can Evidence for Design be Explained Away?', in J. Chandler and V. Harrison (eds.), *Probability in the Philosophy of Religion* (Oxford University Press, 2012), pp. 79–102. Chapter 7 explores the scientific explanations of the origins of religion offered by Dennett and Dawkins, and chapter 8 looks at the relationship between religion, morality and evil. In chapters 9 and 10 the focus is on Christianity, with the former exploring the possibility of a revelation from God and some of the New Atheists' objections to Christianity, while the latter presents a case for the historical value of the Gospels and the resurrection. Finally, chapter 11 explores the significance of these issues.

This book could not have been written without the advice and support of a great number of people. For reading and commenting on all or part of an earlier version, or for offering expert advice on key points, I would like to thank Puran Agrawal, Harry Bunting, Paul Coulter, Gillian Glass, James Glass, Robert Gordon, David Hotchen, Marie Keating, Gilbert Lennox, John Lennox, Ian McChesney, Timothy McGrew, Lydia McGrew, Richard Smith, Conor Spence and Julian Ward. For many helpful discussions about science, philosophy, theology and related topics, over many years, I would like to thank Yueping Fang, George Fleming, Frank Gourley, Jonathan Heggarty, Bill Hendren, Zhiwei Lin and Haiying Wang.

Of those who offered advice and feedback on the book, I would like to single out a few people for particular thanks. I would like to thank Mark McCartney not only for providing feedback on a number of chapters, but also for many very helpful discussions during coffee breaks, which helped me to see whether some of my ideas were worth pursuing. I am very grateful to Patrick Roche for extremely insightful and detailed feedback that proved invaluable when revising the text. I am enormously indebted to Graham Veale who has made an invaluable contribution throughout the writing of this book. Graham and I have discussed these issues for many years and he has been involved at every stage from when I first had the idea of writing a book to making the final revisions. Along the way he has helped me to think through numerous topics, has offered sound advice throughout and has provided very insightful feedback on multiple revisions of the text. I cannot thank him enough for the time and effort he has put into this project.

I was overwhelmed (in both senses of the term) by the comments and suggestions I received on an earlier version of the text. It would have been impossible both in terms of the length of the book and my own ability to do justice to all the feedback, but there is no doubt in my mind that it has resulted in a book which is much better than it would have been otherwise. I take full responsibility, of course, for all remaining problems or mistakes in the final version.

I would also like to thank Philip Duce, Senior Commissioning Editor at IVP, who has been remarkably helpful and efficient throughout the process. Given his own expertise in both science and theology, I was delighted when I discovered that he was to be the editor. I am very grateful to him for the sound advice he has given at each stage. I would also like to express my thanks to Patrick Richmond, who provided extremely helpful and detailed comments in his capacity as a reviewer. The book is much improved as a result of his insights.

I am very grateful to my friends and family for their support and prayers during the project. In particular, I want to express my deepest gratitude to my wife, Cathy, for her love, encouragement and advice throughout the project. Writing this book turned out to be much more difficult than I had anticipated. With a young family to look after, it simply would not have been possible without Cathy's enthusiastic support at every stage. She also, somehow, made time to read through many versions of the text, providing extremely valuable suggestions. I cannot possibly thank her enough. My children too will now see more of me and I hope that one day they will think my time was well spent.

David Glass
Greenisland, Co. Antrim, November 2011

For other resources related to the topics discussed in this book, please visit www.saintsandsceptics.org.

ABBREVIATIONS

BTS   Daniel Dennett, *Breaking the Spell: Religion as a Natural Phenomenon* (New York: Viking, 2006)

GNG   Christopher Hitchens, *God Is Not Great: The Case Against Religion* (London: Atlantic, 2007)

TEF   Sam Harris, *The End of Faith: Religion, Terror, and the Future of Reason* (London: Free Press, 2006)

TGD   Richard Dawkins, *The God Delusion* (London: Bantam, 2006)

tr.   translated by

1. A NEW KIND OF ATHEISM

A new Enlightenment

'We are in need of a renewed Enlightenment' writes Christopher Hitchens in the final chapter of his bestselling book *God Is Not Great*.[1] In his closing sentence he states, 'To clear the mind for this project, it has become necessary to know the enemy, and to prepare to fight it.'[2] The enemy is religion, which, he tells us, 'poisons everything'.[3] We can be grateful that he is not calling on his fellow atheists to take up arms, but to participate in an intellectual and cultural project to marginalize religious belief. Why the antagonism towards religion? The rest of his final chapter identifies at least two main answers to this question. First, religion is dangerous. While discussing the aspirations of President Ahmadinejad for Iran to become a nuclear power, Hitchens comments, 'This puts the confrontation between faith and civilization on a whole new footing,'[4] and he then goes on to discuss the role of religion in the terrible atrocities of 9/11. The second answer is that religious belief is no longer tenable in the light of modern science. He expresses this point as follows: 'Religion has run out of justifications. Thanks to the telescope and the microscope, it no longer offers an explanation of anything important.'[5] How exactly this is supposed to follow from the existence of the telescope and microscope is not immediately obvious, but throughout the closing chapter and in the rest of his book Hitchens is adamant that there is a conflict between science and religion, a conflict with only one winner. Indeed, science has such a central role to play in the new Enlightenment that it almost seems to take the place of religion since it 'offers the promise of near-miraculous advances in healing, in energy, and in the peaceful exchange between different cultures'.[6]

Hitchens's closing chapter provides a summary not only of his own book, which was published in 2007, but also a fairly accurate summary of books published by Richard Dawkins, Daniel Dennett and Sam Harris in the preceding few years.[7] In addition to their content, other factors linking these books are their enormous success in terms of sales and their impact in promoting debate about the existence of God and the place of religion in the modern world. As well as formal debates, there have been many reviews in magazines and journals, a substantial number of book-length responses, numerous TV and radio interviews, and seemingly endless online discussions about their ideas. Their provocative claims about belief in God are such that readers tend to fall into one of two categories, enthusiastic supporters or ardent opponents, with very few lying anywhere in between. In fact, the distinctive nature of the atheism on offer is such that it has become known as the 'New Atheism'.[8] Although other atheistic writers such as Victor Stenger and Michel Onfray could also be described as New Atheists, there is little doubt that Dawkins, Dennett, Harris and Hitchens are the leading figures in this movement and so the focus here will be on their recent books on religion.[9]

But what exactly is so distinctive about the New Atheism? And why has it been so successful? What are its goals, tactics and main arguments? What have the critics had to say? And, given that there have been so many responses to the New Atheists, what is the aim of this particular book? These questions provide the focus for the rest of this chapter.

What is the New Atheism?

There are a number of prominent themes in the writings of the New Atheists. Of course, there are differences as well as similarities between them and so not every point mentioned here will be found in all of their books, but there are certainly common ideas that are characteristic of the New Atheism in general. One of the most important aspects of the New Atheism is that it promotes a rejection of belief in God on scientific grounds with particular prominence given to Darwinism. This is despite the fact that arguments for and against God's existence lie within the domain of philosophy rather than science. So although scientists are quite entitled to offer arguments for or against God's existence, it must be recognized that when they do so they are engaging in philosophy, not science.

It must also be emphasized that many leading atheistic thinkers, both past and present, have seen the need to scrutinize the arguments for God's existence in great detail. Not so the New Atheists. They seem to think that this is unnecessary and that by appealing to science they can circumvent this process. There is very little attempt to engage seriously with any recent philosophical work on the topic of God's existence. In fact, they do not even draw on the best arguments by atheistic philosophers, never mind coming to terms with detailed arguments by theistic philosophers. The most detailed discussion of traditional arguments for God's existence is found in chapter 3 of Dawkins's *The God Delusion*, but it is arguably the weakest part of his book, as some of his critics have pointed out.[10]

Daniel Dennett is a philosopher, but even he does not wish to engage in the traditional kinds of debates about God's existence. He writes, 'I decided some time ago that diminishing returns had set in on the arguments about God's existence, and I doubt that any breakthroughs are in the offing, from either side.'[11] Despite this moderate statement, his discussion of the arguments for God's existence is even briefer than Dawkins's and just as dismissive. Admittedly, the focus of Dennett's book lies elsewhere, but it highlights a shortcoming in the New Atheist books, especially in the light of their confident rejection of God's existence. For reasons that will become clear in due course, it seems to me that this is a deliberate strategy on their part.

The problem with their approach of basing their atheism on science rather than philosophy is that whether science leads to atheism, as they claim, is a philosophical question, not a scientific one. And this means that whether their atheism should be taken seriously depends on how good their arguments are. As we shall see in later chapters, there are plenty of reasons to doubt their assertion that science removes the need for God. In fairness to Dawkins, he has gone well beyond the other New Atheists in proposing a new argument against the existence of God. Ironically, it turns out to be essentially an updated version of an argument proposed by the eighteenth-century philosopher David Hume, and so does not depend on modern science in a significant way. This argument will be considered in detail in chapter 6.

A further way in which the New Atheism is based on science is that it offers a scientific explanation for religious belief. Just as Darwinism is supposed to play a key role in removing the need for God, so it provides the context in which a naturalistic explanation of religious belief is proposed. Both Dawkins and Hitchens include a chapter on the origins of religion, but the main contribution comes from Dennett, whose entire book concentrates on this topic. In fact, Dennett's book is quite different both in content and style from the other New Atheist books being considered here. Nevertheless, his argument plays an important role in the New Atheism. Dennett does not claim that a scientific explanation of religion disproves the existence of God, but it seems clear that its contribution to the New Atheism is to provide a means of explaining away the need for God to account for religious belief and practice. This topic will be explored in chapter 7.

Another important dimension of the New Atheism is that belief in God is viewed not merely as mistaken, but as irrational and delusional. The reason for such a negative assessment is linked to their rejection of God on scientific grounds. There is no evidence, we are told, for God's existence, and so belief that he exists must be irrational. In fact, they claim that faith, by definition, is irrational since it is belief without evidence. Harris opines:

> We have names for people who have many beliefs for which there is no rational justification. When their beliefs are extremely common we call them 'religious'; otherwise, they are likely to be called 'mad', 'psychotic', or 'delusional'.[12]

Similarly, Dawkins claims that 'God, in the sense defined, is a delusion; and, as later chapters will show, a pernicious delusion.'[13] Given this conviction, it is not too surprising that the New Atheists frequently adopt the tactic of ridiculing religious belief. After all, if no rational person could believe in God, what is the point in engaging in serious debate? Wouldn't ridicule be more appropriate and perhaps more effective?

One of the most obvious examples of the use of ridicule is found in Dawkins's discussion of agnosticism, where he states, 'I am agnostic only to the extent that I am agnostic about fairies at the bottom of the garden.'[14] He then approvingly quotes other authors who put God in the same category as the Tooth Fairy, Mother Goose, an invisible, intangible, inaudible unicorn, and the now famous Flying Spaghetti Monster.[15] There are two aspects to this. One is the argument Dawkins is making. The argument is that there is no way of disproving the existence of any of these entities because you cannot prove a negative. But, of course, that does not mean we should be neutral about them; since there is no reason at all for believing that they exist, we should assume that they do not. As an argument against the existence of God this is completely hopeless. Why? Because it simply *assumes* that there is no reason for believing in God, which is precisely what is in dispute in the first place. Of course, Dawkins is entitled to *argue* that there is no reason for believing in God and later in the book he tries to do just that, but in linking God with these other entities he seems to be claiming that it is *obvious* that there is no reason for believing in God. And this just isn't obvious at all. In fact, it is not obvious to many atheists who take the arguments for believing in God's existence much more seriously than does Dawkins. They reach the conclusion that there is no God, but they don't think this conclusion is obvious.

So much for the argument, but what about the second aspect to this comparison with the Tooth Fairy, and so on? As a way of ridiculing belief in God it is very effective. Once the comparison has been made, especially by intelligent people such as the New Atheists, it tends to stick in the mind. As an argument it might be hopeless, but if it is repeated often enough an association is made that influences how people view the debate. How ridiculous it would be for someone to offer sophisticated reasons for believing in the Tooth Fairy? For anyone who makes the mental association offered by Dawkins, however ill-founded it is, it becomes very easy to dismiss, without consideration, any reasons offered for belief in God. Of course, this applies not just to belief in God, but any kind of belief. If I can get an association between your favoured political party and the Taliban, for example, into your mind, arguments become unnecessary.

Of the points mentioned so far, there is nothing completely new in the writings of the New Atheists. Many atheists such as Bertrand Russell and Jacques Monod have drawn on science to defend their atheism, others such as Sigmund Freud and Karl Marx have offered naturalistic explanations for religious belief, and many such as H. L. Mencken have ridiculed religion. So what is new about the New Atheism? And why has it been so successful? No doubt its success is due in part to the readability of their books and perhaps also the extent to which they include the various elements noted, but the political and cultural climate in which they write is almost certainly a key factor.

Consider one of their central themes: that religion is dangerous. As we have already seen, Hitchens draws attention to the events of 9/11 and he has much more to say about the evils of religion, not least in a chapter entitled 'Religion Kills'. On the first page of his book *The God Delusion* Dawkins asks us to imagine a world with no religion, a world with 'no suicide bombers, no 9/11, no 7/7, no Crusades, no witch-hunts',[16] just to mention the first five on his list. He also devotes several chapters to the evils of religion. Harris commences his book *The End of Faith* with a story about a suicide bomber and includes considerable discussion about the dangers of religion, particularly in the form of terrorism. In Dennett's *Breaking the Spell* a key motivation for studying religion scientifically is that such an approach is necessary if we are to make informed political decisions about how to deal with religion in the twenty-first century, especially given the threat from religious terrorism.

The New Atheists are certainly right that religion can play a role in heinous acts of terrorism and other evils. And, of course, many atheists in the past have pointed to such evils so as to undermine religious belief, but although this approach is certainly present in the New Atheist writings there is a clear political dimension to their books. How are we to deal with terrorism in the early twenty-first century? Given the events since 2001 this is an extremely important question, and the New Atheists provide us with an analysis of the problem as well as a solution: religion is the problem and marginalizing religion is the solution, or at least an important part of it. Harris states the problem as he sees it in the starkest of terms: 'We will see that the greatest problem facing civilization is not merely religious extremism: rather, it is the larger set of cultural and intellectual accommodations we have made to faith itself.'[17] He also refers to 'the threat that even "moderate" religious faith, however inadvertently, now poses to our survival'.[18] Dawkins bemoans the fact that in the United States Jews and evangelical Christians exert much more political clout than atheists and agnostics. One of his stated aims in his book is to bolster atheist pride and he hopes that it will help atheists to 'come out', which he thinks would be a good first step towards political influence.[19] This attitude towards religion leads to an intolerance of it. This is especially prevalent in Harris, who states that 'we can no more tolerate a diversity of religious beliefs than a diversity of beliefs about epidemiology and basic hygiene'.[20]

If the cultural and political backdrop is really the key to the success of the New Atheism, then their tactics make sense. A careful and detailed evaluation of reasons for and against belief in God would not help to further this agenda since it would require taking religious belief too seriously and might risk giving it credibility. Pitting science against religion, ridiculing belief in God and emphasizing the most extreme forms of religion, particularly with respect to religious violence, would suit such an agenda much better. If the goal is to bring about the new Enlightenment envisaged by Hitchens, where the influence of religious belief diminishes, it seems that the approach of more moderate atheists is not working. As Harris notes, 'the prospects for eradicating religion in our time do not seem good'.[21]

A more robust form of atheism is called for and that is precisely what is offered by the New Atheism. Nowhere is the contrast between the New Atheism and more moderate atheism seen more clearly than in Dennett and Dawkins's heated dispute with their fellow atheist Michael Ruse on the topic of evolution and Intelligent Design.[22] Ruse is just as opposed to intelligent design as Dennett and Dawkins, but he thinks they make a tactical mistake by linking evolution with atheism and so alienating Christians. Castigating Ruse as an appeaser like Neville Chamberlain, Dawkins makes it clear that the real war is not against Intelligent Design but against religion.

None of this should be taken to imply that the New Atheists do not offer any arguments for their position; they certainly do. Nor can we simply assume that just because they employ ridicule so effectively that their arguments are therefore invalid. We can easily dismiss, for example, the idea that belief in God is obviously mistaken just like belief in the Tooth Fairy, but this still leaves the question as to whether there are good reasons for believing in God or whether the New Atheists have managed to show that there are no such reasons. The goal in this book is to attempt to get behind their rhetoric and assess their underlying claims, but before doing this it is worth looking at some of the criticisms levelled against the New Atheists.

The emperor's new clothes

Given the nature of the New Atheists' attack on religious belief, it is not surprising that they have come in for a lot of criticism. In one of the more irenic books that discusses the New Atheism, professor of divinity at the University of Edinburgh David Fergusson writes, 'the rhetoric employed by the new atheists is often as hostile and shrill as those of the most vehement religionists . . . the recent criticism of religion is at times too rabid and disabling of patient and constructive debate'.[23] One of the key criticisms of the New Atheists by John Haught, a professor of theology at Georgetown University, is expressed as follows: 'Their understanding of religious faith remains consistently at the same unscholarly level as the unreflective, superstitious, and literalist religiosity of those they criticize.'[24] In his scathing review of Dawkins's *The God Delusion* in the *London Review of Books*, Terry Eagleton, professor of English literature at Manchester University, asks us to 'Imagine someone holding forth on biology whose only knowledge of the subject is the Book of British Birds, and you have a rough idea of what it feels like to read Richard Dawkins on theology.'[25] Eagleton later describes Dawkins as 'theologically illiterate'. Philosophy professor Michael Ruse from Florida State University, who as we have seen is an atheist, condemns the New Atheists in the strongest of terms:

> But I think first that these people do a disservice to scholarship. Their treatment of the religious viewpoint is pathetic to the point of non-being. Richard Dawkins in *The God Delusion* would fail any introductory philosophy or religion course. Proudly he criticizes that whereof he knows nothing. As I have said elsewhere, for the first time in my life, I felt sorry for the ontological argument. If we criticized gene theory with as little knowledge as Dawkins has of religion and philosophy, he would be rightly indignant. . . . Conversely, I am indignant at the poor quality of the argumentation in

Dawkins, Dennett, Hitchens, and all of the others in that group. . . . I have written elsewhere that *The God Delusion* makes me ashamed to be an atheist. Let me say that again. Let me say also that I am proud to be the focus of the invective of the new atheists. They are a bloody disaster and I want to be on the front line of those who say so.[26]

Mathematician John Lennox, who like Dawkins is a professor at Oxford University and has debated him on several occasions, is particularly critical of Dawkins's view of faith as belief without evidence:

Dawkins' idiosyncratic definition of faith thus provides a striking example of the very kind of thinking he claims to abhor – thinking that is not evidence based. For, in an exhibition of breathtaking inconsistency, evidence is the very thing he fails to supply for his claim that independence of evidence is faith's joy.[27]

As we shall see in chapter 2, Dawkins is not the only New Atheist who holds this definition of faith.

It is worth noting that the authors quoted above are not merely drawing attention to the ridicule and mockery in the writings of the New Atheists, but to their lack of understanding of the very subject they are criticizing and their poor scholarship in general. Perhaps worst of all is the charge that their approach is just like the extreme forms of religion of which they are so critical.

One response made by Dawkins is that you do not need to study up on leprechology in order to disbelieve in leprechauns.[28] A similar response, which has gained a lot of popularity in New Atheist circles, is due to P. Z. Myers, a professor of biology at the University of Minnesota and author of the popular atheist blog Pharyngula. It is known as the Courtier's Reply and is intended to follow on at the end of the fable of the emperor's new clothes. Theology is the emperor, Dawkins the little boy and theologians the courtiers. It is quoted in part below:

I have considered the impudent accusations of Mr Dawkins with exasperation at his lack of serious scholarship. He has apparently not read the detailed discourses of Count Roderigo of Seville on the exquisite and exotic leathers of the Emperor's boots, nor does he give a moment's consideration to Bellini's masterwork, *On the Luminescence of the Emperor's Feathered Hat*. We have entire schools dedicated to writing learned treatises on the beauty of the Emperor's raiment, and every major newspaper runs a section dedicated to imperial fashion; Dawkins cavalierly dismisses them all. . . . Dawkins arrogantly ignores all these deep philosophical ponderings to crudely accuse the Emperor of nudity. . . . Until Dawkins has trained in the shops of Paris and Milan, until he has learned to tell the difference between a ruffled flounce and a puffy pantaloon, we should all pretend he has not spoken out against the Emperor's taste.[29]

This is wonderful as a piece of rhetoric, but will it really do as a response? Can it be used to excuse the New Atheists' lack of knowledge of theology and their inadequate engagement with arguments for the existence of God? In an article that criticizes Dawkins's argument that God almost certainly does not exist, but defends an atheistic position, philosopher Erik Wielenberg states why he is not impressed with the Courtier's Reply. He writes:

> I do not know exactly how much theology one needs to know to disprove the existence of God, but one needs to know at least enough theology to understand the various widely-held conceptions of God. In general, in order to argue effectively against a given hypothesis, one needs to know enough to characterize that hypothesis accurately. Furthermore, if one intends to disprove God's existence, it is hardly reasonable to dismiss criticisms of one's putative disproof on the grounds that God doesn't exist anyway.[30]

Essentially, the idea behind the Courtier's Reply is that it is *obvious* (or should be to any rational person) that there is no basis for belief in God, just as it is obvious that the emperor has no clothes. But as we saw earlier in the context of Dawkins's references to the Tooth Fairy, it is not at all obvious that there is no basis for belief in God. And even if the New Atheists think otherwise, they cannot sensibly base their arguments on such an idea on pain of circularity.

As the title of this book suggests, my contention is that the situation is almost precisely the opposite of that which Myers describes. It is the New Atheism that is the emperor. The various critics, both theists and atheists, represent the little boy who points out that the emperor has no clothes. But what is the emperor to do? The ending of the original version provides the answer: 'But he thought, "This procession has got to go on." So he walked more proudly than ever, as his noblemen held high the train that wasn't there at all.'[31] Despite numerous criticisms of their arguments, there does not seem to be any recognition among the New Atheists or their followers that their arguments do not work. Admitting this would not necessarily mean conceding that atheism is false – there are plenty of atheists who do not subscribe to the New Atheism – but it isn't just about winning arguments. The New Atheism is a programme to marginalize religion and so the procession must continue, with the New Atheists walking 'more proudly than ever'.

There are a couple of key differences between Myers's version and mine. Unlike Myers I am not claiming that it is *obvious* the New Atheists' arguments are unsuccessful. It is necessary to understand their arguments properly and the objections to them before it becomes clear that this is the case. And since the New Atheism continues to find much support, those of us who think it is unsuccessful need to keep trying to show just where it goes wrong. Another difference is that Myers's view seems to presuppose that *all* versions of theism are obviously without rational basis, whereas my focus is primarily on the New Atheism rather than atheism in general.

The New Theism

When reading the New Atheists it would be easy to get the impression that there is no rational basis for belief in God's existence. They seem to think that science, particularly Darwinism, made God unnecessary a long time ago. And as science has progressed, belief in God has become increasingly untenable. According to Hitchens, belief in God belongs to a long past era when people lived in 'abysmal ignorance and fear'.[32] He claims that we shall 'never again have to confront the impressive faith of an Aquinas or a Maimonides' because 'Faith of that sort – the sort that can stand up at least for a while in a confrontation with reason – is now plainly impossible.'[33] If anyone is to believe in God these days, it could only be on the basis of a blind faith because we should be able to see the traditional reasons for believing in God 'as the feeble-minded inventions that they are'.[34]

Had the New Atheists been writing in the 1950s or 1960s, this mindset would have been understandable because at that time atheism was dominant in academia, especially in philosophical circles. But then in the late 1960s and 1970s things began to change. Christian philosophers showed that many of the reasons given for rejecting belief in God weren't nearly as persuasive as many atheists had assumed. Some, such as Alvin Plantinga, argued that just because God's existence could not be proved logically to the satisfaction of atheists, this did not mean it was irrational to believe in God. He also presented detailed arguments to show that the problem of evil did not disprove God's existence as many had thought.

Around the same time many arguments for God's existence started to make a comeback through the work of people like Richard Swinburne, who has written extensively on the subject. Swinburne's approach has not been to try to prove with certainty that God exists, but instead to show that on the basis of a whole range of features of the universe the cumulative case for

God's existence is strong. William Lane Craig is another leading figure who has presented various reasons for belief in God, most notably, an argument based on the universe having had a beginning. Many other philosophers have also been involved in making a case for the rationality of belief in God and Christian belief as well. These include William Alston, Robin Collins, Stephen Evans, John Hare, J. P. Moreland and Nicholas Wolterstorff, to name just a few.[35]

Developments in science also helped the case for theism. The evidence that the universe is expanding, which in turn provided evidence that the universe had a beginning in the big bang, presented a real problem for many atheistic scientists. Scientists also discovered that there are many features of the universe having just the right values for life to exist and such that, if any of them were slightly different, life would be impossible. This *fine-tuning* of the universe has given great impetus to design arguments.

This does not mean that theism has become dominant either amongst philosophers or scientists. It has not. But these developments have given rise to an environment where belief in God is a viewpoint that is taken very seriously and this is because there is a strong rational and evidential basis for belief in God. The New Atheists completely ignore these developments in philosophy and fail to do justice to the scientific issues. Of the philosophers mentioned above only two even get a mention in the books by the New Atheists: Plantinga in two footnotes by Dennett, and Swinburne is discussed briefly by Dawkins, who completely fails to do justice to Swinburne's arguments.

One important aspect of this book will be to draw on some of the developments in what might be called the New Theism in order to respond to the New Atheism.

A look ahead

The goal of this book is to defend Christian theism and not religious belief in general. It would obviously be utter folly to defend any and every kind of religious belief and practice, just as it would be utter folly to defend any and every kind of political party. Even if the details of the New Atheists' analysis are questionable, there is no doubt that religion is involved in many of the conflicts in the world today. Who could possibly deny such a thing? It would be very difficult in view of this fact to respond by arguing that religion in general is good and beneficial. But it is also too simplistic to say that all religion is bad and dangerous. Of course, many terrible things have been done in the name of Christianity, but again it would be too simplistic to conclude that Christianity should therefore be rejected.

Defending Christian theism will involve defending two things: Christianity in particular and theism in general. Let's start with theism. One area of strong agreement with the New Atheists is on their claim that the existence of God is a factual question. Like them, I shall not use the word 'God' as a metaphor for referring to something else such as having a sense of awe at the beauty of the universe. In fact, Dawkins's definition of the God Hypothesis – 'there exists a superhuman, supernatural intelligence who deliberately designed and created the universe and everything in it, including us'[36] – seems like a reasonable starting point. But I shall also claim that God is good and that he is the God who is revealed in Jesus Christ. My approach will be to argue for theism first and then for the truth of the central claims of Christianity. And I shall assume that these central claims are to be understood in their orthodox sense. For example, I shall take it as axiomatic that if Jesus did not rise from the dead physically, then Christianity is false. The New Atheists view such a position as both honest and indefensible. On the latter point I beg to differ. Indeed, the case for orthodox Christianity is much stronger as the result of developments in the field of biblical studies in the last few decades, as we shall see in chapter 10.

As noted in the preface, in presenting a positive case for Christian theism, one limitation is that it will not be possible to address objections raised by prominent atheist philosophers (such as Richard Gale, Michael Martin, Graham Oppy, William Rowe, J. Howard Sobel, Michael Tooley and others). The focus here is to present criticisms of the New Atheism and to show that there is a case to be made. For a more exhaustive treatment, the reader would need to look into these authors' objections and responses to them from prominent Christian philosophers such as those mentioned in the last section.[37]

Many of those who have criticized the New Atheists have objected to considering God as a hypothesis. At times the New Atheists give the impression that God is to be considered in the same way as a *scientific* hypothesis and if that is what they mean, then the objection seems completely reasonable. But it seems to me that what the New Atheists have in mind is that evidence could count either in favour or against God's existence and if this is what they mean, I fail to see any problem. Of course, Christians could not and should not view God as *merely* a hypothesis, but it does not follow that evidence is irrelevant to the question of God's existence. As we shall see, however, arguably the New Atheists adopt too narrow a view as to what should count as evidence and adopt strategies to rule out the possibility that evidence could count in favour of God's existence, but I shall assume that the general principle that evidence is relevant to the question is correct.

Before exploring evidence for Christian theism, however, a more fundamental question needs to be considered. Is *faith* incompatible with reason and evidence? The New Atheists claim that faith is one of the key problems with religious belief precisely because it involves believing things for which there is no evidence. We shall explore this topic in the next chapter.

Notes

1. Christopher Hitchens, *God Is Not Great: The Case Against Religion* (London: Atlantic, 2007). This book will be referred to as *GNG*.
2. Ibid., p. 283.
3. Ibid., p. 13.
4. Ibid., p. 280.
5. Ibid., p. 282.
6. Ibid.
7. Daniel Dennett, *Breaking the Spell: Religion as a Natural Phenomenon* (New York: Viking, 2006); Richard Dawkins, *The God Delusion* (London: Bantam, 2006); Sam Harris, *The End of Faith: Religion, Terror, and the Future of Reason* (London: Free Press, 2006). These books will be referred to as *BTS*, *TGD* and *TEF* respectively. See also Sam Harris, *Letter to a Christian Nation: A Challenge to Faith* (London: Bantam, 2007).
8. It seems the expression 'New Atheism' was coined in *WIRED* magazine. See Gary Wolf, 'The Church of the Non-Believers', *WIRED* (Nov. 2006), available at http://www.wired.com/wired/archive/14.11/atheism_pr.html (accessed 30 Oct. 2010).
9. For a discussion between the 'four horsemen' see http://richarddawkins.net/videos/2025-the-four-horsemen-available-now-on-dvd (accessed 30 Oct. 2010).
10. According to the philosopher Thomas Nagel, who is himself an atheist, 'Dawkins dismisses, with contemptuous flippancy the traditional a priori arguments for the existence of God offered by Aquinas and Anselm. I found these attempts at philosophy, along with those in a later chapter on religion and ethics, particularly weak . . .' (Thomas Nagel, 'The Fear of Religion', *The New Republic* [Oct. 2006], available at http://www.tnr.com/article/the-fear-religion [accessed 30 Oct. 2010]).
11. *BTS*, p. 27.
12. *TEF*, p. 72.
13. *TGD*, p. 31.
14. Ibid., p. 51.
15. Ibid., pp. 52–53.

16. Ibid., p. 1.

17. *TEF*, p. 45.

18. Ibid., pp. 42–43.

19. *TGD*, pp. 4–5.

20. *TEF*, p. 46. This intolerance is ironic, however, given that one of his criticisms of religion is that intolerance is intrinsic to religion (*TEF*, p. 13). On the other hand, he also takes what he calls 'moderates' to task for taking tolerance to be sacred (*TEF*, p. 22). So it is not entirely clear whether he thinks the biggest problem with religion is its intolerance or tolerance, but in either case the appropriate response from atheists is one of intolerance.

21. Harris, *Letter to a Christian Nation*, p. 87.

22. *TGD*, pp. 67–69.

23. David Fergusson, *Faith and its Critics: a Conversation* (Oxford: Oxford University Press, 2009), pp. 11–12.

24. John F. Haught, *God and the New Atheism: A Critical Response to Dawkins, Harris and Hitchens* (Louisville, Ky.: Westminster John Knox, 2008), p. xiii.

25. Terry Eagleton, 'Lunging, Flailing, Mispunching', *London Review of Books*, 19 Oct. 2006, pp. 32–34.

26. From the blog Science and the Sacred, http://blog.beliefnet.com/ scienceandthesacred/2009/08/why-i-think-the-new-atheists-are-a-bloody-disaster. html (accessed 30 Oct. 2010).

27. John C. Lennox, *God's Undertaker: Has Science Buried God?* (Oxford: Lion Hudson, 2007), p. 16.

28. See Dawkins's website, http://richarddawkins.net/articles/1647?page=27 (accessed 30 Oct. 2010).

29. From Myers's blog, Pharyngula, http://scienceblogs.com/pharyngula/2006/12/ the_courtiers_reply.php (accessed 30 Oct. 2010).

30. Erik Wielenberg, 'Dawkins's Gambit, Hume's Aroma, and God's Simplicity', *Philosophia Christi* 11 (2009), pp. 113–128.

31. Hans Christian Andersen, *The Emperor's New Clothes* (first published 1837), available at http://www.andersen.sdu.dk/vaerk/hersholt/TheEmperorsNewClothes_e. html?oph=1 (accessed 17 Nov. 2011).

32. *GNG*, p. 64.

33. Ibid., p. 63.

34. Ibid., 71.

35. For an introductory overview of these developments see William Lane Craig, 'God Is Not Dead Yet: How Current Philosophers Argue for his Existence', available at http://www.christianitytoday.com/ct/2008/july/13.22.html (accessed 10 Nov. 2011).

36. *TGD*, p. 31.

37. For a recent collection of articles from an atheistic perspective see Michael Martin (ed.), *The Cambridge Companion to Atheism* (Cambridge: Cambridge University Press, 2006); and from a theistic perspective see William Lane Craig and J. P. Moreland (eds.), *The Blackwell Companion to Natural Theology* (Chichester: Wiley-Blackwell, 2009).

2. IS FAITH IRRATIONAL?

According to the New Atheists, the basic problem with religion can be summed up in one word: faith. In fact, as we shall see, many of the problems with religion are claimed to result from faith. Not surprisingly, faith is an extremely important concept in many religions, not least in Christianity where it is a virtue to be sought after and developed rather than a vice to be shunned. Given such a fundamental disagreement, one wonders whether the New Atheists and Christian believers can really be talking about the same concept at all. To investigate the possibility that the disagreement is the result of a misunderstanding we need to ask the question 'What is faith?'

Christian thinkers have written at enormous length about the nature of faith. Is faith to be understood in an intellectual way, as knowledge of some sort? Or is it instead more about trusting someone, like having faith in a friend? How does faith relate to reason? Are they complementary to, or in conflict with, each other? If Christian writers have struggled to articulate the precise nature of faith, the New Atheists have had no such problem. For them the answer is extremely straightforward. So straightforward, in fact, that they see no need to interact with any Christian thinkers on the subject. Faith, according to the New Atheists, is believing something without evidence. In the words of Mark Twain, 'faith is believing what you know ain't so'.

Dawkins provides a dictionary definition of a delusion as 'a persistent false belief held in the face of strong contradictory evidence, especially as a symptom of psychiatric disorder' and adds that 'the first part captures religious faith perfectly'.[1] Later in the book he claims that 'faith is an evil precisely because it requires no justification and brooks no argument'.[2] In similar vein, Harris, while discussing religion, asks, 'How is it that, in this one area of our lives, we have convinced ourselves that our beliefs about the world can float entirely free of reason and evidence?',[3] and goes on to describe religious faith as 'the idea that belief can be sanctified by something other than *evidence*'.[4] Dennett endorses Dawkins's idea that faith is a meme that discourages rational inquiry, enabling incoherent and incomprehensible religious beliefs to be accepted.[5] Dennett even introduces us to an imaginary character, Professor Faith, to make his point.[6] Hitchens sees true faith as *belief without evidence* but, recognizing the arguments that have been offered to support religious beliefs, he claims that religion 'corrupts faith and insults reason by offering evidence and pointing to confected "proofs"'.[7]

Before investigating whether this characterization of faith is accurate, it is worth exploring its importance within the writings of the New Atheists.

Faith, evidence and irrationality

The consensus among the New Atheists is that faith is not only mistaken, but irrational. Their line of reasoning seems to be as follows: rational people form their beliefs on the basis of the evidence; faith involves believing something without evidence; therefore, faith is irrational. The claim that rational people form their beliefs on the basis of the evidence seems highly plausible. However, even this would need to be qualified in certain ways. For example, it would be important to ask what counts as evidence. Is it only evidence that would be suitable in a scientific context? Presumably not, for rational people form beliefs every day on the basis of what their friends tell them. Indeed, arguably the majority of the beliefs we form every day are not the result of weighing up evidence at all, but again this does not mean that our beliefs are irrational. Nevertheless, I shall let this pass for the moment. Whatever qualifications might be involved, it is still correct to say that rational people should take the relevant evidence into account. But this being the case, it seems clear that the New Atheists think faith is irrational precisely because it is not based on evidence.

We have already seen that Dawkins's remarkably strong claim about religious faith being delusional is based on his view that faith is *belief without evidence*. The claim is not so much based on an argument as a definition. To emphasize the point he asserts that 'dyed-in-the-wool faith-heads are immune to argument'.[8] Arguably, Harris has an even more negative view of faith. In a section entitled 'Faith and Madness' he writes, 'The danger of religious faith is that it allows otherwise normal human beings to reap the fruits of madness and consider them *holy*.'[9] Elsewhere he states, 'The only demons we must fear are those that lurk inside every human mind: ignorance, hatred, greed, and *faith*, which is surely the devil's masterpiece.'[10]

And what is the nature of this faith? It is 'simply *unjustified* belief in matters of ultimate concern'.[11] Again, the logic seems clear: the problem with faith is that it involves belief without evidence.

It is worth pointing out something that should be obvious to us, but that could easily be overlooked in the light of the New Atheists' claims. It is simply that atheists need not hold the view that religious belief is irrational or delusional. In fact, many atheists consider religious beliefs to be mistaken, but not necessarily irrational. For example, prominent atheistic philosophers such as Richard Gale, William Rowe and Graham Oppy, who have assessed the evidence and arguments for and against belief in God as fairly as possible, recognize that people could disagree with them without being irrational. The New Atheists, by contrast, are effectively *defining* faith to be irrational and so, given this approach, we might wonder how objective they will be in dealing with the evidence and arguments for theism. After all, if faith is irrational, is there any need to take the arguments of the faithful seriously? In later chapters we shall see that there is indeed a problem with how the New Atheists handle evidence.

The New Atheists also claim that science and faith are irreconcilable. Hitchens, for example, assures us that 'all attempts to reconcile faith with science and reason are consigned to failure and ridicule'.[12] Now this view seems highly implausible since there are many scientists with strong religious beliefs. But if faith is belief without evidence, it seems to follow that conflict with science is inevitable since an important component of science is the evaluation of theories on the basis of relevant evidence. The problem for the New Atheists is to explain how serious scientists can be serious believers as well.

Harris's answer is that they simply fail to think about the conflicting parts of their lives: 'A person can be a God-fearing Christian on Sunday and a working scientist come Monday morning, without ever having to account for the partition that seems to have erected itself in his head while he slept.'[13] This explanation really won't do, however. Even if one disagrees with the views of writers such as Sir John Polkinghorne, a former professor of mathematical physics at Cambridge University who is now an Anglican priest, or Francis Collins, a geneticist who led the Human Genome Project and is now director of the National Institutes of Health in the US, it is obvious that they have thought hard about the relationship between their science and their faith. In fact, a very good case can be made for saying that many religious scientific writers do a much better job of integrating their faith with science than the New Atheists' attempts to integrate their atheism with science. But irrespective of what one thinks of such writers, the idea that they just mentally partition their religious and scientific beliefs is obviously false.

Dawkins's attempt is even worse. He claims that scientists who hold to orthodox Christian beliefs 'stand out for their rarity and are a subject of amused bafflement to their peers in the academic community'.[14] A survey by Larson and Witham in 1996 showed that the attitude of scientists to belief in a personal God was more or less the same as that of scientists surveyed in 1914 (39.6% believed in such a God, 45.5% did not and 14.9% were unsure compared with 41.8%, 41.5% and 16.7% respectively in 1914).[15] Given Dawkins's viewpoint, one might have expected that the wide-ranging developments in twentieth-century science would have resulted in a loss of faith, but this is not supported by the best evidence. So it seems that belief in God is not particularly rare and presumably at least 40% of scientists do not share Dawkins's bafflement!

It is true that in a later survey in 1998 Larson and Witham found that among scientists in the National Academy of Sciences in the United States only 7.0% believed in a personal God, while 72.2% did not, compared with 27.7% and 52.7% respectively in corresponding data from a survey of leading scientists in 1914.[16] What are we to make of these statistics? First of all, Dawkins discusses this topic in the context of arguments for the existence of God in a section entitled 'The Argument from Admired Religious Scientists'. Now, of course, if it is claimed that the existence of admired religious scientists constitutes good evidence for the existence of God, then Dawkins would be quite right to demur. Such an argument would be very weak indeed, but can Dawkins name any significant theologian or philosopher who proposes this as a serious argument? There are interesting questions to ask about the origins of modern science and the motivations of some of its pioneering figures, but simply to point to the views of leading scientists or statistics about such views as evidence for or against God's existence is surely mistaken.

So, as far as arguments for the existence of God are concerned, Dawkins is simply attacking a straw man. As we have seen, Dawkins's claim that belief in God is rare among scientists is not borne out by the statistics. He does, however, make the claim that 'American scientists are less religious than the American public generally, and that the most distinguished scientists are the least religious of all.'[17] This may well be correct, but what follows from it? That this is evidence against the existence of God? Or evidence that traditional religious beliefs are incompatible with science? Astonishingly, having identified the fallacy in the argument for God's existence from admired religious scientists, Dawkins seems to commit the very same fallacy in arguing *against* God's existence from admired *non-religious* scientists!

It must also be remembered that these surveys refer to belief in a personal God and so do not give any indication of the proportion of scientists who could be described as deists, believing in an intelligence that is responsible for the physical universe. Indeed, many prominent scientists hold views along these lines and do so *because* of the scientific evidence. Astonishingly, Dawkins suggests that some such scientists are being disingenuous. After referring to the cosmologist Paul Davies, who holds a view along these lines, Dawkins points out that he won the Templeton Prize, which Dawkins describes as 'a very large sum of money given annually by the Templeton Foundation, usually to a scientist who is prepared to say something nice about religion'.[18] Worse still, commenting on the distinguished physicist Freeman Dyson's claim to be a Christian who is not interested in the doctrine of the Trinity or the truthfulness of the Gospels, Dawkins asks, 'But isn't that exactly what any atheistic scientist *would* say, if he wanted to sound Christian?'[19] Granted, Dyson's views are incompatible with orthodox Christianity, but they are certainly not atheistic either.

Why is Dawkins so resistant to the idea that scientists can believe in God without thereby undermining their scientific integrity, especially when this view leads him to such implausible claims? Dawkins's attitude is all the more surprising since there is a much more sensible line of argument he could take, and that is to hold, as many atheists do, that some scientists have assessed the evidence and come to the sincere but mistaken conclusion that God exists. Of course, to acknowledge the possibility of rational disagreement would undermine his view that belief in God is an irrational delusion.

The New Atheists as theologians

We have seen that the definition of faith as *belief without evidence* leads the New Atheists to make extremely strong claims about the irrationality of religion, but how should faith be defined? There is no doubt that the New Atheists' definition is a popular way of characterizing faith, but does it do justice to the concept of faith as understood within Christianity? After all, there would be no point in the New Atheists coming up with their own definition of faith, and then pointing out how irrational it is. For their claims to be taken seriously their definition must, at the very least, bear some resemblance to faith as Christians understand it.

So how do Christians define faith? Within Christianity there are a range of viewpoints on the nature of faith and how it relates to reason. In fact, faith has such a central role in Christianity that it has been written about endlessly by theologians and philosophers. Despite so much material on the topic, there is no evidence that the New Atheists have made even the slightest effort to come to terms with the Christian understanding of faith. Dawkins, for example, quotes Martin Luther to show that reason is the enemy of faith, but as theologian Alister McGrath points out in response, Dawkins fails to mention that what Luther means by 'reason' is something different from what Dawkins takes it to mean. As McGrath explains:

> What Luther was actually pointing out was that human reason could never fully take in a central theme of the Christian faith – that God should give humanity the wonderful gift of salvation without demanding they do something for him first. Left to itself, human common sense would conclude that you need to do something to earn God's favour – an idea that Luther regarded as compromising the gospel of divine graciousness, making salvation something that you earned or merited.
>
> His inept engagement with Luther shows up how Dawkins abandons even the pretence of rigorous evidence-based scholarship. Anecdote is substituted for evidence; selective Internet-trawling for quotes displaces rigorous and comprehensive engagement with primary sources.[20]

Dawkins, Harris and Hitchens demonstrate a similar level of engagement with Tertullian, Pascal and Kierkegaard. Harris is at least aware that the New Atheist definition of faith is not the only one. He briefly mentions the views of theologian Paul Tillich and goes on to claim that 'anyone is free to redefine the term "faith" however he sees fit and thereby bring it into conformity with some rational or mystical ideal'.[21] Although he is referring to theologians' attempts to 'recast faith', it seems like a perfect description of what the New Atheists have done. Harris even presents an argument for ignoring what theologians have to say, claiming that he is interested in the faith of the faithful, not the theologians. But if the arguments of the New Atheists are to have any force when it comes to the rationality of belief in God, they have an obligation to represent the views of serious Christian thinkers.

This is not to say that there would be no merit in looking at faith as understood by typical believers rather than theologians. It seems to me that there is an issue here since I think that many Christians adopt an approach to faith that takes little cognizance of evidence and to rational thought more generally. An interesting analysis of the problem, investigation into how this attitude came about within evangelical Christianity in North America, and exploration of its consequences in politics and science can be found in *The Scandal of the Evangelical Mind* by the historian Mark Noll.[22] While his focus is on North America, unfortunately the problem is more widespread. For example, many Christians seem to share the view of the New Atheists that there is a serious and inevitable conflict between science and Christianity. So if all the New Atheists wished to claim was that faith is often associated with lack of concern for reason and evidence, this chapter would be unnecessary, except perhaps to reinforce the point. But they make a much stronger claim. The view of the New Atheists is that faith is irrational by definition because it involves believing things for which there is no evidence. So it is not just the faith of the faithful, but *faith itself* that is the problem. Not only that, but because faith is irrational it is also dangerous. Since their view of faith has an impact on many of the claims they make about religious belief, it is important to see whether their account of faith stands up to serious scrutiny.

Harris certainly thinks it does since he claims that his view of faith is the unambiguous view of the Bible. Here is how he arrives at this conclusion:

> Hebrews 11:1 defines faith as 'the assurance of things hoped for, the conviction of things not seen.' Read in the right way, this passage seems to render faith entirely self-justifying: perhaps the very fact that one believes in something which has not yet come to pass ('things hoped for') or for which one has no evidence ('things not seen') constitutes evidence for its actuality ('assurance'). Let's see how this works: I feel a certain, rather thrilling 'conviction' that Nicole Kidman is in love with me. As we have never met, my feeling is my only evidence of her infatuation. I reason thusly: my feelings suggest that Nicole and I must have a special, even metaphysical, connection – otherwise, how could I have this feeling in the first place? I decide to set up camp outside her house to make the necessary introductions; clearly, this sort of faith is a tricky business.[23]

This is probably the clearest example you are ever likely to see of someone making the Bible say what he wants it to say. Note the expression 'read in the right way'. Harris clearly has a flair for creative interpretation, but whatever else can be said about his account, it is certainly not the right way to read the text. It is important to note that the biblical concept of hope does not mean wishful thinking, but is rather trusting God to do what he has promised.[24]

What is faith then according to the passage Harris quotes from Hebrews 11? The translation of this verse quoted by Harris corresponds to that in the

English Standard Version (ESV) of the Bible, but a quick comparison with other versions would be sufficient to indicate that there is disagreement about how the words, which have been translated 'assurance' and 'conviction' in this version, should really be translated. This might have raised some question marks, but it wouldn't have been difficult to find out that he had misunderstood the verse. Here is what theologian David Chapman says about it in *The ESV Study Bible*:

> defining faith as 'assurance' and 'conviction', the author indicates that biblical faith is not a vague hope grounded in imaginary wishful thinking. Instead, faith is a settled confidence that something in the future – something that is not yet seen but has been promised by God – will actually come to pass because God will bring it about. Thus biblical faith is not blind trust in the face of contrary evidence, not an unknowable 'leap in the dark'; rather biblical faith is a confident trust in the eternal God who is all-powerful, infinitely wise, eternally trustworthy.[25]

Although the Greek text of Hebrews 11:1 is notoriously difficult to translate,[26] I very much doubt that New Testament scholars will be persuaded by the 'Kidman' interpretation offered by Harris. So while Harris's account of faith as wishful thinking is certainly a tricky business, the biblical view of faith seems highly rational. And, of course, it wouldn't do for Harris to respond by saying that it is irrational to trust in a God who doesn't exist since the issue is whether the Bible *portrays* faith as irrational.

Faith in the context of Hebrews 11 is about trusting God's promises, but faith of this kind presupposes belief in God's existence. This gives rise to the question of how we know God exists. Does this also require faith? If so, it clearly can't be faith in the sense of believing God's promises and so it must be a broader notion of faith than that in Hebrews 11. We are then left with a question about what kind of faith it is. Is it an irrational faith, as the New Atheists maintain? Is it based on evidence? We must now try to get some idea about how these kinds of questions are addressed within Christianity.

Faith and reason: a selection of views

The New Atheists fail to take into account the enormous body of literature on the nature of faith and the relationship between faith and reason. If we are even to begin to think about this relationship, we must think not only about the nature of faith but also about the nature of reason. Does reason require, for example, that all our beliefs be based on evidence? If so, how strong does the evidence need to be? Does the evidence have to guarantee that the belief is true or establish it beyond reasonable doubt or make it more likely to be true than false or . . .? And what kind of evidence are we talking about anyway? Who decides what should count as admissible evidence?

Keeping these questions in the back of our minds, let us investigate the relationship between faith and reason by considering the views of four Christian thinkers. The first is the great medieval philosopher Thomas Aquinas and the other three are leading contemporary Christian philosophers: Richard Swinburne, Paul Helm and Alvin Plantinga. Aquinas is an obvious choice, and in the case of the three contemporary philosophers I have selected them not only because they are major figures in their field (mainly philosophy of religion, although they have also contributed to other areas of philosophy), who have thought and written very clearly about faith and reason, but also because their contrasting views are, I think, representative of a broad spectrum of Christian thinking on this matter. More attention will be given to Alvin Plantinga's views, not because they are necessarily to be preferred, but because they are much more controversial and raise a lot of questions about the relationship between faith and reason.

Thomas Aquinas

Faith, according to Aquinas, lies between knowledge (*scientia*) and opinion; in cases where we do not have knowledge, we have belief or opinion. But for Aquinas the truths of faith cannot be proved and so do not constitute knowledge. In this sense they are more like belief or opinion. On the other hand, unlike belief or opinion, faith is not characterized by a lack of conviction or commitment, and so in this sense it is more like knowledge. Thus, for Aquinas faith is like a lower form of knowledge.

We must be careful neither to overemphasize Aquinas's contrast between faith and knowledge nor to conclude that his view of faith is in conflict with reason or evidence. First of all, despite Aquinas's use of the term *scientia* for knowledge, this should not be confused with modern science. Aquinas was of course writing before the development of modern science and so, basing his views on Aristotle, he took *scientia* to correspond to certainty either because the truth could be clearly seen or demonstrated using logic.[27] With the rise of modern science came a new approach to acquiring knowledge, an approach based on inference from empirical evidence rather than logical demonstration. A key aspect of modern science, and a point emphasized by the New Atheists, is that it does not give us certainty, well-justified belief perhaps, but not certainty. Thus, it seems clear that in Aquinas's terms modern science, like faith, would lie somewhere between knowledge and opinion.

A second point to bear in mind is that for Aquinas, belief in the existence of God does not constitute faith. Aquinas is perhaps best known for his Five Ways, which offer proofs for the existence of God and so it is a matter of knowledge rather than faith or opinion. So contrary to the New Atheists' idea that belief in the existence of God is irrational because it requires faith, here we have a very significant Christian thinker who does not think that belief in God's existence requires faith at all!

According to Aquinas, faith comes into play when considering specifically Christian beliefs such as the Trinity, the incarnation and so forth. In his book on Aquinas, Brian Davies points out that 'Aquinas takes faith to be something which distinguishes Christians from others who acknowledge the existence of God.'[28] As to what such faith amounts to, Davies puts it like this: 'faith is believing God himself since the truths of faith are revealed by God. [Aquinas] also thinks that to believe God is to share in what God knows, albeit imperfectly.'[29] This raises the question of how we can know that these Christian claims as found in the Bible are really revelations from God. Is this just something to be believed on the basis of blind faith? No, it seems that Aquinas took signs such as miracles as evidences to confirm these revelations as coming from God. Nevertheless, such confirmation does not constitute logical proof and so faith does not constitute knowledge.

The important point here is not whether Aquinas was right or wrong about the nature of faith, about his proofs for God's existence or whether the evidence he cites confirms the Bible as God's revelation. His view is only one of many, but it is clear that he did not think of faith as *belief without evidence* or reasons. Since this is the view of such a major figure in Christian theology, it should give us serious cause for concern about the claims of the New Atheists on the nature of faith.

Before going on to look at the views of some modern writers, it is worth noting two features of Aquinas's view of faith and its relation to reason. First, Aquinas thought of faith as being primarily about belief that certain claims are true, a matter of intellectual assent.[30] In this there is agreement with the New Atheists who also see faith as belief that certain claims are true; it is just that they think such beliefs are in fact false. As we shall see, this aspect of Aquinas's view of faith is not shared by all Christian thinkers. Secondly, Aquinas distinguishes faith from knowledge and although this is understandable given his conception of knowledge it is unfortunate since it suggests that faith is deficient in certain respects compared to other types of knowledge. Since reason, although important, takes us only so far, we might characterize this viewpoint with the slogan *faith beyond reason and evidence*.

Richard Swinburne

In many respects Richard Swinburne can be seen as the modern heir of Thomas Aquinas. He has written extensively on the coherence and rationality of belief in God and in the central claims of Christianity, particularly in the context of modern science. In his book *The Existence of God* he presents versions of the cosmological and teleological arguments as well as arguments from consciousness, providence, history and miracles, and religious experience to show that it is more probable than not that God exists.[31] Note that unlike Aquinas he does not claim to prove God's existence with certainty, but uses probability theory to argue that each piece of evidence counts in favour of God's existence and, when considered cumulatively, they make it probable that God exists.

The conclusion that God's existence can be established as probably, rather than certainly, true would have been a problem for Aquinas since it would not be good enough to count as knowledge. Nevertheless, few things can be established with complete certainty and, of course, Swinburne's approach is quite consistent with modern science, which often proceeds by showing that a range of different pieces of evidence support a theory, but without actually proving it with certainty. Thus, Swinburne's arguments could be seen as an updating of Aquinas's approach for the modern scientific age. Furthermore, Swinburne not only presents evidence for the existence of God, but also for specifically Christian claims such as the incarnation and resurrection.[32]

The implication of Swinburne's approach seems to be that, contrary to the New Atheists, belief in the existence of God is rational *precisely because* it is based on good evidence. It is worth reiterating that the point here is not to assess Swinburne's arguments for God's existence, but to note that a leading Christian thinker claims that belief in the existence of God is not a matter of blind faith but is firmly based on evidence. We shall return to the question of whether there really is good evidence for God's existence in later chapters.

There is a further twist in Swinburne's position, however, since he does not equate faith with belief that God exists or that the claims of Christianity are true. Like Martin Luther, Swinburne emphasizes that faith is not merely belief that certain things are true but also involves trust.[33] According to Swinburne, to trust God involves acting on an assumption about what God will do for us when there is some reason to doubt that this is the case.[34] Thus, having 'some reason to doubt' is essential to faith. Indeed, Swinburne makes it clear that it is the fact that God's existence cannot be proved with certainty that leaves 'abundant room for faith'.[35] So Swinburne agrees with Aquinas that faith comes into play when reasons and evidence are less than fully compelling, although he disagrees on exactly how this occurs. Overall, though,

Swinburne's view on faith and reason could be summed up with the same slogan used for Aquinas: *faith beyond reason and evidence.*

Paul Helm

Like Aquinas and Swinburne, Paul Helm also thinks that reason and evidence have an important role to play, although he has a different characterization of what that role should be.[36] He agrees with Swinburne that trust is an essential component of faith. But faith also involves beliefs including beliefs about God and, according to Helm, these are based on evidence. In fact, he claims that 'the believer should strive to conform the strength of his beliefs to the strength of the evidence',[37] which results in the following relationship between evidence and belief: 'weak evidence, weak belief; strong evidence, strong belief'.[38]

This, of course, leaves a question about how the evidence can be shown to support the beliefs in question. On this point Helm places less emphasis on the traditional arguments for the existence of God and instead focuses on what he calls a web of beliefs. Take God's existence. Helm thinks that a limitation of the traditional arguments is that they tend to treat God in isolation from everything else. Consequently, he prefers an approach that considers how the existence of God relates to a wide range of other beliefs and in particular the way in which the existence of God helps to explain or make sense of the world around us. The idea is that the rational justification for the beliefs making up the web depends on the extent to which the beliefs are coherent, where coherence is to be understood not just in the sense that the beliefs are consistent but that they support each other and provide explanations. This means that each belief does not stand or fall on its own, but must be considered as part of the entire system of beliefs.

Although Helm takes a different approach from Swinburne, they both agree that the extent to which one is rationally justified in believing that God exists (or that various claims of Christianity are true) depends on the evidence. As noted above, both also think that trust is central to faith, but differ on how trust relates to the evidence. We have already seen that Swinburne thinks that having 'some reason to doubt' is essential to trust, but here Helm disagrees. Helm defends what he calls an *evidential proportion* view of faith and so, just as belief should be proportional to evidence, 'trust ought to be proportioned to the strength of the corresponding belief'.[39]

To summarize, here is how Helm defines faith: 'To have faith in God . . . is not to believe, against all the odds, that God exists and in addition to trust him; it is solely to trust him on the basis of evidence and for the fulfilment of certain needs or goals.'[40] Since faith should be in proportion to evidence we might characterize this viewpoint with the slogan *faith with reason and evidence.*

Alvin Plantinga

The New Atheists claim that belief in God is irrational because it is not based on evidence. Aquinas, Swinburne and Helm all disagree with this claim since they think that there is good evidence for believing in God. Alvin Plantinga also rejects the claim of the New Atheists, but for a different reason. The New Atheists accept the presumption of atheism, which is the idea that the burden of proof is on the theist to provide evidence or arguments for the existence of God. Plantinga rejects this view and thinks that belief in God need not be based on arguments. Plantinga's views are often misunderstood or misrepresented, but essentially he is arguing that belief in God should be considered innocent until proven guilty. He argues that theists are within their intellectual rights to believe in God, even when they don't have evidence that could convince a sceptic.

Is it ever reasonable to hold a belief without evidence? Suppose you are accused of a crime and all the evidence points to your guilt even though you know you are innocent.[41] What should you do? Shouldn't you base your beliefs on the evidence and conclude that you must be guilty after all even though you are sure you are innocent? No, clearly it would be rational to maintain your innocence even if you cannot explain why the evidence is against you. This seems like a clear example where it is possible to hold a belief rationally without basing it on the evidence; indeed, the belief is in conflict with the evidence. According to Plantinga, you would be warranted in maintaining your innocence despite the lack of evidence because your belief is appropriately *grounded*.[42] Plantinga's view does not seem unreasonable in this case.

Some might object to the way in which the crime scenario was described. They will maintain that you are warranted in maintaining your innocence, but claim that you *do* have evidence in terms of your own memory. But what do we mean by evidence here? Plantinga will claim that although your memory beliefs constitute *grounds* for believing that you are innocent, they do not constitute *evidence*. For Plantinga, evidence is something you use as part of an argument to infer a conclusion. But in the crime scenario this isn't what happens. You don't use your memory beliefs as part of an argument and conclude you must be innocent; you just know directly you are innocent without having to go through a reasoning process of this kind. But some think this is too narrow a conception of evidence. In fact, in some of his writings Plantinga distinguishes between *propositional* evidence, which consists of other beliefs that could be used as part of an argument for the belief in question, and *non-propositional* evidence, which could be experiential in character. In the crime scenario you do not have propositional evidence, but still have a kind of evidence after all: the evidence of your own experience.

How does this apply to belief in God? Can a person be warranted in believing in God without evidence? Or more precisely, can a person be warranted in believing in God without having good arguments for God's existence? Plantinga thinks that if there is a God, then the answer would probably be 'yes'. He appeals to the idea of God's implanting within us a mechanism (or faculty) called the *sensus divinitatis* that disposes us to believe in him. If this mechanism is functioning properly, then in the right circumstances we shall form the belief that God exists. An analogy with the way in which we form perceptual beliefs might help make sense of this. Someone whose eyesight and relevant brain mechanisms are functioning properly forms true beliefs about her surroundings if the circumstances are right (e.g. if there is adequate lighting). By contrast, she will not be so likely to form true beliefs if her eyesight is poor or the lighting is inadequate.

What are we to make of Plantinga's claims, particularly his idea that the believer is warranted in believing in God because of the operation of a mechanism implanted by God? Isn't this an obvious example of circular reasoning? In order to be warranted in believing in God, wouldn't the believer need to be warranted in believing that God had implanted such a mechanism? And wouldn't this require being warranted in believing in God in the first place? This would be a fair criticism if Plantinga were presenting his views as an *argument* for belief in God or for the truth of Christianity, but he is not. Instead, he is giving an account of *how* people could come to believe in God. It is important to emphasize that Plantinga is not actually claiming to have shown that belief in God is *actually* warranted via the mechanism described, but only that it would be warranted in this way *if God exists*. Plantinga argues that God, if he exists, would want us to know that he exists and also that it is reasonable to believe that he would enable us to come to know this via something like the *sensus divinitatis* rather than requiring that we must make an exhaustive assessment of all the evidence and arguments to come to a tentative conclusion that God exists.

In this way Plantinga claims that the believer would be warranted in believing in God even if he is unaware of the mechanism by which this comes about.[43] By contrast, if there is no God, belief in God would not be warranted. The New Atheists maintain that belief in God is not warranted because there is insufficient evidence, but Plantinga would argue that even if they were right that there is not much evidence, this would not show that belief in God is unwarranted. *The only way to show that belief in God is unwarranted would be to demonstrate that God does not exist* and the New Atheists have failed to do this, as we shall see in later chapters.

It might be objected that not just belief in God but any belief could be claimed to be warranted via some sort of mechanism in the way Plantinga describes, but Plantinga denies this. Consider, for example, the belief that there is no God. Could an atheist use Plantinga's approach to argue that belief in the non-existence of God could be grounded in a similar way? It seems not, because if there is no God, there would be no good reason to think that there would be some sort of reliable, in-built mechanism that would ground atheistic beliefs in the same kind of way.

Is there any place for arguments and evidence within Plantinga's scheme? There are at least two ways in which arguments and evidence are important for Plantinga. First, just because a belief is not based on arguments it does not mean that it is unfalsifiable. Just as I might need to consider evidence that I was mistaken when I thought I saw a friend, so the believer in God would need to consider arguments or evidence that might be considered to undermine belief in God. In such cases, it would be appropriate for the theist to provide counterarguments to support belief in God.[44] In particular, Plantinga has presented detailed arguments in response to the problem of evil, a topic that will be considered in chapter 8.[45]

Secondly, although Plantinga maintains that evidence is not *necessary* for belief in God to be warranted, he does not claim that there is no evidence or arguments for God's existence. In this regard, leading Christian philosopher and apologist William Lane Craig adopts a viewpoint consistent with Plantinga's scheme. Craig maintains that arguments and evidence are unnecessary for the believer to *know* that God exists, but are necessary to *show* that God exists; that is, to convince someone else.[46] The same would apply in the crime scenario described earlier since you need to acquire evidence if you want to *show* other people that you are innocent even though you already *know* you are innocent. In fact, in a recent book, which is a debate about the existence of God with the philosopher Michael Tooley,[47] Plantinga presents arguments against naturalism. In particular, he counters the presumption of atheism, responds to the problem of evil, and argues that naturalism cannot account for consciousness or human knowledge and so leads to scepticism. He also argues that theism is the only sensible alternative to naturalism. Elsewhere he has argued that naturalism cannot account for morality either.[48]

It is not my goal to evaluate Plantinga's view of faith and reason, but just to outline some of the key features of his position. If we were to focus only on the narrow question of whether belief in God can be warranted without arguments or evidence, we would get a rather one-sided view of his position since he also presents an overall case against naturalism and in favour of theism. In summary, he can be viewed as arguing that (1) the presumption of atheism is incorrect and so it is just as legitimate to start from Christian presuppositions as atheistic presuppositions, (2) that Christian theism provides an intellectually satisfying world view, and (3) that atheism provides an unpersuasive and intellectually incoherent world view.

In agreement with Aquinas, Plantinga views faith in relation to specifically Christian beliefs, but in addition to knowledge of these beliefs faith also involves the will, which seems to correspond to trust as discussed by Swinburne and Helm. According to Plantinga, truths that are known by faith do not need to depend on arguments.[49] Since Plantinga holds that faith can be entirely reasonable without the need for arguments, provided it is appropriately grounded, we might characterize this viewpoint with the slogan *faith with reason but without arguments*.

Faith and reason: some key points

Having completed our brief survey of Aquinas, Swinburne, Helm and Plantinga, it is time to try to draw some conclusions. All four put forward serious and clearly defended views. Plantinga's approach is certainly the most controversial and many theists and atheists have disagreed with him, but such disagreements can be carried out in a rational way with objections being raised and counter-arguments provided in response. Before drawing any conclusions, we shall consider some of the relevant issues.

Belief that and belief in
There is a consensus among the four thinkers that faith is not merely an intellectual belief, but this is more prominent in the three contemporary philosophers who emphasize the role of trust. One way to make this point is to notice two ways in which we use the word 'believe'. If I say 'I *believe that* the Prime Minister is the head of the government,' no one will be interested in my statement, except perhaps to enquire as to why I have stated something that is obviously true. If, however, I say 'I *believe in* the Prime Minister,' people will be interested for a very different reason. Similarly, to *believe that* God exists is one thing, but to *believe in* God is something completely different; it is to trust God. Faith involves both these kinds of belief. The New Atheists focus on faith as *belief that* rather than *belief in* as is clear from the fact that they take faith to be belief (without evidence) that God exists.

Belief in, or trust, is an action and so it is different in this respect from *belief that*; you can decide whether to trust someone, but you can't just decide to believe that some statement is true. Even if you have very strong evidence that a rope bridge will support you and you desperately want to get to the other side, the seriousness of something going wrong (no matter how unlikely) might prevent you from acting on your belief; that is, you are not willing to trust the rope bridge by stepping on to it. And, of course, it can work the other way round as well: if the consequences of something going wrong are not so serious, or if the consequences of not trusting are serious, then it can be appropriate to trust someone or something even if the evidence is not so strong.

This is not to say that it is appropriate to *believe in* God even if you don't *believe that* God exists, but it does suggest that faith is not merely about weighing evidence to arrive at a conclusion: there is something we must do. Also, assuming evidence is relevant to *belief that* God exists, it will also be relevant to *belief in* God, but the exact relationship between evidence and *belief in*, or trust, is more complex (and this is true for trust generally, not just trust in God). Furthermore, belief in God rather than belief that God exists is usually what Christians are referring to when they talk about faith. Of course, it presupposes belief that God exists, but this belief on its own is not what faith is all about. This being the case, it is not at all surprising that Christians do not place as much of an emphasis on evidence as the New Atheists would like: most would maintain that there is good evidence that God exists, but they are much more interested in believing *in* God than arguing about his existence. There is nothing irrational about such an attitude to faith.

An obvious but extremely important point is that faith has an object. A person cannot simply have *belief that* or *belief in*: she must have belief that or in *something*. This means that it makes no sense to say, as the New Atheists do, that faith *in general* is irrational. Whether a particular instance of faith is irrational depends on the object of faith in that case. Few will deny that it is rational to have faith in a close friend who has proved to be trustworthy over a long period of time, and irrational to have faith in the Tooth Fairy. What about faith in God – is it rational or irrational? It should now be clear that it cannot be claimed to be irrational merely on the grounds that all faith is irrational. No such simple victory is available to the New Atheists. They need to show that faith *in God* specifically, rather than faith in general, is irrational. Of course, they do offer various arguments along these lines that need to be considered on their merits (and will be in subsequent chapters), but their strategy of claiming that faith in God is irrational because faith is irrational by definition is seriously flawed.

Reason, evidence and belief

Focusing again on the *belief that* component of faith, it is noticeable that there is no consensus among Aquinas, Swinburne, Helm and Plantinga concerning the precise role that reason and evidence should play. There is agreement that belief is reasonable and so they would all contest the claim of the New Atheists that belief is irrational; but while Aquinas, Swinburne and Helm base this reasonableness on evidence, Plantinga does not. Essentially, Plantinga would reject the identification of reason with public, objective evidence that is prominent in the New Atheists.

Despite their differences, however, there is agreement among the authors that reason and evidence are relevant for showing that belief in God or Christian belief is coherent and does not require the believer to accept inconsistent or illogical beliefs. There is also agreement that use of reason and evidence is appropriate for dealing with the objections raised against Christianity by its critics such as the New Atheists. Furthermore, there is agreement that arguments and evidence can be presented in favour of belief in God. As we have seen, Plantinga does not claim that one *cannot* give reasons for believing in God, just that one *need not* do so. Thus, even from Plantinga's perspective there does not seem to be anything wrong with presenting particular reasons and evidences for the existence of God and the truth of Christianity.

Overall, our discussion of faith and reason illustrates that within Christianity it is entirely appropriate to provide arguments and evidence for the existence of God and the truth of Christianity. The four views on faith and reason that have been considered are certainly not exhaustive, but note that the New Atheists fail to engage with any of them or any other well-thought-out view on the subject. Our brief survey is sufficient to show that the claim of the New Atheists that faith is necessarily irrational fails miserably to do justice to Christian viewpoints on the subject. Defining faith in this way enables them to dismiss religious belief easily, but their argument carries no intellectual force whatsoever.

For the purposes of this book it has been important to identify some aspects of the relationship between faith and reason that are consistent with a Christian understanding. However, it is not necessary to come down in favour of one of the four views outlined or to have a fully worked out account of the exact relationship. Having said that, in terms of how to evaluate evidence and arguments for and against the existence of God, the approach I shall adopt is more similar to Swinburne's approach than it is to that of Aquinas, Helm or Plantinga.

Are there limits to reason?

It is quite possible that there are truths that humans could never establish because of our finitude. Perhaps there are truths about other parts of the universe that are beyond our reach, truths about the human mind or truths about the laws of science that we shall never discover because we are not clever enough. In fact, we even know from the field of mathematics that there are limits to reason (defined in a formal sense) that are more fundamental. The Austrian mathematician Kurt Gödel demonstrated that there are certain logical systems in which there are true statements that cannot be proved from the axioms and the rules of inference.[50]

These limitations to human reasoning are due to our finitude and logical factors, but limitations can also arise because of psychological biases. In his book *Faith Beyond Reason*,[51] Stephen Evans notes the relevance to faith of the psychological phenomenon of cognitive dissonance, the idea that there is a tendency to adjust our beliefs to fit our emotions. As an example, he points out that whenever we do something that is morally dubious and that makes us feel guilty, we come up with more respectable explanations for our action. Evans also points out that emotions and desires can affect the way in which we interpret and weigh evidence. It is quite possible, for example, that the victim of a crime will draw different conclusions from evidence against a suspect than will people who had no involvement.

Evans investigates the plausibility of the idea found in many Christian thinkers that human reason is limited or corrupted in some way.[52] He does not claim that reason is irrelevant to questions about faith, but distinguishes between rational and irrational attempts to articulate how reason might be limited. The problem is not with reason per se, but with the fact that reason, affected by our emotions and desires as it often is, may not be neutral when it comes to questions concerning God's existence and other beliefs. Evans finds this kind of thinking in prominent Christians such as Tertullian, Augustine, Luther, Calvin and focuses particularly on Kierkegaard. Although he thinks Kierkegaard was too negative in his assessment of the value of evidence for Christian belief, Evans argues that for the most part he was critical of reason in this restricted sense rather than reason in general.

It must be stressed that the problem with reason according to this way of thinking is not that reason itself is flawed or that there is something wrong with thinking logically about problems. The problem is with us, not with logic. It arises because our emotions and desires can influence how we evaluate evidence and arguments. This being the case, it seems likely that limits to reason will be less significant in areas like mathematics, where emotions and desires are not so relevant. By contrast, emotions and desires are likely to limit our reason more on matters of ultimate concern such as belief in God. The New Atheists would no doubt agree with this assessment wholeheartedly. It's just that according to them it is *believers* in God who are unable to reason and weigh evidence properly, whereas *unbelievers* are not influenced so much. In many respects the views of the New Atheists are similar to those of Feuerbach, who considered belief in God to be a projection of the human mind, and Freud, who considered it to be a form of wish-fulfilment. Indeed, Hitchens claims that Freud's 'critique of wish-thinking is strong and unanswerable'.[53] But what is sauce for the goose is sauce for the gander: if there is no God, perhaps the Feuerbach–Freud approach might provide a possible explanation for why people believe in God, but if there is a God perhaps it is the New Atheists who are engaged in wishful thinking. Just as Feuerbach, Freud and the New Atheists can claim that believers are negatively influenced by non-rational factors in their reasoning, so Augustine, Calvin and Kierkegaard can claim that the reasoning of unbelievers is impeded in a similar way.

The New Atheists seem to assume that in contrast to religious believers they can be objective and unbiased in their assessment of the evidence relating to belief in God because they have no religious commitment, but is this really the case? It is interesting to note that many reviews of the New Atheists have criticized them, not because of their atheism, nor for emphasizing the dangers of religion, but for their inability to handle the arguments and evidence fairly. This failing is all the more glaring because they place so much emphasis on science and the need to treat evidence objectively and fairly. In his review of *The God Delusion* in the *London Review of Books*, Terry Eagleton claims:

> Card-carrying rationalists like Dawkins . . . are in one sense the least well-equipped
> to understand what they castigate, since they don't believe there is anything there to
> be understood, or at least anything worth understanding. This is why they invariably
> come up with vulgar caricatures of religious faith that would make a first-year
> theology student wince. *The more they detest religion, the more ill-informed their criticisms of
> it tend to be.*[54]

Eagleton's point is that Dawkins doesn't even attempt to understand religion seriously or present it fairly because he is already convinced that it is false and because he *detests* it. If Eagleton is correct, it seems that Dawkins, and arguably the other New Atheists as well, illustrate perfectly the limitations to reason that Evans is talking about.

Clearly, it is important to try to deal with the issues as fairly as possible. The

New Atheists would expect nothing less in discussions about science, so why should it be any different when discussing religion? There is no doubt that many Christian writings are likewise affected by bias and prejudice and I am not claiming that my own approach will be free from bias, but we should at least be aware of this and the limits it can place on the potential of even good arguments to convince others.

Here a further issue arises. It might be thought that if we could all just manage to get past our own biases, then we could use our reason to weigh up the evidence properly and reach agreement. This view is somewhat naive, however. Evans draws attention to another way in which reason can be limited that is relevant here. He distinguishes between what he calls *concrete reason* and *ideal reason*. Ideal reason is a *normative* term relating to 'those patterns of thinking that ought to be emulated because they are most likely to lead to truth'.[55] Concrete reason is a *descriptive* term relating to the actual patterns of thinking that are considered to be reasonable in a society. He argues that 'a rejection of concrete reason is not necessarily a rejection of ideal reason, but may in fact be motivated by a commitment to ideal reason'.[56] Suppose God does in fact exist, but what is considered as acceptable modes of reasoning (i.e. concrete reason) makes it impossible to recognize this truth. In such a case Evans claims there would be a tension between concrete reason and ideal reason.

The history of science seems to provide some examples of what Evans has in mind since there have been debates about the kinds of reasoning, explanation and evidence that are admissible within science. The origin of modern science required new approaches to reasoning about the natural world that amounted to a departure from Greek and medieval approaches in which deductive reasoning was predominant. Within science some such as Francis Bacon have favoured an inductive approach as the model of proper scientific reasoning, whereas others have argued for various alternatives such as inference to the best explanation. Clearly, it is possible to criticize Bacon's approach without rejecting scientific reasoning per se, but precisely because an alternative approach provides a better account of scientific reasoning. Disputes can also arise in other ways. Initially, theories such as evolution and the atomic theory of matter were called into question because they went beyond what could be verified directly. In these cases, and many others, progress in science involved criticism of the existing view of what was acceptable in scientific reasoning. In Evans's terms it involved criticism of concrete scientific reason, but not ideal reason. To put it another way, scenarios like these involved conflicting accounts of what constituted acceptable reasoning.

Arguably, something like this is going on in debates between theists and the New Atheists. It is not just that they disagree about the conclusions they reach; they disagree about how to reason properly about belief in God. An obvious example of this concerns the status of evidence in such debates. What can be considered as admissible evidence? The New Atheists often claim that there is no evidence for God's existence, whereas many theists think there is plenty of evidence. What is going on here? It certainly isn't obvious (to most of us) that the New Atheists are correct about this, so how do they arrive at their conclusion?

One factor is that at times they give the impression that they would consider as admissible only evidence that directly verified God's existence, or that was sufficiently similar to evidence acquired in scientific experiments. In chapter 6 we shall see that another factor is that they appear to rule out the possibility that God could be an explanation of anything. Yet we shall see reasons to reject these views and so to reject the New Atheists' conception of evidence as being too narrow. Arguably, it is more general considerations about the universe, about human nature, about meaning and truth that constitute the relevant evidence for belief in God. In rejecting the New Atheists' approach to evidence, the theist is not rejecting evidence per se, but merely the New Atheists' conception of it. The suggestion is that the New Atheists' approach is in conflict with ideal reason since it may well prevent us from getting at the truth. Clearly, if there is a God, this would be a very important fact about our universe, a fact we would want to know. The problem is that if God does in fact exist, the approach to reasoning and evidence adopted by the New Atheists would make it impossible (or almost so) to know this fact.

Consider the following analogy. Joe is very wary about forming false beliefs and so decides not to believe anything unless he can be completely certain about it. Initially, he becomes much more discriminating in terms of which newspapers, television programmes and websites he accepts as reliable sources of information. He then wonders whether he can really be certain about anything in any such sources and so gives up on all newspapers, and so on. After that he concludes he cannot be certain about anything anyone tells him, even his close friends, and decides to believe only what he can work out for himself. The problem with Joe's strategy is that almost all his beliefs go by the board; he ends up a sceptic about almost everything. Of course, there is at least one positive thing about his strategy: he wanted to avoid false beliefs and has certainly achieved this, but only because he hardly believes anything at all. Clearly, there is also merit in being sceptical to some extent by being discriminating in terms of media sources to trust, for example. But it is equally clear that Joe has gone too far since his approach prevents him from knowing all sorts of things; it prevents him from getting at the truth.

No doubt the New Atheists would agree with me about Joe's case, but when it comes to belief in God, it is at least possible that the New Atheists are in a similar position to Joe. Although they are correct to be sceptical to some extent, arguably they go too far by adopting an approach to evidence that would prevent them from believing in God even if God exists; that is, they adopt an approach that could prevent them from getting at the truth. They may be wary that if they were to broaden their approach it would open the door to all sorts of irrational beliefs, but there is no good reason to think that this is the case, just as rejecting Joe's approach to rationality does not lead to irrationality. In fact, it was Joe's approach itself that led to irrationality.

Do these points really apply to the New Atheists? Do they have too narrow a conception of evidence? And even if a broader conception of evidence is adopted, how does theism fare when all the evidence is considered? We shall return to some of these questions in our consideration of the evidence for theism in chapters 4 and 5, but the discussion here should alert us to the fact that it is not merely a matter of weighing up all the evidence since there may be differences of opinion as to what counts as evidence in the first place. It also highlights the fact that in rejecting the reasoning of the New Atheists, the theist need not be rejecting reason itself but may be advocating an approach to reasoning and evidence that is better equipped to discover truth.

Faith and its consequences

So far we have focused on how the New Atheists have failed to do justice to faith as it is understood within Christianity. In essentially defining faith to be irrational they have misrepresented mainstream Christian views on the subject. It might be thought that nothing terribly important hinges on this. After all, even if the New Atheists turn out to be wrong about the nature of faith, surely their main arguments against belief in God and their claims about the dangers of religion are much more significant. Unfortunately, things are not so simple. Here I shall argue that in fact the New Atheists' naive view of faith distorts some of their other views. As we saw earlier, it results in overblown and unhelpful claims about the irrationality of belief in God, which in turn give rise to an unwillingness to engage seriously with the views of their opponents. In this section I consider two further distortions.[57]

Faith and evil

The New Atheists have gone to great lengths to point out the evils carried out in the name of religion and, of course, they are quite right to do so. What is not so clear is the validity of the conclusions they draw, but that is for a later chapter. Here I want to draw attention to one aspect of their analysis, found particularly in Dawkins and Harris: the idea that faith plays a key role in religious violence.

A common attitude towards the evils perpetrated by religion is that the problem lies not so much with religion, but with religious extremism of one variety or another. Dawkins and Harris have no truck with this idea. The problem, as they see it, is religion itself or, to be more accurate, faith. Harris sums up the viewpoint very clearly:

> It is time we recognised that all reasonable men and women have a common enemy. It is an enemy so near to us, and so deceptive, that we keep its counsel even as it threatens to destroy the very possibility of human happiness. Our enemy is nothing other than faith itself.[58]

Similarly, Dawkins tells us that 'we should blame religion itself, not religious *extremism* – as though that were some kind of terrible perversion of real, decent religion'.[59] Much of their discussion is carried out in the context of the Al Qaeda attack on the World Trade Center, but they make it clear that their point applies as much to Christianity as Islam.

Now one can certainly sympathize with some of their claims since it is clear that religion does play a fundamental role in such horrendous atrocities, but the further claim that it is 'religion itself' or 'faith itself' that is the problem is highly implausible and completely unwarranted. Is the faith of the Quakers, a group committed to pacifism, part of the 'enemy' along with Al Qaeda? The very idea is preposterous and one wonders what led the New Atheists to such a conclusion. The problem, according to Dawkins and Harris, seems to be that the rest of us are mistaken in thinking that there is a distinction in kind to be made between a religious suicide bomber and a Quaker because both have *faith*. And indeed, apparently the faith of the Quaker opens the door to the worst kinds of extremism. Dawkins tells us that he does 'everything in [his] power to warn people against faith itself, not just against so-called "extremist" faith. The teachings of "moderate" religion, though not extremist in themselves, are an open invitation to extremism.'[60]

The real problem then is faith. With regard to the notion that Al Qaeda attacks are perversions of true faith, Dawkins asks, 'But how can there be a perversion of faith, if faith, lacking objective justification, doesn't have any demonstrable standard to pervert?'[61] Now, of course, there is an onus on Muslims to demonstrate that such attacks are perversions of Islam and, likewise, for Christians to demonstrate that the Crusades were perversions of Christianity. But Dawkins thinks this is impossible for the simple reason that faith, by definition, is irrational since it involves believing against the evidence and so cannot have any demonstrable standards. It seems that if one opens the door to faith, anything goes.

Once again it appears that their definition of faith leads the New Atheists to very implausible conclusions. And once again there is a much more plausible view that they could adopt. After all, one does not need to be a Christian or even hold to any religious belief to recognize that Christians do have standards that enable them to argue coherently and rationally against religious violence. As we saw earlier, one of the main problems with Dawkins's view is that it makes no sense to say that faith in general is irrational. Whether faith is irrational in a particular case depends on the object (or content) of that faith.[62] It is the content of a particular person's faith that needs to be assessed, not merely the fact that he has faith in something. Furthermore, if faith is not necessarily irrational, there is no need to equate the faith of the Quaker with that of an Al Qaeda terrorist.

It is worth making one final point about faith and evil. Religious people often try to turn the tables on atheists in this argument by pointing to all the evil that has been carried out by atheists. If violence carried out by people in the name of a given religion is taken as counting against that religion, doesn't the same apply to violence carried out by atheists? Don't atheists need to show that violence carried out by their fellow atheists is a perversion of 'true' atheism? At this point Harris makes the following claim: 'Consider the millions of people who were killed by Stalin and Mao: although these tyrants paid lip service to rationality, communism was little more than a political religion.'[63] Similarly, Hitchens claims, 'Totalitarian systems, whatever outward form they may take, are fundamentalist and, as we would now say, "faith-based".'[64] Astonishingly, Harris and Hitchens seem to be saying that even though they were atheists Stalin and Mao held irrational beliefs, and so they were just like people of faith! Thus, even the terrible evil carried out by atheists can be attributed to religion. But, once again, this is based on a definition rather than a serious argument: faith is irrational, 'true' atheism is rational, so atheists who carry out terrible atrocities really belong in the same camp as people of faith.[65] Ironically, this kind of thinking has all the hallmarks of the worst and most narrow-minded religious arguments of which the New Atheists are so critical.

Faith and child abuse

A common concern among the New Atheists is the relationship of religion to children. As in the case of other evils perpetrated in the name of religion, there are legitimate questions to be asked here. One need look no further than the sexual abuse scandals within the Roman Catholic Church in recent years. Here again, however, I want to focus on just one particular aspect of this debate: the role of faith.

Particularly for Dawkins, the problem with teaching religious beliefs to children is not just that the beliefs are false nor that the tactics used are inappropriate, but that children are being taught to have *faith*. Here is how he puts it:

> More generally (and this applies to Christianity no less than to Islam), what is really pernicious is the practice of teaching children that faith itself is a virtue. Faith is an evil precisely because it requires no justification and brooks no argument. Teaching children that unquestioned faith is a virtue primes them – given certain other ingredients that are not hard to come by – to grow up into potentially lethal weapons for future jihads or crusades . . . If children were taught to question and think through their beliefs, instead of being taught the superior virtue of faith without question, it is a good bet that there would be no suicide bombers . . . Faith can be very very dangerous, and deliberately to implant it into the vulnerable mind of an innocent child is a grievous wrong.[66]

As in previous sections, it is faith itself that is the problem, not just the faith of Al Qaeda terrorists. No distinction is made between different kinds of faith since faith, by definition, is believing something without evidence and so it is *always* wrong to teach faith to children. Harris also subscribes to Dawkins's view, claiming that 'every child is instructed that it is, at the very least, an option, if not a sacred duty, to disregard the facts of this world out of deference to the God who lurks in his mother's and father's imaginations'.[67]

Just as before, Dawkins and Harris have opted for the simple, sweeping generalization that faith itself is the problem because it is always irrational rather than distinguishing between different instances of faith based on their respective contents. And so, once again, their definition of faith leads them to a very implausible conclusion, namely that teaching faith to children is wrong irrespective of the particular religion of the parents. And once again, a much more plausible viewpoint is open to them, which is simply to hold that even if all religious beliefs are false, the teaching of at least some of them is not necessarily a 'grievous wrong'.

Conclusion

The New Atheists think that belief in God is not only mistaken, but irrational. Among the New Atheists we also find the claims that religion is inextricably linked to evil and that teaching religious faith to children is akin to child abuse. Of central importance is the concept of 'faith', which for the most part the New Atheists take to be *belief without evidence*. Since belief without evidence is considered to be irrational, the New Atheists tend to adopt a blanket approach to religion: *all* belief in God is irrational and even moderate religion is dangerous because it opens the door to extremism.

A serious problem with this assessment is that the New Atheists have simply assumed that faith is *belief without evidence*. No doubt there is plenty of faith that is of this variety, but they have given little or no attention to what Christian thinkers actually take faith to be and how they relate it to reason. Ironically, their account of faith seems itself to be a belief without evidence to support it or, at least, only a highly selective use of evidence. Hence, their account of faith is an example of irrationality by their own lights.

Our discussion has raised a number of issues that should be borne in mind when discussing Christian faith. First, faith involves both *belief that* and *belief in*. Christian faith is not just the intellectual belief *that* certain things are true but involves belief or trust *in* God. Secondly, it is appropriate to use reason and evidence when considering Christian faith. While there is some disagreement among Christians as to whether it is necessary to provide convincing reasons and evidence for their beliefs, most agree that reason and evidence have some role to play in undermining objections to Christian faith and in making a positive case for it. Thirdly, there may be limits to human reasoning that come into play when considering faith. These limitations can be due to human biases, which can affect both theists and atheists, or they can arise due to the fact that certain approaches to reasoning and evidence may not be well equipped to get at the truth. On this latter point it may be that it is *because* of the importance of evidence in helping us to find the truth that the theist finds it necessary to criticize the New Atheists' approach to evidence.

In this chapter I have made no attempt to argue that there is a God, but have tried only to show that faith is not necessarily irrational, as the New Atheists would have us believe. This clears the way for a discussion of some of the relevant considerations raised by the New Atheists in subsequent chapters since there is no reason to think that such deliberations are somehow inimical to the nature of faith, or at least to Christian faith. But before considering reasons and evidence that might be offered in support of the existence of God, it is worth investigating the claim of the New Atheists that belief in God is irrational because it conflicts with science. This will be the focus of the next chapter.

Notes

1. *TGD*, p. 5.
2. Ibid., p. 308.
3. *TEF*, p. 17.
4. Ibid., p. 29, emphasis in original.
5. Memes will be discussed in chapter 7.
6. *BTS*, pp. 232–233.
7. *GNG*, p. 71.
8. *TGD*, p. 5.
9. *TEF*, p. 73, emphasis in original.
10. Ibid., p. 226, emphasis in original.
11. Ibid., p. 65.
12. *GNG*, pp. 64–65.
13. *TEF*, pp. 15–16.
14. *TGD*, p. 99.
15. Edward J. Larson and Larry Witham, 'Scientists Are Still Keeping the Faith', *Nature* 386 (1997), pp. 435–436.
16. Edward J. Larson and Larry Witham, 'Leading Scientists Still Reject God', *Nature* 394 (1998), p. 313.
17. *TGD*, p. 100.
18. Ibid., p. 19.
19. Ibid., p. 152, emphasis in original.
20. Alister McGrath, *The Dawkins Delusion* (London: SPCK, 2005), p. 6.
21. *TEF*, p. 65.
22. Mark A. Noll, *The Scandal of the Evangelical Mind* (Grand Rapids: Eerdmans, 1994). See also his *Jesus Christ and the Life of the Mind* (Grand Rapids: Eerdmans, 2011).
23. *TEF*, p. 64.
24. 'Hope is that excellent habituation by which one securely trusts that God will be faithful to his promise and will provide the faithful with fit means to receive it' (Thomas C. Oden, *Life in the Spirit, Systematic Theology: Volume Three* [New York: HarperCollins, 1992], p. 146).
25. David W. Chapman, in *The ESV Study Bible: English Standard Version* (Wheaton, Ill.: Crossway Bibles), p. 2379.

26. For a discussion see Ben Witherington III, *The Indelible Image: Part I* (Downers Grove: IVP Academic, 2009), pp. 447–452.

27. As noted above, there is a kind of certainty involved in faith for Aquinas since faith involves conviction about the truth of the belief, but this is different from certainty in the sense of being logically demonstrable.

28. Brian Davies, *The Thought of Thomas Aquinas* (Oxford: Oxford University Press, 1993), p. 275.

29. Ibid, p. 277.

30. That he did not think of faith as *merely* intellectual; see Davies, ibid., pp. 274–296.

31. Richard Swinburne, *The Existence of God*, 2nd ed. (Oxford: Oxford University Press, 2004).

32. See, for example, Richard Swinburne, *The Resurrection of God Incarnate* (Oxford: Oxford University Press, 2003).

33. In addition, Swinburne claims that to have faith one must also have a good purpose for otherwise there is no link between faith and good conduct.

34. Richard Swinburne, *Faith and Reason* (Oxford: Oxford University Press, 1981), p. 112.

35. Swinburne, *Existence of God*, p. 2. In fact, Swinburne also allows for what he calls *pragmatist faith* in cases where someone does not have belief. For a criticism of this viewpoint see Paul Helm, *Faith with Reason* (Oxford: Oxford University Press, 2000), pp. 139–157.

36. Helm, *Faith with Reason*.

37. Ibid., p. 21.

38. Ibid.

39. Ibid., p. 154.

40. Ibid., p. 17.

41. This is based on an example of Alvin Plantinga, *Warranted Christian Belief* (Oxford: Oxford University Press, 2000), pp. 371–372.

42. According to Plantinga, warrant is what distinguishes true belief from knowledge. Someone can have a true belief just by luck, but something extra is needed for it to constitute knowledge.

43. Compare this with perceptual belief. If I see a tree I do not need to have reasons for believing that the relevant brain mechanisms are functioning properly or even know what these mechanisms are in order to be warranted in my belief that I see a tree.

44. See Plantinga, *Warranted Christian Belief*, pt. 4.

45. See, for example, Alvin Plantinga, *God and Other Minds* (New York: Cornell University Press, 1967); and Alvin Plantinga, *God, Freedom and Evil* (Grand Rapids: Eerdmans, 1974).

46. William Lane Craig, *Reasonable Faith: Christian Truth and Apologetics*, 3rd ed. (Wheaton: Crossway, 2008), pp. 43–58.

47. Alvin Plantinga and Michael Tooley, *Knowledge of God* (Oxford: Blackwell, 2008).

48. Alvin Plantinga, 'Naturalism, Theism, Obligation and Supervenience', available at http://www.ammonius.org/assets/pdfs/plantinga.pdf (accessed 26 Sept. 2011).

49. Plantinga, *Warranted Christian Belief*, pp. 241–289.

50. Of particular significance is the fact that this result applies to arithmetic. For an accessible account see E. Nagel and J. R. Newman, *Gödel's Proof* (London: Routledge & Kegan Paul, 1958).

51. C. Stephen Evans, *Faith Beyond Reason* (Edinburgh: Edinburgh University Press, 1998).

52. Alvin Plantinga also explores this topic in *Warranted Christian Belief*, pp. 199–240.

53. *GNG*, p. 103.

54. Terry Eagleton, 'Lunging, Flailing, Mispunching', *London Review of Books*, 19 Oct. 2006, p. 32, emphasis mine.

55. Evans, *Faith Beyond Reason*, p. 93.

56. Ibid., p. 94. Evans argues that various Christian thinkers, particularly Kierkegaard, who appear to be critical of reason are actually critical of concrete reason rather than ideal reason.

57. John Haught, in his book *God and the New Atheism: A Critical Response to Dawkins, Harris and Hitchens* (Louisville, Ky.: Westminster John Knox, 2008), also draws attention to the way in which the New Atheists' naive view of faith influences their overall case. In a very interesting way he describes the New Atheists, especially Sam Harris, as proposing something like a new version of the four noble truths of Buddhism. According to Haught, the first noble truth of the New Atheism is that people are living needlessly miserable lives. The second is that the cause of this distress is faith (defined as belief without evidence), particularly in the form of belief in God. The third is that the way to avoid unnecessary suffering is to abolish faith. Haught points out that this leads them to the view that we need to eliminate even the toleration of faith. The fourth, which replaces the Buddhist eightfold path, is that the way to eliminate faith, and hence to end suffering, is by following the scientific method.

58. *TEF*, p. 131.

59. *TGD*, p. 306, emphasis in original.

60. Ibid.

61. Ibid.

62. It also depends on how faith comes about. For example, trusting someone on the basis of reading a horoscope would be irrational even if the person were trustworthy.

63. *TEF*, p. 78.

64. *GNG*, p. 250.

65. Perhaps the New Atheists would claim that they are not commending atheism alone, but atheism along with evidence-based reasoning, but in that case they should accept that atheists can be just as irrational as anyone else rather than trying to attribute atheistic irrationality to religion or faith.

66. *TGD*, pp. 307–308.

67. *TEF*, p. 65.

3. DOES SCIENCE UNDERMINE BELIEF IN GOD?

The discussion in chapter 2 showed that faith cannot simply be defined as *belief without evidence* and that there is nothing inherently irrational about belief in God. Indeed, there is nothing inappropriate about giving reasons and evidence for belief in God. Of course, this is not to say that *all* religious beliefs are rational, but there is no good reason to think that they are *all* irrational either.

Perhaps it can be granted that religious beliefs cannot be dismissed on the basis of an ill-informed definition of faith, but isn't there still a fundamental problem with religious beliefs? Aren't they incompatible with science? Since science is a rational way to acquire beliefs doesn't this mean that religious beliefs are irrational after all? Perhaps it was rational to believe in God before modern science came along, but surely there is no longer any need to believe in God. And the problem isn't just that science has disproved a few particular religious beliefs, but that conflict between science and religion seems inevitable: the more scientific knowledge we acquire, the less need there is to believe in God. In chapter 2 we explored the idea that faith is irrational in principle, whereas here we investigate the idea that it is *no longer* rational because it is incompatible with science.

The New Atheists present several ways in which they think religious beliefs are incompatible with science. The most prominent is the one noted above: that science renders belief in God redundant. One response to the idea that there is a conflict of this kind between science and religion is to claim that they are completely independent of each other, science dealing with facts and religion with morality. However, the New Atheists think that this position is a cop-out, and in fact I agree with them, but that leaves questions about how science should relate to religious beliefs and how potential conflicts can be handled. Other reasons provided by the New Atheists for the incompatibility of science and religion are based on claims about the incomprehensibility of religious beliefs compared to the clarity of scientific beliefs and miracles as violations of scientific laws. Each of these topics will be considered in turn.

God: a redundant explanation?

In the light of modern science the New Atheists claim that belief in God has become increasingly difficult to sustain. The basic idea is straightforward enough. In the past people were unaware of natural explanations for various phenomena such as thunder and lightning and so attributed them to God. As science progressed it provided explanations of more and more of these otherwise mysterious phenomena, leaving less and less need for God. Theists are left in the position of desperately clutching on to any remaining phenomena that science cannot explain as their only grounds for belief, but this strategy is doomed to failure. Surely it is much more reasonable to believe that science will one day explain all remaining mysteries. And if science can't, surely there is no reason to think that religion can. Or at least so the argument goes.

Hitchens expresses this kind of view clearly by linking religious belief with ignorance and fear. He states that religion

> comes from the bawling and fearful infancy of our species, and is a babyish attempt to meet our inescapable demand for knowledge . . . Today the least educated of my children knows much more about the natural order than any of the founders of religion . . .
>
> All attempts to reconcile faith with science and reason are consigned to failure and ridicule for precisely these reasons . . . there would be no such churches in the first place if humanity had not been afraid of the weather, the dark, the plague, the eclipse, and all manner of other things now easily explicable.[1]

Dawkins also sums up this viewpoint by stating, 'Historically, religion aspired to *explain* our own existence and the nature of the universe in which we find ourselves. In this role it is now completely superseded by science.'[2]

There is no doubt that this idea of inevitable conflict between the rational, progressive forces of science on the one hand and the obscurantist, regressive forces of religion on the other is popular and widespread. But, unfortunately for the New Atheists' cause, research has shown it to be a myth. Historian of science Colin Russell comments:

> The common belief that . . . the actual relations between religion and science over the last few centuries have been marked by deep and enduring hostility . . . is not only historically inaccurate, but actually a caricature so grotesque that what needs to be explained is how it could possibly have achieved any degree of respectability.[3]

Undoubtedly, well-known episodes such as the Galileo affair and responses to Darwin's *The Origin of Species* weigh heavily on the popular psyche. It is certainly true that Galileo came into conflict with church authorities over his defence of the Copernican theory that removed Earth from the centre of the universe, but historians of science have clearly demonstrated that this was far from being the science versus religion confrontation that it is often portrayed to be. For a start, Galileo was a devout believer himself and, more importantly, he faced opposition from outside the church as well as from within. The problem arose from the fact that Galileo's views were in conflict with Aristotelianism, which was the dominant viewpoint, albeit one that was adopted by the church as well as the scientists of the time. As historian of science John Hedley Brooke comments:

> It would, for example, be quite wrong to imagine that opposition to the Copernican theory derived only from religious prejudice. In 1543 an earth-centered cosmos was the physical orthodoxy of the day, supported by philosophical arguments that, at the time, were peculiarly compelling. . . . Certainly the Catholic Church had a vested interest in Aristotelian philosophy, but much of the conflict ostensibly between science and religion turns out to have been between new science and the sanctified science of the previous generation.[4]

As for evolution, it appears to present a more straightforward example of the conflict thesis espoused by the New Atheists, especially in view of the fact that many contest evolution for religious reasons to this day. Even here, however, things are not as simple as they seem. At the time many Christians were sympathetic to evolution, including no less a figure than the biblical inerrantist and leading Princeton theologian Benjamin B. Warfield.[5] And there were scientists who opposed it, including no less a figure than Lord Kelvin, whose estimates for the age of Earth posed a serious problem for evolution, although subsequent scientific developments showed his estimates to be incorrect. Today, of course, the position is different with evolution being generally accepted in the scientific community and most of the opposition coming from religious believers, but is this a straightforward example of science versus religion?

Apart from some atheists (although certainly not all) and some creationists (although certainly not all), hardly anyone thinks that acceptance of evolution is incompatible with belief in God.[6] So if it is not an example of science versus belief in God, is it an example of science versus the Bible? Well, the Roman Catholic Church thinks not, as do many prominent evangelicals.[7] Whatever one thinks about this, it seems clear that the disagreement is primarily one *between Christians* over their interpretations of the Bible rather than a straightforward example of science in conflict with religion. Furthermore, irrespective of one's view of the Intelligent Design movement, it is clear that their opposition to evolution stands or falls on the basis of their scientific criticisms, not their interpretation of the Bible.[8] We shall return to the question of evolution and design in chapter 6.

If Galileo and Darwin do not conform to the conflict stereotype of the New Atheists, it is not obvious what other aspects of science would make the case more clearly. In fact, most scientific developments do not seem to pose any real threat to belief in God. The development of electromagnetic theory or quantum theory, for example, seem to be neutral and there are even some aspects of science such as big bang cosmology that arguably point in the opposite direction as we shall see in chapter 4. But perhaps there is a more subtle way in which science might be thought to undermine belief in God. Despite the points made above, perhaps the New Atheists are right to maintain that belief in God is no longer necessary. One could continue to believe in God while accepting evolution and various other scientific explanations, but there is no longer any need to do so.

Dawkins refers approvingly to Peter Atkins's notion of a lazy creator. Atkins's idea is that as science progresses there is less left for God to do. If evolution is 'God's way of achieving creation', then God wouldn't need to do anything except let evolution get on with its work. Dawkins writes, 'Step by step, Atkins succeeds in reducing the amount of work the lazy God has to do until he finally ends up doing nothing at all: he might as well not bother to exist.'[9]

Essentially, this is a criticism of the so-called God-of-the-gaps, the idea that God is to be found at the gaps in scientific explanation. The objection to this approach is that as the gaps are filled by science, God is gradually removed from the picture. This is also the focus of Hitchens's comments about Laplace. When Napoleon asked Laplace where God fitted into his mathematics he replied, 'I have no need of that hypothesis.'[10]

Ironically, Dawkins is aware that to attack the God-of-the-gaps is to attack a straw man since he points out that it was criticized by the theologian Dietrich Bonhoeffer. Despite the fact that the God-of-the-gaps approach is rightly criticized as bad theology, Dawkins seems to think that scientific progress removes the need not only for the God-of-the-gaps, but for God as well. Before responding to Dawkins and Hitchens on these points and, in particular, to their comments about Laplace and Atkins's lazy creator, we shall consider the limits of scientific explanation.

What science can and cannot explain

It is well known that many of the leading figures of modern science such as Galileo, Kepler, Boyle, Newton, Faraday and Maxwell were believers in God and most of them were orthodox Christians. Is this just a coincidence? The New Atheists' response seems to be that almost everyone believed in God back then. This seems inadequate, however, as the real question is why science took root in a monotheistic, and specifically Christian culture, rather than in a polytheistic or pantheistic culture. Many claim that science developed at least partly because of their religious beliefs and, in particular, a belief in the intelligibility of the natural world arising from the doctrine of creation. Certainly this seems to have been the motivation of many of these scientists. Kepler, for example, believed, 'The chief aim of all investigations of the external world should be to discover the rational order which has been imposed on it by God and which he revealed to us in the language of mathematics.'[11]

The question here is how such scientists could really have engaged in their work if science by its very nature removes the need for God as the New Atheists maintain. When Kepler proposed his laws of planetary motion did he think that there was one less reason for believing in God? When Maxwell discovered his theory of electromagnetism did he too think that God had become redundant in one more respect? A gap had been filled in terms of a scientific account and so God was no longer needed? One less thing for a lazy creator to do? Certainly not. They thought of their work as expressing how the universe behaves in accordance with laws God had put in place. The fact that the universe can be described by mathematics is just what they would have expected given their belief in an intelligent creator. God was not brought in just to account for the crumbs from the scientists' table. It was belief in

God that helped them to make sense of the whole thing. They were 'thinking God's thoughts after him'.

The attitude of these founding fathers of science is a far cry from the God-of-the-gaps approach criticized by Dawkins and Hitchens or to the claim of Dawkins that 'one of the truly bad effects of religion is that it teaches us that it is a virtue to be satisfied with not understanding'.[12] Dawkins's claim is undoubtedly correct of some religions, but it is most emphatically not the religion of Kepler or Maxwell.

Could it be claimed that in fact these scientists did not properly understand the relationship between their religious beliefs and science? Is it possible that they somehow (and fortunately for us) thought their beliefs were conducive to their scientific work, but if they had only known the truth they would have realized that their work was undermining belief in God? Presumably, had they grasped this insight they would have either stopped their scientific work straightaway or else relinquished their religious beliefs. Needless to say, the burden of proof lies with anyone claiming that these scientists were fundamentally mistaken about the relationship between science and religion. I am unaware of any attempt that has been made to argue the case.

Fortunately, there is a very straightforward way to make sense of the approach of these pioneers of science. It is the simple idea that a scientific account of an event can be completely compatible with an alternative account of the same event. Suppose you are out for a drive in your car and see your friend Jack walking along the road. Jack happens to see you and waves at you as you drive past. Would an explanation of *how* this happened in terms of the functioning of Jack's brain and the subsequent physiological processes in his arm resulting in the movement of his hand undermine your belief that the reason *why* Jack waved at you was because he recognized you and wanted to great you? Clearly not. The scientific account does not *explain away* the reason *why* Jack waved at you, but explains *how* Jack waved at you.[13] In a similar way, the pioneers of science believed that by providing scientific accounts of natural phenomena they were in no way removing God from the picture. As mathematician John Lennox puts it:

> It is . . . a category mistake to suppose that our understanding of the impersonal principles according to which the universe works makes it either unnecessary or impossible to believe in the existence of a personal Creator who designed, made, and upholds the universe.[14]

But perhaps there is an objection to the line of reasoning offered so far since there is quite a difference between Jack and God. In Jack's case you know

why he waved because you know how people normally behave when they recognize someone, but it might be argued that there is no corresponding way of
knowing that God created and upholds the universe. According to this objection, maybe the existence of God is compatible with science, but the problem
is just that there is no reason to believe in God in the first place. In response,
many theists will argue that there are plenty of good reasons for believing in
God. Whether that is the case or not, the point here is that this disagreement
cannot be resolved by the atheist's making a simple appeal to the progress of
science. The atheist might have a point if the only reasons offered for belief
in God were due to gaps in science, but that was not the view of the scientists
mentioned earlier and is not the view I shall defend here either.

Let's suppose that you did not recognize Jack when he waved at you. It
is true that the scientific account of the various mechanisms involved does
provide an explanation of the fact that he waved at you, but this is clearly
not the full story. Indeed, the most important question for you is *why* this
person waved at you; that is, you want to know what the *reason* was for his
waving at you. On being informed that it was your friend Jack, the explanation is obvious. This explanation in terms of Jack's reason for waving is clearly
compatible with the scientific account and is not intended to fill a gap in
the science. It is apparent that your question as to why this person waved at
you does not require further scientific research into brain function. To think
otherwise would be, as Lennox puts it, a category mistake.[15]

The idea that it would be a category mistake essentially amounts to saying
that there are really two distinct kinds of explanation in the example. In
addition to *scientific explanations* there are also *personal explanations*. The former
generally refer to physical states and scientific laws, whereas the latter refer to
desires and intentions of a person. The philosopher Keith Ward claims that
personal explanation

> is a perfectly satisfactory form of explanation, and it does not seem to be reducible
> to scientific explanation. If it is, no one has yet plausibly suggested any idea how to
> reduce it. How can my talk of knowledge, desires, intentions and awareness translate
> into statements of physics that only refer to physical states and general laws of their
> behaviour?[16]

Like Ward, Richard Swinburne argues for the existence of God on the
grounds that God's existence provides a good *personal* explanation of various
features of the universe, including a personal explanation as to why the
universe exists in the first place.[17] Here we see the problem with Dawkins's
considering God to be a scientific hypothesis. As pointed out in chapter 1 my

objection to this is not to the word *hypothesis* but to the word *scientific*. Arguably, the New Atheists reject the idea that God's existence explains anything on the grounds that God is not a good scientific explanation, but they fail to do justice to the possibility that God's existence could provide a good personal explanation. Yet this issue lies at the heart of the whole debate, as Ward points out. Which of the two kinds of explanation is more fundamental? The New Atheists would claim that scientific explanation is more fundamental because there is a scientific explanation for the existence of persons with desires and intentions. By contrast, the theist claims that personal explanation is more fundamental because there is a personal explanation for the existence of the physical universe and scientific laws in terms of the desires and intentions of God. It would clearly be begging the question in favour of atheism to require that all explanation must be scientific in nature.

One response to this line of reasoning would be to point out that a lot of progress has been made in fields like neuroscience and to claim that future science might enable us to reduce personal explanations to scientific explanations. The problem with this response is that the reasons put forward by Swinburne and Ward for thinking that personal explanation cannot be reduced to scientific explanation are not based on the limitations of current science, but on showing that it cannot be done even in principle because these are fundamentally different types of explanation.[18] If they are right about this, then personal explanation takes us beyond the limits of science. Even if we possessed complete scientific accounts of the history of the universe, the origin of life, of conscious life, and so on, an important, and perhaps even the most important, question would still remain: is there some ultimate reason for all of this to have taken place? Whether or not belief in God provides a good answer to this question, it is not merely a question that can be answered by filling a gap in our scientific knowledge, although that is not to say that science is completely irrelevant to answering it. We shall return to this topic in the next chapter.

Another way in which scientific explanation appears to be limited is in terms of its own success. Why is it that science is able to explain so many natural phenomena? The world behaves in a sufficiently regular and orderly way that we are able to study it and in many cases describe its behaviour by scientific laws expressed in terms of mathematical equations. But why should this be so? As we have seen, the pioneers of science accounted for the success of science in theistic terms. Once again the key point is that this question takes us beyond the limits of science for it is science itself that is to be explained.[19] A modern defender of this approach is Richard Swinburne, who puts it like this:

> I am not postulating a 'God of the gaps', a god merely to explain the things which science has not yet explained. I am postulating a God to explain what science explains; I do not deny that science explains, but I postulate God to explain why science explains.[20]

A related question concerns not only the fact that the natural world can be described by scientific laws, but the fact that the laws, and in particular the relevant constants, have values that are suitable for life to exist. Why should this be so? Many think that theism provides a good explanation. It may also be the case that the origin of the universe provides a limitation to scientific explanation that may be relevant to theism. We shall return to these issues in chapters 4 and 5.

It is also possible that there will turn out to be other ways in which science is found to be limited. For example, cosmologist Stephen Hawking and others have claimed that Gödel's incompleteness theorem might rule out the possibility of a theory of everything.[21] Quantum theory places a limitation on our knowledge of any system via the Heisenberg uncertainty principle. It may also provide a limitation in the further sense that there are various interpretations of the theory that appear to be empirically equivalent so that no conceivable experiment could provide reason to favour one interpretation over another.[22] It seems unlikely that such limitations have any direct implications for belief in God, but they do suggest that it may not be possible, even in principle, for science to answer some questions within its own domain. This being so, one cannot rule out the possibility that science will encounter some limitations in principle that are relevant to theism.

There are, of course, plenty of gaps in our scientific understanding of the universe. It certainly seems that a strategy of basing one's belief in God merely on the fact that there are such gaps is misguided and it also seems appropriate for scientists to try to fill the gaps. Nevertheless, it would be a mistake to conclude that there are therefore no gaps. The claim that no gaps exist certainly goes beyond the available evidence. John Lennox distinguishes between 'bad gaps', which we would expect to be closed by science, and 'good gaps' that might 'be revealed by science as not being within its explanatory power'.[23] He notes that if mathematicians cannot prove a conjecture true, one strategy is to try to prove that it is false. He draws attention to the fact that this approach can also work in physics as illustrated by the fact that the law of conservation of energy excludes the possibility of perpetual-motion machines. He suggests that there could be a corresponding law of conservation of information, which might make it possible to infer the existence of 'good gaps'. Whether his suggestion will ever be shown to be correct, one cannot rule out the possibility that science might indeed reveal 'good gaps'.

The philosopher of science Bradley Monton, who is an atheist, points out:

> Just because gaps in the past were filled in with further naturalistic scientific investigation, it doesn't follow that every gap in the future will be similarly filled. [An] argument to the contrary is a relatively weak inductive argument . . . it's also the case that the history of science is full of seemingly insoluble gaps in our understanding that have never been filled in naturalistically.[24]

He refers to examples such as the nature of consciousness, how the brain produces conscious experience, what the nature of 'mass' is, what the universe is made of, and goes on to say, 'One can't just say: all gaps in the past have been naturalistically filled in, so future gaps will be naturalistically filled in as well, because in fact there are some persistent gaps that have never been naturalistically filled in.'[25]

In this context it is worth distinguishing between causal gaps and explanatory gaps. Consider a chain of events where each event is an effect of the one before it and a cause of the one after it. This could be a chain of events in a chemical reaction, for example. Suppose that all of the events in the cause-and-effect chain are well understood scientifically, except for one step in the process. In that case, we could say that there is a causal gap in our scientific knowledge. Now consider an explanatory gap. In debates about the nature of consciousness some people have claimed that there is an explanatory gap in the sense that consciousness cannot be explained in terms of the physical processes taking place in the brain. In general, this explanatory gap is not considered to be a gap in a cause-and-effect chain of events. The philosopher David Chalmers argues that there is an explanatory gap even though he believes that there are no causal gaps in the physical world.[26] Furthermore, while some advocates of the explanatory gap think that one day the gap might be closed, Chalmers argues that this gap cannot be closed in principle because of the difference between conscious experience and physical processes.[27] It seems to me that appealing to God in the context of a causal gap in a cause-and-effect chain of events describing a regularly occurring natural process is highly problematic. But appealing to God in the context of an explanatory gap might be feasible in some cases where there are good reasons for believing that the gap is one that cannot be closed in principle.

Irrespective of whether such gaps, either causal or explanatory, exist within science, it is clear that there are limitations to scientific explanation that arise from science itself; questions concerning whether there is a reason for the world to be the way it is, questions about why science explains and questions about why scientific laws take on the specific forms they do thus making the universe suitable for life. Let us call these *limitations beyond science* and contrast them with *limitations within science* such as those arising from Gödel's theorem, quantum theory or Lennox's good gaps. It also seems clear that there are other important *limitations outside science*, such as questions about how we should live our lives, questions that science simply cannot answer. Sam Harris appears to dispute this since he has proposed a scientific account of morality, but we shall see in chapter 8 that there are serious problems with his proposal.

Dawkins appears to be sceptical about whether there are any meaningful questions that science cannot answer, but concedes:

> Perhaps there are some genuinely profound and meaningful questions that are forever beyond the reach of science. Maybe quantum theory is already knocking on the door of the unfathomable. But if science cannot answer some ultimate question, what makes anybody think that religion can?[28]

The first point to note in response is that there is no 'perhaps' about it. Many of the questions that are of greatest importance to most people's lives are beyond the reach of science. Given their emphasis on scientific knowledge over and above other types of knowledge, the New Atheists come close to what is known as *scientism*, the belief that science is the only rational approach for acquiring knowledge. According to scientism, if there are meaningful questions outside science, it is not possible to know the answers, at least not with the kind of justification found in science. As many have pointed out, however, scientism is self-defeating in the sense that if it is true there could be no good reason to believe it to be true.[29] John Lennox explains the problem:

> But what destroys scientism completely is the fatal flaw of self-contradiction that runs through it. Scientism does not need to be refuted by external argument: it self-destructs. . . . For, the statement that only science can lead to truth is not itself deduced from science. It is not a scientific statement but rather a statement about science . . . Therefore, if scientism's basic principle is true, the statement expressing scientism must be false. Scientism refutes itself. Hence it is incoherent.[30]

Dawkins may well be right that religion is irrelevant to limitations within science such as those arising from quantum theory. But his dismissal of the relevance of religion to questions beyond science and outside science is not at all convincing, as we shall see in later chapters. For the moment, however, it should be clear that progress in science in no way undermines belief in God.

This would be the case only if belief in God is confined to the God-of-the-gaps.

The above discussion enables us to respond to Atkins's lazy creator charge and Hitchens's reference to Laplace. Atkins's lazy creator is simply the God-of-the-gaps, who becomes irrelevant as science fills the gaps. The God of serious believers is unaffected by such developments. As for Laplace's claim that he had no need of God in his equations, this is certainly correct. If God appeared in the equations, it would again be the God-of-the-gaps, brought in because of scientific ignorance. Lennox asks us to suppose the following:

> Napoleon had posed a somewhat different question to Laplace: 'Why is there a universe at all in which there is matter and gravity and in which projectiles composed of matter moving under gravity describe the orbits encapsulated in your mathematical equations?'[31]

This question involves *limitations beyond science* since it asks for the reason for the existence of the universe and of scientific laws. Lennox claims that 'it would be harder to argue that the existence of God was irrelevant to that question'.[32]

While it is important to recognize the problems of the God-of-the-gaps approach, we also need to be aware of a tendency on the part of some atheists to dismiss all theistic arguments as God-of-the-gaps arguments. Theistic arguments often involve appealing to God as an explanation for something that science cannot explain. In response, it is often claimed that appealing to God in this way is just the God-of-the-gaps strategy. We must be careful here, however. If the theist appeals to something that science cannot explain at present, but for which there are good reasons to believe that future science will provide an explanation, the God-of-the-gaps charge seems justified. If, on the other hand, the theist offers reasons for believing that science will not, in principle, be able to provide an explanation or that it is very unlikely that future science will undermine the argument and might even enhance it, then the atheist cannot simply dismiss the argument by attributing it to the God-of-the-gaps strategy. Consider the earlier discussion about personal and scientific explanation. Since good reasons have been provided by Swinburne and others for thinking that personal explanation cannot be reduced to scientific explanation, it would be inappropriate for an atheist to dismiss this as a God-of-the-gaps argument. To assume that there must always be a scientific explanation even if it is not known at present is essentially a 'naturalism of the gaps' and just takes us back to scientism.

The separation of science and religion

Instead of viewing science and religion as being in conflict with each other, an alternative approach is to see them as being completely independent of each other. According to this approach, they deal with different subject matters and so there is no possibility of conflict between them. The late Stephen Jay Gould articulated this in terms of what he called non-overlapping magisteria (NOMA), the idea that science deals exclusively with the empirical realm (including facts and theory) while religion deals exclusively with questions of ultimate meaning and moral value.[33]

Needless to say, all of the New Atheists reject NOMA and are right to do so, although not necessarily for the right reasons. Dawkins, for example, asks, 'But does Gould really want to cede to *religion* the right to tell us what is good and what is bad?'[34] As I read Gould, the answer is clearly 'no'. Gould states:

> I most emphatically do not argue that ethical people must validate their standards by overt appeals to religion . . . But I do reiterate that religion has occupied the center of this magisterium [of ethical discussion and search for meaning] in the traditions of most cultures.[35]

Gould's point seems to be that religion should deal only with questions of meaning and morality rather than factual matters, but that is not to say that *only religion* can address questions of meaning and morality. Given Gould's own non-religious perspective it is hard to see what else he could have had in mind. A more significant problem for Gould's position, which both Dawkins and Dennett draw attention to, is that many religions do make factual claims. Christian claims about the existence of God and the life of Jesus, for example, can hardly be reduced solely to claims about meaning and morality. Dennett sums up responses to NOMA:

> Although Gould's desire for peace between these often warring perspectives was laudable, his proposal found little favor on either side, since in the minds of the religious it proposed abandoning all religious claims to factual truth and understanding of the natural world . . . whereas in the minds of the secularists it granted too much authority to religion in matters of ethics and meaning.[36]

But if NOMA is incorrect, what is the alternative? Must we return to the viewpoint where science and religion are considered to be in continual conflict? Much has been written about the relationship between science and religion (or theology), but few defend either of these approaches. A leading contributor on this topic, Ian Barbour, has outlined four ways of relating the two fields: *conflict, independence, dialogue* and *integration*.[37] We have already discussed the first two and it is unnecessary for our purposes here to consider the dialogue and integration approaches in detail. The key point, however, is that they allow for a much more positive relationship than that advocated by either the New Atheists or Gould. For example, John Polkinghorne refers to a *consonance* where 'the scientific and theological accounts of the world must fit together in a mutually consistent way' and that they can do so 'not as a mere matter of compatibility, but with a degree of mutual enhancement and enlightenment'.[38]

There are various respects in which a positive relationship can be articulated. For example, Barbour discusses the order and intelligibility of the world as a presupposition of science that cannot be explained by science but makes sense from a theistic perspective. Another possible link arises from the fact that truth is important for religious believers as well as scientists, a point recognized by the New Atheists. But contrary to the New Atheists, many writers on science and religion go further and claim that there is some similarity in the approaches used for acquiring truth.[39] A particular example of this is the claim that both science and religion use an approach known as inference to the best explanation,[40] whereby they try to find the best explanation of the facts in question. In the scientific case this might be some body of evidence such as that amassed by Darwin, whereas in religion it might be more general features of the universe, human nature, morality, and so on. For example, science, like religion, often tries to make sense of the observable world by appealing to entities like quarks that cannot be observed. And just as in science, it is factors such as explanatory power, coherence and comprehensiveness that are used to argue, for example, that God exists.[41] None of this is to say that science and religion have the same methodology. Clearly, it is often possible to test scientific theories, particularly in physics, to a high degree of accuracy. Despite such differences, however, there are more similarities than some might be prepared to admit.[42]

This brief discussion of approaches to the relationship between science and religion highlights the fact that, despite the impression given by the New Atheists, conflict on the one hand or independence on the other are not the only two options. In fact, the idea that there might be a single, correct approach to the relationship between science and religion seems unlikely. Instead, the two disciplines can interact in a variety of ways. For example, scientists undertaking experiments in atomic collisions do not need to draw on their religious views before doing the experiments and so science and religious views are independent in this case. In other cases conflicts seem possible. Suppose, for example, that big bang cosmology is rejected and replaced by a new theory proposing that the universe always existed, something like an updated version of the steady state theory perhaps. This would not worry some theologians, but it would come into conflict with the Christian doctrine of creation as traditionally understood.

It is worth noting that there is nothing particularly unique about the relationship between science and religion since similar issues arise with other disciplines. How do science and history relate, for example? Or science and philosophy? Philosophers and scientists usually ask very different questions and so do not need to consult each other very much. This means that in most cases the two disciplines are independent, but not always since there are areas where they interact.[43] For example, research on the foundations of quantum mechanics raises philosophical as well as scientific issues and there is no simple way to separate the two. In such cases, scientists cannot ignore philosophical questions and philosophers cannot ignore scientific questions.

Since conflicts cannot be ruled out, what should one do if or when conflicts between science and a religion such as Christianity arise? Here there are no easy answers, but there is a range of fairly straightforward options to be considered rather than simply rejecting Christianity. First, it is possible that even from a Christian perspective the theological reasons for holding the belief are dubious, if it is based on a misinterpretation of the Bible, for example. This would have been the case when some Christians mistakenly took the Bible to teach that Earth was at the centre of the universe. Secondly, it is possible that what is presented as science is really going beyond what science can reliably tell us. This would apply when we are told that science shows that our existence was not planned but is the result of an unguided, purposeless process. Even most atheists will acknowledge that statements of this kind are philosophical in nature and go far beyond the scientific evidence. Thirdly, in some cases it is possible to remain agnostic as to how to resolve the conflict. Suppose there are good theological reasons for holding on to a Christian belief, but that the conflicting scientific claims have good evidential support. Perhaps, however, new evidence or theories will shed new light on the conflict or a new theory will come along that is better supported by the evidence and that does not conflict with Christianity. The bigger the conflict the less the third approach seems acceptable, especially over a long period of time. But for minor conflicts, such as claims that some archaeological discovery disproves a passage in the Bible, this approach is often the best one to adopt.

Once again, it is also worth noting that these strategies for dealing with conflict are not unique to science and religion. Scientists themselves often have to deal with a similar situation when evidence arises that seems to conflict with the currently accepted theory. They may decide to revise the theory or to question its validity or to wait and see whether new research will throw further light on the matter. The apparent conflict between the orbit of the planet Uranus and Newton's theory of gravitation provides a famous example. The evidence was too well confirmed to reject, but the Newtonians did not decide to reject the theory either. Instead, a new planet was postulated that would enable Newton's theory to account for the orbit of Uranus. Neptune was duly discovered. However, this approach failed when the orbit of Mercury was also found to be in conflict with Newton's theory. The moral of the story is that there is no straightforward way of deciding how to resolve a conflict in science that will be appropriate in all cases. The same applies to conflicts between science and religion.[44]

Science, religion and incomprehensibility

A common claim of the New Atheists is that religion, particularly in monotheistic religions, revels in incomprehensibility. Dennett in particular emphasizes the role of incomprehensibility in the survival and propagation of religion. The idea is that people can demonstrate their belief merely by professing it and to do this they do not need to understand it. In fact, incomprehensibility can help in this regard since 'People's discomfort with sheer incoherence is strong, so there are always tantalizing elements of sense-making narrative, punctuated with seriously perplexing nuggets of incomprehensibility.'[45] Dennett's point is that a prosaic account of religious beliefs would give rise to scepticism, but the use of incomprehensibility adds mystery, which makes them more appealing. Dennett and Dawkins also link incomprehensibility with faith, the idea being that faith enables the religious believer to embrace the incomprehensible and paradoxical.

It is important to emphasize that by incomprehensible they mean 'not just *counterintuitive* . . . but downright unintelligible'.[46] And of course this fits in with their idea that theology is obscurantist, and they seem to think that it is deliberately so, trying to cover up its lack of evidential support. Furthermore, they contrast this obscurantist approach with the clarity of scientific ideas. But Dennett is familiar with the response that science, particularly physics, also appeals to incomprehensible and mysterious concepts. Dennett asks, 'isn't my faith in the truth of the propositions of quantum mechanics that I admit I don't understand a sort of *religious* faith in any case?'[47] He responds by drawing attention to an important difference between the two cases in that predictions of quantum mechanics have been confirmed to a high degree of accuracy in experiments. Furthermore, it is not just a matter of professing the propositions of quantum mechanics; you can build a device that depends on it for its operation.

Dennett is of course right that this is a very important difference, but it fails to address the issue fully, which was not about the evidence for quantum mechanics as opposed to theological claims but the incomprehensibility of quantum mechanics. Here we must be careful, for in one sense quantum mechanics is comprehensible. The mathematical formalism is certainly comprehensible and can be used to make remarkably accurate predictions of atomic structure, for example; but in terms of understanding what the quantum world is like it is safe to say that no one really knows. Numerous interpretations of quantum mechanics have been proposed, but none has been generally accepted and all are to a greater or lesser extent paradoxical. The famous Schrödinger's cat paradox illustrates one of the problems. A quantum process has a 50:50 chance of triggering the release of cyanide inside a box. Unfortunately, there is a cat in the box, which will die if the cyanide is released. Afterwards we open the box and find that the cat is either dead or alive (of course), but what is the state of the cat just before we opened the box? Intuitively it will be either dead or it will be alive depending on the outcome of the chance process; it is just that we don't know which. But if the cat is described by quantum mechanics, this intuitive answer seems to be ruled out. So what is going on?

There seems to be some sense in which it is in a very strange combination of being *both dead and alive*, a combination that makes perfect sense mathematically but not in terms of what is really going on.[48] According to the many worlds interpretation, there are really two worlds, the cat being dead in one and alive in the other, and so when we open the box there are two versions of us as well; in one world we see that the cat is alive and in the other we see that it is dead. If this isn't paradoxical enough, another interpretation claims that it is our act of merely opening the box that results in the cat changing from being in its weird quantum state to being alive or dead. Dawkins rightly describes this account as 'equally preposterous' and 'shatteringly paradoxical'. It seems that incomprehensibility and paradox lie at the heart of one of the pillars of modern science.

It is important to clarify the point of this discussion. Sometimes religious commentators seem to argue that modern physics is mysterious, just as religion is mysterious, and so it is just as rational to believe the latter as the former. That is certainly not my point. The point is rather that just because some ideas in theology are difficult, if not impossible, to express clearly, that is no reason to dismiss them as ploys introduced to help people believe the unbelievable. In fact, the comparison with science suggests a much more charitable interpretation of what is going on in at least some cases. In the scientific case it should not surprise us that we find it difficult to comprehend how the world works at the most fundamental level. There is no guarantee that our concepts, which are appropriate in ordinary everyday circumstances, will also apply to quantum mechanics. It might be desirable if they did, but reality forces us to appeal to metaphors or seemingly paradoxical and coun-terintuitive ideas instead. This in no way contradicts the view expressed earlier that belief in God gives us reason to think that the world is intelligible and so provides a basis for science. It does not follow from this idea that it will be easy for us to understand what the world is like nor that we shall be able to make sense of it in terms of ordinary everyday concepts; perhaps it is intel-ligible mathematically, but not intuitively. Also, the general intelligibility of the universe does not preclude the possibility that there will be some fundamental aspects of reality that are forever beyond our understanding. As finite crea-tures, that seems like a distinct possibility.

If there is a God, it seems quite likely that the same limitations would apply in the theological case. If, as finite creatures, we find it difficult to comprehend the natural world, it would surely not be surprising if we also find it difficult to comprehend the creator of the world. There is every reason to think that some of our ordinary concepts would no longer apply and so an appeal to metaphor or apparently paradoxical ideas might be necessary. It would be a mistake to dismiss the idea of God on the grounds that, if God exists, he does not fit in easily to the familiar world of experience. Modern physics would suggest that dismissing ideas on such grounds is a poor strategy. Yet, as we shall discuss, in chapter 6, part of Dawkins's case against God seems to rest on the idea that God, if he exists, would have to fit in with our experi-ence since he thinks that God would have to possess some sort of complex structure analogous to the human brain.

But there is a danger in going too far in the direction of emphasizing the limitations of our concepts. Just because things are difficult to understand does not mean that anything goes. If the language we use to talk about God is meaningless or contradictory, then it really isn't worth talking about God at all. And it must be acknowledged that some religious writing does fall into this category. But the main doctrines of Christianity do not. The doctrines of the Trinity and the incarnation cannot easily be grasped in terms of ordinary concepts, but they are hardly meaningless or contradictory.[49] Furthermore, there are many Christian claims that are perfectly intelligible, such as that God exists, that God created the world, that Jesus rose from the dead, and so forth.

Indeed, the New Atheists think these claims are false and so they must think they are meaningful.

Overall, there is no good reason to think that there is some fundamental conflict between science and religion, with the former being the paradigm of clarity and the latter delighting in incomprehensibility. Many of the beliefs in Christianity are perfectly clear and those that are much more difficult to understand can be thought of in terms of trying to make sense of a reality (i.e. God) that is greater than our limited minds can fully comprehend.

Miracles

The New Atheists reject all belief in God, but they reserve a special contempt for religious belief that involves miracles. In their view the idea of a deistic creator who gets the universe off and running and leaves it to its own devices thereafter is bad enough, but a God who is personal, loving, all-knowing, and so on, and who performs miracles or answers prayers is beyond the pale; surely no rational person could believe in such a God. The impression is given that the more sophisticated and rational religious believers have rejected this kind of theism, but just haven't had the courage to take the final step to embrace atheism. And, of course, they are partly right in the sense that many theologians have indeed rejected belief in any kind of miraculous intervention in favour of a more deistic viewpoint.

But why do the New Atheists (and indeed the theologians in question) take such a dim view of miracles? At least part of the answer is that they think there is some kind of inconsistency between science and belief in miracles, that it is somehow inappropriate to believe in miracles in the light of modern science. Dawkins puts it like this:

> Sophisticated theologians aside (and even they are happy to tell miracle stories to
> the unsophisticated in order to swell congregations), I suspect that alleged miracles
> provide the strongest reason many believers have for their faith; and miracles, by
> definition, violate the principles of science.[50]

Note the expression 'violate the principles of science'. What does Dawkins mean by this? It seems clear from the context that he takes this to be an extremely negative feature of miracles. His view seems to be that science is the most rational way to acquire knowledge about the world, but miracles violate the principles of science and so belief in miracles is tantamount to a rejection of science.

If this is Dawkins's view, it faces an obvious rejoinder. A common way of thinking about miracles is that they are events brought about by God that could not have been brought about by natural processes. In one sense such events do violate scientific laws, but it is not because there is anything wrong with the laws in question; it is just that there is something else going on, namely God's acting in a direct way. In general, scientific laws tell us what will happen under certain circumstances, other things being equal, such as there being no interfering effects that would render the law inapplicable. In the case of miracles the relevant laws cannot be applied because other things are not equal. So one can accept the validity of scientific laws, but also maintain that on occasion God decides to act in a different way. There is nothing even remotely contradictory about such a viewpoint.[51]

To maintain that belief in miracles requires rejecting science presupposes that all events are brought about by natural processes in accordance with scientific laws. Of course, this seems like a very reasonable viewpoint if the natural world is all there is, that is, if there is no God. But if there is a God, there would be no obvious reason to reach this conclusion. Thus, rejecting miracles because of science seems to amount to saying that it is irrational to believe in miracles if there is no God (or no other supernatural beings). But who ever thought otherwise?

So there is no way of ruling out the very possibility of miracles by appealing to science. To rule out the possibility of miracles would require the further assumption that the natural world is all there is, but that would be begging the question against miracles. Dawkins seems to be aware of this since, despite his claim that belief in miracles is unscientific, he does not quite close the door on the miraculous. In fact, he thinks that whether a particular alleged miracle occurred is a 'strictly scientific question with a definite answer in principle: yes or no'.[52] This is a very revealing claim for it suggests that all factual questions are scientific questions. In fact, there are questions in almost every area of human thought that have 'a definite answer in principle: yes or no'. Questions about common-sense beliefs and factual beliefs we form every day as well as beliefs in detective cases, history, morality, music, poetry, literature, sport, and so on can have definite yes or no answers but most people would not think of these as part of science. This seems like a clear statement of Dawkins's scientism. He even allows for the possibility in principle that scientific evidence might lend support to a miraculous claim. Dennett goes further and claims:

> the only hope of ever demonstrating [that a miracle occurred] to a doubting world would be by adopting the scientific method, with its assumption of no miracles, and showing that science was utterly unable to account for the phenomena.[53]

It is not at all obvious how one could demonstrate any such thing. Based on the writings of the New Atheists, it seems highly likely that they would give short shrift to any miraculous claim no matter what the evidence. The reason for this is that they appear to have an absolute commitment to the view that all events can be accounted for, in principle if not in practice, in terms of purely natural explanations.

To some readers the story so far will sound familiar: miracles as violations of laws of nature, the idea that these laws count against miracles, but do not completely rule them out, and yet in practice miraculous claims are always likely to be ruled out. This is all very similar to the argument against miracles proposed by the great Scottish philosopher David Hume. In fact, Hitchens tells us that 'the last word on the subject was written by . . . Hume'.[54] In his book *Hume's Abject Failure* the leading philosopher of science John Earman, who is an agnostic, begs to differ:

> It is not simply that Hume's essay does not achieve its goals, but that his goals
> are ambiguous and confused. Most of Hume's considerations are unoriginal,
> warmed over versions of arguments that are found in the writings of predecessors
> and contemporaries. And the parts of *'Of Miracles'* that set Hume apart do not
> stand up to scrutiny. Worse still, the essay reveals the weakness and the poverty
> of Hume's own account of induction and probabilistic reasoning. And to cap it
> all off, the essay represents the kind of overreaching that gives philosophy a bad
> name.[55]

If Earman is right, far from having the last word on the subject, it seems that Hume really didn't have very much of substance to say on the subject at all. Despite its weaknesses, it is worth considering Hume's argument briefly to understand an approach to miracles that is very similar to that adopted by the New Atheists.

Hume claims that 'a wise man . . . proportions his belief to the evidence'.[56] In the case of an alleged miracle, there is testimonial evidence of witnesses supporting it, but he claims that the laws of nature count against it. Since laws of nature are based on numerous observations, this means that there is substantial evidence against the miracle. So the wise man must weigh up the evidence on both sides and Hume leaves us in no doubt as to what the rational conclusion should be:

> A miracle is a violation of the laws of nature; and as firm and unalterable experience
> has established these laws, the proof against a miracle, from the very nature of the
> fact, is as entire as any argument from experience can possibly be imagined.[57]

Hume does not completely close the door on miracles, but allows the possibility that it could be rational to believe that a miracle had occurred if rejecting the testimony would be even more incredible than believing the miracle. That at least is the theory, but when it comes to practice he discusses a particular case where he considers the credibility and integrity of numerous witnesses to be unquestioned and yet claims:

> And what have we to oppose to such a cloud of witnesses, but the absolute
> impossibility or miraculous nature of the events, which they relate? And this surely,
> in the eyes of all reasonable people, will alone be regarded as sufficient refutation.[58]

The door is quickly closed. It seems that no amount of evidence would be considered adequate to make it reasonable to believe a miracle had occurred. And so it seems with the New Atheists as well.

Essentially, Hume's argument amounts to saying that because any alleged miracle is so improbable to start with (since it is at odds with a law of nature), no amount of evidence supporting the miracle can compensate for this and so it is always more probable that the miracle did not occur. But if this is correct, the same principle seems to apply in non-miraculous cases. As Earman makes clear, an event that initially seems very improbable need not remain so once the relevant evidence is taken into account. In addition to the initial probability of the event, the probability of the evidence if the event had not taken place also needs to be considered. To illustrate Earman's point, suppose my friend Tom enters the lottery every week. Suppose also that the winning numbers have just been announced in a particular week. Although it is initially very unlikely that he won, the next day Tom arrives at my house and is driving a new BMW. He tells me that he hit the jackpot in the lottery the previous night, he shows me a newspaper that has a picture of him receiving the cheque and later I see him on the local news on television. All of this evidence would be very improbable if he had not won the lottery, but is just the kind of evidence that would be expected if he had won. This is sufficient to overcome the initial improbability of Tom's having won and, in fact, I can be virtually certain that he did win.

There doesn't seem to be any reason why this kind of reasoning could not apply in the case of miracles. Perhaps we think that a particular miraculous claim is very improbable, but it could become probable (and perhaps highly probable) once reliable testimonial evidence is taken into account. This is particularly so if there are numerous independent, reliable witnesses. An objection might be that the two cases are not really analogous because a miracle involves a supernatural event that cannot be explained in terms of scientific laws, whereas this is not the case for Tom's winning the lottery. But that just amounts to a refusal to allow the evidence to overturn the initial improbability of the miracle and so is clearly begging the question against miracles.

Suppose, taking various witness testimonies into account, we conclude that an extremely unusual event has taken place, one that cannot be accounted for in terms of scientific laws. Would that be sufficient to establish it as a miracle? Perhaps instead we should just treat it as an unexplained event or maybe an event that motivates us to look for a new and better scientific theory to account for the evidence. Here the context of the event is important.[59] The idea is not that any inexplicable occurrence should be labelled as a miracle, but if it seems plausible to think that God would have had a good reason to bring the event about and if it is an event that seems unlikely to be explained by future science, then a miracle seems like a distinct possibility.[60]

None of the foregoing discussion presents any reason for believing that any miracles have ever occurred, but is simply to show that there need not be anything irrational in doing so. In particular, there is nothing unscientific about belief in miracles. Indeed, if there is good evidence in favour of a miracle having occurred, the proper scientific attitude should be to accept it as such.[61] We shall consider evidence for a particular miraculous claim, the resurrection of Jesus, in chapter 10.

Conclusion

The goal in this chapter has been to show that there is no intrinsic conflict between science and belief in God, even a God who intervenes in the world to perform miracles. Scientific progress does not remove the need for God unless it is the God-of-the-gaps whose role is merely to account for things that science cannot yet explain. In Christianity, God is just as much the God of what science does explain as what it does not. Furthermore, the scientific enterprise is certainly consistent with a belief in a God who created a universe that behaves in an orderly way and that is intelligible to humans. Of course, science and religion are different, but this difference does not mean that they must inevitably be in conflict or that they must be treated as completely independent of each other. Finally, we have also seen that there is no foundation to the ideas that in general religious concepts are deliberately made incomprehensible in contrast to the clarity of scientific concepts and that science somehow renders belief in miracles irrational.

Perhaps science and belief in God are not in conflict, but this does not amount to an argument that God exists. After all, it is possible for belief in God to be compatible with science and yet false. In the next chapter we consider some reasons for believing that God does in fact exist.

Notes

1. *GNG*, pp. 64–65.

2. *TGD*, p. 347, emphasis in original.

3. C. A. Russell, 'The Conflict Metaphor and its Social Origins', *Science and Christian Belief* 1 (1989), pp. 3–26 (quoted in John C. Lennox, *God's Undertaker: Has Science Buried God?* [Oxford: Lion Hudson, 2007], pp. 26–27).

4. John Hedley Brooke, *Science and Religion: Some Historical Perspectives* (Cambridge: Cambridge University Press, 1991), p. 37.

5. See David N. Livingstone, *Darwin's Forgotten Defenders* (Edinburgh: Scottish Academic Press, 1987). Livingstone draws attention to a number of prominent evangelicals, such as the scientist Asa Gray and theologians James McCosh and A. H. Strong, who embraced evolution. The extent to which Warfield supported evolution has been questioned by Fred Zaspel, 'B. B. Warfield on Creation and Evolution', *Themelios* 35.2 (2010), pp. 198–211. However, he at least seems to have been sympathetic towards evolution even if he questioned the Darwinian mechanism for it.

6. One particular issue here arises from the existence of suffering and death, which a theistic evolutionist must accept as being part of God's creation. We shall consider this question as part of the problem of evil in chapter 8.

7. See, for example, Tim Keller, 'Creation, Evolution, and Christian Laypeople', available at http://biologos.org/uploads/projects/Keller_white_paper.pdf (accessed 14 Sept. 2011).

8. Many critics, including the New Atheists, think that advocates of Intelligent Design (ID) are being disingenuous and that ID is just biblical creationism in disguise. This seems incorrect for three reasons. First, some advocates of ID, particularly Michael Behe, hold views that are much closer to theistic evolution with God guiding the evolutionary processes rather than biblical creationism. Secondly, they make no appeal to the Bible in any of their arguments and so their arguments really ought to be taken at face value. Thirdly, even if their motivation is based on the Bible, why should this present a problem if they make no appeal to the Bible? The key point would be that they claim to have *independent* scientific confirmation of ID. This is a scientific claim, not a biblical one. See Michael J. Behe, *The Edge of Evolution: The Search for the Limits of Darwinism* (New York: Free Press, 2007); William A. Dembski, *No Free Lunch: Why Specified Complexity Cannot Be Purchased without Intelligence* (Lanham, Md.: Rowman & Littlefield, 2007).

9. *TGD*, p. 118.

10. According to historian of science Colin Russell, in his *Cross-Currents: Interactions Between Science and Faith* (Leicester: IVP, 1985), p. 91, the story is probably apocryphal, the alleged reply is not about theism but only science, and Laplace was a practising Roman Catholic.

11. Quoted in Lennox, *God's Undertaker*, p. 20.

12. *TGD*, p. 126.

13. For more on this topic, see chapter 6.

14. Lennox, *God's Undertaker*, p. 44.

15. Lennox gives an illustration that in some respects is similar to that of Jack's waving. He asks us to imagine a team of scientists asked to investigate a beautiful cake. They all draw on their respective disciplines to give a description of the cake. But this still leaves the question as to why the cake was made in the first place and that is a question the scientists cannot answer. Only Aunt Matilda who made it can reveal the answer to us.

16. Keith Ward, *Why There Almost Certainly Is a God: Doubting Dawkins* (Oxford: Lion Hudson, 2008), p. 23.

17. Richard Swinburne, *The Existence of God*, 2nd ed. (Oxford: Oxford University Press, 2004). See especially his discussion of scientific and personal explanation on pp. 26–47.

18. Swinburne provides a detailed argument that personal explanation cannot be analysed in terms of scientific explanation. In addition to the idea that both scientific and personal explanations are required to give the whole story in a scenario such as that of Jack's waving, Swinburne argues that personal explanation cannot be reduced to explanation in terms of passive states (as would be appropriate in a scientific explanation) causing an effect because such states could bring about the corresponding effect without the person intending to do so. He writes, 'Having an intention is not something that happens to an agent, but something she does . . . When one explains an occurrence as brought about by an agent having some intention, one is not by the word "intention" describing some state or event that caused the occurrence, but one is stating that the agent brought about that occurrence and did so because he meant to do so' (ibid., p. 43).

19. In some cases lower-level laws can be explained in terms of higher-level laws, such as Kepler's laws by Newton's laws, but the highest-level laws cannot be explained in this way. If it turns out that there is a fundamental theory of everything, the question would still remain as to why this theory describes our universe.

20. Richard Swinburne, *Is There a God?* (Oxford: Oxford University Press, 1996), p. 68.

21. See, for example, Stephen W. Hawking, 'Gödel and the End of Physics', available at http://www.hawking.org.uk/index.php/lectures/91 (accessed 14 Sept. 2011). Others have questioned this conclusion, however. See, for example, Solomon

Feferman, 'The Nature and Significance of Gödel's Incompleteness Theorems', available at http://math.stanford.edu/~feferman/papers/Godel-IAS.pdf (accessed 14 Sept. 2011).

22. See, for example, Euan Squires, *The Mystery of the Quantum World*, 2nd ed. (Bristol: Institute of Physics, 1994).

23. Lennox, *God's Undertaker*, p. 169.

24. Bradley Monton, *Seeking God in Science: An Atheist Defends Intelligent Design* (Peterborough, Ont.: Broadview, 2009), pp. 115–116.

25. Ibid., p. 116.

26. David J. Chalmers, *The Conscious Mind* (Oxford: Oxford University Press, 1996), p. 125.

27. We shall consider the topic of consciousness again in chapter 5.

28. *TGD*, p. 56.

29. See Paul Moser, *The Evidence for God* (Cambridge: Cambridge University Press, 2010), pp. 76–83; J. P. Moreland and William Lane Craig, *Philosophical Foundations for a Christian Worldview* (Downers Grove: IVP, 2003), pp. 346–350.

30. Lennox, *God's Undertaker*, p. 42.

31. Ibid., p. 45.

32. Ibid.

33. Stephen Jay Gould, *Rock of Ages: Science and Religion in the Fullness of Life* (New York: Ballantine, 1999).

34. *TGD*, p. 57, emphasis in original.

35. Gould, *Rock of Ages*, p. 58.

36. *BTS*, p. 30.

37. Ian G. Barbour, *Religion in an Age of Science* (New York: HarperCollins, 1990).

38. John C. Polkinghorne, *Scientists as Theologians: A Comparison of the Writings of Ian Barbour, Arthur Peacocke and John Polkinghorne* (London: SPCK, 1996), pp. 6–7.

39. See, for example, John C. Polkinghorne, *Reason and Reality* (London: SPCK, 1991).

40. Michael C. Banner, *The Justification of Science and the Rationality of Religious Belief* (Oxford: Clarendon, 1990).

41. An approach along these lines will be adopted in subsequent chapters.

42. For a good account of various approaches to relating science and theology with a particular focus on methodology in science and biblical interpretation, see Philip Duce, *Reading the Mind of God: Interpretation in Science and Theology* (Leicester: Apollos, 1998). Duce proposes a common framework based on the philosophy of Michael Polanyi, which has some features in common with inference to the best explanation but emphasizes personal involvement and commitment in the acquisition of knowledge.

43. Similar points could be made about the relationship between philosophy and theology. For an account of the interaction between philosophy and theology

in the Middle Ages and how modern science was born out of this interaction see James Hannam, *God's Philosophers* (London: Icon, 2009).

44. For an in-depth discussion in the context of conflicts between science and the Bible see Duce, *Reading the Mind of God*, pp. 79–100.

45. *BTS*, p. 230.

46. Ibid., p. 229, emphasis in original.

47. Ibid., p. 232, emphasis in original.

48. The standard interpretation of quantum mechanics seems to lead to the conclusion that it would be a mistake to say that the cat is both dead and alive, just as it would be a mistake to say that it is alive or to say that it is dead or to say that it is neither dead nor alive. That seems about as paradoxical as it can get. See David Z. Albert, *Quantum Mechanics and Experience* (Cambridge, Mass.: Harvard University Press, 1994), pp. 73–79.

49. See, for example, Moreland and Craig, *Philosophical Foundations*; Richard Swinburne, *The Christian God* (Oxford: Clarendon, 1994).

50. *TGD*, p. 59.

51. For a philosophical defence of miracles see Richard Swinburne, *The Concept of Miracle* (New York: Macmillan, 1970); for a biblical perspective see C. John Collins, *The God of Miracles: An Exegetical Examination of God's Action in the World* (Wheaton, Ill.: Crossway, 2000).

52. *TGD*, p. 59.

53. *BTS*, p. 26.

54. *GNG*, p. 141.

55. John Earman, *Hume's Abject Failure* (Oxford: Oxford University Press, 2000), p. 3.

56. David Hume, *Enquiries Concerning Human Understanding and Concerning the Principles of Morals*, ed. P. H. Nidditch, 3rd ed. (Oxford: Clarendon, 1975; first published 1777), p. 110.

57. Ibid., p. 114.

58. Ibid., p. 125.

59. Richard Swinburne considers the importance of religious significance in his discussion of miracles in *Concept of Miracle*, pp. 7–10.

60. The resurrection of Jesus would be a good example. If there is evidence to support the resurrection, it should not be considered merely as an inexplicable event, but as a miracle.

61. It might be objected that this is a God-of-the-gaps argument and, indeed, that it involves a *causal gap*, which I noted earlier is highly problematic. However, there is no causal gap in our scientific knowledge in this case. The point about a miracle is that we *do* know what would normally happen, but it does not happen on this occasion. For this reason, God is not filling in the missing piece in a scientific explanation, but bringing about something that the scientific processes

on their own would not have brought about. Also, by definition, miracles are not
regularly occurring events that we would expect to be able to explain scientifically.
Furthermore, inferring that a miracle occurred requires that there would have to be
some good reason for God to bring it about and not merely that it is scientifically
inexplicable.

4. EVIDENCE FOR GOD – PART 1: THE EXISTENCE AND BEGINNING OF THE UNIVERSE

If the New Atheists are to be believed, this should be a very short chapter. It's not just that they think the balance of evidence is against God's existence; they don't think there is any evidence *at all* in favour of God's existence. It's not that they think the case against God is stronger, all things considered, than the case for God; they don't think there is a serious case for God's existence and they think the case against is overwhelming. In the light of the discussion in earlier chapters it will not come as a surprise that the New Atheists' views are much more extreme than most of their fellow atheists and agnostics. Many atheists would concede that the arguments against God's existence are not quite as decisive as the New Atheists believe.[1] Of course, having weighed all the arguments they still reject belief in God, but are prepared to recognize that others could come to a different conclusion on the basis of the same evidence. The New Atheists have no truck with such a compromising attitude. Instead, they maintain that belief in God is irrational and results not from the fact that believers come to a different conclusion on the basis of the evidence, but because they *ignore* the evidence.

Dawkins, of course, considers belief that God exists to be a delusion and claims that 'there is no evidence to favour the God Hypothesis'.[2] This is a remarkably strong claim, for it is one thing to claim that *overall* the evidence does not favour the God hypothesis, but quite another to claim that there is *no* evidence that counts in its favour. By way of analogy, consider a murder trial.

It is clearly not necessary for the defence to claim that there is *no* evidence against the accused, but only that overall the evidence is not strong.

As we saw in chapter 1, Dawkins does not claim to be able to prove absolutely that there is no God, but lest we get the impression that he may be wavering in his unbelief, he states, 'I am agnostic only to the extent that I am agnostic about fairies at the bottom of the garden.'[3] When considering evidences proposed in favour of belief in God, Hitchens is equally uncompromising, claiming:

> The 'evidence' for faith, then, seems to leave faith looking even weaker than it
> would if it stood, alone and unsupported, all by itself. What can be asserted without
> evidence can also be dismissed without evidence. This is even more true when the
> 'evidence' eventually offered is so shoddy and self-interested.[4]

Note the quotes around evidence indicating, like Dawkins, that in fact there is no evidence or at least no good evidence.

The New Atheists' attitude to evidence for God can be summarized by the view expressed by the philosopher Bertrand Russell in a story to which Dawkins alludes. Russell was asked what he would say if, after death, God asked him why he had not believed. To which he replied, 'Not enough evidence, God, not enough evidence.' Strictly speaking, however, Russell's response is a bit weak for the New Atheists since they claim there is not just insufficient evidence, but none at all.

So convinced are the New Atheists that there is no case for the existence of God, that either they do not bother considering the arguments for the existence of God or else they mention them only briefly and in some cases only to ridicule them. Although Harris makes many sweeping statements about the irrationality of belief in God because he claims it is based on faith rather than evidence, he does not present any discussion of the traditional arguments for the existence of God. Hitchens confidently asserts that 'it is within the compass of any human being to see these evidences and proofs [for the existence of God] as the feeble-minded inventions that they are'.[5] Unfortunately, he does not tell us exactly where the arguments go wrong, but instead makes claims about religion arising from human ignorance and about science ruling out belief in God. He thinks that pointing to the merits of evolution is sufficient to rebut the design argument, but does not address the evidence of fine-tuning (see chapter 5).

Dawkins's chapter on arguments for God's existence must be an embarrassment to most informed atheists and agnostics. As we saw in chapter 1, the philosopher Michael Ruse has stated that '*The God Delusion* makes me ashamed to be an atheist'.[6] Dawkins makes no attempt to engage with the arguments for God's existence or any contemporary advocates of them. In fact, the hypothesis that he wrote this chapter purely for entertainment value receives confirmation when he starts listing humorous arguments for God obtained from a website.[7] He does take a much more serious approach to the design argument, which we shall return to in due course. Dennett assures those of us interested in how he will deal with the arguments for God's existence that we shall have our 'day in court', but when we arrive in court in chapter 8 we find that the purpose is not so much to consider the evidence as to pass judgment. As far as the design argument is concerned, the wise judge informs us that he had reached his verdict in an earlier book and quotes from it to let us know the outcome. The cosmological argument is dealt with in just one paragraph and, rather surprisingly, Dennett gives the impression that one of the problems with it is that it is too difficult to understand.[8] Not a very convincing objection!

Overall, the New Atheists fail miserably to do justice to the evidence and arguments for the existence of God. Perhaps this is not so surprising, however. If they are fully convinced that God does not exist, it scarcely seems like it would be worth taking much time to investigate the evidence seriously. In this chapter and the next I shall try to redress the balance by presenting some evidence and arguments that might be offered in favour of belief in the existence of God, but before doing so two matters need to be addressed. First, if no convincing argument is forthcoming does this mean that we should reject belief in God just as Russell did? Or should we believe in God unless there is a convincing argument to show that God does *not* exist? Secondly, what kind of evidence is appropriate and/or reasonable to look for? Must it be evidence that establishes the existence of God beyond reasonable doubt? Or must it just make it more plausible than not to believe in God? And would it need to be evidence that everyone would find convincing?

Atheism, agnosticism and celestial teapots

It may come as a surprise to some, but the New Atheists are not really atheists at all! Strictly speaking they should be called the 'new agnostics' since they do not claim they can prove with certainty that God does not exist. We must be careful about the term 'agnostic', however, since the 'New Atheists' are not neutral about the existence of God, but are convinced that he *almost certainly* does not exist. Dawkins explains his belief in terms of a scale from 1 to 7. Number 1 on the scale is the *strong theist* who believes with complete certainty that God exists. Number 7 is the *strong atheist* who is just as certain that God does not exist, while number 4 is the *completely impartial agnostic* who considers God's existence and non-existence to be equally likely. The other numbers on the scale represent other intermediate viewpoints with numbers 2 and 6 being the de facto theist and atheist respectively who are very confident in their beliefs although not quite as confident as the strong theist or strong atheist.[9]

If an agnostic is someone who is not sure whether God exists, then strictly speaking number 6, the de facto atheist, is really an agnostic. Dawkins puts himself at number 6, but leaning towards number 7. As we saw earlier, he is agnostic only to the degree that he is agnostic about fairies. Dawkins is completely correct to distinguish between different types of agnosticism and he makes a further point that also seems right. Some people maintain that the question of God's existence could never be settled one way or the other and so are permanently agnostic in principle. Dawkins rightly points out that even if we can neither prove nor disprove God's existence, this does not mean that we can say nothing about it. In fact, Dawkins thinks it can be shown that God's existence is extremely improbable; I disagree with Dawkins's assessment of the evidence, but not with his claim that evidence is relevant to the question of God's existence.

Even if one adopts the viewpoint that evidence is irrelevant to God's existence, Dawkins does not think that the rational viewpoint is that of number 4 on the spectrum, the view that considers the existence and non-existence of God equally likely. Instead, he thinks that in the absence of evidence the rational viewpoint is one of disbelief. To make his point, he refers to Bertrand Russell's story about a celestial teapot. Suppose it is claimed that between Earth and Mars there is a teapot orbiting the Sun, but that it is too small to be observed even by the most powerful telescopes. On the other hand, its existence cannot be disproved either. Since there is no evidence either way, does this mean we should be agnostic about the existence of the teapot? In particular, should we take the view that the existence and non-existence of the teapot are equally likely? Clearly not. In the absence of evidence, it is overwhelmingly unlikely that it exists. According to Dawkins, the same attitude should be adopted when it comes to God's existence; if there is no evidence to support belief in God, then we should adopt position number 6 (or perhaps closer to 7) instead of number 4 and conclude that God's existence is very unlikely indeed.

The implication of this is that our default position should be one of de facto atheism just as it is in the case of the celestial teapot. This is an extremely important point because we ought to have some idea about how convincing the evidence would need to be before considering specific pieces of evidence that might be relevant to God's existence. If Dawkins is right, then it might still be rational to disbelieve in God even if there is moderately good evidence that seems to support his existence. Consider the teapot again and suppose that some indirect evidence were to become available that pointed to its existence (perhaps a passing satellite photographs something vaguely teapot shaped). Would this be sufficient to make us believe? Hardly. The teapot hypothesis is so improbable that we would not change our minds unless there was overwhelming proof for its truth. Dawkins is assuming that belief in God is just as ridiculous as belief in the celestial teapot and so overwhelming proof is required for God's existence. If, by contrast, it is reasonable to start out with the belief that the existence and non-existence of God are equally likely, then moderately convincing arguments might make it very likely indeed that he does exist.

Dawkins's viewpoint is known as the presumption of atheism, the idea that the burden of proof lies with the theist to show that God exists rather than with the atheist to show that he does not. Perhaps the most prominent defence of this viewpoint was given by the former atheist Antony Flew. Interestingly, it seems that Flew eventually found the evidence in favour of God's existence to be so overwhelming that it was sufficient to overcome his default atheism.[10] Hence, even if Dawkins's uneven playing field is adopted, it is not impossible to make a convincing case for God's existence. But this still leaves the question as to whether his position should be adopted.

There are at least two scenarios in which the absence of any evidence might be relevant in deciding whether to believe in something. The first case is where there definitely should be evidence, but in fact there is none. For example, suppose I tell you that I have a pet elephant in my back garden. If you go to look for the elephant but don't see it, then clearly there is no elephant (my garden is not too big!). The second case is where no evidence would be expected either way. Suppose instead that I tell you I have a pet ant in my back garden. If, in addition to thinking I am a very strange person, you go to look for it but don't see it, you could not be so sure that it does not exist.

Dawkins's own view is that the first scenario is correct; that is, if there is a God there should be evidence of his existence, but in fact there is none. He states that 'a universe with a supernaturally intelligent creator is a very different kind of universe from one without',[11] and that 'NOMA [non-overlapping magisteria] is popular only because there is no evidence to favour the God Hypothesis.'[12] His idea seems to be that the universe does not have certain characteristics that would be expected if God existed. If this view is right, then it appears that default atheism would make sense. But it is far from obvious that this view is right. It can be contested in two ways. The most obvious response is to claim that there is evidence to support belief in God despite Dawkins's assertion to the contrary. This is the approach I shall adopt.

Alternatively, some will respond by saying that there is no good reason to think that the evidence should be clear cut either way; perhaps the evidence is irrelevant to God's existence or only relevant in a very subtle way. It is difficult to see what argument the atheist can produce that shows that God would be obliged to create evidence to satisfy philosophers and scientists. After all, Christians typically think that the belief that God exists is of no value without a personal relationship with God. And it is simply a fact that many people develop a deep personal faith without an academic consideration of the evidence.

It is to counteract this second response that Dawkins introduces the celestial teapot. He wants to show that such faith is intellectually irresponsible, as it would allow us to believe in any ridiculous proposition. But is the celestial teapot a good analogy for belief in God? Consider instead the Higgs boson, which many physicists believed to exist before any evidence had been obtained (like the celestial teapot) despite numerous attempts (unlike the celestial teapot).[13] Why does it seem acceptable to presume non-existence with respect to the celestial teapot, but not the non-existence of the Higgs boson? Obviously the difference lies in terms of how the existence of the Higgs boson would help to make sense of other things given its key role in the standard model of particle physics. By contrast, there is no reason whatsoever to think that the celestial teapot exists, and even if it did its existence would not help to make sense of anything else; it would just be one more object in the universe.

Which of the analogies is better when considering the existence of God, the celestial teapot or the Higgs boson? If God exists, he is clearly not just one more thing in the universe, but plays a much more fundamental role in terms of creating everything else that does exist. Now some atheists, including probably the New Atheists, will deny that the existence of God would help make sense of anything, but other atheists will disagree. In fact, in the absence of a convincing argument to the contrary, it seems that the rest of us – atheist, agnostic and theist alike – are at least as entitled to presume that God, if he existed, would play a fundamental role in making sense of the universe. Of course, it hardly needs to be stated that there are also enormous differences between the Higgs boson and God. For example, the former gives rise to precise predictions that can be tested experimentally. Nevertheless, in terms of the presumption of atheism the analogy with the Higgs boson seems much more appropriate than the analogy with the celestial teapot.

The upshot of all this is that the presumption of atheism is untenable.

First, even if the evidence is irrelevant to God's existence or only relevant in a very indirect way, it still does not follow that one should presume that God does not exist nor even that his existence is very improbable.[14] Secondly, if there should be evidence for God's existence (if he exists) as Dawkins maintains, then the question is whether the evidence actually exists. In this case the only way to make a judgment is to determine whether there is any evidence and, if there is, how good it is; presumptions are not much help.[15]

What kind of evidence?

The New Atheists seem to be convinced that there is no evidence that counts in favour of God's existence, but this raises the question of what would count as acceptable evidence. If they maintained that there could be no such evidence *even in principle*, their claim would be a very hollow one indeed. Similarly, their demand that theists provide evidence for belief in God only makes sense if they have some idea about the kind of evidence that would be acceptable to them. If every conceivable piece of evidence for the existence of God were to be countered with the retort that it is always irrational to believe in a supernatural being, there would be little point in trying to meet their demand.

Do the New Atheists completely rule out the possibility of evidence for God's existence? Their view that if God existed there should be evidence for his existence seems to suggest that they do not rule out the possibility of such evidence in principle.[16] In terms of what evidence would count as acceptable or, to put it another way, what evidence would be required to change their minds, the New Atheists fail to provide much by way of detail. Commenting on the philosopher Richard Swinburne, Dawkins says:

> He rightly suggests that if God wanted to demonstrate his own existence he would find better ways to do it than slightly biasing the recovery statistics of experimental versus control groups of heart patients. If God existed and wanted to convince us of it, he could 'fill the world with super-miracles'.[17]

What would constitute convincing evidence of God's existence for Dawkins? Would a voice speaking to him from the sky and other events of that sort be sufficient? Would such events really be convincing? One suspects that anyone as sceptical about the supernatural as the New Atheists would not be convinced. Surely a conspiracy by fundamentalists to convert sceptics would be a much more plausible hypothesis to such an anti-supernatural mindset.

More important, however, is that even if they do not rule out the possibility of evidence, one suspects they would set the bar impossibly high. Despite the reservation noted above, one can imagine all sorts of 'super-miracles' that might be convincing were they to occur, but it would be unreasonable to claim that one should not believe in God *unless* such miracles occurred. After all, we can speculate about what evidence we would like, but we have to deal with the evidence we actually possess. And, of course, this is true in science as well. Physicists would like evidence for the Higgs boson to be much easier to acquire, but reality is sometimes not as accommodating as we would like.

An example of setting the bar too high would be to demand that there be some sort of direct experimental proof of God's existence. This need not worry us, however, since most of the beliefs we hold are not amenable to this kind of proof. In fact, even most of our scientific beliefs cannot be proved in this way. This claim is in no way intended to undermine science; it just is not the way science works. Typically, scientists propose theories to account for a range of data and try to find ways to test them. But supposing that the test turns out as the theory predicted, does that prove that the theory is true? No, for a new theory could come along that would also make the same prediction, but would also account for failings of the old theory. The replacement of Newton's theory of gravity by Einstein's is a case in point. It would be more appropriate to say that the test *confirmed*, or *supported*, rather than proved the theory.

The same thing applies when scientists are unable to make predictions that can be tested experimentally. For example, what caused the extinction of the dinosaurs? By considering how well various hypotheses account for the evidence, it is possible to reach a judgment as to which is best supported. Of course, this applies not just in science but elsewhere as well, history providing an obvious example. Similarly, detectives have to take into account all the relevant evidence in determining the identity of the murderer. In all of these cases it is important to note that a single piece of evidence might not give the whole picture. Perhaps it confirms or supports a particular hypothesis, but overall the evidence supports a different hypothesis. For example, if a reliable witness identified Jones at the scene of the crime, it might support the hypothesis that Jones is the murderer even if it turns out that overall the evidence points to Smith's guilt. Alternatively, a particular piece of evidence might confirm a hypothesis only to a small extent, yet when all the evidence is taken into account the case for the hypothesis might be very strong.

Trying to articulate how science works is a notoriously difficult subject, but many scientists and philosophers of science would agree that something along the lines described above is correct. One particular way of spelling this out is in terms of what is known as *inference to the best explanation*,[18] which is basically the idea that scientists propose alternative hypotheses to explain some phenomena and try to determine which one does the best job by looking at their explanatory power, simplicity, coherence, scope, and so on.[19] Although much more could be said on the topic, the approach described in the last paragraph will suffice for our purposes and so will be used to investigate possible evidence that might support the existence of God. It is important to emphasize that this approach is not confined to scientific contexts, but is a more general reasoning strategy that is appropriate when evidence is being used to assess hypotheses.[20] In particular, it is relevant when considering personal explanations, which involve the intentions, knowledge and desires of intelligent agents. This is particularly relevant here since theistic explanations are better thought of as personal, rather than scientific, explanations as pointed out in chapter 3.

The goal then is to consider various pieces of evidence to determine whether they count in favour of God's existence. Perhaps no single piece of evidence will prove conclusive on its own, but I shall argue that the combined weight of all the evidence is sufficient to make a strong case for God's existence. To start with, we shall consider the very existence of the universe itself.

The existence of the universe

The great German mathematician and philosopher Gottfried Wilhelm Leibniz famously asked, 'Why is there something rather than nothing?' Or as cosmologist Stephen Hawking asks, 'Why does the universe go to all the bother of existing?'[21] What, in other words, is the explanation for the existence of the universe? There is no obvious reason for thinking that there had to be a universe; there might just as easily have been nothing at all. So, it certainly seems reasonable to ask for an explanation for its existence. Just as it makes sense for scientists to seek explanations for the things within the universe, it makes sense to seek for an explanation for the very existence of the universe itself.

Could the universe somehow explain its own existence? There are reasons for thinking that the answer must be 'no'. Science, of course, offers explanations for all sorts of things. Why does a particular species exist? Or life, or the solar system, or the Milky Way, or atoms? Scientific explanations for such things typically involve relevant scientific laws and a description of what the universe (or some relevant part of it) was like before the entity in question came into existence. This approach is appropriate for explaining various *parts of the universe*, but what about the *universe as a whole*? We might be able to explain the current state of the whole universe in terms of past states of the whole universe, but that still leaves the question as to why it existed in the past. Even if the universe has always existed, this would not explain why it, rather than something else or nothing at all, exists. And explaining the current state of the universe in terms of its past states presupposes the existence of scientific laws to get from one state to another, but then what is the explanation for these laws? It seems clear that no explanation for the existence of the universe can be given in terms of the universe itself. So the universe appears to require an explanation, but neither the universe itself nor presumably any part of it can provide an explanation. It follows that the explanation must be something distinct from the universe. The theist, of course, claims that God is the explanation.

A response of the New Atheists to this line of reasoning is to ask, 'If God explains the universe, who explains God?' As Hitchens puts it, 'Thus the postulate of a designer or creator only raises the unanswerable question of who designed the designer or created the creator. Religion and theology and theodicy . . . have consistently failed to overcome this objection.'[22] Despite Hitchens's confident assertion, there is a straightforward answer: no one, since God is not explained in terms of anything external to himself. But then Hitchens could reply that if theists can say this about God, why can atheists not just say that the universe does not require an explanation? In fact, a common atheistic response to the argument being put forward here is to deny that the universe has an explanation at all and to claim instead that its existence is just a brute fact.

Notice that since this response asserts that the universe has no explanation in terms of anything external to it, the objection to theism cannot be that it is unreasonable for the theist to say that God has no explanation of this kind. Rather, the theist and the atheist both accept that there is something that cannot be explained by reference to anything external to itself: God in the case of the theist and the universe in the case of the atheist. This raises the question as to the most suitable terminating point for explanation – is it with the universe itself or with God? There are a number of reasons for thinking that God is a better terminating point. Theists postulate a Supreme Being who is the creator of the universe, and from this conception of God certain attributes follow.[23] First, if God exists (and most atheists are willing to grant that this is a possibility), there could not be any cause of his existence and so his existence could not be explained by anything outside himself. By contrast, it seems entirely possible that the universe could have a cause and hence an explanation. Most atheists agree with this statement. Those who deny that the universe has an explanation are typically not claiming that it could not *in principle* have an explanation, but just that in reality it does not.

Secondly, if God exists, there could not have been a beginning to his exist-ence, whereas there could have been a beginning to the universe. Whether or not the universe had a beginning, it certainly seems *possible* that it did. As we shall see in the next section, there are good reasons for thinking that it did in fact have a beginning, but even if that were not the case, there do not appear to be any convincing reasons for thinking that such a beginning would be impossible. Again, most atheists agree with this.

Thirdly, many theists (although not all) have argued that if God exists, he does not merely happen to exist, but his existence is necessary in the sense that he could not have failed to exist.[24] By contrast, the universe appears to be contingent, which means that there is no reason why it must exist. You and I are contingent since we might not have existed had things worked out differ-ently, if our respective parents had not met, for example. Indeed, the existence of humanity as a whole is also contingent and it is difficult to see any reason why the universe is not contingent too. Again, most atheists agree that the universe is contingent.[25]

These three differences between God and the universe strongly suggest that God is a suitable terminating point for explanation since, if he exists, he *must* be the terminating point. By contrast, the universe seems like an arbitrary terminating point. Furthermore, if entire universes can exist without adequate explanation, what does this do to rational enquiry? What else might occur for no reason at all? It might be objected that the theist is in the same boat since God would exist without explanation, but if God is necessary in the sense described above then there would be an explanation for God's existence in terms of the necessity of his nature.

A further objection can be raised at this point by the atheist. Even if it is granted that there is an explanation (or cause) of the universe, this does not establish that God is the explanation. Describing the explanation for the universe as a terminator of explanation, Dawkins claims that even if we grant that such a terminator exists,

> there is absolutely no reason to endow that terminator with any of the properties normally ascribed to God: omnipotence, omniscience, goodness, creativity of design, to say nothing of such human attributes as listening to prayers, forgiving sins and reading innermost thoughts.[26]

It is certainly true that the argument does not establish all of these character-istics, but of course it was never intended to. If the universe is explained by something external to itself that in principle cannot be explained by anything else, this certainly seems difficult to square with atheism. It cannot simply be dismissed on the grounds that the argument fails to tell us whether God answers prayers or not. It would be a bit like a detective dismissing DNA evidence that linked Jones to the murder weapon on the grounds that the evidence fails to tell us how Jones acquired the weapon. Furthermore, philosopher William Lane Craig claims that the argument can establish more than Dawkins thinks. He argues that the cause of the universe transcends space and time and so cannot be physical. He claims that the only kind of possible cause is a mind and hence the cause must be personal.[27]

One way of looking at this point is by thinking about evidence again. Recall that a single piece of evidence can count in favour of one hypothesis (and against another) without establishing conclusively that the hypothesis is true. This may apply here. Perhaps the evidence considered here, that is, the existence of the universe, does not conclusively prove that God exists. The atheist can avoid this conclusion, but this still leaves the question as to whether the existence of the universe counts as evidence in favour of God's existence.

To answer this question, let's consider how well the two main hypotheses explain the evidence. First of all, atheism has no explanation to offer for the existence of the universe. The most plausible viewpoint for the atheist is to say that the universe is just a brute fact, but this is simply a frank admission that no explanation is available. On the other hand, the existence of God does provide an explanation in terms of a being who is not part of the universe and who is also a natural stopping point for explanation. So the existence of the universe is a mystery to the New Atheists and explicable to theists. This means that the evidence considered here, the existence of the universe, weighs in favour of the existence of God.[28]

The beginning of the universe

The point of the previous section was that the mere existence of the universe provides evidence for the existence of God, irrespective of whether the universe had a beginning. The argument does not conclusively prove that God exists; but if the universe had a beginning, an atheistic viewpoint would be even harder to sustain than if the universe had no beginning. For this reason it would seem that a beginning to the universe would provide additional evidence for the existence of God.

The central question is then, did the universe have a beginning? Although philosophical arguments can be adduced to support a beginning, our focus here will be on scientific evidence. The question of whether the universe had a beginning has been discussed throughout history, but until relatively recently there was no scientific evidence to suggest a beginning; as far as science was concerned the universe might have been infinitely old. This situation changed dramatically as a result of one of the most important discoveries of twentieth-century science, the expanding universe.

Scientists had assumed that the universe was static rather than expanding or contracting, there being no evidence to the contrary. Most famously, Albert Einstein was so committed to this view that when he discovered that his general theory of relativity did not seem to permit such a static universe, he introduced a cosmological constant to ensure that his theory would predict a static universe after all. He later considered this to be his greatest mistake.

By contrast, Alexander Friedmann and Georges Lemaître independently used Einstein's theory without his cosmological constant to predict an expanding universe. Experimental evidence for the expansion of the universe was discovered by the astronomer Edwin Hubble in 1929. Hubble found that light from distant galaxies was red-shifted; that is, the light was shifted to longer wavelengths. This was explained by the fact that such galaxies were moving away from us. In fact, he found that the speed with which they are moving away increases with their distance from us. His work showed that the expansion of the universe is the same in all directions just as Friedmann and Lemaître had predicted.[29]

Since the universe is expanding and hence becoming less dense, this means that in the past it was much more dense. If we extrapolate back far enough, we reach a state when the universe was extremely dense and hot and finally a state of infinite density where the theory of general relativity breaks down (a state known as a singularity). The big bang theory describes the expansion of the universe from this early hot, dense phase, which is currently estimated to have occurred about 13.7 billion years ago. It is worth emphasizing that it is not just energy and matter that originate in the standard big bang theory, but space and time as well. This strongly suggests creation *ex nihilo* (out of nothing). Cosmologists John Barrow and Frank Tipler clearly state what the implications of this theory would be: 'At this singularity, space and time came into existence; literally nothing existed before the singularity, so, if the Universe originated in such a singularity, we would truly have a creation *ex nihilo*.'[30] The similarity with the Christian doctrine of creation *ex nihilo* is striking, especially given the traditional Christian understanding that not only did God create the universe out of nothing rather than pre-existing material, but that God created space and time as well.

This similarity has not been lost on physicists and astronomers. The astronomer Sir Arthur Eddington stated that 'The beginning seems to present insuperable difficulties unless we agree to look on it as frankly supernatural.'[31] The astronomer Robert Jastrow is even more explicit:

> For the scientist who has lived by his faith in the power of reason, the story ends like a bad dream. He has scaled the mountains of ignorance; he is about to conquer the highest peak; as he pulls himself over the final rock, he is greeted by a band of theologians who have been sitting there for centuries.[32]

Not surprisingly, many scientists have resisted the idea of a beginning precisely because of its theological implications. Cosmologist Stephen Hawking pointed out that 'Many people do not like the idea that time has a beginning, probably because it smacks of divine intervention.'[33] Similarly, science writer John Gribbin claimed that 'The biggest problem with the Big Bang theory of the origin of the universe is philosophical – perhaps even theological.'[34]

Such negative attitudes have provided a strong motivation for replacing the big bang theory. Most notably, Hermann Bondi, Thomas Gold and Fred Hoyle proposed a steady state theory in which an infinitely old universe continually creates new matter as it expands so that its overall state remains the same. Hoyle was explicit about his anti-theological motives:

> Unlike the modern school of cosmologists, who in conformity with Judaeo-Christian theologians believe the whole universe to have been created out of nothing, my beliefs accord with those of Democritus who remarked 'Nothing is created out of nothing'.[35]

The steady state theory has now been decisively rejected because of evidence that did not fit with the theory but which can be explained by the big bang theory. The relative abundance of hydrogen to helium and the cosmic microwave background radiation are two key pieces of evidence. In the former, the relative abundance of hydrogen to helium is about three to one as the big bang theory predicts. In the latter, in 1965 Arno Penzias and Robert Wilson discovered microwave radiation at a temperature of about 3 degrees Kelvin (i.e. 3 degrees above absolute zero, which is −273 degrees C) and found that it was of the same intensity in all directions. This had been predicted on the basis of the big bang theory, according to which the background radiation is essentially a remnant of the heat from the early phase of the universe when it was very dense and at a very high temperature. Needless to say, the steady state theory did not predict such radiation.

Overall, there is convincing evidence in favour of the big bang theory. This is summed up by the astronomer Sir Martin Rees:

The empirical evidence for a Big Bang ten to fifteen billion years ago is as compelling as the evidence that geologists offer on Earth's history . . . A few years ago, I already had ninety per cent confidence that there was indeed a Big Bang . . . The case now is far stronger: dramatic advances in observations and experiments have brought the broad cosmic picture into sharp focus during the 1990s, and I would now raise my degree of certainty to ninety-nine per cent.[36]

However, although the big bang theory's account of the history of the universe is widely accepted, this does not mean that there are no alternatives. In fact, numerous alternatives have been proposed and there is little doubt that at least part of the motivation for such theories is a desire to avoid the theistic implications of the big bang. One example is the oscillating universe model in which the universe expands, then collapses back on itself, then expands again, and so on for ever. Various versions of this model have been proposed. Ironically, a version of it tends to appear every once in a while, it then disappears, then a new version reappears, and so on, just like the model itself! One of the main problems with such models is that on current evidence it seems that the universe (or the current oscillation according to this model) will not collapse, thus counting against the theory. Further problems concern the mechanism that is supposed to bring about the expansion of each oscillation after the collapse of the preceding one and the fact that many such models are incompatible with there being an infinite number of cycles and so a beginning cannot be avoided anyway.

Other alternatives appeal to quantum theory in one way or another. The standard big bang theory is based on Einstein's general theory of relativity, but during the first fraction of a second of the universe this theory is no longer adequate and quantum theory becomes relevant. One problem is that there is as yet no accepted theory that brings quantum theory and general relativity together, a so-called quantum theory of gravity. Nevertheless, scientists have some ideas about the features such a theory might possess. It must be said, however, that the specific proposals as to the role quantum theory might play in the earliest moments of the universe are extremely speculative. Of course, the speculative nature of such proposals is not necessarily a problem from a scientific point of view since theories that start out as speculative can end up being successful and in a field such as cosmology some aspect of speculation seems necessary if progress is to be made. However, if a proposal is intended to undermine the idea that the universe had a beginning, there must be some good reason to think that the proposal is true or likely to be true. Merely appealing to the possibility that the universe might not have had a beginning would be a very weak response to the argument being proposed here.

For the moment, let us focus on whether quantum theory undermines the claim that the universe had a beginning. The most prominent proposal of this kind is the Hartle–Hawking model, which was popularized by Stephen Hawking in his best-selling book *A Brief History of Time* and is also a key component in his more recent book *The Grand Design*, which was co-authored with his fellow cosmologist Leonard Mlodinow.[37] For the purposes of our discussion, the most salient feature of this model is that quantum effects come into play in the earliest moments of the universe (prior to the Planck time[38]) in such a way as to eliminate the singularity of the standard big bang theory. According to the Hartle–Hawking model, quantum effects mean that time becomes indistinguishable from space and a consequence of this is that there is no singularity in their model and so, they claim, no beginning to the universe. The idea is that although time and space are finite they have no boundary analogous to the way in which the surface of Earth is finite in extent but has no boundary. As Hawking puts it, 'if you sail off into the sunset, you don't fall off the edge or run into a singularity'.[39] Similarly, there is no 'edge' to the universe in the sense that it did not have a beginning. Hawking clearly thinks that his model has implications for God:

> So long as the universe had a beginning, we could suppose that it had a creator. But if the universe is really completely self-contained, having no boundary or edge, it would have neither beginning nor end: it would simply be. What place, then, for a creator?[40]

What are we to make of Hawking's claim? It is worth emphasizing that in rejecting a beginning to the universe, Hawking is not claiming that the universe is infinitely old. In fact, Hawking's model is in agreement with the standard big bang account about the age of the universe. It is only in the first fraction of a second that there is disagreement.[41] Hawking's astonishing claim is that the universe has existed for a finite amount of time, but had no beginning.

Things are not quite so straightforward, however. Central to the Hartle–Hawking model is the notion of imaginary time, the idea that in the earliest moments of the universe time is represented not just by ordinary real numbers but by imaginary numbers such as the square root of minus one. Imaginary numbers are widely used in physics, but since they play an essential role in removing the singularity in the Hartle–Hawking model, we must ask how such numbers are to be interpreted in this context. A lot hinges on this since, as Hawking has pointed out, if we consider the history of the universe in ordinary real time, then it did have a beginning. So which is it? Did the universe have a beginning or not, according to the Hartle–Hawking model?

The answer to this question depends on whether Hawking's notion of imaginary time gives a correct representation of reality or whether it is just a useful mathematical idea that should not be considered as an accurate representation of reality. The philosopher William Lane Craig has pointed out that the notion of imaginary time is physically unintelligible;[42] perhaps it is useful mathematically, but not as a realistic feature of the universe.[43] If so, then even if Hawking's model is accepted, the history of the universe should be understood in terms of real rather than imaginary time, in which case the universe had a beginning after all.

There are other problems as well. If imaginary time were to be taken as a representation of reality, there is also a question of how the transition from imaginary time to ordinary time took place and whether such a transition even makes sense.[44] A further problem is that it is in conflict with the evidence because the type of universe that is most likely to arise in the Hartle–Hawking model is very different from the kind of universe we observe.[45] So, there are a number of reasons for thinking that the model is not viable. Even if it is viable, there are two further problems. First, there is no good reason to think that it is true; it is at best a possibility. The problem with this is that in order to reject the claim that the universe had a beginning it is not sufficient to point to the mere possibility of there having been no beginning. Secondly, even if the model were correct, it is not clear that it would avoid a beginning for the reasons discussed above.

Although there are many other alternative cosmological proposals that avoid a beginning, none has gained widespread support and all are speculative in nature.[46] Philosophers Bradley Monton and Graham Oppy correctly point out that we do not know all the relevant physics and so there is no guarantee that a theory of quantum gravity will include a beginning of the universe, but Monton's claim that 'we ought to conclude that it's unknown whether there's a big bang and hence we ought to conclude that it's unknown whether the universe began to exist' seems too sceptical.[47] The evidence is highly suggestive of a beginning. There is widespread agreement that the evidence confirms the big bang model to within a fraction of a second of the beginning. The relevant evidence is what we would expect if the universe had a beginning and so rival theories are in the difficult position of having to account for this evidence while also denying that such a beginning occurred. More scepticism would be warranted if we had good reason to believe that a quantum gravity approach would avoid the need for a beginning, but that does not seem to be the case. Furthermore, research by Borde, Guth and Vilenkin points in the opposite direction since they have shown that certain kinds of models are expected to have a beginning.[48] Overall, on the basis of the evidence, there is plenty of reason to affirm, and little, if any, to deny, that the universe had a beginning.

The idea that the beginning of the universe provides a reason for believing in God is summed up in the Kalām argument for God's existence,[49] which can be stated as follows:

1. Whatever begins to exist has a cause.
2. The universe began to exist.
3. Therefore, the universe has a cause.

Clearly, if premises 1 and 2 of the argument are true, then the conclusion 3 follows. If this argument is sound, it would point to a cause of the universe that is not part of the universe itself and that transcends space and time. This is certainly consistent with the cause being God, although we shall return to this point later.

Given their claim that there is no evidence in favour of God's existence, you might have thought that the New Atheists would have plenty to say about this. You might at least have expected them to outline how the beginning of the universe fits in with their atheism, yet they have remarkably little to say on the matter in their recent books. Astonishingly, Dawkins seems to think that the big bang removes the need for God. In discussing Aquinas's cosmological argument for the existence of God as the cause of the universe, Dawkins claims that 'it is more parsimonious to conjure up, say, a "big bang singularity", or some other physical concept as yet unknown'.[50] He seems completely oblivious to the fact that it is precisely the big bang that is the problem for atheism since it denotes the beginning of the universe and so only confirms premise 2 of the argument above. If Dawkins accepts the big bang theory, which seems likely as it is the dominant theory in cosmology, does he then reject premise 1? In other words, does he think that things can come into existence without a cause? He certainly doesn't offer any reason for thinking that they can.

Dennett is the only one of the four New Atheists who really attempts to address the issue, although he also has very little to say on the matter. Here are some of his comments on the argument:

> The Cosmological Argument, which in its simplest form states that since everything must have a cause the universe must have a cause – namely, God – doesn't stay simple for long. Some deny the premise, since quantum physics teaches us (doesn't it?) that not everything that happens needs to have a cause. Others prefer to accept the premise and then ask: What caused God? The reply that God is self-caused (somehow) then raises the rebuttal: If something can be self-caused, why can't the universe as a whole be the thing that is self-caused?[51]

In response it must first be noted that at least in the Kalām version of the cosmological argument it is not that everything must have a cause, but that *whatever begins to exist* has a cause. So his question 'What caused God?' misses the point since if God exists, then he had no beginning, whereas we know, or at least have very good reason to believe, that the universe did have a beginning. Furthermore, theism typically does not maintain that God is *self-caused*, but rather *uncaused*. How could anything be self-caused? In order for anything to cause itself to come into existence it would already need to exist in the first place to do the causing. The very notion of self-causing is contradictory and so the suggestion that the universe as a whole is self-caused is a non-starter. Equally contradictory is Dennett's notion of self-creation. He puts it like this:

> What does need its origin explained is the concrete Universe itself, and as Hume's Philo long ago asked: Why not stop at the material world. *It*, we have seen, does perform a version of the ultimate bootstrapping trick; it creates itself *ex nihilo*, or at any rate out of something that is well-nigh indistinguishable from nothing at all. Unlike the puzzlingly mysterious, timeless self-creation of God, this self-creation is a non-miraculous stunt that has left lots of traces.[52]

Once again, theists do not think of God as *self-created*, but rather that he was not *created* at all. It is interesting to note that Dennett does seem to agree with the argument presented earlier that scientific evidence confirms the notion of creation *ex nihilo*. But instead of drawing the plausible conclusion that the universe had a creator who is not part of the universe, he appeals to the contradictory idea that the universe created itself out of nothing.

Perhaps Dennett would respond that if the theist wants to claim that God is uncaused, why can the atheist not just claim that the universe is uncaused? But a major difference is that the universe had a beginning, whereas God, if he exists, did not. And the point of premise 1 of the Kalām argument stated earlier is that things do not come into existence completely uncaused. It seems that Dennett acknowledges this point since he thinks that the 'concrete Universe' does require an explanation, and instead of claiming that it simply popped into existence out of nothing he appeals to his notion of self-creation.

Earlier we saw that there was no good reason to think that the second premise of the Kalām argument, that the universe had a beginning, could be rejected by appealing to quantum theory; but what about the first premise?[53] Does quantum theory teach us, as Dennett maintains, 'that not everything that happens needs to have a cause'? There is no doubt that the world of quantum theory is a weird and wonderful place and that it is generally taken to be indeterministic, so that the state of the world at an earlier time does not guarantee what its state will be at a later time.[54] Quantum theory enables us to calculate the probability that a certain event, such as the decay of a radioactive particle, will occur within a certain period of time, but not to predict exactly when it will occur. Are such events uncaused? The answer will depend on exactly how cause is to be defined and this is a much-debated issue. Fortunately, for our purposes the relevant question is not whether quantum theory teaches us that certain events can occur uncaused in some sense of that term, but whether quantum theory gives us any reason to believe that something can spontaneously come into existence out of nothing.

Often discussed in this context is what is known as a quantum vacuum. In such a vacuum subatomic particles can appear briefly and then disappear again. There have been a number of ingenious suggestions as to how the universe might be the result of such a quantum fluctuation. Despite the fact that these models for the origin of the universe are extremely speculative to say the least, it might be thought they show that it is possible for something to come into existence out of nothing. This is certainly what some of their advocates have claimed. The problem with this idea is that a quantum vacuum is not the same as nothing. As John Polkinghorne has pointed out, 'the quantum vacuum is a hive of activity, full of fluctuations, random comings-to-be and fadings-away'.[55] He goes on to say, 'suppose for a moment that such a fluctuation was the actual origin of our universe. It would certainly not have come from something which without great abuse of language could be called "nothing".'[56] So although quantum theory does allow for particles to appear in a quantum vacuum, it does not give us any reason to believe that particles (or universes for that matter) can spontaneously come into existence out of literally nothing. A particular example of this kind of claim is found in the account of the origin of the universe by Hawking and Mlodinow. They contend that 'the universe can and will create itself from nothing' and that this occurs spontaneously via a quantum process.[57] The problem is that quantum theory gives the probability that a system will make a transition from one state to another, but is inapplicable in the case of a transition from absolutely nothing to something.[58]

In general, claims that the universe could have come into existence spontaneously out of nothing involve equivocating between a so-called nothing, which can be described by quantum theory on the one hand and literally nothing at all on the other. Physicist Victor Stenger even goes so far as to claim:

> Since 'nothing' is as simple as it gets, we cannot expect it to be very stable. It would
> likely undergo a spontaneous phase transition to something more complicated, like

a universe containing matter. The transition of nothing-to-something is a natural one, not requiring any agent.[59]

The problem with this is that what Stenger calls 'nothing' is in fact something that can be described by the laws of physics – it is not very stable, for example – and so can undergo a transition to something else. But whatever this 'nothing' is, the term 'nothing' is clearly inappropriate. If Stenger really meant nothing, literally nothing, then he would be denying that anything exists. In this case it would make no sense to describe nothing as unstable. The problem with these kinds of claims is aptly summed up by the philosopher Keith Ward. When referring to a book by the scientist Peter Atkins, Ward wrote, 'One of its poetic features is Atkins' use of the word "nothing" to mean "huge numbers of very complicated things".'[60]

One objection to the argument for God's existence based on the beginning of the universe is that it is a God-of-the-gaps argument. The idea is that God is simply being introduced to fill a gap in science. However, as pointed out in the last chapter, we must be careful about dismissing theistic arguments too hastily by labelling them God-of-the-gaps arguments. In the current case, the God-of-the-gaps charge is a very weak response for two reasons. First, if God were being introduced as a cause in a context where a physical cause would be appropriate, the God-of-the-gaps charge might have some merit. But in the big bang we are talking about the very origin of the universe and there is reason to believe it involves the origin of space and time so that physical causes are not possible.

Secondly, the argument is not based on scientific ignorance, but depends only on whether the universe had a beginning, which is a question science can address. As we have seen, there is reason to believe that good scientific evidence does point to a beginning. So, the argument is based on science, not scientific ignorance. Of course, it is possible that future science could show that the universe did not have a beginning despite this evidence. In this case, the argument would no longer work, but that is just how things are when dealing with evidence since new evidence can point in a different direction. This applies whether the evidence is for belief in God, for a scientific theory or in any other evidential context. However, it is not a serious objection to the argument to point out the mere possibility that it might turn out that the universe had no beginning; some good reason would need to be given for thinking that to be the case.

To summarize the main argument, there is good scientific evidence that points to the universe having had a beginning and there is no basis in science for thinking that something (never mind a universe) could come into existence out of literally nothing without being caused to do so. Thus, there is good evidence to support the first premise of the Kalām argument and the second premise should be accepted unless one is prepared to believe without any scientific justification that things can simply come into existence out of nothing completely uncaused. There is then good reason to accept the conclusion that the universe had a cause that is not a part of the physical universe and transcends space and time.[61]

As in the previous section, it is clear that the argument does not seek to establish all the characteristics of God;[62] but once again the key question is how well the argument supports theism as opposed to atheism. It seems clear that just as in the previous section the argument does not conclusively prove the existence of God. For example, despite all the evidence amassed in support of the universe having had a beginning, it may be possible that a new theory will obviate the need for a beginning. But this does not mean that the argument has no merit? Far from it. Based on the intuitively obvious assumption, which has not been undermined by science, that things don't spontaneously pop into existence out of nothing, theism provides a much better explanation of the scientific evidence relating to the beginning of the universe than atheism. This means that the evidence provides support for the existence of God.

Conclusion

In this chapter we have considered two pieces of evidence: the existence of the physical universe and the beginning of the universe. It has been granted that neither of these features of the universe proves with 100% certainty that God exists, but this should not provide much comfort to the atheist. After all, many atheists put a lot of emphasis on science, yet scientific theories are never proven to be true. Instead, evidence is put forward which supports the theory, and if the evidence is sufficiently strong the theory can be accepted. So the question is whether these pieces of evidence provide support for the existence of God, or equivalently, whether they would be more likely if there is a God than if there is not. Arguments have been presented to show that both the existence of the universe and its beginning are actually much more likely if there is a God. Hence, they provide strong evidence for the existence of God.

It is also worth noting that certain atheistic responses to these arguments might actually undermine science. With regard to the existence of the universe, some have maintained that the existence of something (the universe) rather than nothing is not in need of explanation. But if this approach can be adopted for the universe, why not for entities within the universe. Yet one of the goals of science is to find out why the universe contains the entities it does. With regard to the beginning of the universe, some atheists have maintained that the universe popped into existence out of literally nothing. But if one can accept this, there might be a danger of reaching a premature conclusion that there is no cause for the coming into existence of certain entities within science when there are causes to be found. Similarly, for atheists who believe that things that come into existence *do* require a cause, there is a danger that they will always seek to find ways to deny that the universe had a beginning no matter how much evidence for a beginning becomes available.

We have considered two fundamental aspects of reality that seem to require explanation, but there are also other features of the universe that are often proposed as providing evidence for the existence of God. We shall turn to some of these in the next chapter.

Notes

1. For example, Graham Oppy, who is a leading atheist philosopher, argues that there are 'no arguments that ought to persuade those who have reasonable views about the existence of orthodoxly conceived monotheistic gods to change their minds' and he contends that 'there is a very wide range of reasonable views' on this topic (*Arguing About Gods* [Cambridge: Cambridge University Press, 2006], p. xv).

2. *TGD*, p. 59.

3. Ibid., p. 51.

4. *GNG*, p. 150.

5. Ibid., p. 71.

6. From the blog Science and the Sacred, http://blog.beliefnet.com/scienceandthesacred/2009/08/why-i-think-the-new-atheists-are-a-bloody-disaster.html (accessed 30 Oct. 2010).

7. *TGD*, p. 85.

8. 'Unless you have a taste for mathematics and theoretical physics on the one hand, or the niceties of scholastic logic on the other, you are not apt to find any of this compelling, or even fathomable' (*BTS*, p. 242).

9. *TGD*, pp. 50–51.

10. See Antony Flew and Gary R. Habermas, 'My Pilgrimage from Atheism to Theism: A Discussion between Antony Flew and Gary R. Habermas', *Philosophia Christi* 6 (2004), pp. 197–212.

11. *TGD*, p. 58.

12. Ibid., p. 59.

13. The Higgs boson is an elementary particle predicted by the standard model of particle physics. If it exists it would resolve certain problems in the standard model. In particular, the role of the Higgs boson is to mediate the Higgs field, which is postulated to permeate the universe and which provides a mechanism whereby elementary particles can acquire their mass. Some evidence for the existence of the Higgs boson has recently been acquired, but at time of writing the jury is still out.

14. A good argument would be required to show that God's existence is highly improbable and on this count Dawkins and Russell's appeal to the celestial teapot will not suffice. Dawkins does provide another argument to support the claim that God's existence is highly improbable. It will be considered in chapter 6.

15. For a more in-depth discussion see my 'Probability and the Presumption of Atheism', *Yearbook of the Irish Philosophical Society* (2010), pp. 58–68.

16. As we shall see in chapter 6, at times Dawkins gives the impression that God could not provide a good explanation for anything, which seems to imply that there could be no evidence for God's existence even in principle.

17. *TGD*, p. 65.

18. For a detailed account see Peter Lipton, *Inference to the Best Explanation*, 2nd ed. (London: Routledge, 2004).

19. Another way of spelling it out is in terms of Bayesianism, which draws on probability theory to consider how likely a piece of evidence would be if a given hypothesis were true. In particular, if a piece of evidence were more likely given hypothesis A than hypothesis B, then this would confirm hypothesis A; that is, it would count in favour of A. Although inference to the best explanation and Bayesianism have some differences, they also have some similarities and may be compatible with each other. For our purposes, the differences between them are not important.

20. This seems to fit quite well with Dawkins's approach, since in considering the existence of God he wants to consider it as a scientific question, yet he also seems to realize that it is inappropriate to look for direct experimental proof through prayer experiments, for example, where one group receives prayers and a control group does not.

21. Stephen W. Hawking, *A Brief History of Time* (London: Bantam, 1988), p. 174.

22. *GNG*, p. 71.

23. See, for example, J. P. Moreland and W. L. Craig, *Philosophical Foundations for a Christian Worldview* (Downers Grove: IVP, 2003), pp. 501–535; Richard Swinburne, *The Existence of God*, 2nd ed. (Oxford: Oxford University Press, 2004), pp. 93–109.

24. See, for example, Moreland and Craig, *Philosophical Foundations*, pp. 502–504.

25. This point is more controversial, however, since not all theists consider God to be necessary in this sense.

26. *TGD*, p. 77.

27. William Lane Craig, 'In Defence of Theistic Arguments', in R. Stewart (ed.), *The Future of Atheism: Alister McGrath and Daniel Dennett in Dialogue* (London: SPCK, 2008), p. 70.

28. I have considered only two hypotheses here, atheism and theism. Perhaps it could be argued that some other hypothesis such as deism or pantheism is even better than theism. It is worth making three brief points. First, I'm not aware of any convincing arguments to this end. Secondly, even if there are, it doesn't offer much comfort to the atheist. Thirdly, even if one of these rivals is better than theism, it may still be the case that theism receives some support from the evidence and that once all the evidence is taken into consideration theism would still come out on top. Of course, none of this undermines the main claim that the evidence supports theism over atheism. For a detailed atheistic perspective on this argument see J. Howard Sobel, *Logic and Theism: Arguments for and Against the Existence of God* (Cambridge: Cambridge University Press, 2004), pp. 200–237; for a detailed theistic perspective see Alexander R. Pruss, 'The Leibnizian Cosmological Argument', in William Lane Craig and J. P. Moreland (eds.), *Blackwell Companion to Natural Theology* (Chichester: Wiley-Blackwell, 2009), pp. 24–100.

29. In fact, this should be thought of as the expansion of space itself and not merely the galaxies moving away from each other in a pre-existing space.

30. John Barrow and Frank Tipler, *The Anthropic Cosmological Principle* (Oxford: Oxford University Press, 1986), p. 442.

31. Quoted in William Lane Craig, *Reasonable Faith: Christian Truth and Apologetics*, 3rd ed. (Wheaton, Ill.: Crossway, 2008), p. 128.

32. Robert Jastrow, *God and the Astronomers*, 2nd ed. (New York: Norton, 1992), p. 107.

33. Hawking, *Brief History of Time*, p. 46.

34. John Gribbin, 'Oscillating Universe Bounces Back', *Nature* 59 (1976), p. 15.

35. Fred Hoyle, *Facts and Dogmas in Cosmology and Elsewhere* (Cambridge: Cambridge University Press, 1982), pp. 2–3 (quoted in C. Southgate [ed.], *God, Humanity and the Cosmos* [Edinburgh: T. & T. Clark, 1999], p. 36).

36. Martin Rees, *Just Six Numbers* (London: Phoenix, 2000), p. 11.

37. Stephen W. Hawking and Leonard Mlodinow, *The Grand Design: New Answers to the Ultimate Questions of Life* (London: Bantam, 2010).

38. Approximately 10^{-43} sec.

39. Hawking, *Brief History of Time*, p. 136.

40. Ibid., pp. 140–141.

41. Sometimes it is claimed that the big bang theory has been rejected in favour of more recent cosmological models, but this is misleading. It is correct if it refers to the standard big bang model, which does not involve quantum theory, but the general

big bang account going right back to within the first second of the universe is generally accepted.

42. See pp. 279–300 in William Lane Craig and Quentin Smith, *Theism, Atheism and Big Bang Cosmology* (Oxford: Clarendon, 1995).

43. In fact, in a sense, Hawking himself seems to agree, for he claims that 'a scientific theory is just a mathematical model we make to describe our observations: it exists only in our minds. So it is meaningless to ask: Which is real, "real" or "imaginary" time? It is simply a matter of which is the more useful description' (Hawking, *Brief History of Time*, p. 139). This is a succinct summary of Hawking's positivism. Yet, as Craig points out, Hawking's claim that his model removes the need for a creator only makes sense if it is interpreted realistically.

44. See Robert J. Deltete and Reed A. Guy, 'Emerging from Imaginary Time', *Synthese* 108 (1996), pp. 185–203.

45. See Alexander Vilenkin, *Many Worlds in One: The Search for Other Universes* (New York: Hill & Wang, 2006); Don N. Page, 'Susskind's Challenge to the Hartle–Hawking No Boundary Proposal and Some Resolutions', *Journal of Cosmology and Astroparticle Physics* (2007), 0701:004, http://arxiv.org/abs/hep-th/0610199 (accessed 30 Sept. 2011).

46. An excellent debate on the relevant issues is found in the book by Craig and Smith, *Theism, Atheism*, even though some more cosmological models have been proposed since it was published.

47. Bradley Monton, *Seeking God in Science: An Atheist Defends Intelligent Design* (Peterborough, Ont.: Broadview, 2009), p. 98. See also Oppy, *Arguing About Gods*, pp. 146–147.

48. They have shown that under reasonable assumptions expanding universes will have a finite past, 'Inflationary Spacetimes Are Incomplete in Past Directions', *Physical Review Letters* 90.15 (2003), p. 151301. Vilenkin comments that 'With the proof now in place, cosmologists can no longer hide behind the possibility of a past-eternal universe. There is no escape, they have to face the problem of a cosmic beginning' (A. Vilenkin, *Many Worlds in One: The Search for Other Universes* [New York: Hill & Wang, 2006], quoted in Craig, 'In Defence of Theistic Arguments', p. 75).

49. See William Lane Craig, *The Kalām Cosmological Argument* (London: Macmillan, 1979). Traditionally, the Kalām argument is supported by logical arguments to demonstrate that the universe *must* have had a beginning. Here I focus on empirical arguments to show that the universe *actually* had a beginning, but not that it must have had one. Craig uses both logical and empirical arguments to support premise 2.

50. *TGD*, p. 78.

51. *BTS*, p. 242.

52. Ibid., p. 244.

53. Perhaps this is what he meant by 'well-nigh indistinguishable from nothing at all'.

EVIDENCE FOR GOD — PART I

54. In fact, arguably the problem is more fundamental since there is no such thing as the precise state of the universe due to intrinsic uncertainty.

55. John Polkinghorne, *Science and Creation* (London: SPCK, 1988), p. 59.

56. Ibid., p. 60.

57. Hawking and Mlodinow, *Grand Design*, p. 180.

58. For a detailed response to Hawking and Mlodinow, see John C. Lennox, *God and Stephen Hawking: Whose Design Is it Anyway?* (Oxford: Lion Hudson, 2010).

59. Victor J. Stenger, *God: The Failed Hypothesis* (New York: Prometheus, 2008), p. 133.

60. Keith Ward, *Why There Almost Certainly Is a God: Doubting Dawkins* (Oxford: Lion Hudson, 2008), p. 107.

61. Of course, much more could be said both for and against. For example, various authors have claimed that a cause must precede its effects and so the first premise (that everything that begins to exist has a cause) does not apply to the universe since there can be no cause prior to the universe (since time begins at the big bang). Some theists have responded by claiming that God is causally prior, but not temporally prior, to the universe and that his causing the universe to exist is simultaneous with its beginning. Similarly, some atheists have argued that it is conceivable that something could begin to exist without a cause and so theists need to demonstrate that this is impossible in reality. Advocates of the argument have responded that it is much more plausible to accept the first premise than to deny it, and so the burden of proof lies with the atheist. For a detailed atheistic perspective see Oppy, *Arguing About Gods*, pp. 137–168; for a detailed theistic perspective see William Lane Craig and James D. Sinclair, 'The Kalām Cosmological Argument', in William Lane Craig and J. P. Moreland (eds.), *Blackwell Companion to Natural Theology* (Chichester: Wiley-Blackwell, 2009), pp. 101–201; for a discussion by an atheist who finds the argument somewhat persuasive see Monton, *Seeking God in Science*, pp. 86–99; and for an in-depth debate between a theist and atheist see Craig and Smith, *Theism, Atheism*.

62. Although William Lane Craig argues that in addition to transcending space and time the cause must be changeless, immaterial, without beginning, uncaused, unimaginably powerful and personal. See his 'In Defence of Theistic Arguments'.

5. EVIDENCE FOR GOD – PART 2: THE ORDER OF THE UNIVERSE AND THE EXISTENCE OF CONSCIOUS MINDS

As we saw in the last chapter, the New Atheists' belief that there is no evidence for God's existence has been formed without any serious consideration of the evidence that has been proposed by theists. In particular, it was argued that the very existence of the universe itself and the evidence for the universe having had a beginning are better explained by the existence of God than by atheism and so they both count as evidence in favour of God's existence. Even if there were no other evidence for God, these two pieces of evidence are so fundamental that they cannot be dismissed lightly. In this chapter we shall consider three further pieces of evidence. The first of these, like the previous two, is concerned with a general feature of the universe: its order. The third is much more specific since it is not about the universe as a whole, but relates to conscious beings such as ourselves. These two are related since we could not exist unless the universe was sufficiently well ordered. However, it turns out the conditions necessary for our existence and indeed for the existence of life in general are much more specific than we might have guessed. This provides the focus for the second piece of evidence to be considered in this chapter, the fine-tuning of various features of the universe, which provides a bridge between the first and third pieces of evidence.

An orderly universe

It hardly needs saying that science is about much more than collecting empirical facts. Scientists strive to find order behind these facts, scientific laws that make sense of a range of facts. For example, scientists were not content simply to chart the trajectories of different planets, but wanted instead to find a law that would make sense of the motions of all the planets. And, of course, Newton's law of gravity was able to account not only for the motion of heavenly bodies, but objects falling to earth as well. The bringing together of diverse phenomena under a single scientific law is a key component of science.

In chapter 3 we saw that many pioneers of modern science expected to find such order in nature because they believed the universe was the product of a rational creator. Here I want to focus on a basic result of science, for if science tells us anything it tells us that there is a great deal of order in the universe. From the large-scale structure of the universe to the microscopic world of subatomic particles we find laws of nature in operation so that diverse phenomena can be understood in terms of general laws rather than in isolation. And, furthermore, it seems that these laws apply throughout the universe and not just in our own region of it. As John Polkinghorne puts it,

> We are so familiar with the fact that we can understand the world that most of the time we take it for granted. It is what makes science possible. Yet it could have been otherwise. The universe might have been a disorderly chaos rather than an orderly cosmos. Or it might have had a rationality that was inaccessible to us. . . . There is a congruence between our minds and the universe, between the rationality experienced within and the rationality observed without.[1]

Philosopher Richard Swinburne makes the same point: 'The orderliness of the universe in this respect is a very striking fact about it. The universe might so naturally have been chaotic, but it is not – it is very orderly.'[2]

Perhaps the most important aspect to this order concerns what the Nobel prize-winning physicist Eugene Wigner referred to as the 'unreasonable effectiveness of mathematics in the natural sciences'. Why is it that the laws of physics can be 'written in the language of mathematics' as Galileo put it? The fact that mathematics plays such a fundamental role in physics and has given rise to so many precise predictions that have been verified experimentally makes it very difficult to deny that there is an underlying explanation for this state of affairs. Another theoretical physicist, Paul Davies, writes, 'Yet the fact that "mathematics works" when applied to the physical world – and works so stunningly well – demands explanation, for it is not clear we have any absolute right to expect that the world should be well described by mathematics.'[3] Polkinghorne discusses the role that looking for beauty, or elegance, in their equations played in the work of Nobel Prize-winning physicists Paul Dirac, Erwin Schrödinger and Albert Einstein. Dirac famously said that 'it is more important to have beauty in one's equations than to have them fit experiment'.[4] Ironically, this strategy yielded remarkably accurate agreement with experiment. Polkinghorne writes:

> There is no a priori reason why beautiful equations should prove to be the clue
> to understanding nature; why fundamental physics should be possible; why our
> minds should have such ready access to the deep structures of the universe. It is a
> contingent fact that this is true of us and our world, but it does not seem sufficient
> simply to regard it as a happy accident. Surely it is a significant insight into the nature
> of reality.[5]

One particular example of order concerns the orbits of planets in the solar system. The orbits of the planets are governed by the law of gravity, which is what is known as an inverse square law. This means that if the distance between two objects were to be doubled the gravitational force between them would be reduced by a factor of four. As physicists John Barrow and Frank Tipler show, 'Only in universes in which gravity abides by an inverse square law could the solar system remain in a stable state over long time-scales.'[6] Astronomer Martin Rees points out that if gravity satisfied an inverse cube law, then a slight modification in the speed of a planet would result in its plunging into the Sun or else spiralling out into darkness.[7] Interestingly, the inverse square law is a direct consequence of there being three spatial dimensions in the universe.[8] Hence, the dimensionality of the universe seems to be necessary for this aspect of the order of the universe and consequently for the existence of complex life.

Before going on to investigate how this order might be relevant to belief in God, it is first worth pausing to see whether such order is really a feature of the universe. It might be thought that quantum theory shows otherwise; isn't the quantum world a place where randomness and chaotic behaviour reign? Not really. Quantum theory is certainly very different from Newtonian mechanics, which it replaced. Although there is an intrinsic uncertainty in the quantum world, this does not mean that it is completely chaotic. On the contrary, the equations of quantum theory enable us to make remarkably accurate predictions that have been verified experimentally as noted above. Quantum theory is a prime example of the effectiveness of mathematics in science.

Order in the quantum world is very different from order in the Newtonian world, but it is order nonetheless.

Is it possible that the order is not really a feature of the world itself, but instead exists in our minds? In other words, do we impose order on the world that is not really there in the world itself? Some postmodern attitudes to science seem to go in this direction, denying that science is any more than a human construction with little or no relation to reality. Such a view is difficult to take seriously since it would leave us unable to account for scientific progress and would provide no reason for thinking that scientific laws that have worked so well in the past will continue to work in the future. A more plausible view would be to say that scientific theories enable us to account for the phenomena and make predictions, but do not (at least, not necessarily) give an accurate description of what the world is really like.[9] Even if such a view is correct, which I doubt, it seems that the world would still have to be sufficiently orderly for our theories to make accurate predictions.

So there doesn't seem to be any reason to deny that the world is orderly, as Polkinghorne, Swinburne and others maintain. And it seems clear that the New Atheists agree with this. Needless to say, they would have no truck with the idea that the order is imposed by us on the world since they continually emphasize that science gives an accurate picture of what the world is really like.

Does the order of the universe count as evidence in favour of theism over atheism? It certainly seems plausible to hold, as the pioneers of science did, that if God were to create a universe he would create an orderly one. One reason for believing this is that we know from observation and direct experience that minds create order and so it would seem reasonable to believe that a universe created by God would be orderly. Other reasons can be found in Swinburne's claims that order is a necessary condition of beauty and that order means rational beings can perceive the order so as to utilize it to achieve certain goals.[10] He then argues that these are both reasons for God to make an orderly universe. Since order is necessary for intelligent beings to exist, it also seems likely that this would provide a further reason for God to create an orderly universe.

What about atheism? How could it account for the order in the universe? Could a scientific explanation be given for it? It seems not, since the order is found in the scientific laws themselves. In principle, if a Theory of Everything were to be discovered it might account for all other scientific laws, but what about the Theory of Everything itself? It would clearly represent the order in the universe so it would still need to be accounted for. In Swinburne's comment that the 'universe might so naturally have been chaotic' is the suggestion that if there is no God it would be very unlikely that the universe would be orderly. Could it be argued in response that the universe somehow had to be orderly? There doesn't appear to be any good reason to think that this is the case; it at least seems unlikely that it had to have as much order as it actually does.

This seems to leave the atheist with just one option, that the order of the universe is just an inexplicable brute fact. But this seems unsatisfactory since there is a great deal of order in the universe and so it is highly improbable that this should have occurred without any explanation. According to theism the order is not at all improbable and so theism offers a much better explanation of the evidence. As in the previous cases this means that the evidence provides support for the existence of God.

This is not quite the end of the matter, however, with this piece of evidence. This is a type of design argument and so is open to a couple more objections that are relevant to some other design arguments. One of these is the 'who designed the designer' objection. This is not quite the same as the 'who created the creator' objection dealt with earlier. Since much has been made of this objection by Richard Dawkins it will be considered in the next chapter. A further objection is the so-called anthropic principle objection, which says that we should not be surprised at observing order in the universe since if it was not orderly we would not be here to observe it. This is often raised in the context of the fine-tuning argument and so will be discussed in the next section.

Fine-tuning

In the last few decades scientists have increasingly become aware that the universe is 'just right' for life. If any one of a number of features of the universe had been even slightly different, life as we know it would be impossible. Although there are different types of features to which this applies, most attention is focused on the physical constants.[11] Some of the physical constants determine the strengths of the fundamental forces in physics (the gravitational, electromagnetic, weak nuclear and strong nuclear forces). For example, the gravitational force between two objects depends not only on their masses and the distance between them but also on the gravitational constant G.

One of the most striking examples of fine-tuning is due to the fact that life depends crucially on the degree to which the electromagnetic force is stronger than the gravitational force. According to Paul Davies, a change in the ratio of these forces of about 1 part in 10^{40} (that's a 1 with 40 zeroes after it, or ten thousand billion billion billion billion) would mean that stars such as the Sun, capable of supporting life, could not exist.[12] The precision involved in this example of fine-tuning is quite incredible on its own,[13] but it may not be the most impressive example.

In chapter 4 we came across Einstein's dubious reasons for introducing a cosmological constant; that is, he wanted a static universe. We now know this cannot be right because the universe is expanding, but there are now much more credible reasons for thinking that such a constant has a role to play. The role of the constant is such that if it is positive, it causes space to expand. Indeed, since we now know that the universe is not only expanding but accelerating, this suggests that the cosmological constant has a positive value. This means that if it is too big, galaxies could not form and, in fact, it must be remarkably close to zero. Physicist turned philosopher Robin Collins has explored the fine-tuning of the cosmological constant, as well as other instances of fine-tuning, in some detail.[14] He discusses how there are various contributions to what he calls the effective cosmological constant. These include contributions from various fields in physics, which give rise to the energy density of empty space, and also an intrinsic component not based on these fields. The problem is that theoretical estimates of the contributions from the various fields give values between 10^{53} and 10^{120} higher than the maximum value that would be possible in a life-permitting universe. However, once all the components, including the intrinsic component, are factored in, obviously the effective cosmological constant does lie within the life-permitting range (otherwise we wouldn't be here). Collins argues that the possible range of values is at least 10^{53} greater than the life-permitting range, and so estimates a fine-tuning of at least one part in 10^{53}.

Here are a few other examples. If the strong nuclear force had been weaker, this could have resulted in the instability of elements necessary for carbon-based life; while if it had been stronger, this could have had a negative impact on the production of carbon and oxygen. The existence of hydrogen is sensitive to the strength of the weak nuclear force. A decrease in the weak force would mean that there would be no hydrogen-burning stars like the Sun. Other types of physical constants also feature in fine-tuning scenarios. For example, if the difference between the neutron and proton masses had been slightly greater, then, once again, there would be no stars like the Sun. A number of examples of fine-tuning relate to the initial conditions of the universe. For example, the low entropy condition of the early universe seems to require extremely precise fine-tuning for stars and planets to exist.[15]

Other examples could be cited,[16] but the general picture is clear.

Cosmologists Stephen Hawking and Leonard Mlodinow summarize the findings:

> The emergence of complex structures capable of supporting intelligent observers seems to be very fragile. The laws of nature form a system that is extremely fine-tuned, and very little in physical law can be altered without destroying the possibility of the development of life as we know it. Were it not for a series of startling coincidences in the precise details of physical law, it seems, humans and similar life-forms would never have come into being.[17]

Collins illustrates the extent of the fine-tuning, and asks us to think of the

> values of the initial conditions of the universe and constants of physics as co-ordinates on a dart board that fills the whole galaxy, and the conditions necessary for life to exist as an extremely small target, say less than a trillionth of an inch: unless the dart hits the target, complex life would be impossible.[18]

No wonder Paul Davies says 'the impression of design is overwhelming'.[19] 'Overwhelming' is the right word since the degree of precision required for life to exist is so great that intuitively it seems utterly ludicrous to think that all of these different features of the universe have just the right values for life to exist without an intelligent agent having been responsible. If you want scientific evidence for the existence of God, it is difficult to imagine what more you could ask for.

Standard responses to fine-tuning

Before looking at some of the main responses from atheists, it is worth looking at one consideration that Richard Dawkins asks us to bear in mind. He appeals to Darwinism as a consciousness-raiser. Relating this to the idea that the improbability of certain features of the world, such as the fine-tuning examples, should be taken as evidence for design, Dawkins says:

> Darwinian natural selection shows us how wrong this is with respect to biological improbability. And although Darwinism may not be directly relevant to the inanimate world – cosmology, for example – it raises our consciousness in areas outside its original territory of biology.[20]

Just to be clear, Dawkins is completely correct that Darwinism is not directly relevant to the fine-tuning evidence. Darwinism can draw on the fact that natural selection is a non-random process and on vast timescales to account for biological complexity. By contrast the fine-tuning evidence considered above applies to the first second of the universe, and so timescales are irrelevant, and there is no corresponding mechanism to select appropriate values.

But what are we to make of Darwinism as a *consciousness-raiser*? Even if Darwinism undermines design in biology, a point we shall return to in the next chapter, it does so by providing an explanation that does not appeal to design. But how can Darwinism undermine design in the context of fine-tuning without giving an explanation of fine-tuning? And, if there is no convincing explanation of fine-tuning that does not appeal to design, why should design still be ruled out, especially given the incredible degree of fine-tuning? Dawkins's view seems to be a bit like saying that no one should ever be convicted of murder because some people in the past have been wrongly convicted. Of course, the fact that innocent people have been convicted of murder should make us cautious about convicting someone on insufficient evidence. But if the evidence is overwhelming in a particular case, it would be a huge mistake *not* to convict.

One type of objection to fine-tuning is that although at present there is no scientific reason for the physical constants to have the values they do, perhaps this will change in the future; perhaps a Theory of Everything (TOE) will be discovered that will explain the values of these constants and show that they could not have been otherwise. In reply it must be said that while this possibility cannot be ruled out, there is no good reason to believe it and so to depend on this as a response seems like wishful thinking on the part of the atheist. Indeed, in M-theory,[21] which is currently the best candidate for a TOE, recent work shows that far from predicting the physical constants uniquely there could be 10^{500} different possibilities.[22] Furthermore, even if a TOE were to be discovered that did predict the physical constants uniquely, it would still be an amazing coincidence that the predicted constants were those that support life. This is the reason that Dawkins provides for rejecting this first response to the fine-tuning evidence.[23]

Even in the absence of a TOE it might be argued that future developments in science will provide explanations for the evidence of fine-tuning without any need to appeal to design. For example, physicist Victor Stenger claims that the cosmological constant may turn out to be zero and that the acceleration of the universe may be accounted for in some other way.[24] One suggestion is that it might be due to a neutral matter field known as quintessence. But there are problems with this response. First, it requires some new principle to show why the cosmological constant is zero and it is not clear what that would be. A particular difficulty is that inflationary cosmology, which says that there was an extremely short-lived and incredibly rapid expansion of the early universe, requires a large, effective cosmological constant to drive it and that presents a problem if the cosmological constant is zero. If inflation were to be abandoned, this would give rise to another example of fine-tuning, which inflation was supposed to account for. Furthermore, for quintessence to act as an effective cosmological constant and for this effect to be small enough to lie within the life-permitting range may well require further fine-tuning. So while some sort of explanation along the lines suggested by Stenger could not be ruled out, it seems very likely that fine-tuning would be required elsewhere or that it would merely push the case for design back to the underlying principles or laws appealed to.[25]

One way of expressing this first kind of response, that is, that future science might account for the evidence without having to appeal to design, is to say that the argument from fine-tuning is a God-of-the-gaps argument. The suggestion is that we should not appeal to God as an explanation just because of a gap in current science. This is a very weak objection to fine-tuning for several reasons. First, as discussed in chapter 3, we need to distinguish between causal gaps and explanatory gaps. The fine-tuning argument is not appealing to God to fill in causal gaps, but is pointing to something in need of explanation. Secondly, what needs to be explained is not something arising from scientific ignorance, but is due to evidence gathered at the frontiers of modern science since the 1970s or so. Thirdly, what needs to be explained are very fundamental features of the universe, such as constants and initial conditions. Fourthly, it is not a matter of appealing to design to explain a single piece of evidence since there are many different instances of fine-tuning arising in different areas of science. This kind of diversity of evidence is very important in science itself and so should not be dismissed lightly in the context of fine-tuning. Fifthly, in the case of God-of-the-gaps arguments, it has often been the case that subsequent science has filled in the gaps and so invalidated the arguments; but, as we have seen, in the case of fine-tuning there are reasons to think that future science will not undermine the argument and may well enhance it.[26]

A second objection is to say that the fine-tuning is only necessary for life as we know it; perhaps other types of life that we cannot even imagine would have developed if some of the physical constants had been different. One point to note is that for a number of examples of fine-tuning, if the constants had been different, no galaxies, stars or planets could have formed and there is no reason to believe that any kind of intelligent life could exist in such a universe, so this approach is extremely speculative. It is also quite plausible to believe that the conditions that would permit other types of life to exist would also be fine-tuned. This means that had the physical constants been different and yet some exotic kind of life existed, the existence of such life would depend crucially on the physical constants in that universe (just as our existence depends on the constants in the real universe). Overall, this means that the range of values of the constants that permit life would still be extremely small compared to the total range of possible values.

Also, as Robin Collins points out,[27] for the fine-tuning evidence to count in favour of design it is not required that no other values of the physical constants would support life, but only that the *surrounding* range of non-life-permitting values is large compared to the life-permitting range. To illustrate the point he returns to his dartboard analogy. Suppose the dart hits a very small target surrounded by a much larger blank area. This would still count in favour of the dart's having been aimed even if there might be other targets elsewhere on the board.

A third objection to fine-tuning is to appeal to what is called the anthropic principle.[28] The basic idea is that we should not be surprised that we observe fine-tuning because if the universe were not finely tuned, we would not be here to observe it; a finely tuned universe is the only kind we could observe. Initially, this approach appears to have some plausibility. A defender of this approach, the philosopher of science Elliott Sober, draws on the following example.[29] Suppose I catch fifty fish from a lake. Does the fact that all the fish I catch are more than ten inches long support the hypothesis that all the fish in the lake are more than ten inches long more than the hypothesis that only half the fish in the lake are more than ten inches long? It is tempting to think that it does since otherwise it might seem like a remarkable coincidence that all the fish caught were more than ten inches long. But suppose that the net I used could only catch fish more than ten inches long because of the size of the holes. It is now clear that the evidence does not support the first hypothesis because it would have been impossible to observe fish of any other length. The size of the holes in the net gives rise to an *observational selection effect*.

But now consider another example.[30] You are to be executed by a firing squad of 12 excellent marksmen who fire 12 rounds each. All 144 shots are fired, yet you are still alive – because all have missed. Initially you think that the marksmen must have missed deliberately, but then you recall the anthropic principle and reason as follows: 'The fact that all the shots missed me does not tell me anything about the intentions of the marksmen. After all, if they hadn't all missed, I wouldn't be here to consider the matter.' This response is clearly inadequate since it still seems entirely legitimate to ask why all the shots missed and perfectly reasonable to conclude that it was deliberate.

Intuitively, the fine-tuning case is much closer to this example than the fishing example. In particular, in the firing squad case the observation that I am still alive is much more likely if the marksmen missed deliberately because otherwise I wouldn't be around to make the observation. Similarly, in the fine-tuning case the observation that the constants are suitable for life is much more likely given design because otherwise it is unlikely that anyone would be here to make the observation. By contrast, in the fishing example, the type of net used has no bearing on whether the observation will be made and guarantees that if an observation is made, all the fish caught will be more than ten inches long.[31] This means that just as anthropic reasoning does not undermine the conclusion that the marksmen missed deliberately, it cannot be used to undermine the conclusion that fine-tuning is due to design. This conclusion seems to be generally accepted. Indeed, Dawkins rejects the anthropic principle as a response to the fine-tuning evidence based on the firing squad analogy.[32]

A multiverse response to fine-tuning

There is a further response that is open to opponents of design. It certainly seems improbable that our universe should have just the right values of the physical constants for life to exist, but what if our universe is not unique? What if it is only one of many that together constitute a multiverse? Consider an analogy. Suppose you are the only person who buys a lottery ticket and your numbers come up. Because this outcome is vastly improbable, it might be reasonable to wonder whether it really occurred by chance. Suppose, however, that you are just one of millions of people to buy a ticket (most with different numbers) and your numbers come up. While you would still be surprised, there doesn't seem to be any reason to question chance as an explanation. After all, so many people bought tickets that it was reasonably likely that one or more people would win.

Similarly, the fine-tuning of the physical constants in our universe might point to design if ours is the only universe, but if there are a large number of universes with different physical constants, then perhaps there would be no need to appeal to design. Anthropic reasoning would then come into play since it would not be surprising that we find ourselves in the universe (or one of the universes) that has suitable physical constants; we could not exist in a universe that did not have suitable constants. Thus, anthropic reasoning on its own does not offer an adequate atheistic reply to the fine-tuning evidence, but perhaps anthropic reasoning together with a multiverse does.

Before going any further it is worth pausing to consider how there could be more than one universe. If we think of the universe as simply everything physical that exists, then clearly there couldn't be more than one, but if we think of the universe as the observable universe the picture is very different. Earlier, we ran across inflation theory, which postulates an extremely short-lived and rapid expansion of the early universe. According to inflationary scenarios, the observable universe is just one region in a much larger domain. In the simplest case, these other regions would have the same physical laws and constants, but different initial conditions. While some would refer to these regions as separate universes that together constitute a multiverse, others would consider them to be parts of a single universe and would reserve the term 'multiverse' for scenarios in which the different universes can have different physical constants. It is this kind of multiverse that is relevant here since in principle there might be a large number of universes with different physical constants. In the vast majority of these the values will not be fine-tuned to support life, but perhaps in some of them (including ours of course) they will.

Do these multiple universes exist? No one knows. And, of course, there is no way to observe them since they are not part of our observable universe. Could we ever know whether multiple universes exist? Physicists disagree about whether multiverse theories are testable and, closely related to this, whether they should have a legitimate place in science. Cosmologist George Ellis is sceptical.[33] He points out that some kind of causal connection between an object and experimental apparatus is required for testing to be possible and so this rules out the testability of certain types of multiverse scenarios that lack a causal connection with our own universe. For multiverse scenarios where other universes had a common origin with our own, he argues that although they could not be detected directly, a case could be made if their existence was a consequence of well-established physical laws or processes. However, for one of the main proposals, his concern is that the underlying physics has not been tested and may be untestable. In particular, he is concerned that it involves unwarranted extrapolations that go far beyond the domain where current physics can be tested. Overall, his assessment is that the 'existence of multiverses is neither established nor scientifically establishable'.[34]

Others are not so sceptical. Cosmologist Don Page argues that multiverse theories may be able to make predictions that can be tested experimentally, although he identifies certain requirements that need to be met.[35] Martin Rees is also more optimistic about the prospects for multiverse theories. Essentially, his reasoning is based on the idea that if there is evidence to support a scientific theory, this evidence can also be taken to support other things that the theory says even if those other things cannot be tested directly. He points out that we can give credence to what current theories predict about quarks or the region inside black holes because of other evidence to support the theories.[36] Similarly, suppose there is a scientific theory that predicts the existence of multiple universes and that makes other predictions as well. If evidence confirms these other predictions, and so confirms the theory, this could be taken as confirming the existence of multiple universes as well. In principle, Ellis would probably agree, but Rees seems more hopeful that the relevant assumptions required to predict multiple universes could become better established.

It is true that indirect evidence is often taken to support scientific claims that cannot be tested directly, but it is far from clear at what point we would be justified in believing that a multiverse is likely to exist. Page claims that 'if we find a multiverse theory that is simpler and more explanatory and predictive of what is observed than the best single-universe theory, then the multiverse theory should be preferred'.[37] As Page is aware, though, it is difficult to decide how we should weigh the simplicity of the multiverse and single-universe theories. Even if the multiverse theory explains certain pieces of evidence well, this may be outweighed by its much greater complexity. Furthermore, if a theory that was supported by evidence predicted a multiverse, we might wonder whether there is a simpler single-universe theory that can account for all the evidence without having to appeal to multiple universes. In that case, we might be tempted to accept the successful theory as a working hypothesis while remaining agnostic about its more extravagant claims. However, given the approach in this book, these considerations do not present too much of a problem for multiverse hypotheses since if a multiverse hypothesis explains the evidence better than single-universe hypotheses, the evidence would still count in favour of the multiverse hypothesis, even if we were still inclined to reject it all things considered.

At present all multiverse proposals are highly speculative. As pointed out in chapter 4, the speculative nature of such proposals is not necessarily a problem from a scientific point of view since theories that start out as speculative can end up being successful. However, if the fine-tuning evidence is to be explained by the existence of a multiverse rather than design, there must be some good reason to think the proposed multiverse actually exists or is likely to exist. Merely appealing to the possibility that some multiverse theory might be true would be a very weak response to design. By way of analogy, suppose that Joe stands accused of robbing a bank on grounds that include an eyewitness having seen him at the scene of the crime. Detectives are not likely to be impressed at the suggestion that it was really Joe's identical twin brother if they have no good reason to believe that he has a twin brother. The mere possibility that there might be an alternative explanation would not be good enough.[38]

The speculative nature of multiverse hypotheses has not stopped some of the New Atheists from appealing to them in order to reject design. Both Dawkins and Dennett refer to two possible multiverse scenarios.[39] One is

an oscillating universe that has an endless sequence of big bangs, each followed by expansion, contraction and a big crunch before the next big bang,
and with a different set of physical constants in each case. The other is Lee
Smolin's hypothesis that black holes can give rise to offspring universes with
constants that have been mutated from the parent universe. Not surprisingly,
Dawkins and Dennett are both taken with Smolin's account, which is a kind
of cosmic Darwinism. Needless to say, however, both scenarios are extremely
speculative, there is no evidence to support them (in fact, there is evidence
against at least the first scenario as Dawkins points out), and neither has many
supporters even among multiverse advocates.

Interestingly, both Dawkins and Dennett are fully aware of the speculative nature of these (and other) multiverse proposals. Their reasoning seems
to be that the mere fact that some such scenario might be *possible* is all that is
required to make it preferable to theism as an explanation for fine-tuning.[40]
Dawkins reasons as follows:

> The key difference between the genuinely extravagant God hypothesis and the
> apparently extravagant multiverse hypothesis is one of statistical improbability. The
> multiverse, for all that it is extravagant, is simple. God, or any intelligent, decision-
> taking, calculating agent, would have to be highly improbable in the very same
> statistical sense as the entities he is supposed to explain. The multiverse may seem
> extravagant in sheer *number* of universes. But if each one of those universes is simple
> in its fundamental laws, we are still not postulating anything highly improbable. The
> very opposite has to be said of any kind of intelligence.[41]

This is a key argument in Dawkins's book and is fraught with difficulties, but
these will be dealt with more fully in the next chapter. For the moment, let us
ask whether there is any multiverse hypothesis that Dawkins would consider
less favourable than theism. Would the proposal, due to theoretical physicist
Max Tegmark, that everything that can happen does happen somewhere in
the multiverse be preferable to theism?[42] If so, this may commit Dawkins to
the view that miracles such as the resurrection occur *naturally* somewhere in
the multiverse without God having to bring them about.[43] Would Dawkins
really find this preferable to theism? Surely not. Would he really consider this
multiverse scenario 'simple' and 'not postulating anything highly improbable'?
If Dawkins does not find the above scenario preferable to theism, he needs
to explain, at least in general terms, where he would draw the line between
multiverse hypotheses that are preferable to theism and those that are not.
Merely pointing out that some multiverse hypothesis might be feasible is not
good enough.

Although not antagonistic towards theism, astronomer Martin Rees also opts for a multiverse as a rival to theism as an explanation for the fine-tuning evidence.[44] His reason seems to be that although the existence of other universes is 'conjectural' and the theories that predict them are 'speculative', he thinks that 'the multiverse genuinely lies within the province of science, even though it is plainly no more than a tentative hypothesis'. Rees thinks that the multiverse is part of science because we know what questions need to be addressed to put it on a more credible footing and it is capable of being refuted. This view can be questioned, but let us accept that Rees is correct, as many scientists believe. What follows from this? That it is probably true? Or that it is more plausible than theism? Hardly. The mere fact that a theory could be shown to be false doesn't give us reason to believe that it is probably true! At the very least there would need to be significant confirmation of some kind.

Now, to be fair, Rees does not claim that it is probably true, but merely that he finds it 'compellingly attractive'; yet he does think it is to be preferred over theism. Rees does offer a more plausible account of how multiple universes could arise than Dawkins or Dennett, but his basic starting point seems little better than their claim that the very possibility of a multiverse is sufficient to make it preferable to theism. At best Rees shows that the possibility of a multiverse should be taken seriously rather than simply dismissed, but that is a long way short of demonstrating that it undermines the evidence for design.

Hawking and Mlodinow base their multiverse proposal on a particular interpretation of quantum theory known as the Feynman 'sum over histories' approach, which is named after the Nobel prize-winning physicist Richard Feynman. In the everyday world, if an object travels from A to B, there is a definite path that it takes to get there. By contrast, in the quantum world, things are not so simple and if a particle travels from A to B, it is generally agreed that a definite path cannot be defined. What happens to the particle? How does it get from A to B? No one really knows, but even so physicists are able to perform calculations to find out the probability that the particle will arrive at B. A very useful technique for performing these calculations is due to Feynman and it involves taking into account all the paths from A to B. Most people just think of this as a mathematical technique, but Hawking and Mlodinow think that the particle really takes all the different paths simultaneously. They then apply this to the beginning of the universe as follows:

> In this view, the universe appeared spontaneously, starting off in every possible way. Most of these correspond to different universes. . . . Some people make a great

mystery of this idea, sometimes called the multiverse concept, but these are just different expressions of the Feynman sum over histories.[45]

This leads them to the following astonishing claim: 'histories in which the moon is made of cheese do not contribute to the present state of the universe, though they might contribute to others. That might sound like science fiction, but it isn't.'[46] Is this really where modern science takes us? That's where it takes Hawking and Mlodinow, but fortunately it doesn't follow from science. There are plenty of other interpretations of quantum theory that don't require thinking that a particle really travels along all or possible paths or that the universe starts off in every possible way or that there might be a moon made of cheese in another universe. So why do Hawking and Mlodinow adopt this view? They don't say. The reasons presented in support of their multiverse proposal are not at all persuasive.

Arguably the most plausible multiverse proposals are those based on inflationary theory. According to some versions of inflation, our universe is only one of many 'bubble' universes that arise from separate big bangs.[47] However, if these separate universes are to differ from each other there must be some way for them to acquire different constants in their laws of physics. Here M-theory can come into play.[48] As we saw earlier, it seems that M-theory does not uniquely predict the constants of physics, but in this context that is an advantage because the different values for the constants might be realized in different universes. In a small proportion of these universes the constants will be appropriate for life and, not surprisingly, we find ourselves in such a universe.

What are we to make of this scenario? First of all, like other multiverse proposals it is extremely speculative. While inflation theory is widely accepted as part of big bang cosmology, the idea that inflation can give rise to separate universes with different laws of physics is much more controversial. And M-theory is currently taken seriously because it is the best candidate for a Theory of Everything, but at present there is no experimental evidence for it. As noted earlier, just because a multiverse scenario is speculative it does not mean that it is unscientific; but if there is no good reason to believe it to be true, it would have little impact on design. Secondly, even if some evidence were forthcoming that indirectly supported this approach, it is very doubtful whether it would seriously undermine the claim that fine-tuning provides evidence for design. In order to achieve that, we would need strong evidence to convince us that the multiverse scenario was true, and not merely some evidence in its favour. At best, we might conclude that there is evidence for both, but not be sure which to opt for. Thirdly, it is not at all obvious that such a scenario would enable us to avoid design anyway, so even if we knew it to be true there would be no reason to opt for it *rather* than design. One reason for this is identified by George Ellis, who thinks that a multiverse would not provide a final explanation, but

> just pushes the ultimate question back one stage further. For if one assumes the existence of a multiverse, the deeper issue then becomes: Why this multiverse rather than another one? Why an ensemble [of universes] that allows life rather than one that does not? The only multiverse proposal that necessarily admits life is Tegmark's extreme version of 'all that can happen does happen'. But why then should this be the one that exists, with its extraordinary profligacy of infinities? The crucial existential questions recur and the multiverse proposal *per se* cannot answer.[49]

More specifically, inflation itself seems to require fine-tuning,[50] and Robin Collins argues that the inflationary multiverse scenario requires a number of components to be in place, without any one of which it would still 'almost certainly fail to produce a single life-sustaining universe'.[51] These components are a mechanism to supply the energy needed for the bubble universes (the inflaton field), a mechanism to form the bubble universes, a mechanism to convert the energy of the inflaton field to normal mass/energy, and a mechanism that allows enough variation among the universes.[52] In addition, appropriate background laws, such as gravity, and physical principles, such as the Pauli exclusion principle, would need to be in place to support life. Thus, even if indirect evidence became available to support the existence of other universes it would not obviate the need for design.

In summary, there is well-established evidence that a wide range of features of our universe are fine-tuned to support life. In particular, various physical constants have the right values to an astonishingly high degree of accuracy. Does this evidence support theism over atheism? This evidence is extremely suggestive of design; indeed, so unlikely does the evidence seem in the absence of design that it makes the case for design compelling. Various attempts to account for this evidence in straightforward ways compatible with atheism are generally agreed to have failed. The only feasible rival to design is some sort of multiverse scenario, but this faces serious difficulties. First, all such scenarios are extremely speculative and so fail to undermine design. Secondly, it is doubtful whether we could ever have convincing evidence for the existence of other universes. And thirdly, far from removing the need for design, multiverse scenarios require it if they are to account for life-permitting universes.

Just as with the previous pieces of evidence, the fine-tuning does not logically entail the existence of God,[53] but the evidence weighs heavily in favour of theism and against atheism. The New Atheists often claim that there is no evidence for God's existence, but this leaves one wondering whether they have really understood the fine-tuning evidence at all. If one wants scientific evidence for God's existence, it is difficult to conceive what could be stronger evidence than fine-tuning.

The conscious mind

When you think about it, the existence of thinking beings is a very odd feature of the universe. We have no evidence of life anywhere else in the universe and yet here on Earth there is not only life but intelligent beings capable of thought, capable of contemplating the nature of the universe itself. There are many things in the universe such as stars, planets, mountains, oceans, trees and many other forms of life that seem to be capable of being understood purely in terms of their physical properties, but minds appear to be very different. As we shall see, there are serious objections to *physicalism* (or materialism), which holds, roughly speaking, that everything is ultimately physical. According to this view, everything that exists has the properties it does because of the properties of its physical constituents (atoms, molecules, etc.). Atheism, however, is usually wedded to physicalism and so this constitutes a problem for atheism. The general idea in this section is that the existence of minds and associated mental phenomena, such as thinking, holding beliefs, having desires and experiencing pain, would be much more probable if God exists than if atheism were true. As such, this provides additional evidence for the existence of God.

One problem for physicalism is the existence of conscious experience. When tasting food or feeling pain, for example, we have an experience that is characterized by its subjective, qualitative nature. This is sometimes put by saying that there is something it is like to be in pain, a *felt* quality that cannot be captured in the language of physics or mathematics. Scientists know a lot about the structure and properties of atoms and molecules and also of much more complex physical entities such as the human brain, but nowhere in this knowledge is there anything even remotely like the sort of experience you have when you taste a lemon, for example. The problem for physicalism is to explain experiences of this sort, which are intrinsically subjective and qualitative, in terms of physical phenomena, which are intrinsically objective and quantitative. The prospects don't look good.

Another problem for physicalism concerns the very different ways in which we can acquire knowledge about physical and mental phenomena. If you are hungry, you know this directly by experience, whereas I can only know that you are hungry if you tell me or if I can infer it from your behaviour. Your experience is *private* to you and you have *privileged access* to it. Contrast this with how we acquire knowledge about a physical object such as a piece of metal. Anyone with the right equipment and knowledge can measure its dimensions, weigh it, determine its melting point, find out how it reacts with certain acids, and so on. This knowledge is acquired by performing certain operations rather than being acquired directly and so there is no privileged access to these properties of the metal that are public, equally accessible in principle to everyone. Notice also that if I acquire knowledge that you are hungry, I still do not have *your* experience of being hungry. This highlights the subjective nature of conscious experience. In general, our knowledge of physical phenomena is knowledge acquired from an objective, third-person point of view, whereas we have knowledge of our own mental states from a subjective, first-person point of view.

These points highlight fundamental differences between mental phenomena and physical phenomena and suggest that the gap between them is not capable of being bridged by further scientific research. No matter how much knowledge we acquire about the physical properties of the brain, we would still be lacking a subjective, first-person account of conscious experience. The points raised so far against physicalism are illustrated by what is known as the 'knowledge argument'.[54] Suppose that a neuroscientist called Mary knows all of the brain processes involved in vision and that, using various instruments, she is able to monitor all the relevant processes in your brain when you are observing a red flower. She knows all the relevant physical facts, so does this mean that she knows everything relevant to your observation? Let's suppose she is colour-blind and has never had the experience of seeing the colour red. It seems clear that she can have no knowledge of the *experience* of seeing red. We can assume that she is able to *predict* that you will experience seeing red (since we can assume that in previous studies other people have reported seeing red when their brains have been in the same state), but that is a very different matter from *having knowledge* of what the experience is like. She is lacking a piece of knowledge that cannot be acquired by knowing all the facts about the brain; the only way this knowledge can be acquired is by having the experience. The point of this illustration is that there are facts (which can be acquired only by experience) that are not physical facts. If this is correct, physicalism is false.[55]

Although these are not the only challenges facing physicalism, they do seem to be the most pressing.[56] Many physicalists will of course grant that *at the moment* we do not have a full explanation, but will claim that this gives us no reason to think it impossible. Pointing to the enormous progress science has made in understanding the functioning of the brain, some will claim that an understanding of mental phenomena is a realistic possibility. It is certainly true that neuroscience has made a lot of progress in identifying brain processes *associated with* various mental phenomena, the so-called neural correlates of consciousness, but this falls a long way short of *explaining* mental phenomena. The problem for the physicalist is that brain processes can be described in terms of physical processes, but mental phenomena are a very different kind of thing. This is not to suggest that there is no value to such research; clearly, it could be extremely beneficial from a medical point of view. But as we have seen, there must be more to explaining mental phenomena than giving a detailed account of physical processes in the brain since the former have a subjective, qualitative, experiential character that is completely lacking in the latter.

The idea that the problems with physicalism are not merely due to limitations in current science is argued convincingly by the philosopher of mind David Chalmers, who takes a naturalistic approach to the mind but nevertheless rejects physicalism. He argues that there is 'an *explanatory gap* between the physical level and conscious experience'.[57] He claims:

> Physical explanation is well suited to the explanation of *structure* and of *function* . . .
> But the explanation of consciousness is not just a matter of explaining structure
> and function. Once we have explained all the physical structure in the vicinity of the
> brain, and we have explained how all the various brain functions are performed, there
> is a further sort of explanandum: consciousness itself. Why should all this structure
> and function give rise to experience? The story about the physical processes does not
> say.[58]

The reason Chalmers claims that there is an explanatory gap that cannot be filled even in principle is because physical explanations are not the right kind of explanations and the fundamental reason for this is because 'facts about consciousness in our world are further facts about our world, over and above the physical facts'.[59]

The philosopher Thomas Nagel also raises an objection to physicalism in a famous article entitled 'What Is it Like to Be a Bat?'[60] Bats navigate their way around using sonar, but having knowledge of all the physical facts about bats does not tell us what their conscious experiences are like, if they have them at all. Again, the difficulty is that there seem to be facts that are not physical facts and are not entailed by physical facts either. Sometimes physicalists claim that consciousness is a higher order, or emergent, physical property of brains. Just as solidity is not a property of atoms and molecules but is a property of certain arrangements of them (e.g. in a chair), so consciousness is an emergent property of the complex physical structure of the brain.[61] But if Chalmers and Nagel are correct, there is a serious problem with this kind of reasoning. Solidity (and other emergent properties of this kind) is a consequence of the physical properties of the microstructure of the chair in the sense that given all the physical facts about its microstructure it could not fail to be solid. If Chalmers and Nagel are correct, consciousness is not a consequence of the physical properties of the microstructure of the brain in this sense. It is a further fact about the world over and above the physical facts.

What do the New Atheists have to say about all of this? Dennett has a lot to say and is extremely critical of the kinds of arguments presented here.[62] He would claim that these arguments appeal to common-sense intuitions about the mind that have no place in a proper scientific account, but are merely part of an inadequate approach often referred to as *folk psychology*. The problem is, as we have seen, that the subjective, qualitative character of mental phenomena do not seem to fit in with the objective, quantitative character of physical phenomena. The difficulty for Dennett, however, is that by claiming that our common-sense intuitions about these matters have no place in science, he seems to be getting things the wrong way round. In the case of the mind, subjective, qualitative mental phenomena are the data that scientific theories should be trying to explain. This point is made forcibly by the philosopher Dean Zimmerman:

> In effect, Dennett turns traditional empiricism on its head. The old-fashioned
> empiricist says that science brings hypotheses before the tribunal of sensory
> experience for confirmation or falsification. Dennett puts the judges on trial:
> everything we say about our awareness of colours, sounds, smells, etc. is, as likely
> as not, unreliable confabulation. None of it should be accepted until independently
> confirmed by impersonal scientific investigation; and the scientists who would study
> consciousness are solemnly warned not to slip into the habit of trusting even their
> own judgments about what experience is like.[63]

By contrast, if we do trust our own judgments about what experience is like, which it seems to me we should since that constitutes the data, and if we have reason to believe that these judgments do not fit in with a physicalist account of the mind, as I have been arguing, then we have a good reason to reject physicalism.

Astonishingly, my scepticism about physicalism is shared by one of the

New Atheists and by the one who works in neuroscience, Sam Harris. Here is what he has to say:

> Most scientists consider themselves *physicalists*; this means, among other things, that they believe that our mental and spiritual lives are wholly dependent upon the workings of our brains. On this account, when the brain dies, the stream of our being must come to an end. Once the lamps of neural activity have been extinguished, there will be nothing left to survive. Indeed, many scientists purvey this conviction as though it were itself a special sacrament, conferring intellectual integrity upon any man, woman, or child who is man enough to swallow it.
>
> But the truth is that we simply do not know what happens after death. While there is much to be said against a naïve conception of a soul that is independent of the brain, the place of consciousness in the natural world is very much an open question. The idea that brains *produce* consciousness is little more than an article of faith among scientists at present, and there are many reasons to believe that the methods of science will be insufficient to either prove or disprove it.[64]

You might want to read that again. Given that Dawkins and Dennett adopt the views criticized by Harris here, they are presumably in the group who 'purvey this conviction as though it were itself a special sacrament'. And leaving open the option of some kind of existence after death? Atheism is not what it used to be! Harris thinks that the self is an illusion, but consciousness is not. Instead of being conscious individuals, he seems to think that we are all part of a universal consciousness. This illustrates the lengths to which even one of the New Atheists is prepared to go in order to accommodate mental phenomena.

How does all of this relate to belief in God? As noted earlier, atheism is usually wedded to physicalism and since physicalism has such serious short-comings this constitutes a real problem for atheism. Perhaps, however, the atheist could reject physicalism and accept the existence of mental phenom-ena as something fundamental and non-physical. This would be incompatible with the atheism of Dawkins, Dennett and Hitchens, but Harris moves in this direction. Harris suggests that 'Consciousness may be a far more rudimen-tary phenomenon than are living creatures and their brains.'[65] In the light of the arguments against physicalism, it might be thought that this means that consciousness is scientifically inexplicable. Harris would deny this, as would David Chalmers, whose arguments against physicalism were considered earlier. Chalmers too thinks there must be some fundamental non-physical properties of the world as well as fundamental laws that specify how these non-physical properties depend on the physical properties of the world. He acknowledges that we have very little idea about these laws at present, but thinks that it should be possible in principle to discover them.

Philosopher Richard Swinburne begs to differ. He argues that the existence of such laws relating physical and mental properties is highly improbable.[66] He does not deny that there could be a long list of causal connections between the two, just that there could be underlying laws from which these causal connections could be derived. One of his main objections to such laws is due to the fact that physical objects differ from each other in measurable ways, whereas thoughts and other mental phenomena do not. So although there are laws relating measurable quantities such as mass and velocity, it is very unlikely that there could be laws relating measurable quantities and mental phenomena such as thoughts. In fact, arguably much of the success of modern science is due to the fact that it restricts its attention to measurable quantities, while separating off qualitative properties such as colours and tastes from the physical world and assigning them to the mental world. Consider the case of colour. The wavelength of light is a measurable quantity and so can appear in physical laws, but the conscious experience of colour, to which it gives rise, cannot.

If Swinburne is right, mental phenomena are inexplicable scientifically and yet it is very improbable that such phenomena would exist unexplained. This being the case, the existence of mental phenomena is extremely improbable if there is no God. By contrast, according to theism, the mental is more fundamental than the physical since there is a mind, God's mind, that does not depend on any physical structure and is responsible for bringing the physical universe into existence. If theism is true, the existence of mental phenomena within the universe does not seem at all surprising. There would be no requirement on God to bring creatures with minds into existence, but it is not at all implausible that he would. So although there is no scientific explanation, there is a personal explanation in terms of the action of God. Clearly, mental phenomena do exist and so count as evidence in favour of theism.

But let's suppose that Swinburne is wrong. Let's suppose that there are fundamental non-physical features of the world and that it is somehow possible to discover laws relating them to physical phenomena as Chalmers envisages. This would leave the question of why these non-physical features exist, why there are any such laws and why these particular laws hold in our universe resulting in the mental life we all experience. These would be unexplained brute facts about the world if atheism is true; but, as before, it seems very improbable that these things should exist unexplained and so they are very improbable if atheism is true. In this case the argument from consciousness could be seen as an extension of the design argument relating to the order found in the universe as presented earlier in this chapter.

As with the previous pieces of evidence, the existence of mental phenomena does not logically prove the truth of theism, but that is not the goal. The goal is to compare theism with atheism. Given that a physicalist approach to the mind faces formidable objections in principle and given the close connection between atheism and physicalism, this presents a problem for atheism. But there is also a problem for atheists who reject physicalism since such a view requires features of the world that are very improbable in the absence of God. In both cases the evidence clearly points to theism.[67]

Conclusion

In this chapter we have considered three more pieces of evidence for the existence of God: the order of the universe, fine-tuning and the existence of conscious minds. As with the two pieces of evidence considered in the last chapter, it has been argued that each of these features of the universe counts in favour of the existence of God. While no single piece of evidence logically proves the existence of God, arguably several provide extremely strong evidence, even when considered on their own. Overall, however, it is the cumulative weight of all five pieces of evidence that makes a substantial case for the existence of God.

It is also worth noting that several of the pieces of evidence considered in these two chapters are based on the findings of modern science (the beginning of the universe, the order of the universe and fine-tuning). Far from being in conflict with science, theism is supported by it and it is atheism that is in tension with scientific findings. As in the last chapter, certain atheistic responses to the arguments presented in this chapter might actually undermine science. With regard to the fine-tuning, some appeals to multiverse scenarios might well undermine parts of science such as origin-of-life research. If such scenarios can account for fine-tuning, why could they not also account for the origin of life in terms of blind chance? If there are enough universes, then life would develop by chance somewhere and, of course, we should not be surprised to find ourselves in one of the lucky universes. Also, with regard to the mind, some atheists want to deny the significance given to the subjective, qualitative nature of mental phenomena in the scientific study of the mind, but there may be a danger that this fails to do justice to the data that stand in need of explanation. So it seems that at least some atheistic responses to the arguments presented in this chapter are potentially in conflict with science.

Why have only five reasons for believing in God's existence been presented?

Does biological complexity point to God as well? Or morality? Or religious experience? Or the evidence surrounding Jesus of Nazareth? The New Atheists have had much to say about all these topics and so their views will be considered in subsequent chapters. Whatever conclusions are reached, however, it will not negate the argument of these two chapters, that a number of features of the universe provide strong evidence for the existence of God.

Despite all this evidence, however, Dawkins claims to have an argument to show that no such evidence counts in favour of God's existence and that God almost certainly does not exist. We turn to this argument in the next chapter.

Notes

1. John Polkinghorne, *Science and Creation* (London: SPCK, 1988), pp. 20–21.
2. Richard Swinburne, *The Existence of God*, 2nd ed. (Oxford: Oxford University Press, 2004), p. 154.
3. Paul Davies, *The Mind of God* (London: Simon & Schuster, 1992), p. 150.
4. Quoted in ibid., p. 176.
5. John Polkinghorne, *Belief in God in an Age of Science* (New Haven, Conn.: Yale University Press, 1998), p. 4.
6. John Barrow and Frank Tipler, *The Anthropic Cosmological Principle* (Oxford: Oxford University Press, 1986), p. 261.
7. Martin Rees, *Just Six Numbers* (London: Phoenix, 1999), p. 150.
8. Barrow and Tipler also argue that the stability of atoms depends on the existence of three spatial dimensions.
9. The most plausible defence of this position of which I am aware is found in the work of Bas van Fraassen. See, for example, *The Scientific Image* (Oxford: Clarendon, 1980).
10. Swinburne, *Existence of God*, pp. 188–191.
11. In addition to fine-tuning of physical constants, Robin Collins refers to fine-tuning of the laws of physics, the initial conditions of the universe and higher-level features such as properties of chemical elements ('God, Design and Fine-Tuning', in R. Martin and C. Bernard [eds.], *God Matters: Readings in the Philosophy of Religion* [New York: Longman, 2002], pp. 119–135). An example of fine-tuning of the laws of physics is that if any of the fundamental forces of physics did not exist, life would be highly improbable. An example of fine-tuning of initial conditions arises from the rate of expansion of the universe, which in turn depends on the ratio of the actual density of the universe to the critical density. If this ratio had been slightly less than one in the early universe, expansion would have dominated over gravity and no galaxies could have formed. If it had been slightly greater than one,

gravity would have won out over expansion and the universe would have collapsed too quickly. Although the present value of this ratio is not known exactly, it is not too far from one. For this to be the case it must have been exceedingly close to one in the early universe. It has been estimated that at the Planck time this ratio must have been one to an accuracy of about one part in 10^{60}. However, cosmologists generally believe that this example of fine-tuning can be accounted for in terms of inflationary models, according to which the universe underwent an extremely rapid and brief expansion within the first second of the universe. Nevertheless, even if this is correct it may well be the case that inflation itself requires fine-tuning. An example of the last of Collins's types of fine-tuning is the way in which the synthesis of carbon in stars crucially depends on the existence of a resonance at the right energy level.

12. Paul Davies, *Superforce* (New York: Simon & Schuster, 1984), p. 242.

13. Robin Collins estimates the fine-tuning in this case to be 1 in 10^{36}.

14. See Robin Collins, 'The Teleological Argument: An Exploration of the Fine-Tuning of the Cosmos', in William Lane Craig and J. P. Moreland (eds.), *Blackwell Companion to Natural Theology* (Chichester: Wiley-Blackwell, 2009), pp. 202–281; by the same author, 'Evidence for Fine-Tuning', in N. A. Manson (ed.), *God and Design: The Teleological Argument and Modern Science* (London: Routledge, 2003), pp. 178–199; see also Rees, *Just Six Numbers*, pp. 102–114.

15. In his book *The Emperor's New Mind* (Oxford: Oxford University Press, 1989), Oxford mathematician and theoretical physicist Roger Penrose claims that the accuracy would have to have been one part in $10^{10^{(123)}}$, that is, 10 raised to the power of 10^{123}. If this can be identified as the probability of the low entropy state occurring by chance, this would be the strongest example of fine-tuning by a long way. However, there are a number of objections to this identification. For discussion of this point, see Collins, 'Teleological Argument', pp. 220–222. Collins claims that this provides a strong qualitative example of fine-tuning even if it cannot be quantified. In his article 'How to Rigorously Define Fine-Tuning', available at http://home.messiah.edu/~rcollins/Fine–tuning/FT.htm (accessed 10 Nov. 2011), Collins also responds to a more general objection to the definition of relevant probabilities in fine-tuning arguments due to T. McGrew, L. McGrew and E. Vestrup, 'Probabilities and the Fine-Tuning Argument: A Skeptical View', *Mind* 110 (2001), pp. 1027–1037. For another response see J. Koperski, 'Should we Care about Fine-Tuning', *British Journal for the Philosophy of Science* 56 (2005), pp. 303–319.

16. Bernard Carr presents an up-to-date scientific account summarizing key examples in 'The Anthropic Principle Revisited', in B. Carr (ed.), *Universe or Multiverse?* (Cambridge: Cambridge University Press, 2007), pp. 77–89. A detailed discussion of examples of fine-tuning as well as philosophical issues can be found in *Universes* by John Leslie (London: Routledge, 1989) and in *The Anthropic Cosmological Principle*

by John Barrow and Frank Tipler (Oxford: Oxford University Press, 1986), while a very accessible account can be found in *Just Six Numbers* by Martin Rees (London: Phoenix, 1999).

17. Stephen W. Hawking and Leonard Mlodinow, *The Grand Design: New Answers to the Ultimate Questions of Life* (London: Bantam, 2010), p. 161.

18. Collins, 'God, Design and Fine-Tuning', pp. 4–5; page numbers refer to a version of this paper available at http://home.messiah.edu/~rcollins/Fine-tuning/FT.htm (accessed 16 Nov. 2010).

19. Paul Davies, *The Cosmic Blueprint* (New York: Simon & Schuster, 1988), p. 203.

20. *TGD*, p. 114.

21. See Brian Greene, *The Elegant Universe: Superstrings, Hidden Dimensions, and the Quest for the Ultimate Theory* (New York: Vintage, 1999).

22. See Carr, *Universe or Multiverse?*, p. 5.

23. *TGD*, p. 144.

24. Victor J. Stenger, *God: The Failed Hypothesis – How Science Shows that God Does Not Exist* (Amherst, N. Y.: Prometheus, 2008), pp. 151–153; *The New Atheism: Taking a Stand for Science and Reason* (Amherst, N. Y.: Prometheus, 2009), pp. 95–97.

25. For a detailed response to Stenger on these points and other objections he raises against fine-tuning, see Collins, 'Teleological Argument'.

26. This is not to say that science could not disconfirm the fine-tuning argument. For example, it is possible that science could show that we are mistaken about the evidence for fine-tuning and so the various constants are not as finely tuned as current evidence suggests.

27. Ibid., p. 10.

28. In fact, my focus here is on the weak anthropic principle. See Barrow and Tipler, *Anthropic Cosmological Principle*, for details.

29. Elliott Sober, 'The Design Argument', in W. Mann (ed.), *The Blackwell Guide to the Philosophy of Religion* (Oxford: Blackwell, 2004), pp. 117–147.

30. This example is based on Richard Swinburne, 'Arguments from the Fine-Tuning of the Universe', in J. Leslie (ed.), *Physical Cosmology and Philosophy* (New York: MacMillan, 1990), pp. 160–179. See also Leslie, *Universes*, pp. 13–14.

31. There has been a lot of discussion in the literature about these and other examples, often involving a lot of technical details about probability theory. For a more detailed response see Jonathan Weisberg, 'Firing Squads and Fine-Tuning: Sober on the Design Argument', *British Journal for the Philosophy of Science* 56 (2005), pp. 809–821.

32. *TGD*, pp. 144–145.

33. George Ellis, 'Multiverses: Description, Uniqueness, Testing', in Carr, *Universe or Multiverse?*, pp. 387–409.

34. Ibid., p. 407.

35. Don N. Page, 'Predictions and Tests of Multiverse Theories', in Carr, *Universe or Multiverse?*, pp. 411–429. In particular, he discusses the need for multiverse theories to include a well-defined measure for observations.

36. Rees, *Just Six Numbers*, p. 168.

37. Page, 'Predictions and Tests', p. 413.

38. This suggests, however, that I am claiming that design is to be preferred over a multiverse hypothesis unless the latter can be shown to be likely to be true. But someone might deny this and claim that there is no reason to prefer design in this way. If we treat them on an equal footing instead, then the evidence of fine-tuning provides some evidence for *both* design and a multiverse since both are much better explanations than alternatives such as blind chance. Notice, however, that in this case fine-tuning *does* provide evidence for design, which is what I'm trying to argue. To deny this, it would need to be shown not merely that a multiverse hypothesis is possible, but that there are good reasons to believe it to be true.

39. *TGD*, pp. 145–146; Daniel C. Dennett, *Darwin's Dangerous Idea* (London: Penguin, 1996), pp. 177–180.

40. Arguably, they might also think that such scenarios must be experimentally testable in order to be preferable to theism, but this is not entirely clear. Dawkins does not appeal directly to such an idea and while Dennett thinks that Smolin's hypothesis might make testable predictions, concerning the oscillating universe scenario he says, 'It is hard to believe that this idea is empirically testable in any meaningful way, but we should reserve judgment' (*Darwin's Dangerous Idea*, p. 179).

41. *TGD*, pp. 146–147.

42. See Max Tegmark, 'The Multiverse Hierarchy', in Carr, *Universe or Multiverse?*, pp. 99–125.

43. From a naturalist's point of view, a resurrection could occur if the brain, heart, and so on, started to function again and arguably this, although ludicrously improbable from a purely natural point of view, is not strictly impossible since all the atoms and molecules could spontaneously come into the right configurations. So, if everything that can possibly happen will happen somewhere in the multiverse, a resurrection will occur somewhere.

44. Rees, *Just Six Numbers*, pp. 164–179. See also his 'Cosmology and the Multiverse', in Carr, *Universe or Multiverse?*, pp. 57–75.

45. Hawking and Mlodinow, *Grand Design*, p. 136.

46. Ibid., p. 140. They also draw on M-theory, but M-theory does not generate the different universes; it defines what universes are possible.

47. See Alan Guth, *The Inflationary Universe: The Quest for a New Theory of Cosmic Origins* (Cambridge, Mass.: Perseus, 1997).

48. See Andrei Linde, 'The Inflationary Multiverse', in Carr, *Universe or Multiverse?*, pp. 127–149.

49. Ellis, 'Multiverses', p. 406.

50. See, for example, Carr, 'Anthropic Principle Revisited', pp. 80–81.

51. Robin Collins, 'The Multiverse Hypothesis: A Theistic Perspective', in Carr, *Universe or Multiverse?*, pp. 459–480.

52. Having a large number of universes all with the same constants of physics would not account for the fine-tuning evidence. This is where M-theory might fit the bill.

53. After all, an atheist could appeal to sheer luck to account for it. Nevertheless, this is a hopeless strategy and I am unaware of any atheist who adopts it.

54. Due to Frank Jackson, 'Epiphenomenal Qualia', *Philosophical Quarterly* 32 (1982), pp. 127–136. The version presented here is slightly different.

55. For further discussion of the knowledge argument and for a defence of it against various objections that have been raised, see David J. Chalmers, *The Conscious Mind* (Oxford: Oxford University Press, 1996), pp. 140–146.

56. A further difference between the mental and the physical is that thoughts can be *about* things, about sport or food or the universe, for example. But if our thoughts are ultimately to be understood in physical terms, how could a complex arrangement of atoms and molecules be (or possess properties that are) *about* anything? This is known as 'intentionality' and it represents a further challenge for physicalism, but will not be pursued further here. Another argument is based on a thought experiment involving zombies, who look and behave just like humans but lack conscious experience. Chalmers argues that there is nothing in the physical laws governing our universe that necessitates the existence of conscious experience and so facts about consciousness are not physical facts. For details, see Chalmers, *Conscious Mind*, pp. 94–99.

57. Ibid., p. 107, emphasis in original.

58. Ibid., emphasis in original.

59. Ibid, p. 123.

60. Thomas Nagel, 'What Is it Like to Be a Bat?', *Philosophical Review* 83 (1974), pp. 435–450.

61. See, for example, John Searle, *The Rediscovery of the Mind* (Cambridge, Mass.: MIT Press, 1992).

62. See especially Daniel C. Dennett, *Consciousness Explained* (Boston: Little Brown, 1991).

63. Dean Zimmerman, 'Dispatches from the Zombie Wars', *Times Literary Supplement*, 28 Apr. 2006, p. 9. A similar point is made by the philosopher of mind John Searle in a very interesting exchange with Dennett that took place in the *New York Review of Books*; see John Searle, *The Mystery of Consciousness* (London: Granta, 1998), p. 120. This book also contains another interesting and heated exchange between Searle and David Chalmers.

64. *TEF*, p. 208, emphasis in the original.

65. Ibid., p. 209.

66. Swinburne, *Existence of God*, pp. 192–218.

67. As with all the other arguments for the existence of God, much more could be said both for and against. For a detailed atheistic perspective see Graham Oppy, *Arguing About Gods* (Cambridge: Cambridge University Press, 2006), pp. 382–400; for a detailed theistic perspective see Swinburne, *Existence of God*, pp. 192–218; and for an in-depth debate between a theist and atheist see Alvin Plantinga and Michael Tooley, *Knowledge of God* (Oxford: Blackwell, 2008).

6. DAWKINS'S DILEMMA

The New Atheists are convinced not merely that God does not exist but that atheism is vindicated by science. As we saw in chapter 3, they believe that science explains away the need for God. Darwinism is particularly important because it is supposed to have explained away the need for design.[1] According to Dawkins, as far as arguments for God's existence are concerned, only the design argument merits serious consideration. He writes:

> The argument from design is the only one still in regular use today, and it still sounds to many like the ultimate knockdown argument. The young Darwin was impressed by it when, as a Cambridge undergraduate, he read it in William Paley's *Natural Theology*. Unfortunately for Paley, the mature Darwin blew it out of the water. There has probably never been a more devastating rout of popular belief by clever reasoning than Charles Darwin's destruction of the argument from design.[2]

Similarly, Dennett thinks that apart from the design argument the other arguments are 'intellectual conjuring tricks or puzzles rather than serious scientific proposals'.[3] And once again it is Darwin who is supposed to have finished off the design argument, as Dennett makes clear in his earlier book, appropriately entitled *Darwin's Dangerous Idea*.[4]

There is an obvious problem, however, with depending too much on

Darwin as a response to design arguments: even if Darwinism defeats design in the case of biology it leaves untouched design arguments based on the order in the universe or the fine-tuning of the physical constants considered in the last chapter. It appears that the Darwinian response to the design argument is incomplete and needs to be supplemented. But the Darwinian response to design is not the only one offered by atheists. An alternative approach is to follow in the path of the Scottish philosopher David Hume who attempted to identify fundamental flaws in design arguments. If this philosophical approach works, it is much more robust since it does not require the atheist to produce an alternative explanation to design and so it is not restricted to the biological case.

Given the advantages of such a philosophical response to design arguments, it is perhaps not surprising that Dawkins and the other New Atheists supplement their scientific Darwinian response with a philosophical Humean response. In particular, Dawkins has put forward what he calls the ultimate Boeing 747 gambit, which, it is claimed, turns the tables on design by showing that the kinds of assumptions underlying design arguments actually lead to the conclusion that 'there almost certainly is no God'. Before trying to determine whether Darwinism really does explain away the need for design and whether Dawkins's extremely ambitious gambit works, we need to consider the Humean and Darwinian responses to design in more detail.

Hume versus Darwin

As we have seen, Darwinism is particularly important for the New Atheists because it is claimed to have removed the need for design as an explanation of complex life. Their point is not just that Darwinism *explains*, but that it *explains away*, evidence that otherwise might have provided support for design. At times Dawkins gives the impression that there is some initial plausibility to the idea that complex life points to a designer. The reason for this is that the extraordinary complexity of living organisms demands a special kind of explanation. If there were no scientific explanation, he seems prepared to acknowledge that belief in a designer would make sense, and indeed that it did before Darwin. Dawkins asks:

> Who, before Darwin, could have guessed that something so apparently *designed* as a dragonfly's wing or an eagle's eye was really the end product of a long sequence of non-random but purely natural causes?[5]

As we saw earlier, Dawkins refers to the young Darwin as having been impressed by the case for design put forward by William Paley, but then goes on to claim that the mature Darwin 'blew it out of the water'. Hitchens expresses a similar view:

> Before Charles Darwin revolutionized our entire concept of origins, and Albert Einstein did the same for the beginnings of our cosmos, many scientists and philosophers and mathematicians took what might be called the default position and professed one or another version of 'deism,' which held that the order and predictability of the universe seemed indeed to imply a designer . . .[6]

The general point seems clear: complex life would provide evidence for design if we didn't have a scientific explanation, but since Darwin we do have such an explanation and so there is no longer any need for design. This is what I shall call Dawkins's *Darwinian Response* to design.

Writing before Darwin, the philosopher David Hume presented a number of objections to the design argument in his *Dialogues Concerning Natural Religion*.[7] Of particular relevance here is his objection that if an explanation is required to account for the order in the universe, an explanation would also be required to account for the order in the mind of the designer.[8] Or to put it in other words, 'Who designed the designer?' If we suppose that the existence of complex living organisms provides evidence for the existence of a designer, then Hume's argument amounts to saying that such a designer would be as complex as the organisms he is supposed to explain and so would be just as much in need of explanation. And if someone responds that the designer does not need to be explained, Hume would ask why we cannot say the same thing about the living organisms in the first place.

The point at this stage is not to evaluate Hume's objections to design, but to contrast them with the Darwinian response. Hume's objections are not based on the findings of modern science but on more general considerations, which purport to show that the design argument is flawed. If Hume's objections are valid, it is unnecessary to have a scientific explanation of order in the universe to reject design and so there was no need to infer design even before Darwin. By contrast, the Darwinian response to design is dissatisfied with the philosophical arguments of Hume, but is only confident in rejecting design when a scientific explanation of the order in question is in place. The philosopher of science Elliott Sober contrasts the two approaches as follows:

> Philosophers who now criticize the organismic design argument often believe that the argument was dealt its death blow by Hume. . . . the design argument after Hume was

merely a corpse that could be propped up and paraded. Hume had taken the life out if it.

Biologists often take a different view. For them, Hume's skeptical attack was not the decisive moment; rather it was Darwin's development and confirmation of a substantive scientific explanation of the adaptive features of organisms that really undermined the design argument (at least in its organismic formulation). Philosophers who believe that a theory can't be rejected until a better theory is developed to take its place often sympathize with this point of view.[9]

Sober himself rejects many of Hume's criticisms of design, but nevertheless his rejection of design does not depend on 'seeing the merits of Darwinian theory'.[10]

For present purposes, I shall consider *Humean responses* to the design argument to be those that, like Sober's, do not depend on 'seeing the merits of Darwinian theory' and contrast them with the *Darwinian response*, which does depend on Darwinism and considers Humean responses to be inadequate. It is clear that the two types of responses are incompatible since the Darwinian response claims that Darwinism is *necessary* for rejecting design while Humean responses claim that it is not. Another way of putting this is to say that the Darwinian response *requires an alternative explanation* (i.e. Darwinism) to explain away the need for design, whereas Humean responses attempt to show that design does not really provide an explanation and so design fails irrespective of whether an alternative explanation is available or not. Of course, there would be no incompatibility involved in adopting Humean responses and also claiming that Darwinism provides an independent reason for rejecting design, but someone who takes this view is not adopting the *Darwinian response* since he does not think Darwinism is *necessary* for rejecting design. As we shall see, although Dawkins espouses the Darwinian response, in reality he seems to reject it in favour of Humean responses. In fact, his main argument against design closely follows Hume's argument concerning the need for an explanation of the mind of the designer.

Dawkins's arguments against design

In a chapter entitled 'Why There Almost Certainly Is No God' Dawkins presents a response to the design argument that is supposed to show that the existence of God is extremely improbable. He refers to his argument as the 'Ultimate Boeing 747 gambit'. The name comes from the claim, attributed to cosmologist Fred Hoyle, that the probability of life emerging on Earth is no greater than the probability that a Boeing 747 would be assembled by a hurricane sweeping through a scrapyard. The core idea is, 'However statistically improbable the entity you seek to explain by invoking a designer, the designer himself has got to be at least as improbable. God is the Ultimate Boeing 747.'[11] To put it another way, he says:

> the designer hypothesis immediately raises the larger problem of who designed the designer. The whole problem we started out with was the problem of explaining statistical improbability. It is obviously no solution to postulate something even more improbable.[12]

Elsewhere he writes, 'A designer God cannot be used to explain organized complexity because any God capable of designing anything would have to be complex enough to demand the same kind of explanation in his own right.'[13] Throughout the chapter where Dawkins presents his argument, he draws attention to the importance of Darwinism in undermining the design argument, but it is not immediately obvious why Darwinism is relevant. In fact, Dawkins really seems to be offering distinct arguments, which can be expressed as follows.[14]

Argument 1: the ultimate Boeing 747 gambit. This argument can be divided into two parts. The first is the 'Who designed the designer?' argument. It starts with the idea that it is extremely improbable that organized complexity would exist unexplained and so we should look for an explanation of organized complexity in nature. But if God exists he must have organized complexity, the very same property we wanted to explain in the first place, and indeed he would be even more complex. Therefore, God's organized complexity would be even more in need of explanation than that found in nature. (Or equivalently, according to Dawkins, God is not a good ultimate explanation of organized complexity in nature.)

The second part of the argument is the 'Improbability of God' argument. The idea here is that if God exists, there would be no explanation of his organized complexity. Since it is extremely improbable that organized complexity would exist unexplained, it is therefore extremely improbable that God exists.

Argument 2: the Darwinian argument. Dawkins claims that the design argument depends on the claim that 'nothing that we know looks designed unless it is designed'.[15] He argues that Darwinism shows that this is false by explaining apparent design in the living world. Consequently, the design argument is flawed and hence provides no basis for belief in God.

From Dawkins's writing it seems clear that he would defend both arguments. Argument 1 summarizes his argument in chapter 4 of *The God Delusion*. Argument 2 is the response he gives to the design argument in chapter 3 of the same book.[16] Note the all-encompassing nature of argument 1 since it purports to show that no matter what degree of organized complexity is found in the universe, it would still be inappropriate to appeal to God as an explanation. This reveals the Humean nature of this argument since it is not dependent on particular scientific claims or theories such as Darwinism. In fact, it is very similar to Hume's argument and so in no way depends on the findings of modern science. Dennett confirms that Dawkins is really just using Hume's argument, describing it as 'an unrebuttable refutation, as devastating today as it was when Philo used it to trounce Cleanthes in Hume's *Dialogues* two centuries earlier'.[17] Hitchens and Harris also endorse arguments along the lines of argument 1. Hitchens claims that 'the postulate of a designer or creator only raises the unanswerable question of who designed the designer or who created the creator'.[18] Similarly, Harris writes, 'If God created the universe, what created God? To say that God, by definition, is uncreated simply begs the question. Any being capable of creating a complex world promises to be very complex himself.'[19]

In contrast to the 747 gambit, the Darwinian argument essentially claims that Darwinism provides an alternative explanation of design. It is also a more modest argument than the 747 gambit in that it does not purport to show that God probably does not exist, but just that the evidence cited in design arguments does not provide a good reason for believing in his existence.

Given these differences between the Humean argument (the 747 gambit) on the one hand and the Darwinian argument on the other, it is worth noting that in a sense the former renders the latter unnecessary. The Darwinian argument would be necessary only for someone who rejected the 747 gambit. Dawkins seems to think that the 747 gambit is sufficient to establish the conclusion that God cannot be an explanation of organized complexity and that God's existence is extremely improbable, but these conclusions in no way depend on Darwinism. If the 747 gambit is valid, these conclusions follow solely from certain claims about complexity and the kind of being God would be; Darwinism is simply irrelevant from a logical point of view.

Now, of course, Dawkins is quite entitled to put forward both arguments. From the fact that the Humean argument makes the Darwinian argument unnecessary it does not follow that it is unsound or that it cannot be proposed as an additional argument. Dawkins could take the attitude that his opponents might be persuaded by the Darwinian argument if they are not persuaded by the Humean argument (or vice versa). This parallels the approach adopted by some theists of proposing both logical proofs and scientific arguments for the existence of God. What Dawkins is not entitled to do is to defend the Humean argument while also maintaining that Darwinism is *necessary* for rejecting design and so imply that the Humean argument is inadequate on its own. This gives rise to a dilemma for Dawkins: should he adopt Humean arguments like the 747 gambit, and so maintain that Darwinism is unnecessary for rejecting design; or should he reject Humean arguments, claiming that Darwinism is necessary, and so place all his emphasis on the Darwinian argument instead?

The problem with adopting the latter strategy is that the Darwinian argument is rather weak as a response to design, as we shall see later. If it works at all, it still seems to require support from Humean arguments such as the 747 gambit. But there is also a problem for Dawkins in adopting the former strategy of opting for a Humean response to design that does not depend on Darwinism or the findings of modern science. The problem is that there are a number of prominent themes in his writings which strongly suggest that a Humean response is inadequate and that Darwinism is indeed necessary for rejecting design. We shall briefly consider four such themes. First, he has made many explicit comments about Darwinism defeating design and these would make no sense if he really thought that a Humean response was adequate to rule out design and that Darwinism was unnecessary. For example, as quoted at the start of the chapter, he refers to 'Charles Darwin's destruction of the argument from design'. In other words, it was Darwin, rather than Hume, who defeated design.[20]

Secondly, Dawkins believes there is insufficient evidence to support belief in God's existence.[21] There is a potential problem for Dawkins here, however, because of his views on whether God could provide a good explanation of *anything*. Although argument 1, even if sound, would only establish the conclusion that God would not be a good ultimate explanation of *organized complexity*, at times Dawkins appears to want to rule out God as an explanation of anything. In an earlier article he states, 'The hypothesis of God offers no worthwhile explanation for anything, for it simply postulates what we are trying to explain. It postulates the difficult to explain, and leaves it at that.'[22] If Dawkins does not wish to rule out the possibility of God as an explanation, as this comment suggests, then there must be circumstances in which he thinks God would provide an explanation, but I am not aware of his having provided an account of the kind of circumstances in which this would be the case. The problem is that if God cannot be an explanation of anything, then *nothing* could count as evidence for God, even in principle. And if this is Dawkins's view, it sheds a very different light on his claim about there not being enough evidence. It is natural to assume that he intends this to be an empirical claim, that there could be evidence for God, but that as a matter of fact there is not. His claim is rather hollow if he believes that no *conceivable* evidence could count in favour of God's existence because God is always more complex than the evidence he is supposed to explain. Similarly, there seems little point in trying to meet his demand for evidence for God if he is going to respond by saying that God cannot be an explanation no matter what evidence is offered.

Thirdly, Dawkins considers the existence of God to be a scientific hypothesis since a universe created by God would be very different from one that was not created by God. But, as with the previous point, if the 747 gambit is sound and if Dawkins believes that no evidence could count in favour of God's existence, this would undermine the idea that his existence is a scientific hypothesis.

Fourthly, and related to the previous points, is Dawkins's claim that science provides justification for atheism. He holds that scientific progress makes belief in God unnecessary as an explanation; with the progress of science there is simply less and less for God to explain. Once again, this does not make much sense if Dawkins believes that God *cannot* be an explanation even in principle. The idea seems to be that although God does, or did, provide an explanation, science now provides *better* explanations. This is a very Darwinian response.

These four reasons do not sit easily with a Humean response to design because they suggest that Darwinism and modern science are necessary for rejecting design. They seem to indicate that we can be confident in rejecting design and the existence of God because science has given us better explanations and so makes God unnecessary. Consequently, it would make more sense for Dawkins to throw all his weight behind the Darwinian response to design rather than the Humean response, yet he does not do so. As we have already seen, the 747 gambit is Humean, and therefore philosophical, in nature. It does not depend on Darwinism or modern science more generally. As we shall see below, when he does appeal to Darwinism he ends up falling back on a Humean approach. For consistency he should adopt the Darwinian response, but in practice he relies on a Humean response; in responding to design, he wishes to have his scientific Darwinian cake, but can't resist eating it with philosophical Humean arguments.

Of course, it is not that there is anything wrong with using philosophical arguments, but it is important to realize that this is what Dawkins is doing. Since his case is based on philosophical arguments, he cannot claim that science defeats theism nor can he object to theists using philosophical arguments. This still leaves the question of whether the Darwinian or Humean responses to design are any good. Before trying to answer this question we need to take a detour into the topic of explanation.

Explaining or explaining away?

As we have seen, Darwinism is particularly important for the New Atheists because it is claimed to have removed the need for design as an explanation of complex life. Their point is not just that Darwinism *explains* the existence of complex life, but that it *explains away* complex life as evidence for design. They also claim that it is not just Darwinism but science as a whole that explains away the need for God as we saw in chapter 3. The idea is that although it might have been plausible to believe in God in the past, this is no longer the case. Now it is one thing to say that science explains, but quite another to say that it explains away the need for God. Why not accept both God and science? More specifically, why in embracing evolution do the New Atheists shun design? Why not embrace design *and* evolution? After all, there is no incompatibility between them in the sense that God could, if he wished, have used evolution.

In chapter 3 we considered a scenario where scientific and personal explanations complement each other and where it would be a category mistake to think that one explanation made the other unnecessary. In many cases this complementary approach is the right one to adopt when considering scientific and theistic explanations and so there is no problem with accepting God and science. Can this approach be adopted in the context of evolution? Theistic evolutionists can appeal to the idea that God created a world where evolution is possible. This is reasonable, but it seems to amount to saying that complex life does not provide any evidence for design over and above the evidence from the order in the laws of nature, fine-tuning, and so on. It seems to grant that evolution explains away evidence for design in biology, but not in astronomy. Interestingly, many creationists as well as theistic evolutionists and atheists seem to agree that this kind of conflict exists between evolution and design in biology.[23] Here I want to question that consensus.

Why should there be any conflict between evolution and design in biology? The obvious reply is that there is no need to accept two explanations when one will do. This, of course, applies to all sorts of cases, not just design and evolution. When I learn that the battery in my car is flat, there is no longer any reason to think that the fact that it won't start is due to an engine problem. One way of putting this is to say that although the flat battery explains the fact of the car not starting, it also *explains away* this fact as evidence for an engine problem. But when is one explanation good enough to explain away evidence for another explanation? Is it ever appropriate to accept two explanations? Let's consider the following example.

On arriving home, I discover that the study in my house is very untidy: books are lying on the floor instead of on the shelves, papers are spread all over the room, drawers have been pulled out of the desk, the lamp has been knocked over, and so on. There are two possible explanations of this evidence that spring to mind: the first is that there has been a burglary; the second is that my children have been playing in the study. The evidence is just what I would expect if either explanation actually occurred and I am confident that there is no other explanation that is even remotely plausible. In such a scenario the evidence supports *both* explanations to some extent.[24] Of course, this does not mean they are both equally likely to be true. Even though my children don't play in the study often, this explanation is more likely than a burglary. This is not because it accounts for the evidence any better than the burglary, but just because it is more likely to begin with.

Furthermore, it is possible that both explanations are true. If there had been a burglary when my wife and children were out, it is possible that my children would have wandered into the study later and played in the mess the burglar had left. Likewise, my children could have made the mess and the burglar could have entered later when my wife and children were out. (We'll not consider the realistic possibility that the study might have been tidier *after* a burglary in this case!) But suppose now that I learn that my children had in fact been playing in the study. This is sufficient to explain away the untidiness as evidence for the burglary explanation; the explanation in terms of a burglary is no longer needed.

Let's modify this example a little bit. Let's suppose the evidence of the untidy study is unlikely to have come about as a result of my children playing in the study mainly because it is unlikely (although not impossible) that they would have been able to pull the drawers out of the desk. So the evidence is more or less as I would expect if a burglary had taken place, unlikely if my children had been playing in the study and extremely unlikely otherwise. As before, the evidence provides some support for each of the possible explanations, burglary and children playing, but in this case the evidence counts much more strongly in favour of the burglary explanation. However, suppose that just as in the previous version I learn that my children had in fact been playing in the study. Does this explain away the untidiness as evidence for a burglary as before? Only partially. It no longer explains away the need for the burglary explanation as well as it did in the first scenario because the evidence (i.e. of drawers being pulled out of the desk) is quite unlikely to have come about by my children playing in the study.

Let's add one further twist. Suppose there's a very basic lock on the door of the study. It would almost certainly prevent my children from getting in, but not a burglar. However, if a burglar had gained access, he presumably wouldn't have locked the door after him, so then my children could walk in unhindered. Otherwise, let's suppose everything is as described in the last paragraph. As before, the evidence provides some support for each of the explanations, but what happens now when I discover that my children had in fact been playing in the study? It actually makes it *more likely* in this case that there had been a burglary. In this case, learning that one explanation is true (children playing in the study) not only fails to explain away the untidiness as evidence for the other explanation (a burglary), but it actually makes it more likely. The reason for this is that the presence of a burglar makes it much more likely that the door would have been unlocked and so that the children would have ended up playing in the study later in the day.[25]

Admittedly, the example is rather contrived, but let's be clear about the point being made. The intention of these examples is to illustrate that just because one explanation of a piece of evidence is known to be true (children playing in the study in the above scenarios), we cannot automatically assume that another explanation (burglary) is unnecessary. Let's call the burglary explanation the *initial explanation* and the children playing the *alternative explanation*. We cannot automatically assume that the alternative explanation explains away the evidence for the initial explanation. In some cases it does and so makes the initial explanation unnecessary (as in the first scenario above), in some cases it does not make it unnecessary even though it makes it slightly less likely (as in the second scenario) and in some cases it makes the initial explanation even more likely (as in the third scenario). Which of these cases applies depends on two issues: first, whether the evidence is likely to have occurred given the truth of the alternative explanation; secondly, whether the alternative explanation makes the initial explanation more likely to be true. Let's see how this all applies to the New Atheists' claim that Darwinism explains away the need for design.

Does Darwinism explain away evidence for design in biology?

The central point of Dawkins's Darwinian argument against design is that Darwinism explains the existence of apparent design in the living world. In doing so it falsifies a key premise of the design argument, that apparent design (by which Dawkins means organized complexity) requires actual design. This renders God unnecessary as an explanation of organized complexity and so the design argument fails. In other words, Darwinism *explains away* the need for design. How might the proponent of design address this response?

Two strategies will be considered here. One is to argue that even if Darwinism defeats design in biology, it does not defeat it in other contexts. This will be the main approach and will be considered in the next section. First, however, we shall consider whether Darwinism even explains away the need for design in biology. Similar to the example in the last section on explaining away, the idea is that there are two possible explanations for organized complexity: design and Darwinism. Now suppose, for the sake of the argument, that we do not know initially whether design or Darwinism (or neither or both) is true, just as we did not know initially whether the untidy study was due to children playing or a burglary (or neither or both). Would organized complexity provide support for both hypotheses as in the previous case? The answer seems to be 'yes'. If either design or Darwinism were true, that would give us some reason to expect organized complexity. In other words, they both seem to provide explanations of organized complexity and so both are supported to some extent by its existence. But now suppose other evidence comes to light that provides further support for Darwinism. For simplicity, we shall assume not just that there is evidence for Darwinism, but that it is known to be true. (This is analogous to finding out that the children were in the study.) What are the implications for design?

From the last section we know that there are three possibilities and so we must ask, does Darwinism *explain away* the evidence for design (making it *unnecessary*), or does it *partially explain away* the evidence for design (in which case organized complexity provides some evidence for design but not as much as it did before the evidence for Darwinism was accumulated), or does it make design *more likely*? Dawkins assumes that the first answer is correct, but it is not at all obvious that he is right about this.

Before going any further, it is worth pausing to anticipate a possible objection. The opponent of design might claim that even if we did not know whether Darwinism was true, organized complexity would provide no support for design. This objection is likely to be based on the claim that design is not an explanation at all. In response it must be noted that this is a Humean objection to design, not a Darwinian objection. The idea in this section is to see whether the Darwinian response *on its own*, without the assistance of Humean arguments, can defeat design. The Darwinian response is that although design had some plausibility before Darwin, it has now been explained away.

In order to find out which of the three possible answers is correct, we must ask how likely it is that organized complexity would exist if Darwinism is true and there is no design. To put it another way, given the laws of physics and the initial state of the early universe, does Darwinism make it likely that organized complexity would come into existence without design? First of all, we need to consider the origin of life. Although Darwinism does not account for the origin of life, we could broaden out the discussion to ask how likely it is that natural processes in general, without design, would give rise to life? Even though various theories have been proposed, at present there is no scientific consensus as to how life developed.[26] But the organized complexity found in even the most basic living organisms does suggest that the probability of life arising from purely natural processes is very low. This does not mean it is impossible, but interestingly Dawkins seems to concur that it is improbable since he refers to the 'initial stroke of luck' involved in the origin of life.[27]

Once life has got started, this still leaves the question of how likely it is that more complex forms of life, including intelligent life, would develop. There are a number of reasons for thinking that it is not very likely at all. The late Stephen Jay Gould, in books such as *Wonderful Life*,[28] emphasized the way in which evolution is extremely sensitive to contingent events, particularly in terms of extinctions. He claims that if the history of life were to be rerun, it would be very unlikely to give rise to creatures such as human beings. This view has been challenged by others including Simon Conway Morris,[29] who emphasizes the role of convergence in evolution and claims that the evolution of intelligence was almost inevitable. Nevertheless, despite the significance of convergence, it certainly seems plausible that there have been important transitions in the history of life that would be very improbable given our knowledge of the mechanisms of evolution and the complexity involved in the transitions. Indeed, this does not seem to be controversial. In addition to the origin of life, Dawkins acknowledges that certain steps in the development of more complex life are improbable. He says that 'it may be that the origin of life is not the only major gap in the evolutionary story that is bridged by sheer luck, anthropically justified'.[30] He suggests two further hurdles as well:

> Mark Ridley . . . has suggested that the origin of the eucaryotic cell . . . was an even more momentous, difficult and statistically improbable step than the origin of life. The origin of consciousness might be another major gap whose bridging was of the same order of improbability.[31]

It seems clear that Dawkins thinks the probability of complex life evolving is very low due to certain hurdles along the way.[32] He appeals to the anthropic principle and considerations about the size of the universe and number of

possible planets in an attempt to lessen the force of these factors, but ultimately reverts to a Humean response:

> [Natural selection] needs some luck to get started, and the 'billions of planets'
> anthropic principle grants it that luck. Maybe a few later gaps in the evolutionary
> story also need major infusions of luck, with anthropic justification. But whatever
> else we may say, *design* certainly does not work as an explanation for life, because
> design is ultimately not cumulative and it therefore raises bigger questions than it
> answers – it takes us straight back along the Ultimate 747 infinite regress.[33]

What is astonishing about this is that Dawkins appeals to this philosophical
Humean argument to help him in the context of discussing *design in biology.*

It must be emphasized that these points are not intended to undermine
Darwinism.[34] Dawkins presumably did not mean them that way and neither
do I. In fact, here I'm making the assumption that Darwinism is true. The
question we want to answer is whether Darwinism explains away the need for
design in biology and to find an answer we need to get some idea about how
likely it is that complex life would arise without design. The answer seems to
be that it is very unlikely and although this does not undermine Darwinism,
it does raise a serious question mark over Dawkins's claim that Darwinism
explains away the need for design.

Let's try to relate this to the three scenarios in the last section. The evidence of the untidy study corresponds to the evidence of complex life and the
hypotheses of the children playing and a burglary correspond to Darwinism
and design respectively. In the last section, we made the assumption that it
was discovered that the children had in fact been playing in the study and
here we are assuming that Darwinism is in fact true. In the first scenario, the
evidence of the untidy study was very likely to occur given that the children
had been playing in the study and this was sufficient to explain away the need
for the burglary hypothesis. Similarly, if complex life is very likely to arise as a
result of Darwinian processes this would explain away the need for design, but
we have seen that there are good reasons to doubt that this is the case.

In the second scenario, the evidence of the untidy study was very unlikely
to occur given that the children had been playing in the study (because of
the heavy drawers) and so the fact that they had been playing there only
partially explained away the evidence for the burglary hypothesis. This may
well be analogous to the situation with respect to Darwinism and design.
Since the probability of organized complexity arising given Darwinism is low,
Darwinism only partially explains away the evidence for design.

What about the third scenario? In that case not only was the evidence of the untidy study unlikely to occur given that the children had been playing in the study (because of the heavy drawers), but it was unlikely they would have been in the study unless there had been a burglary (because of the lock). In this case the fact that the children had been playing in the study actually provided further support for the burglary hypothesis, because this would provide an explanation of why the children were able to get into the study later in the day. So the question here is whether Darwinism itself requires design. Or, to put it another way, would design provide an explanation for the occurrence of Darwinian evolution? There are some reasons for thinking that it would since evolution requires the existence of living organisms in the first place and we have already seen that the probability of life arising from unguided natural processes may well be very low. Furthermore, evolution could not occur in a universe without finely tuned laws and, as argued in chapter 5, this also points to design.

So there are some reasons for thinking that Darwinism might actually provide support for design. However, it is not clear that these considerations are sufficient to compensate for the partial explaining away considered in scenario 2. Nevertheless, the discussion here suggests that at best Darwinism only partially explains away the need for design in biology. In other words, Darwinism has not explained away the need for design and so the existence of complex life still counts as evidence for a designer.[35]

Why the Darwinian argument doesn't work

There is, however, a much more fundamental objection to Dawkins's Darwinian argument. It seems clear that even if Darwinism explained away the need for design in biology, it would not follow that design can be ruled out in general. There are many theists who argue for design in the context of cosmological fine-tuning, but would nevertheless agree with Dawkins (and so disagree with my argument in the last section) that Darwinism has explained away the need for design in the context of biological complexity. The design argument does not depend on the belief that 'nothing that we know looks designed unless it is designed' as Dawkins claims it does.[36] Design arguments are not based merely on the appearance of design, but typically involve arguing for design on the basis of an inference to the best explanation of the evidence. Just because we cannot infer design *everywhere* does not mean that we cannot infer it *anywhere*.

Actually, despite Dawkins's claims about Darwinism defeating design, he writes:

Far from pointing to a designer, the illusion of design in the living world is explained with far greater economy and with devastating elegance by Darwinian natural selection. And, while natural selection itself *is limited to explaining the living world, it raises our consciousness* to the likelihood of comparable explanatory 'cranes' that may aid our understanding of the cosmos itself.[37]

As we saw in the last chapter, the most plausible way to understand his idea that Darwinism raises consciousness against design is that we should be cautious about inferring design. The problem is that it is one thing to claim that Darwinism should make us cautious about inferring design, but to claim that Darwinism has defeated design is another matter altogether.

It is worth reiterating Dawkins's response to the fine-tuning of the physical constants, which was discussed in the last chapter. Dawkins appeals to a multiverse to account for fine-tuning and addresses the claim that this is no more satisfactory than design as follows:

People who think that have not had their consciousness raised by natural selection. The key difference between the genuinely extravagant God hypothesis and the apparently extravagant multiverse hypothesis is one of statistical improbability. The multiverse, for all that it is extravagant, is simple. God, or any intelligent, decision-taking, calculating agent, would have to be highly improbable in the very same statistical sense as the entities he is supposed to explain.[38]

Here Dawkins appeals to natural selection as a consciousness-raiser, but wisely he is not content to rest his case on the Darwinian argument. He appears not to be entirely convinced by the alternative multiverse explanation in this case, but nevertheless thinks it is to be preferred to design. What is the reason for this? Clearly, Dawkins has reverted to his ultimate Boeing 747 gambit by claiming that God is too improbable to be a satisfactory explanation. It is not just that one should be cautious about inferring design, but that design should *never* be considered as a legitimate explanation. This clearly goes far beyond anything that Darwinism as a consciousness-raiser could establish.

Overall, the Darwinian argument against design is extremely weak. And Dawkins seems to realize this; hence his appeal to the ultimate Boeing 747 gambit, which is definitely Humean rather than Darwinian in nature. Now it is time to evaluate this argument, which purports to show that 'there almost certainly is no God'.

Why the ultimate Boeing 747 gambit doesn't work

Recall that this argument has two components: the *who designed the designer argument* and the *improbability of God argument*. The former concludes that God's organized complexity would be even more in need of explanation than that found in nature, while the latter concludes that it is extremely improbable that God exists. Has Dawkins really managed to turn the tables on the design argument and show that belief in God is untenable? The idea is that God's organized complexity would require explanation and yet none can be given because God is the stopping point for explanation. So if God possesses organized complexity, there seems to be a difficulty for the theist. Can the theist give an adequate response?

Consider first of all the claim that links organized complexity with improbability: that it is extremely improbable that organized complexity would exist unexplained. Why does Dawkins think this is true? To answer this, we must consider what he means by organized complexity. Basically, according to Dawkins, a system has organized complexity if it is composed of a variety of parts arranged in a highly specific manner so that it is able to function.[39] Living organisms provide an obvious example as does a Boeing 747. The link with improbability is due to the fact that organized complexity is highly unlikely to arise by chance. Dawkins puts it like this: 'The argument from improbability states that complex things could not have come about by chance.'[40] This statement seems straightforward enough. Take the Boeing 747. The chances of a Boeing 747 coming about by a hurricane in a scrapyard are extremely low because a Boeing 747 has a highly specific complex structure that requires all the components to be in the right place for it to function. So we can certainly agree with Dawkins on this point. But all that follows from this is that it is extremely improbable that that organized complexity would *come about* by chance. This does not establish what his argument requires, namely that it is extremely improbable that that organized complexity would *exist* unexplained. If God possesses organized complexity, all Dawkins's argument establishes is that God is highly unlikely to have *come about* by chance; few theists will be worried by this conclusion! For living organisms and Boeing 747s, which have a *beginning to their existence*, Dawkins's link between organized complexity and improbability seems reasonable, but that is because the various components must be assembled in the right way, whereas this is clearly not the case for God.

Even though Dawkins has not presented an argument to support his contention that it is extremely improbable that organized complexity would exist unexplained, let us nevertheless grant him this for the sake of the argument.[41] Does this mean that Dawkins's *who designed the designer argument* would work?

That depends on whether God possesses organized complexity.[42] Consider another premise in Dawkins's *who designed the designer argument*: that if God exists he must have organized complexity, the very same property we wanted to explain in the first place, and indeed he would be even more complex. Here is what Dawkins has to say: 'A God capable of continuously monitoring and controlling the individual status of every particle in the universe *cannot* be simple.'[43]

Here we must be careful about the words 'simple' and 'complex'. If 'simple' is taken to mean something like simple-minded or only capable of performing simple tasks, it is clear that God cannot be simple in this sense. Of course, if 'complex' just means 'not simple', then clearly God is complex, but this does not even come close to establishing that God is complex in the sense relevant for Dawkins's argument, that is, organized complexity. Similarly, when theologians or philosophers point out that there is a long tradition of understanding God to be simple rather than complex, it is not always clear that this is relevant to Dawkins's argument either; perhaps it is just a different use of the terms 'simple' and 'complex'.[44]

What is required then for Dawkins's argument is to show not just that God, if he exists, would have complexity in some sense, but that he would have *organized complexity* since only this type of complexity can be linked with improbability. What is Dawkins's argument that God would possess organized complexity? He seems to think that any being capable of doing the amazing things God is supposed to be able to do must possess organized complexity. Recall that organized complexity requires an arrangement of parts in a highly specific way that enables the system to function. But why think that God must have such an arrangement of parts? In the biological case, organized complexity is due to highly specific arrangements of physical parts; but if God exists he is non-physical and so clearly his organized complexity cannot be of this type. Is there some reason for thinking that God, if he exists, must therefore have a highly specific arrangement of *non-physical* parts? What exactly is the argument for this? And what are these parts supposed to be anyway? Here is one reason Dawkins provides for thinking that God would have organized complexity:

> God may not have a brain made of neurones, or a CPU made of silicon, but if he has
> the powers attributed to him he must have something far more elaborately and non-
> randomly constructed than the largest brain or the largest computer we know.[45]

Granted, humans have complex brains and perhaps all embodied intelligent agents must have complex brains of some sort, but it is not at all clear that an unembodied intelligence must have what effectively amounts to a non-physical brain. So it is not obvious that Dawkins's claim is true and he does not provide an argument for it. Perhaps he is advancing an inductive argument: what we might call the 'Big Brain' objection to God's existence:[46]

1. Every example of intelligent agency that we observe has an organized and complex structure.
2. God, if he exists, is an intelligent agent.
3. Therefore it is probable that God would have an organized and complex structure.

But this would be a specious piece of reasoning. Every example of intelligent agency that we observe is resident on Earth. Does this prove that it is improbable that intelligent agents exist elsewhere in the universe? We need to be very careful when using inductive arguments of the form 'every x we have observed is y, therefore the next x we observe will be a y', since they can lead us to reject good evidence for claims that run counter to our experience. If an explorer testifies to the existence of black swans, it is unreasonable to disregard his evidence because every swan you have encountered is white.

As Alvin Plantinga points out, 'The materialist thinks of thought as generated by the physical interaction of such things as neurons.'[47] Dawkins seems to carry this idea over to immaterial minds as well, so that if such minds exist they would also have to generate thought by interaction of non-physical parts. By contrast, as Plantinga goes on to say, 'An immaterial self doesn't have any parts; hence of course, thought isn't generated by the interaction of its parts.'[48] It is important to emphasize that the dispute at this point is not about the *existence* of an immaterial mind like God's. It is rather that Dawkins is claiming that if God did exist, he would have to possess organized complexity, which would amount to a complex arrangement of non-physical parts. Theologian Patrick Richmond provides what is perhaps the most plausible construal of Dawkins's position, which is to adopt Hume's approach of identifying the non-physical parts with ideas in God's mind. The difficulty with this approach is that a mind needs to be distinguished from an arrangement of ideas. As Richmond puts it:

> we cannot make much sense of a conscious idea existing independently of a
> mind; ideas are not independent, separable entities like physical parts, but are
> logically inseparable from a mind. . . . [Divine ideas] are all essential aspects of the
> single act of God's comprehension of his power, not independent entities. God's
> consciousness can be a non-composite, irreducible mental state.[49]

Philosopher Keith Ward adopts a very similar approach when he writes:

> God is not complex in the sense of being composed of separate and separable parts.
> The ideas in God's mind are not separately existing ideas that are added together to
> form the mind of God. They only exist as part of the mind of God, which is one
> consciousness. . . . The mind comes first, and its ideas are parts that are inseparable
> from that mind.[50]

Richmond and Ward are not denying that God is complex in some sense, but just that he does not have organized complexity.

Now, of course, Dawkins might be incredulous at the suggestion that such an immaterial mind exists, but he finds arguments from 'personal incredulity' flawed and is entirely correct in this regard. As pointed out in chapter 3, we shouldn't reject what might otherwise be a good explanation just on the grounds that it does not fit with our experience. We saw that quantum theory throws up many strange and counter-intuitive ideas – far stranger, and at further remove from our experience, than the concept of a non-embodied agent – but that does not mean it should be rejected. The central point here, however, is that Dawkins has provided no reason for believing that God, if he exists, would possess organized complexity and so his argument fails.

Dawkins's problems with probability

As we have seen, Dawkins tends to revert to Humean arguments (i.e. his ultimate Boeing 747 gambit) whenever Darwinian arguments run into trouble. Furthermore, we have also seen that there are serious problems with his ultimate Boeing 747 gambit. But let's now assume for the sake of argument that somehow Dawkins can reinstate his gambit. Should Dawkins then adopt this Humean approach? As pointed out above, there would be a significant price to pay for such a move since it would seem to require rejecting his claim that atheism has an evidential basis in modern science. Still, perhaps he should be willing to pay the price if it would really make his atheism secure. But would it? Certainly, it seems so since the conclusion of his *improbability of God argument* is that 'it is extremely improbable that God exists'. However, this conclusion should not worry the theist because it is based on a seriously problematic application of probability theory.

Now we must ask what Dawkins means when he says that God's existence is extremely improbable. It is important here to distinguish between the *prior probability* of a belief *before* a piece of evidence has been considered and the *posterior probability*, which is the updated probability *after* the evidence has been taken into account.[51] So when Dawkins says that God's existence is extremely improbable, we must ask whether he is referring to a prior probability or a posterior probability? It seems clear from Dawkins's ultimate Boeing 747 gambit that even if it were sound it would at best establish that the prior probability of God's existence, before any specific evidence is taken into account, is extremely low. The reason for this is that it appeals to what God must be like if he exists, that is, that he must have organized complexity, and that organized complexity is improbable if unexplained, and so on. It does not appeal to any evidence that theists might appeal to as supporting belief in God. Now here is Dawkins's problem: *it is very common for a belief to have a very low prior probability and yet a very high posterior probability*. We have already come across this issue in the context of miracles in chapter 3, but here it crops up in the context of God's existence.

Consider again the story from chapter 3 about my friend Tom who enters the lottery every week. Suppose that the winning numbers have just been announced in a particular week. What is the probability that Tom has hit the jackpot? Well, either he has or he hasn't, but without knowing what numbers he selected it is very reasonable for me to assign an extremely low probability: 1 in 10,000,000 perhaps. However, the next day Tom arrives at my house, driving a new BMW, and he tells me that he hit the jackpot in the lottery the previous night. Initially, I am suspicious because Tom is a bit of a practical joker, but then he shows me a newspaper that has a picture of his receiving the cheque and later I see him on the local news on TV, which again confirms his story. What is the probability now? Although, the prior probability was low, the posterior probability after taking all the evidence into account is extremely high; in fact, I can be virtually certain he hit the jackpot.

Could something similar be the case in terms of the probability of God's existence? Suppose Dawkins is right that the prior probability of God's existence is extremely low, even lower than the probability of Tom's winning the lottery, say 1 in 100,000,000. Is it conceivable that there could be any evidence for God's existence that could overturn such a low probability? One possibility is the evidence from fine-tuning that was considered in the last chapter. There is at the very least a prima facie case for saying that such extreme precision would have been very unlikely to occur if there were no God (let's say 1 in 10^{12}, which arguably is not nearly improbable enough), while it is not all that improbable if there is a God (let's say 1 in 100). With these values, the probability of God's existence gets updated to a *posterior* probability just above 0.99, so it becomes *almost certain that God does exist*.[52] Clearly, these particular numbers should not be taken too seriously, but they do illustrate the point that overall the probability of God's existence might be high even if its prior probability is very low.

Now, of course, Dawkins would claim that he has considered all the evidence and has discovered that there is no evidence that would count in favour of God's existence. Hence, even if the above scenario is possible in principle, in practice the probability of God's existence will remain extremely low. The problem is that when we consider how Dawkins handles the evidence, it is clear that this response is inadequate. Consider the fine-tuning evidence as a case in point. As we saw earlier, Dawkins considers a multiverse as an alternative to design, but ultimately falls back on a Humean response: even if the atheist cannot offer a satisfactory explanation, God is not a good explanation because he would be even more complex and hence improbable.

There is a confusion here, however. Even if we grant that God's existence is improbable (in the sense of a low prior probability), it does not follow that God's existence would not explain certain features of the universe. Consider again the story about my friend Tom. Even though it is improbable (in the sense of a low prior probability) that he won the lottery, nevertheless if he did win the lottery this fact would account for all the evidence (new BMW, etc.) very well. Similarly, even if the prior probability of God's existence is extremely low because of his complexity, it still seems perfectly plausible to reason as follows: let's suppose that God does actually exist (improbable as it might be), then his existence would account for the evidence of fine-tuning.

In fact, Dawkins implicitly seems to assume that if God existed his existence would explain the evidence of fine-tuning; it's just that he thinks it is very unlikely that God exists in the first place. But if he grants this, he cannot claim that there is no evidence for God. On the contrary, if the evidence of fine-tuning is more probable if God exists than it would be without God's existence, then there is evidence for God and so it makes it more likely that God exists. In this case Dawkins's position would amount to saying that he does not find the evidence sufficiently convincing, but this raises the question *why* is it insufficient? If the fine-tuning evidence is not convincing enough, what kind of evidence would be required? No doubt, he would claim it is insufficient because God's existence is highly improbable to begin with, but that is just to revert to Humean arguments and, as we have seen, there are good reasons to think that these arguments fail. This being the case, it is difficult to see how Dawkins can rule out the possibility that God's existence might be highly probable overall, just as it was highly probable overall that Tom won the lottery.

A number of reasons for rejecting Dawkins's ultimate Boeing 747 gambit have been presented, but the problem lies with the conclusion and not just the argument. Even if his argument were successful it would only establish that the *prior* probability of God's existence is low, but this is insufficient to establish that the *posterior* probability is also low. Thus, he has not provided any good reason to believe that God's existence is improbable.

Conclusion

Richard Dawkins is faced with a dilemma between scientific Darwinian and philosophical Humean responses to the design argument. He wishes to give the impression of grasping the Darwinian horn of the dilemma as is clear from his direct claims about the importance of Darwinism (and science more generally) to his atheism. However, there are serious problems with the Darwinian response to design. Arguably, it does not even explain away the evidence for design in biology, but more significantly it has very little to offer by way of a response to design outside biology. Dawkins claims that Darwinism raises our consciousness against design outside biology, but far from ruling out design this would amount to little more than the claim that we should exercise caution when inferring design.

Interestingly, Dawkins seems to be very much aware that the Darwinian response is exceedingly weak, particularly in view of the evidence from fine-tuning, and so he falls back on a Humean approach instead. In doing so it is clear that Darwinism plays an insignificant role in his argument since it is Humean arguments that are really doing the work. Thus, in fact Dawkins is really grasping the Humean horn of the dilemma, which thoroughly discredits the idea that his atheism is based on the findings of modern science since the Humean approach is a philosophical approach that does not depend on Darwinism. Nevertheless, this would be a sensible move for Dawkins to make if his arguments worked, but in fact there is good reason to think that they are flawed. In particular, his ultimate Boeing 747 gambit is supposed to show that God's existence is very improbable, but it does nothing of the sort. All of the key premises to the argument are highly questionable but, worse still, even the conclusion is misleading because it is compatible with there being a very high probability for God's existence once all the evidence is taken into account.

Notes

1. Here I use the term 'Darwinism' as a shorthand for the neo-Darwinian synthesis.
2. *TGD*, p. 79.

3. *BTS*, p. 241.

4. Daniel C. Dennett, *Darwin's Dangerous Idea: Evolution and the Meanings of Life* (London: Penguin, 1995).

5. *TGD*, p. 116, emphasis in original.

6. *GNG*, p. 65.

7. David Hume, *Dialogues Concerning Natural Religion*, ed. H. Aiken (New York: Hafner Library of Classics, 1948; first published 1779).

8. Ibid., pp. 33–34.

9. Elliott Sober, 'The Design Argument', in W. Mann (ed.), *The Blackwell Companion to the Philosophy of Religion* (Oxford: Blackwell, 2004), p. 15. The quotation is taken from an expanded version of the paper available at http://philosophy.wisc.edu/sober/design%20argument%2011%202004.pdf, to which the page numbers refer. Interestingly, in the original version of this text Sober cites Dawkins as an example of the Darwinian position.

10. Ibid., p. 15.

11. *TGD*, p. 114.

12. Ibid., p. 158.

13. Ibid., p. 109.

14. My formulation of the argument draws on the formulation of Patrick Richmond, 'Richard Dawkins' Darwinian Objection', *Science and Christian Belief* 19 (2007), pp. 99–116. Richmond, however, presents it as a single argument.

15. *TGD*, p. 79.

16. Ibid.

17. Dennett, *Darwin's Dangerous Idea*, p. 155. Furthermore, Dawkins seems to accept that his argument is no different from Hume's, and so presumably no more dependent on science, since he quotes these remarks of Dennett with approval (*TGD*, p. 157). Dennett points out that Hume could not think of an alternative explanation and so in the end 'caved in' to the design argument, but the clear implication is that Hume's arguments had shown that the design argument was flawed and so his caving in was a failure of nerve on Hume's part that was not grounded on rational considerations.

18. *GNG*, p. 71.

19. Sam Harris, *Letter to a Christian Nation: A Challenge to Faith* (London: Bantam, 2007), p. 73.

20. He clearly emphasizes the importance of Darwin over Hume in defeating design in his earlier book *The Blind Watchmaker* (London: Penguin, 1986), pp. 5–6.

21. In fact, he believes there is no evidence at all, but the same point applies: he gives the impression that there could in principle be evidence for God's existence, but that as a matter of fact no such evidence exists.

22. From 'Lecture from "The Nullifidian" (Dec 94)', available at http://richarddawkins.net/articles/89 (accessed 5 July 2010).

23. Theistic evolution is the idea that God used evolution to bring about complex life, so it is clear that theistic evolutionists do not see any conflict between evolution and the existence of God. Most theistic evolutionists, however, think that evolution rules out an argument for design from the existence of complex life, and it is this claim that I wish to question.

24. Recall the discussion in chapter 4 about when evidence confirms or supports a hypothesis.

25. I am, of course, simplifying things here for the sake of the illustration. For example, a more realistic possibility would be that I had forgotten to lock the study on this particular occasion.

26. See, for example, Paul Davies, *The Fifth Miracle* (London: Penguin, 1999).

27. *TGD*, p. 140.

28. Stephen J. Gould, *Wonderful Life: The Burgess Shale and the Nature of History* (New York: Norton, 1989). Hitchens refers to Gould's work and seems to concur with Gould that this shows that intelligent life is an accident of history (*GNG*, pp. 92–93). For our purposes, it is significant that Hitchens seems to accept that intelligent life is highly unlikely to arise as a result of unguided evolution.

29. Simon Conway Morris, *Life's Solutions: Inevitable Humans in a Lonely Universe* (Cambridge: Cambridge University Press, 2003).

30. *TGD*, p. 140. It could be argued that the probability of complex life without design would not be low when the size of the universe and the possibly large number of planets capable of supporting life are taken into account, which is presumably what Dawkins has in mind when he refers to 'sheer luck, anthropically justified'. Without more detailed knowledge of the probabilities involved in evolutionary processes and the number of suitable planets, it is difficult to evaluate this claim, but given our current knowledge of the complexity in even the simplest living organisms it is not clear that these kinds of considerations would make it at all probable that complex life would appear. Nevertheless, let us suppose that the origin of life somewhere in the universe is quite probable once these factors are taken into account. Whether the probability of complex life is low now depends on what kind of complex life is being considered. If it is just any kind of living organism, then clearly the probability would be quite high. If it refers to eukaryotic life, it might not be so high. Given the improbability of the transition to eukaryotic life, this transition may well only occur on a small proportion of planets where life exists and so unless the number of such planets is large, the transition might not occur at all. Similarly, the probability of complex life becomes lower as the complexity under consideration increases. Hence, this strategy for increasing the probability of complex life will run out of steam quite quickly as the level of complexity increases. For example, if we take complex life to refer to animals that are conscious, it is reasonable to think that the probability would remain extremely low. At the very least, given our knowledge

about the complexity of life and the improbability of various transitions towards greater complexity, the onus would be on those wishing to claim that the probability of complex life is not low to make their case.

31. Ibid., p. 140.

32. In his review of Conway Morris's book *Life's Solutions*, Elliott Sober writes, 'Imagine a long sequence of evolutionary transitions . . . Even if each transition in this chain – from the first to the second, from the second to the third, and so on – were highly probable, it would not follow that the transition from the first to the last is highly probable. The problem is that probabilities multiply; multiply a big probability like 9999/10000 by itself enough times and you obtain a probability that is very small indeed,' available at http://philosophy.wisc.edu/sober/morris%20review%20for%20NYT.pdf (accessed 30 Sept. 2011).

33. *TGD*, p. 141.

34. This point is relevant to the objection that this is a God-of-the-gaps argument. In chapter 3 we distinguished between causal and explanatory gaps. The argument here is not based on the existence of causal gaps that would be filled in by God. In fact, the argument says nothing about the way in which design operates. The argument is based on our scientific knowledge about the complexity of living organisms and it is compatible with continued scientific investigation into the evolution of complexity.

35. For a much more in-depth discussion of this argument see my paper 'Can Evidence for Design be Explained Away?', in J. Chandler and V. Harrison (eds.), *Probability in the Philosophy of Religion* (Oxford: Oxford University Press, 2012), pp. 79–102.

36. See *TGD*, p. 79.

37. Ibid., p. 2, my emphasis.

38. Ibid., pp. 146–147.

39. See Dawkins, *Blind Watchmaker*, pp. 1–18.

40. *TGD*, p. 114.

41. Patrick Richmond provides an argument in support of this claim in 'Richard Dawkins' Darwinian Objection', pp. 108–109.

42. Actually, that isn't quite right. There is another response open to the theist, which is to grant that organized complexity is very unlikely to exist unexplained and that God does possess organized complexity, but then argue that there is an explanation for God's existence. The theist can argue that if God exists, he does so necessarily. That is, given the kind of being God would be, if he exists, he could not have failed to exist. As such, God, even if he possesses organized complexity, would not require explanation from anything external to himself. Or, to put it another way, his organized complexity would be explained in terms of the necessity of his being. Arguably, this response is fatal on its own to Dawkins's argument. This is the view of both the theist Gregory Ganssle ('Dawkins's Best Argument: The Case Against God in The God Delusion', *Philosophia Christi* 10 [2008], pp. 39–56) and non-theist

Erik Wielenberg ('Dawkins's Gambit, Hume's Aroma, and God's Simplicity', *Philosophia Christi* 11 [2009], pp. 113–128). A detailed discussion of this approach would take us too far from the main focus of this chapter.

43. *TGD*, p. 149, emphasis in original.

44. This point is discussed by Keith Ward in his book *Why There Almost Certainly Is a God: Doubting Dawkins* (Oxford: Lion Hudson, 2008), pp. 48–50. He accepts that God is complex in the sense of the complexity of ideas in God's mind and the actions of which he is capable, but argues that this does not make God's existence improbable. He also argues that God is simple in three respects: first, God is not composed of separate and separable parts; secondly, God acts on the basis of one general principle (for the sake of goodness); thirdly, God is the cause of all existence except the divine existence itself, which can have no cause. The first of these is the most important for the present discussion since it is relevant to the question of whether God has organized complexity.

45. *TGD*, p. 154. Note Dawkins's expression 'far more elaborately and non-randomly constructed'. Perhaps this suggests that Dawkins has some doubts about linking organized complexity to improbability except for entities that had a beginning to their existence.

46. I owe this argument to Graham Veale (personal communication).

47. Alvin Plantinga and Michael Tooley, *Knowledge of God* (Oxford: Blackwell, 2008), p. 58.

48. Ibid.

49. Richmond, 'Richard Dawkins' Darwinian Objection', p. 115.

50. Ward, *Why There Almost Certainly*, p. 48.

51. Prior and posterior probabilities are part of the Bayesian approach to probability. This seems to be the approach to probability that Dawkins has in mind because he takes probabilities to represent rational degrees of belief and so it is entirely reasonable to have a probability for God's existence that lies between 0 and 1. Although not everyone agrees with this approach to probability, it is a mainstream approach. On the prior and posterior probabilities, the prior probability will depend on what background knowledge has been taken into account and the posterior probability will depend on exactly what evidence is included before updating. And even taking into account the background knowledge, there is still a question of whether it makes sense to ask what the prior probability of God's existence is. The question assumes there is a single value, but this will be denied by subjective Bayesians who think that the probability values an individual assigns to his beliefs should only be constrained by the probability calculus and Bayesian rules for updating. Nevertheless, many reject this subjectivity and so again Dawkins's position here is mainstream.

52. Probabilities are updated using Bayes's theorem, which can be expressed as $P(G \mid E) = P(E \mid G) \times P(G) / P(E)$, where $P(G)$ is the prior probability of God's existence,

$P(G \mid E)$ is the posterior probability based on evidence E, $P(E \mid G)$ is the probability of the evidence given that God exists and $P(E)$ is the overall probability of the evidence. Given the values in the main text we have $P(G) = 1/10^8$ and $P(E \mid G) = 1/100$ and, since $P(E \mid {\sim}G)$ is the probability of the evidence given the non-existence of God, we also have $P(E \mid {\sim}G) = 1/10^{12}$. We also know that $P({\sim}G) = 1 - P(G) = 1 - 1/10^8$. Since $P(E) = P(E \mid G) \times P(G) + P(E \mid {\sim}G) \times P({\sim}G)$, this gives $P(E) = (1/100) \times (1/10^8) + (1/10^{12}) \times (1 - 1/10^8) \approx 1.01 \times 10^{-10}$. Using Bayes's theorem, we get $P(G) = (1/100) \times (1/10^8) / (1.01 \times 10^{-10}) \approx 0.9901$.

The vast majority of people who have ever lived have believed that there is a supernatural dimension to reality. The atheist maintains that all of these people have been mistaken, while the New Atheist goes one step further and claims that they have been deluded. Of course, religious beliefs differ dramatically and so they cannot all be true, but in general religious believers have held that the physical universe depends on a supernatural reality. Is it possible that almost everyone has been so thoroughly mistaken about the fundamental nature of reality and that the physical universe is all there is? Atheists will quickly respond with a 'yes' and will rightly point out that truth is not determined by majority vote. But still, if most people disagree with you on a given topic, it might be worth asking why they disagree? Perhaps they are all irrational or deluded, but it might also be worth considering the possibility that you are the one who is mistaken.

There are, however, precedents for discovering that a widely held belief is false. The discovery that Earth goes round the Sun rather than vice versa is an obvious case where the majority viewpoint was shown to be incorrect. So perhaps atheists can maintain that in the same way the majority viewpoint is incorrect in the case of the supernatural. There is a difference between the two cases, however. As philosophers Peter Kreeft and Ronald Tacelli point out, for people who did not believe that Earth went round the Sun, it was not their *experience* of reality that was at fault, but their belief that the Sun was moving rather than the earth. They go on to ask, 'But if God does not exist, what is it that believers have been experiencing? The level of illusion goes far beyond any other example of collective error. It really amounts to collective psychosis.'[1] The New Atheists would probably concur, but in that case one would expect them to present convincing reasons for believing that there is no supernatural dimension to reality before drawing such a radical conclusion. As we have seen in earlier chapters, they do nothing of the sort.

Furthermore, if so many people are in error about the supernatural, atheists need to provide an explanation, for how did so many people come to hold these beliefs in the first place? Needless to say, the New Atheists do offer an explanation for the origins of religious belief and, not surprisingly, it is an evolutionary explanation. Below I shall attempt to give an overview of the account offered by Dennett and Dawkins,[2] before responding to it in the following section.

Genes, memes and belief in God

In providing an evolutionary explanation for religion, the starting point for Dennett and Dawkins is the fact that religion is an expensive business; just think of the time, energy and money involved in religious rituals, devotion, music, literature, art and architecture. What accounts for such extravagance? Dennett expresses the basic issue as follows:

> Whatever else religion is as a human phenomenon, it is a hugely costly endeavor, and evolutionary biology shows us that nothing so costly just happens. Any such regular expenditure of time and energy has to be balanced by something of 'value' obtained, and the ultimate measure of evolutionary 'value' is *fitness*: the capacity to replicate more successfully than the competition does.[3]

Dennett's point is not that we ought to value fitness above other things, but that unless there is something that pays for religion in terms of fitness it would not have survived. So what does pay for religion? Or, to put it another way, we can ask what Dennett calls the *cui bono* question:[4] who benefits from it?

Before answering the question, Dennett draws attention to a number of different ways in which evolution might provide an answer. He asks us to 'put ourselves into the (three bright green) shoes of a "Martian"' who has come to Earth to investigate religion.[5] We may presume that the Martian does not believe in God or is at least setting aside any belief in God for the purposes of investigating religion scientifically. Furthermore, the Martian is well read on evolutionary theory and comes armed with a set of possible ways in which evolution might explain religion. The first of these is what Dennett calls *Sweet-tooth theories*.

The idea in Sweet-tooth theories is that there are cognitive mechanisms in our brain that predispose us to religious belief even though religion had nothing to do with the evolution of these mechanisms in the first place. Dennett's suggestion is that just as we have an evolved receptor system to respond to sugar and other substances that is now overstimulated by products like chocolate that contain the same substances in high concentration, perhaps we have a mechanism in our brain that evolved to 'respond to *something* that religions provide in intensified form'.⁶ This proposal is based on *genetic* evolution and is consistent with there being a gene (or number of genes) or 'god centre' in the brain that predisposes us to religious belief.⁷ Sweet-tooth theories are incomplete on their own since they leave the question as to why the relevant cognitive mechanisms evolved in the first place.

The second category of theories on the Martian's list is *Symbiont theories*. Parasites provide an example of symbionts since they take advantage of the environment provided by their host to enhance their own survival. According to this approach, religion is a cultural symbiont that thrives by spreading from one human host to another. So what benefits from religion in evolutionary terms? In Symbiont theories it is not (primarily) human fitness that benefits, but the fitness of religion itself. Religion may thrive as a *mutualist*, which enhances human fitness, as a *commensal*, which has no impact on human fitness, or as a *parasite*, which is detrimental to human fitness; but the key point is that it is religion itself that benefits. What does the fitness of religion itself mean? In biological evolution we talk about the fitness of organisms, not cultural phenomena like religion. In order to address this issue we need to take a short detour into the world of memes.

The term *meme* was introduced by Dawkins in his book *The Selfish Gene* and has been the subject of much discussion and debate ever since.⁸ Very roughly, the idea is that memes are to cultural evolution what genes are to biological evolution – the basic unit of inheritance. Both genes and memes represent information that can be copied,⁹ but the copying process is imperfect and so results in variation, with some variants having greater fitness and hence being more likely to survive. It is then claimed that memes provide the basis for a Darwinian account of cultural evolution. Dennett cites words and languages as examples as well as various behaviours, such as shaking hands and cooking methods, and artefacts, such as shelters and tools. Memes play a central role in both Dennett's and Dawkins's accounts, but do memes actually exist? Dennett provides a very confident answer: 'Yes, because words exist, and words are memes that can be pronounced.'[10] Others such as anthropologist Dan Sperber are much more sceptical, however, raising questions about their existence, how they are copied and the usefulness of such a Darwinian approach to cultural evolution. This is not to say that these questions cannot be answered – Dennett responds to a number of objections, including those of Sperber, in two appendices in his book[11] – but it does illustrate that memes are controversial and that scientific opinion is divided over their existence and usefulness. It is surely ironic that one of Dawkins's most significant contributions to human thought is a concept that cannot be detected directly, which many people think does not exist in reality because the evidence for it is unconvincing, and that many think is of no use as an explanation – precisely the same criticisms he levels against the existence of God.

The next possibility on the Martian's list is *Sexual-selection theories*. Dennett gives the example of male bowerbirds, which go to great lengths to develop impressive bowers that are assessed by females before selecting a mate. According to this approach, something similar might have occurred in the case of religion with females selecting on the basis of religion-enhancing psychological traits such as sensitivity to music and ceremony. Or perhaps it was not a genetically transmitted trait, but a cultural analogue of sexual selection or some combination of genetic and cultural transmission.

Money theories represent the next alternative. Dennett claims that monetary systems are cultural artefacts that have evolved on a number of occasions. He also argues that money did not result from deliberate human invention, but had instead what he calls a *free-floating rationale*, which basically means that it evolved because it was beneficial in evolutionary terms. If the evolutionary explanation of religion is similar to that for money, who benefited? Dennett suggestions three possibilities: 'everybody in the society benefits, because religion makes society more secure, harmonious, efficient';[12] the elite who are in control benefit at the expense of others; societies as wholes benefit at the expense of rival groups. The last of these options is known as *group selection* and has received considerable attention particularly through the work of evolutionary biologist David Sloan Wilson.[13] However, the significance of group selection as an evolutionary process is controversial and is shunned by both Dennett and Dawkins. This still leaves open the possibility of other Money theory explanations, which in one sense represent the most straightforward evolutionary explanation since they claim that religion enhances fitness.

Dennett concludes the Martian's list with *Pearl theories*, which are the default to be adopted if none of the other theories is tenable. The idea is that just as pearls start out as a speck of foreign matter but end up as something considered valuable by humans, so religion starts out as a by-product of something else but ends up captivating us. Evolution gives rise to mechanisms that are meant 'to respond to irritations or intrusions of one sort or another',[14] but then something new comes along which triggers a response that ultimately leads to religion. Dennett claims that, according to Pearl theories, nothing benefits from religion in terms of biological fitness; it is just a by-product and nothing more.

With this array of theories Dennett then proceeds to outline a possible evolutionary account of religion over the course of several chapters. The resulting account does not appeal to a single theory, but draws on several of them at different stages. It would be impossible to do justice to Dennett's account in just a few paragraphs, but I shall attempt to give a very brief summary.

Cognitive science of religion is a relatively new field of research that has developed over the last few decades and has amongst its leading figures scholars such as Scott Atran, Justin Barrett and Pascal Boyer.[15] The goal of this discipline is to study religious thought and action using theories from the cognitive sciences. Dennett's book draws on and popularizes some of the research that has been undertaken, particularly the work of Boyer and Atran,[16] who emphasize the evolution of certain cognitive mechanisms which in combination can give rise to something like religion. He focuses in particular on a mechanism for agent detection. The idea is that many animals have a mechanism that enables them to distinguish the motion of another *agent*, which might be a predator or prey, from motion that is insignificant, such as the rustling of leaves. According to Dennett, this is a useful mechanism that can overshoot so that sometimes an agent is detected when none is present, a so-called *hypersensitive agent detection device*, or HADD. Dennett then links this with what he calls the intentional stance, which is a stance adopted by humans and some other animals whereby they treat other things in the world as rational agents who act in accordance with their beliefs and desires. He claims that we have difficulty turning off the intentional stance and that this presents problems when someone close to us dies. How does this relate to the origins of religion? Dennett's suggestion is that the intentional stance led those who knew the deceased to conceive of 'the unseen presence of the agent as a *spirit*, a sort of *virtual person* created by the survivors' troubled mind-sets, and almost as vivid and robust as a live person'.[17]

This provides the starting point for Dennett's account, but it is still some way from religion. At this stage memes become more important. The overshooting of our ability to detect agency resulted in all sorts of agent-ideas (about demons and fairies, etc.), out of which only a few survived because they were not too absurd and had greater ability than the others to captivate the human imagination. These memes mutated and improved through time as they spread, but, according to Dennett, this only accounts for superstition, not religion, since there was no belief in these agent-ideas. Dennett's idea, following Boyer, concerns the complex information humans had to deal with in making decisions. He suggests that belief in a 'full-access agent' who had knowledge of all the important information might have helped. These full-access agents turn out to be ancestors; but why ancestors? His answer is that evolution results in children having a tendency to believe whatever their parents tell them and do whatever they command. Once genetic evolution has established this tendency, it can be used (or abused) by agents with agendas of their own or memes that benefit from it. Dawkins also draws attention to the evolutionary advantages of the trusting obedience of children, but also claims that the flipside is gullibility. 'The inevitable by-product', he tells us, 'is vulnerability to infection by mind viruses.'[18]

With full-access agents in place, Dennett asks how knowledge could be acquired from the gods, and this is where divination comes in. The whole point of full-access agents and divination is that they might have helped, or at least appeared to help, in decision-making. These (perceived) benefits enabled the full-access agent and divination memes to propagate. Dennett also suggests that shamanic healing rituals might be explained in a similar way to divination. His idea here is that such rituals may well work because of the placebo effect or, more specifically, the power of hypnotism. And those with a genetic tendency to hypnotizability would be more likely to survive because they would benefit from the shamans' rituals.[19] In effect, healing rituals would pay for themselves in evolutionary terms because of the benefits they bestowed.

All of this, Dennett claims, accounts for folk religion, but what about organized religion? Basically, his answer is that religion became more sophisticated as people became increasingly cultured. He suggests that 'alongside the domestication of animals and plants, there was a gradual process in which the wild (self-sustaining) memes of folk religion became thoroughly domesticated'.[20] This was in large part due to 'stewards' who deliberately brought about changes to help propagate the memes of religion. An important aspect of this, he claims, was innovations to protect religious memes from their opponents by making them immune to confirmation or disconfirmation through secrecy and mystery.

Much more could be said about Dennett's account, but the above description outlines at least some of the main points. Which of the Martian's list of theories does he subscribe to? Well, it is a combination of several, particularly the Pearl (i.e. by-product) theory, which is particularly relevant in terms of the overshooting of agent detection in the early stages, and the Symbiont theory, which is basically a memetic account that becomes dominant once the by-product account has generated relevant memes in the first place. Sweet-tooth theories also seem relevant in so far as Dennett appeals to mechanisms to enable hypnotizability as a potential god centre. Dawkins also accounts for religion in terms of a combination of the by-product and memetic approaches, and overall their approaches are very similar. But what are we to make of these evolutionary explanations and what is their significance for belief in God? We shall now turn to these questions.

Evaluating the Dennett–Dawkins account

Dawkins is not in any doubt about the ramifications of his account of the origin of religion for belief in God. The analogy he uses to describe religious belief as an evolutionary by-product highlights the point. Why do moths fly into candle flames? Moths are known to use light from the moon and stars to help them steer an accurate course. The problem is that when they use the same rules of thumb with light from a candle instead it results in what Dawkins calls 'self-immolation behaviour'. His basic thesis is that this behaviour is a misfiring by-product of a mechanism that evolved because it enhanced the fitness of moths. He then claims that a similar misfiring by-product account can explain the existence of irrational religious belief and practice. He also describes religion as a 'mental virus', which is part of his by-product account since the mental viruses of religion exploit mechanisms in the brain.[21] We shall return to Dawkins's moth analogy in the next section.

Dennett is more circumspect, but he also seems to think that his account undermines the rationality of belief in God. He does not endorse Dawkins's view of religion as a mental virus, although he does consider it a 'major pos-sibility'.[22] He claims that his account is compatible with the existence of God, but mocks sociologist Rodney Stark for claiming that the evolutionary explanation of the origins of religion does not undermine religion but may in fact describe the process through which humans discovered the truth.[23] It is clear that he sees his entire project of explaining religion in purely scientific terms as a component of an atheistic understanding of reality that is intended to explain away the need for God. And, of course, he is perfectly entitled to attempt to do this. But this raises two questions. First, is there any good reason to believe that his account, or some account along these lines, is true? Secondly, even if it is, does it undermine belief in God?

In answering the first of these questions it is important to point out that even Dennett and Dawkins would not claim that their accounts are true. In describing what he is trying to do, Dennett says:

I will try to tell *the best current version* of the story science can tell about how religions have become what they are. I am not at all claiming that this is what science has already established about religion. The main point of this book is to insist that we *don't* yet know – but we can discover – the answers to these important questions if we make a concerted effort.[24]

Dennett's primary goal is to persuade us that religion is a natural phenomenon involving only events that do not involve any violation of scientific laws.[25] He nevertheless claims that this view is not necessarily in conflict with the existence of God since even if God exists, religion itself might be a natural phenomenon. Furthermore, he claims that 'no deeply religious person should object to the scientific study of religion with the presumption that it is an entirely natural phenomenon'.[26] His basis for this is his claim that the only way to demonstrate the occurrence of miracles is by showing that there are certain phenomena that cannot be explained scientifically.

I certainly agree with Dennett that there is nothing to fear about the scientific investigation of religion, but for slightly different reasons. Consider Dennett's claim that religion being a natural phenomenon is compatible with God's existence. For most religious phenomena this seems right. As a Christian I believe that when I read the Bible and meditate upon what it says, God speaks to me, sometimes encouraging me, sometimes correcting or rebuking me, and so on. But there is no voice that I hear and I very much expect that there is nothing supernatural going on in my brain! If scientists were to study my brain at the time, I would not expect them to find evidence of miraculous activity! In that sense then it is a natural phenomenon, but Dennett seems to assume that because something is a natural phenomenon it must have a scientific explanation, or at least that it is in principle explicable in scientific terms. At this point I disagree. No doubt all natural phenomena are capable of being explained by science at least in part. In the case of reading and meditating on the Bible, science could presumably explain the various processes that take place in my brain, but if there is a God who communicates with me through Scripture, and Dennett does not rule out the possibility, then any scientific explanation of what is going on will not be a complete explanation. In fact, it will leave out the most important factor, namely God. To revert to the terminology from chapter 3, there is a personal explanation in terms of God's communicating to me, but in this case this need involve no incompatibility with a scientific explanation of the physical processes in my brain.[27] But to claim that the scientific account gave a complete explanation would be like trying to explain a woman's reaction to reading a letter without referring to the fact that it was written by her son whom she hadn't seen for years. Again, science could tell us a lot about what is going on at the neurophysiological level, but this provides only a very incomplete explanation at best.[28]

Dennett is very keen to *break the spell* of religion, by which he means we should reject the idea that religion be kept immune from scientific study. Some people are opposed to the scientific study of religion because they think religion is outside the scope of science or that scientific approaches will inevitably fail. Dennett portrays such people as obscurants who are opposed to scientific progress. Well, perhaps some people do fall into that category, but my own view is that Dennett is right in thinking that there is no good reason to preclude science from studying religion. My reason for thinking that scientific explanations will be incomplete in at least some cases is not based on obscurantism, but on logic: if God exists and communicates or in some way interacts with humans, purely scientific explanations of these interactions would be necessarily incomplete.

At this point it is worth drawing attention to a viewpoint that seems quite common among atheists at a popular level, although presumably Dennett would not endorse it. It is the idea that science has already explained religion and so science has shown religious belief to be irrational. We shall consider soon whether such explanations could in principle undermine the rationality of religious beliefs, but first I want to focus on the claim that science has explained religion. The mere fact that scientific explanations of religion have been offered is no indication that such explanations are true. Science often seems to involve various rival explanations being proposed for some particular phenomenon. Scientists then try to discriminate between these explanations to determine which is best and, if the best one is sufficiently good, then perhaps they come to believe it to be true or probably true.

Just because scientists propose a *possible* explanation of religion does not mean that science has explained religion. As Dennett says in the passage quoted earlier, his goal was to set out what he considers to be the best scientific account at present, but he certainly does not think it has been established as the true explanation. Furthermore, not only has science not explained religion, but even if it had, that would not necessarily explain away belief in God even in the sense of the *partial explaining away* considered in chapter 6. I shall return to this point later. Indeed, if there is a God, science *cannot* provide a complete explanation of religion for the reasons outlined above. Of course, if we knew on other grounds that there was no God, these kinds of scientific explanations might help explain why so many people do believe in the supernatural.

Now back to our question, although now in a slightly modified form. Is there any good reason for thinking that Dennett's account, or something similar, is true even as a partial account of the origins of religion? The first thing to say is that it is extremely speculative. There is discussion of evidence relating to various psychological phenomena that might have had a role to play, but very little evidence as to whether they actually played the role Dennett suggests. Are hypersensitive agent detection devices (HADDs) relevant in the way Dennett claims? Did divination come about as a result of the utility, or perceived utility, of full-access agents in decision-making? What is the evidence one way or the other? A second issue concerns the all-encompassing scope of Dennett's thesis since he claims that it covers all religions which involve belief in the supernatural. Admittedly, the account is quite general and so has plenty of scope for differences between religions to arise, but is it really the case that *all* religion ultimately derives from the overshooting of HADDs in our ancient ancestors that caused them to think of deceased people as still being present in some sense? Again, what is the evidence?

A related point concerns the failure on Dennett's part to engage with the actual historical development of particular religions, especially in the case of a religion such as Christianity that depends on the historicity of particular events. It is clearly not possible to account for the formation of beliefs about the person of Jesus of Nazareth by appealing to a general account of the origins of religion in terms of HADDs and memes rather than asking serious historical questions. Of course, Dennett only claims to have painted a general picture and would no doubt think that his general approach could be applied in such a way as to do justice to historical questions. One suspects, however, that in attempting to account for belief in the resurrection of Jesus, Dennett would have a lot more to say about belief in resurrection as a powerful meme rather than discussing the actual evidence in the context in which the belief actually arose.

The tendency to want to provide an all-encompassing account rather than undertake a serious historical assessment of the evidence in the case of Christianity is also found in Dawkins and Hitchens. It is particularly exemplified by the fact that they, along with Dennett, seem to think that so-called 'cargo cults' are prototypical of how religions develop. These cults sprang up on various islands in the South Pacific in the nineteenth and twentieth centuries. The general pattern is that islanders were amazed at the possessions of technologically advanced immigrants. When they discovered that new 'cargo' arrived by plane, they assumed it must have been of supernatural origin. They then copied what they perceived to be the rituals of the immigrants, such as building landing strips, radio masts out of bamboo, dressing in the same kinds of clothes, and so on, in order to persuade the gods to bring them some cargo. A famous example from the island of Tana in the New Hebrides is based on the messianic figure called John Frum, although he may not have existed as an actual person. Frum is believed to have made various prophecies, including one about his second coming when he would bring plenty of cargo for the islanders. Apparently, the islanders held a celebration every year in which they performed various rituals in anticipation of Frum's return.

What is the relevance of these cults? At the end of his discussion of them, Dennett sarcastically addresses the person who thinks that these cases have no relevance to their religion: 'These cases may be exceptional. Your religion, you may believe, came into existence when its fundamental truth was revealed by God to somebody, who then passed it along to others.'[29] Dawkins goes much further: 'It is fascinating to *guess* that the cult of Christianity *almost certainly* began in very much the same way [as cargo cults], and spread initially at the same high speed.'[30] No need for evidence; all you have to do is *guess* if you want to be *almost certain* about the origins of Christianity! Why bother worrying about the details of the historical Jewish context in which Christianity arose or carrying out research on the historical value of ancient Christian texts when a quick appeal to cargo cults and a guess will do? Astonishingly, Dawkins later claims that he doesn't 'want to make too much of the cargo cults of the South Pacific',[31] which leaves us wondering what conclusions he might have drawn if he had been making too much of them. But he soon returns to form, telling us that 'Christianity and other ancient religions that have spread worldwide presumably began as local cults like that of John Frum.'[32] Guesses and presumptions rather than evidence seem to go a long way.

So despite the fact that I agree with Dennett that there is no good reason to think that religion is out of bounds to science, the writings of the New Atheists give every reason to believe that there is a real danger of veering off into wishful, evidence-free thinking. On the other hand, perhaps we shouldn't rule out scientific accounts of the origins of religion just because the New Atheists get carried away. After all, as a Christian I do not believe that all religious beliefs are equally valid and so I would expect there to be a diversity of explanations for the origins of religions, and perhaps science can shed some light here. I must, however, be careful. Dennett asks the person willing to consider scientific accounts of other religions, 'Wouldn't it be hypocritical to claim that your own religion was somehow out of bounds?'[33] Yes, it would and so that is not what I am suggesting. I have no objection to scientists offering explanations of the origins of Christianity, although I think such explanations will always be at best incomplete. And obviously, just because I believe Christianity is true, that does not mean that *all* beliefs of *all* other religions are false. Clearly, other religions can have insights about human nature, the value of life, creation, and so forth that agree to a greater or lesser extent with

Christian beliefs. Certainly, some of the mechanisms Dennett discusses could in principle tell us something about the origins of the diversity of religious beliefs as well as some of the similarities between religions.

Furthermore, there is a lot of diversity in terms of belief and practice within Christianity and perhaps here too a scientific account can teach us something. One example of this is the the application of marketing principles in some quarters, which can result in church members being treated as consumers of a product and in less attention being given to doctrine and devotion.[34] So I don't expect science either to provide a fully satisfactory account of the origins of non-Christian religions or to fail to say anything useful about Christianity. The picture is likely to be much more complex, with science perhaps shedding light on some aspects of religion. However, I doubt whether such accounts are likely to be of much help in assessing the truth claims of various religions since this is an issue that would need to be considered on the merits of those claims rather than their origins.

Do evolutionary explanations of belief undermine belief?

So far we have been considering the question of whether there is good reason to believe that the Dennett–Dawkins account is true. Given the highly speculative nature of the account, the lack of evidence cited in its favour, its all-encompassing nature and its failure to tackle historical questions relating to specific religious claims, the answer seems to be 'no'. Let's now turn to another question: *could* scientific explanations of belief in God undermine belief in God? That is, could scientific accounts of the origin of belief in God show that belief in God is irrational or unreasonable or less plausible than it might otherwise have been. We have seen that *if there is a God*, scientific accounts of belief in God will be at best incomplete. But, of course, if there is no God then it seems possible that there could be a complete scientific explanation. Could such scientific explanations of belief help us to decide whether it is reasonable to believe in God in the first place?

It is often assumed that scientific explanations of religious belief undermine belief in God and this assumption is not found just at a popular level but also among some researchers working in the area. In order to see whether there is any basis for their viewpoint, we shall focus on some general features of scientific explanations of religion rather than all the details proposed by Dennett and Dawkins. As we have seen, Dennett and Dawkins both place a lot of emphasis on the idea that religion is a *by-product* of evolution. In other words, religion did not provide a survival advantage and so evolution did not select for it. Instead, evolution selected for something else which gave rise to certain mechanisms in our brains that give us a disposition to religious belief.

Could a by-product account undermine belief in God? Consider again Dawkins's analogy with moths that fly into flames because of a misfiring of a mechanism that evolved for another purpose. If the moth provides a fair analogy for all religious belief, then it certainly looks as if belief in God is irrational. But is it a fair analogy? Clearly, the moth's behaviour is self-destructive, but it seems obvious that not all religious belief is similarly self-destructive. Dawkins might argue otherwise, but his arguments leave a lot to be desired, as we shall see in chapter 8. And in any case, it is an independent argument. Even if religious belief is an evolutionary by-product, it does not follow that such belief *must* be self-destructive. The mere fact of being a by-product would tell us nothing about whether it would be helpful or harmful to us. Also, the issue as to whether a belief is helpful or harmful is separate from the question as to whether it is true or false. We must be careful not to let terms such as 'accident', 'by-product' or 'misfiring' mislead us here since they might seem to suggest that the resulting beliefs would be unjustified. All that these terms mean in this context is that the beliefs in question were not selected for by evolution.

As Justin Barrett points out, theists do not justify their beliefs 'on the grounds that such beliefs conferred a selective advantage in our evolutionary history. As no weight rests on this foundation, to remove it does no harm to these beliefs.'[35] Barrett then goes on to point out that many other beliefs, including scientific beliefs, are also evolutionary by-products in the sense that they were not selected for their evolutionary benefits: 'Evolution did not select for calculus, quantum theory, or natural selection. Are these beliefs then suspect for being "accidents" or "byproducts" of evolution? With this line of reasoning, Darwinism would face the ax alongside theism.'[36] No doubt Dawkins and Dennett would be quick to distinguish between scientific theories and religious beliefs, claiming that the former are rational and based on evidence while the latter are not. But in doing so they would be conceding Barrett's point because they would no longer be criticizing religious beliefs on the grounds that they are evolutionary by-products.

As we shall see in chapter 8, Dawkins also provides a by-product account of morality so that it too results from misfirings of mechanisms that evolution programmed into our brains. However, after referring to our 'Good Samaritan urges' as misfirings, Dawkins quickly clarifies this when he says, 'I must rush to add that "misfiring" is intended only in a strictly Darwinian sense. It carries no suggestion of the pejorative.'[37] He also refers to these misfirings as 'Darwinian mistakes', but adds that they are 'blessed, precious mistakes'.[38] We must ask, what is it that leads Dawkins to conclude that belief in God is an evolutionary mistake and so it is irrational, whereas morality is also an evolutionary mistake but it is a 'blessed, precious mistake'? Clearly, terms such as 'misfiring' or 'accident' or 'mistake' are only to be understood in a Darwinian sense. Hence the idea that the resulting beliefs and behaviours are evolutionary by-products tells us nothing about whether they are true or false, good or evil.

Another problem with the idea that a belief is irrational because it is an evolutionary by-product can be seen by considering an opposite line of attack that is sometimes used to challenge religious belief. This is based on an account of the origins of religious beliefs and practices that considers them to have bestowed a selective advantage. Clearly, accounts of this sort, such as the group selection accounts mentioned earlier, stand in direct contrast to by-product accounts. However, it is sometimes suggested that these accounts undermine the rationality of religious beliefs. The suggestion is that religious beliefs were favoured by natural selection because they enhanced fitness and not because they were true. Barrett summarizes the conflicting claims: 'If a belief is an accident of evolution, it cannot be trusted. If it is a legitimate product of evolution, it still cannot be trusted.'[39] It seems to be a case of 'heads we win; tails you lose'. Obviously, this cannot be correct. It seems clear that whether beliefs are evolutionary by-products or legitimate products of evolution tells us nothing *on its own* about the rationality of those beliefs.

At this point it is worth asking whether Darwinism plays a significant role in the explanation proposed by Dennett and Dawkins. A group selection account appeals directly to natural selection to account for religion in terms of its selective advantage, but as Dennett emphasizes, a by-product explanation is the default position and is to be adopted if none of the other evolutionary explanations is satisfactory. One problem with this is that it seems too easy since it is always possible to provide a by-product explanation by saying that evolution may well have given rise to some mechanism that later gave rise to religion. In chapter 6 we saw that Darwinism does not play any significant role in Dawkins's response to design, despite his claims to the contrary. We also saw that even in the context of biology non-Darwinian factors come into play in his rejection of design. And now it seems that Darwinism is not doing as much work as Dennett and Dawkins would have us believe in their explanation of the origins of religion.[40]

Setting this point aside, however, perhaps the by-product approach can be extended so as to challenge the rationality of belief in God. Given Dawkins's analogy of a moth flying into a flame, perhaps his point is that we can see that the cognitive mechanisms involved in theistic belief are unreliable. Consider again the HADD mechanism on which Dennett bases part of his account.

The idea was that HADD provided an evolutionary advantage by enabling detection of predators, but it also misfired in some cases by generating false beliefs about non-existent agents, for example the false belief that a predator was present. Is HADD unreliable? In other words, does HADD typically give rise to false beliefs?

Philosopher Michael Murray points out that we need to take into account the context in which HADD operates.[41] It seems to be reliable in many contexts, enabling us to detect the presence of other intelligent agents, for example other people, when they are in fact present. For example, when we hear a knock on the door we form a belief (usually correctly) in an agent before we have looked to see whether there is anyone there. No doubt there are other contexts in which HADD results in false beliefs, but then we need to ask whether we can determine the conditions under which this is the case. In particular, is HADD unreliable in contexts where it leads to religious beliefs, as Dennett and Dawkins imply? How could this be shown to be the case? There would need to be some independent way of establishing whether such beliefs are true or false. Suppose that someone looks at the order and beauty in the world and HADD triggers the belief that there is an intelligent agent behind it all. Is this an instance of HADD's yielding a true belief or a false one? The theist will say it is true, the atheist will say false, but the point is that the mere fact of HADD's having triggered the belief does not answer the question. It would be begging the question to assume that HADD is unreliable when it gives rise to religious beliefs of this kind.

Perhaps, however, it could be argued that the cognitive mechanisms involved in generating religious beliefs must be unreliable because they generate religious beliefs that are incompatible with each other, as is obvious from the different and inconsistent beliefs found in different religions. In response to this line of reasoning, Murray argues that the kind of cognitive mechanisms identified by scientists would need to be shown to give rise to these inconsistent beliefs *all on their own*. HADD tells us only that there is an agent, but what kind of an agent we take it to be will depend on cultural influences. He says, 'If you conclude that [an agent] is a bear and I conclude that it is the bogeyman, this doesn't show HADD to be unreliable, it just shows that my mom was wrong to teach me that there is a bogeyman.'[42]

It is also very important to note that HADD does not operate in isolation. Barrett draws attention to other cognitive mechanisms, including our ability to consider evidence, which can override HADD. So even if HADD were shown to be unreliable in a wide range of circumstances, this would still leave the question as to whether our overall ability to form beliefs in intelligent agents is unreliable. Once again, it is difficult to see how Dennett and Dawkins could claim that we are unreliable when it comes to belief in God without begging the question.

Let's consider one final reason for thinking that scientific accounts of religious belief could undermine the rationality of those beliefs. This is the objection that belief in the supernatural is unjustified because religious beliefs can be explained without reference to the supernatural. By analogy, if I claim to have seen a UFO, but you show that my belief can be explained by light from street level reflecting off clouds it seems clear that my belief is no longer justified. Or to give a less loaded example, suppose I believe I saw John in town yesterday, but he explains to me that he was out of the country and that his identical twin was in town, then it seems clear that my belief, although understandable, is no longer justified. Could something similar be happening with regard to belief in God? At present, scientific explanations are certainly nowhere near capable of explaining away the need for belief in God, but could they do so in the future? An immediate problem is that in these examples the alternative explanation is clearly incompatible with my explanation. If I just saw light from street level reflected off the clouds, then I did not see a UFO, and, similarly, if it was John's twin I saw, then clearly it was not John. By contrast, no such incompatibility arises with belief in God. It is certainly possible that God has created certain mechanisms in my brain, either directly or via evolutionary processes, whether as by-products or not, that lead to my forming a belief in God. If this is the case, then the scientific explanation of my belief in God would be incomplete, as we saw earlier.

A further difference is that in the UFO and twin examples, what has been explained away was my *only* reason for holding the belief. Once you explain what I saw without reference to a UFO in the first case or John in the second case, I have no further reasons for my beliefs. In the terminology of chapter 6, the new explanations *completely explain away* the evidence for my beliefs. But in the case of belief in God, I can cite plenty of other reasons for my belief. In fact, it is not even clear that a scientific account would explain away *any reasons* for my belief. Or again, in the terminology of chapter 6, it is not clear that such an explanation would even *partially explain away* evidence for my belief in God. The reason for this is that I'm not at all sure that there is anything about the origins of belief in God that I would consider to be a convincing reason for believing in God in the first place. What about religious experience, though; is that not one of the reasons for believing in God? And if so, wouldn't a scientific explanation of religious experience remove this reason for belief in God?

The argument from religious experience considers the testimonies of a great number of people who claim to have had experiences of God as evidence for the existence of God. The philosopher Richard Swinburne gives a detailed account of this argument, including a discussion of various kinds of religious experiences that could occur in a miraculous or non-miraculous way. He also discusses the reasons for considering such experiences in general as evidence for God's existence, the circumstances under which such experiences would not provide evidence, and the significance of religious experience for an overall case for the existence of God.[43] The New Atheists give short shrift to religious experience, with Dawkins and Harris in particular dismissing all such experiences as psychological illusions and drawing our attention to the claims of people in asylums or people like the Yorkshire Ripper.[44] Clearly not all claims about religious experiences need to be accepted at face value or taken as equally valid, just as not all claims about perceptions (e.g. of colour) or morality need be taken as equally valid. Just because some people are colour-blind, this does not cast doubt on the perceptions of colour by other people. Dawkins and Harris seem to assume that all religious experiences must be illusions because they are already convinced that there is no God or supernatural realm that could be the object of such experiences. Of course, if we already *know* that there is no God, then claims about experiences of God are clearly mistaken, but if we are trying to assess the evidence for God's existence such a straightforward approach is not feasible.[45]

My goal here is not to try to use the argument from religious experience as part of my overall case for God's existence, but rather to explore how scientific explanations of religious experience might be relevant to it. If there is some merit to the argument from religious experience, how could it be undermined? One way would be to show that religious experiences were not brought about by God. As we have already seen, the problem with this is that even if a scientific account of typical religious experiences could be given in terms of the functioning of mechanisms in the brain this would not show that God had not brought it about. The best way to show that God was not responsible would be to provide convincing arguments to show that God does not exist, but the attempts of the New Atheists on this front fail miserably.[46] Another approach would be to provide reasons for thinking that the cognitive mechanisms involved in religious experiences are unreliable. If it could be shown that such mechanisms are generally unreliable in the context of other beliefs, that would provide some reason for thinking they were unreliable in the case of religious experiences as well. So it seems that there could be some potential here for undermining the argument from religious experience. However, it should be pointed out that current research does not achieve this, that it is also quite possible that future research would lead to the opposite conclusion, that is, that such mechanisms are in fact generally reliable, and that even if this argument were to be undermined it would not have much impact on other reasons for believing in God.

Overall, there do not seem to be any good reasons for believing that scientific explanations for belief in God undermine or are likely to undermine that belief. Nevertheless, while such explanations do not present much of a threat to belief in God on their own they could potentially provide part of a larger case for atheism. If there were strong arguments against belief in God, it is undoubtedly the case that scientific accounts of religious belief would form part of the overall picture. In the absence of such a convincing case for atheism and persuasive scientific explanations of religious belief, there is not much to concern the theist.

Do evolutionary explanations of atheism undermine atheism?

So far our focus has been on scientific explanations of religious beliefs, but what about atheism itself? Was it selected by evolution because it enhanced fitness or was it an evolutionary by-product, a cognitive misfiring of some sort? Since memes are central to the Dennett–Dawkins account we should also ask whether they would consider atheism to be a meme. In a dialogue with Alister McGrath, Dennett provides a clear answer: 'Is atheism a meme? Of course it's a meme. And so is science. I mean, it's not as if memes are just the irrational, bad ideas.'[47] As discussed earlier, the idea is that memes are units of cultural inheritance that can be copied and mutated with some having greater survival potential than others. Given this understanding there is no reason to think that atheism cannot be considered in memetic terms. Arguably the reason why many people associate memes with irrationality is because of the way Dawkins uses memes in his discussion of religious belief and, in particular, his characterization of it as a mental virus. Certainly Dawkins does not mean that his reason for describing religious belief in this way is *because* it is a meme, although it is understandable how people might get that impression. Wherever he gets his idea that religious belief is irrational, it is clear that it does not follow from the fact that it can be considered as a meme since otherwise he would have to put atheism in the same irrational category. It is an idea that Dawkins *brings to* the discussion, not one that he *gets from* it.

Before moving on from this point about memes, it is worth considering briefly Dennett's claims about what he calls 'memetic engineering'. A key part of Dennett's account is that in the development of organized religion people took deliberate steps to make their religion more successful in an increasingly competitive marketplace of religions. This included, so he claims, making religions more secretive, deceptive and invulnerable to dis-confirmation. The idea is that just as deliberate manipulations can be intro-duced through genetic engineering rather than simply leaving things to run their natural course, so memetic engineering can be carried out to enhance the fitness of memes rather than leaving them to their natural fate. Dennett considers religious leaders who attempt to reform and improve their reli-gion as memetic engineers.[48] It is not clear whether Dennett is claiming that all such changes are intended to make a given religion more market-able or successful in numerical terms, but in many cases he may be right. Doctrine, truth and devotion to God can easily be given a lower priority than numerical success.

If atheism is a meme, who are its memetic engineers? It seems to me that the New Atheists are the atheistic counterparts of the memetic engineers of religion. The reasoning of the New Atheists seems to be something like this. The more traditional atheists get into all the detailed arguments about the existence of God. They study the atheistic arguments of David Hume and make sure they are familiar with the theistic arguments of Thomas Aquinas. And what is more, such atheists encourage other atheists to do likewise because they think all atheists need to know the reasons for their beliefs and to 'understand the enemy'. But this traditional approach hasn't gained many converts and is largely restricted to more academically minded people who want to read Hume and Aquinas anyway. Atheism needs to get its message out to a more popular audience, it needs a better and less academic image, it needs to go on the offensive and to make itself more marketable. How can this be done? One way is to write popular books that avoid all the detail of the traditional atheism since the focus should be on gaining converts, not experts in philosophy. Quick appeals to science, caricatures of belief in God, plenty of talk about the Flying Spaghetti Monster and an emphasis on the evils of religion should all help. As should getting the message on TV, radio and the Internet, and placing atheistic slogans on buses.

If there are such things as memes, it is hard to avoid the conclusion that the New Atheists are very adept memetic engineers. The New Atheists are quick to point out that atheism is not a religion; perhaps they are right, but the irony is that in their capacity as memetic engineers they adopt similar methods to those they criticize in religion. But have they thought through the conse-quences of their new, populist approach? Perhaps it will backfire or, worse still, succeed and give rise to a kind of religion that is more intolerant and dog-matic than any of the religions of the old variety, even though that is not what the New Atheists intend. As Dennett himself says, 'Memetic engineering, like genetic engineering, can spawn monsters if we're not careful.'[49] Alternatively, if the New Atheists aren't as successful as they hope, they could use their skills to help failing religions raise their game.

Let's return to the issue of evolutionary explanations of atheism. As we have seen, there is no reason for the New Atheists to deny that atheism is a meme or that it can be explained in evolutionary terms.[50] However, given that not much follows about the truth of religious belief from evolutionary explanations, it would seem that the same must be true of atheism as well. Whether it is adaptive or maladaptive would not tell us much about its truth or falsity. So it looks as if we have reached a stalemate. Evolutionary explanations, although very interesting, are of little or no use when it comes to the truth or falsity of belief in God.

There is, however, one further angle on this topic that is worth pursuing. One reason for rejecting the idea that the by-product account of religious belief undermines belief in God was that many of our other beliefs are by-products of evolution as well. Moral and scientific beliefs, for example, might fall into this category. And we know that our moral and scientific beliefs, as well as many of our other beliefs, are true, don't we? We have also seen that there is no good reason to think that the cognitive mechanisms that give rise to belief in God are unreliable. Or at least no more reason to think that they are any more unreliable than other cognitive mechanisms. And we know that most of our cognitive mechanisms are reliable, don't we? But can we be confident about the reliability of these mechanisms and the truthfulness of most of our beliefs? Or should we be sceptics who doubt that we form our beliefs in a reliable way that leads to truth in most cases?

Scepticism has a long history, but here I want to focus on the idea that atheism is particularly vulnerable to scepticism. C. S. Lewis offered an argument along these lines in his book *Miracles*. Central to his argument is the idea that human knowledge depends on the validity of human reasoning. He writes:

> no account of the universe can be true unless that account leaves it possible for our thinking to be a real insight. A theory which explained everything else in the whole universe but which made it impossible to believe that our thinking was valid, would be utterly out of court. For that theory would itself have been reached by thinking, and if thinking is not valid that theory would, of course, be itself demolished. It would have destroyed its own credentials.[51]

He claims that atheism or naturalism is more or less in this position: '[Naturalism] discredits our processes of reasoning or at least reduces their credit to such a humble level that it can no longer support Naturalism itself.'[52] Lewis's argument is basically that if our mental processes are to be understood in physical terms, as the New Atheists would maintain, there is no good reason, from an atheistic perspective, to think that such processes would result in true beliefs. He puts it like this: 'If there is nothing in Nature but Nature, therefore, reason must have come into existence by a historical process. And of course, for the Naturalist, this process was not designed to produce a mental behaviour that can find truth.'[53]

The philosopher Alvin Plantinga has defended what is essentially a more philosophically nuanced version of Lewis's argument.[54] Just as Lewis claims that naturalism undermines our reasoning processes to such an extent that it undermines a belief in naturalism itself, so Plantinga contends that naturalism is 'self-defeating'. In particular, it is evolutionary naturalism that is self-defeating. According to evolutionary naturalism, our cognitive mechanisms are the result of a blind, purposeless process and were selected because they enhanced fitness (or were genetically associated with something that did). In either case, he argues, there is no reason to expect such mechanisms to produce true beliefs reliably. Interestingly, Darwin himself expressed a similar opinion in what has become known as *Darwin's doubt*: 'With me the horrid doubt always arises whether the convictions of man's mind, which has been developed from the mind of lower animals, are of any value or at all trustworthy.'[55] Essentially, Plantinga argues that there is no good reason for the naturalist to reject Darwin's doubt. He argues that if this is the case, then the naturalist has reason to doubt all her beliefs, including naturalism itself. Belief in naturalism gives rise to doubt about naturalism; it is self-defeating.[56]

Perhaps the naturalist will respond by saying that cognitive mechanisms that reliably yield true beliefs would have a survival advantage and so evolution, far from being a problem, provides the reason why we *can trust* our cognitive mechanisms. Lewis is not impressed with this line of reasoning and neither is Plantinga. They point out that natural selection is interested in adaptive behaviour, not true belief. But wouldn't true beliefs result in adaptive behaviour and false beliefs in maladaptive behaviour? Surely the ability to form true beliefs would help to find food, avoid predators, and so on. Whether this is so depends on how beliefs are related to behaviour.

Intuitively, we are inclined to think that our beliefs have a very substantial role to play in causing our behaviour. You want to go to town and you believe that the bus will take you there, so you decide to catch the bus and it does indeed take you to town. So it looks as though beliefs cause behaviour, but there is a problem for the naturalist. Plantinga discusses a variety of ways in which belief and behaviour can be linked, but argues that from a naturalist point of view it is more likely that beliefs cannot cause behaviour at all. What are beliefs from a naturalistic perspective? One answer is that they are neural events of some sort in the brain. Suppose, for example, that I have the belief that I see a tiger and then I run to escape. How does this happen? How does the belief influence my behaviour? According to this naturalistic viewpoint, there is a neural event in my brain corresponding to my belief that I see a tiger. Like all neural events, this particular one will have electrochemical properties associated with it. However, it will also have the content of the belief that I see a tiger associated with it. The question is, what causes me to run? Plantinga argues that the electrochemical properties of the event have a causal influence, but that from a naturalistic viewpoint there is no reason to think that the content of the belief has a causal influence. If that is correct, then whether I have true or false beliefs it will have no impact on my behaviour. If this is so, there is no reason to think that adaptive behaviour requires true beliefs.

So evolution doesn't seem to help, but perhaps the naturalist can appeal to experience or other evidence to support the claim that our cognitive mechanisms produce true beliefs. At this point Plantinga, and Lewis too, would point out that such experience and evidence, as well as the conclusions we want to draw from them, are also the product of the very cognitive mechanisms whose reliability is in question. There seems to be no way in which the naturalist can avoid scepticism and, in particular, his belief in naturalism itself can no longer be maintained. It is worth emphasizing that Plantinga's argument is not supposed to show that naturalism is false, but that it is self-defeating and so it is not rationally acceptable. In other words, if naturalism is true, there can be no way of knowing it to be true.

Needless to say, the arguments of Plantinga and Lewis are highly controversial. Various objections to Plantinga's argument have been proposed, including attempts to show that there are other ways to establish the reliability of our cognitive mechanisms or that even if we cannot be confident of their reliability, that does not undermine all our beliefs. And, of course, Plantinga has responses to these objections.[57] It would be impossible to do justice to all of these responses and counter-responses here, but is it possible to draw any sensible conclusions? Or will theists and atheists simply have to agree to disagree on this topic?

It seems to me that Plantinga has made a strong case that makes the atheist's task of accounting for the reliability of our cognitive mechanisms a very difficult one. Nevertheless, I can certainly understand why an atheist would wish to resist the conclusion that atheism is self-defeating and perhaps there are some strategies atheists might adopt that may have some potential. Furthermore, Plantinga's conclusion is a shocking one: can it really be the case that if an atheist accepts Darwin's doubt, it leads to scepticism about all his beliefs? The mere fact that it is a shocking conclusion for the atheist does not mean it is incorrect, but it would certainly be understandable if the atheist wished to explore every possible avenue before accepting it.

However, even if Plantinga's shocking conclusion can be resisted, he also has another argument.[58] Let's suppose, as we do in practice, that our cognitive mechanisms are generally reliable in terms of giving rise to true beliefs. This reliability is what we would expect if there is a God since it is very plausible to believe that he would create us in such a way that our cognitive mechanisms would be reliable. But it is much less to be expected, for the reasons Plantinga proposes, if atheism is true. If so, then the reliability of these mechanisms provides evidence in support of belief in God. This fits in very well with the approach adopted so far in this book. It is not that particular pieces of evidence prove the existence of God or disprove atheism, but that they count in favour of God's existence. The reliability of our cognitive mechanisms is just one more piece of evidence to support belief in God. Arguably, it is quite a strong piece of evidence since it is much more easily accounted for by theism than atheism.

Conclusion

Scientific explanations of religious belief play a central role in the world view of the New Atheists. What are the consequences of such explanations for belief in God? First of all, their explanations are highly speculative and lacking in evidential support, so there is no convincing reason to believe that they provide a true, or even approximately true, explanation of the origins of religious belief. So nothing follows directly from their views. In principle, though, could a scientific explanation undermine belief in God? Merely giving a scientific explanation of the origins of a belief does not tell us anything about the truth or falsity of the belief. Even the evolutionary by-product accounts of Dennett and Dawkins are not very significant in this respect since they acknowledge that other beliefs such as moral beliefs are by-products as well, but they do not consider our moral beliefs to be thereby false or irrational. This does not mean that there are no circumstances under which a well-established scientific explanation of the origins of particular religious beliefs could undermine those beliefs, but in general the theist has nothing to fear from the scientific study of religion.

Given the widespread nature of belief in a supernatural dimension to reality, atheism has a lot of explaining away to do, but the explanations that have been offered are at best only partially up to the task. We have also seen that although evolutionary explanations of the origins of beliefs do not necessarily undermine those beliefs, there are arguments to suggest that the combination of atheism and evolution can actually undermine atheism itself. Even if the atheist does not find such arguments completely persuasive, there is good reason to think that the reliability of our cognitive mechanisms is much more to be expected given theism than atheism. As such, this is an additional piece of evidence that supports belief in God.

Notes

1. Peter Kreeft and Ronald K. Tacelli, *Handbook of Christian Apologetics* (Downers Grove: IVP, 1994), p. 84. Their discussion is in the context of the common-consent argument for the existence of God. I am not attempting to defend this argument, but merely pointing out that the New Atheists have some explaining to do.
2. The main focus will be on Dennett's account, which is much more detailed.
3. *BTS*, p. 69, emphasis in original.
4. Ibid., pp. 56–69.
5. Ibid., p. 75.
6. Ibid., p. 82, emphasis in original.
7. Dennett prefers to call it a *whatsis* centre rather than a god centre since its original target may have had nothing to do with religion (ibid., p. 83).
8. Richard Dawkins, *The Selfish Gene* (Oxford: Oxford University Press, 1976).
9. *BTS*, p. 81.
10. Ibid., 80.
11. Ibid., appendix A and appendix C where he focuses particularly on objections raised by Dan Sperber, 'An Objection to the Memetic Approach to Culture', in R. Aunger (ed.), *Darwinizing Culture* (Oxford: Oxford University Press, 2000), pp. 163–174.
12. *BTS*, p. 90.
13. David Sloan Wilson, *Darwin's Cathedral: Evolution, Religion, and the Nature of Society* (Chicago: University of Chicago Press, 2002).
14. *BTS*, p. 91.
15. For a concise introduction see Justin L. Barrett, 'Cognitive Science of Religion: What Is it and why Is it?', *Religion Compass* 1 (2007), pp. 1–19.
16. Pascal Boyer, *Religion Explained: The Evolutionary Origins of Religious Thought* (New York: Basic, 2001); Scott Atran, *In Gods we Trust: The Evolutionary Landscape of Religion* (Oxford: Oxford University Press, 2002).
17. *BTS*, p. 113, emphasis in original.
18. *TGD*, p. 176.

19. Dennett also speculates that the mechanism that enables hypnotizability might be a plausible candidate for the god centre as discussed earlier in the context of sweet-tooth theories. In other words this mechanism might have evolved and then have been 'over-stimulated' by religion.

20. *BTS*, p. 170.

21. *TGD*, pp. 186–188. See also his essay 'Viruses of the Mind', in *A Devil's Chaplain* (London: Weidenfeld & Nicolson, 2003), pp. 128–145.

22. *BTS*, p. 184.

23. Ibid., p. 192. See also Rodney Stark, *One True God: Historical Consequences of Monotheism* (Princeton: Princeton University Press, 2001).

24. *BTS*, p. 103, emphasis in original.

25. Ibid., p. 25.

26. Ibid., p. 26.

27. Of course, this does not mean that God never acts in a miraculous way that results in scientifically inexplicable physical events.

28. This is not to say that the two cases correspond exactly. The son's communication is mediated solely through the letter, whereas God's communication may involve more than this. However that further component might be spelled out, it is not obvious that it would require any miraculous activity in my brain.

29. *BTS*, pp. 100–101.

30. *TGD*, p. 202, emphasis added.

31. Ibid., p. 206.

32. Ibid.

33. *BTS*, p. 92.

34. Ibid., pp. 225–226.

35. Justin L. Barrett, 'Is the Spell Really Broken? Bio-psychological Explanations of Religion and Theistic Belief', *Theology and Science* 5 (2007), p. 62.

36. Ibid., p. 63.

37. *TGD*, p. 221.

38. Ibid.

39. Barrett, 'Is the Spell Really Broken?', p. 65.

40. In his discussion of the origins of religion, theologian John Haught claims that Dawkins has left 'Darwin almost completely behind' (*God and the New Atheism: A Critical Response to Dawkins, Harris and Hitchens* [Louisville, Ky.: Westminster John Knox, 2008], p. 57).

41. Michael J. Murray, 'Four Arguments that the Cognitive Psychology of Religion Undermines the Justification of Religious Belief', in J. Bulbulia, R. Sosis, E. Harris, R. Genet, C. Genet and K. Wyman (eds.), *The Evolution of Religion: Studies, Theories, and Critiques* (Santa Margarita, Calif.: Collins Foundation, 2008), pp. 394–398.

42. Ibid., p. 395.

43. Richard Swinburne, *The Existence of God*, 2nd ed. (Oxford: Oxford University Press, 2004), pp. 293–327.

44. See *TGD*, pp. 87–92; and *TEF*, pp. 71–72.

45. A common objection to the argument from religious experience arises from the conflicting nature of such claims. Defenders of the argument will claim that there is often a lot of commonality among religious experiences even though the people having them might describe them in different ways that are shaped by their own culture and traditions.

46. In chapter 8 we shall consider the problem of evil, which is the strongest argument against the existence of God.

47. R. Stewart (ed.), *The Future of Atheism* (London: SPCK, 2008), p. 37.

48. *BTS*, p. 196.

49. Ibid., p. 187.

50. Perhaps the New Atheists would claim that being an atheist is simply not being a theist and so if the origins of theism can be explained there is no need also to explain the origins of atheism since it would just be the default position. There would, however, still be some explaining to do. Did (or does) atheism enhance fitness in some way? Or is it maladaptive? If so, why has it survived? Is it a by-product of some kind? Perhaps it is due to a mechanism that inhibits the triggering of HADD. If so, is it a reliable mechanism or does it frequently misfire, resulting in denial of agency even when there is obvious evidence for it?

51. C. S. Lewis, *Miracles: A Preliminary Study* (London: Fontana, 1960), pp. 18–19.

52. Ibid., p. 19.

53. Ibid., p. 22.

54. See Alvin Plantinga, *Warrant and Proper Function* (Oxford: Oxford University Press, 1993), pp. 216–237; *Warranted Christian Belief* (Oxford: Oxford University Press, 2000), pp. 227–240.

55. This is from a letter Darwin sent to William Graham, 3 July 1881.

56. See also Barrett, 'Is the Spell Really Broken?' In discussing the view that the cognitive mechanisms that give rise to belief in God are error-prone, Barrett argues that this gives rise to *collateral damage*, affecting non-theistic beliefs as well. Moreover, he argues that such views can have a *suicidal tendency* since they cast doubt upon the reasons for holding these views in the first place. His arguments are rather different from Plantinga's, however, since Barrett does not claim that this suicidal tendency follows necessarily from naturalism.

57. For detailed objections to Plantinga as well as replies from him see James Beilby (ed.), *Naturalism Defeated? Essays on Plantinga's Evolutionary Argument against Naturalism* (Ithaca, N. Y.: Cornell University Press, 2002).

58. This is the revised form of what he calls his preliminary argument, which is found in *Warranted Christian Belief*, pp. 229–231.

8. RELIGION, MORALITY AND EVIL

Does religion result in increased moral behaviour or encourage violence? Does belief in God provide a basis for morality or undermine it? Does evolution provide a basis for morality or undermine it? Does the existence of evil disprove the existence of God or does belief in God give us a reason for responding to evil? Discussions about the relationship between religion and morality have a long history, but have received renewed attention since the terrible attacks of 9/11. In fact, the New Atheism can be seen in large part as a response to the events of that fateful day. Richard Dawkins asks us to imagine a world with no religion where events like 9/11 do not occur, Sam Harris thinks that we should no longer tolerate religious diversity, Christopher Hitchens calls for a new Enlightenment as a response to the 'confrontation between faith and civilization',[1] while Daniel Dennett advocates science as the proper way to study religion in order to get a better idea about its potential consequences for the future of life on Earth.

Of course, one can certainly understand their concerns. Religion is certainly a major factor in a lot of conflicts around the world. Since this is a prominent theme in the writings of the New Atheists, it will provide the starting point for this chapter. In particular, we shall consider whether their claims about religion and violence do justice to the evidence. We shall then turn our attention to the attempts of the New Atheists to account for morality in purely naturalistic terms before considering how belief in God might be relevant to morality. Finally, we shall consider whether the existence of evil undermines belief in God.

Religion, atheism and evil

In an often quoted passage from the preface of *The God Delusion*, Richard Dawkins sets the scene:

> Imagine, with John Lennon, a world with no religion. Imagine no suicide bombers, no 9/11, no 7/7, no Crusades, no witch-hunts, no Gunpowder Plot, no Indian partition, no Israeli/Palestinian wars, no Serb/Croat/Muslim massacres, no persecution of Jews as 'Christ-killers', no Northern Ireland 'troubles', no 'honour killings' . . .[2]

No one could deny that religion has a lot of blood on its hands. In a chapter entitled 'Religion Kills', Hitchens provides examples from Belfast, Beirut, Bombay, Belgrade, Bethlehem and Baghdad and this is just places starting with 'B'. Many will respond by saying that it is not religion itself that is the problem, but particular kinds of religions or religious extremism. However, as we saw in chapter 2, some of the New Atheists identify faith as the problem. Harris expresses the point clearly: 'the greatest problem confronting civilization is not merely religious extremism: rather, it is the larger set of cultural and intellectual accommodations we have made to faith itself'.[3] This view is far too simplistic since it is based on equating faith with irrational belief, which certainly does not do justice to the concept of faith within Christianity, as we saw in chapter 2. Nevertheless, the New Atheists are correct in their basic contention that religion is involved in a lot of violence. And although, as a Christian, I would like to be able to say that Christianity is different, unfortunately the evidence is against this position.

Having said all of this, we must ask about the role religion plays in the sorts of examples cited. Can all or even most of the blame be laid at the door of religion? In particular, would the world really be largely free of conflict if there were no religion in the way that Dawkins asks us to imagine? The idea that it would seems remarkably naive. Take the Northern Ireland troubles as an example. Was it primarily a religious dispute between Protestants and Catholics as Dawkins, Hitchens and Harris portray it? Having grown up in Northern Ireland during the troubles, this assessment seems to me to be a gross oversimplification. Dawkins's claim that the terms 'Nationalist' and 'Loyalist' are merely euphemisms for 'Catholic' and 'Protestant' respectively betrays an astonishing ignorance of the reality since the former labels reflect

more accurately what it was all about.[4] Even as a child it was obvious that
the people who were murdering others and yet considered themselves to
be Catholics or Protestants could not be considered Christian in any sense.
Furthermore, in cases where religion was used to justify such heinous acts,
it was clear how perverted such religion was from anything that could
meaningfully be called Christianity.

On the other hand, I certainly don't want to give the impression that
religious differences did not have a role to play. They certainly did. Political
divisions more or less coincided with religious divisions and so religion was
a factor in reinforcing differences and stereotypes. It also has to be said that
Protestants who took their faith seriously were often more critical of attacks
on their own community (i.e. on other Protestants) than they were of attacks
on the other community and the same could be said for Catholics. So the
picture is not a simple one. In fairness to Dawkins, he acknowledges the
non-religious dimensions to the troubles later in his book. His assessment
is much more accurate when he states, 'Religion is a *label* of in-group/out-
group enmity and vendetta, not necessarily worse than other labels such as
skin colour, language or preferred football team, but often available when
other labels are not.'[5] However, he does go on to claim that 'without religion
there would be no labels by which to decide whom to oppress and whom to
avenge',[6] and that 'without religion, and religiously segregated education', the
divide simply would not be there'.[7] The first point is clearly incorrect since
there are plenty of other labels, Nationalist and Loyalist for example. On the
second point, it is certainly true that religious differences played a significant
role historically, but does this mean that there would have been no divide if
there had been no religious difference? We can't rerun the tape of history to
find out, but the evidence from elsewhere certainly suggests that humans are
more than capable of finding other factors over which to divide: political
allegiance, skin colour and territory to name but three examples.

Perhaps religion cannot be isolated as the sole or even predominant
cause of conflict in many cases, but could it be argued that the intolerance
of religion exacerbates disputes in a way that secularism would not? Harris
sums up this attitude when he says that 'certainty about the next life is simply
incompatible with tolerance in this one'.[8] After citing a number of conflicts,
including Northern Ireland, where he identifies religion as the 'explicit cause'
he says:

> Give people divergent, irreconcilable, and untestable notions about what happens
> after death, and then oblige them to live together with limited resources. The result
> is just what we see: an unending cycle of murder and cease-fire.[9]

By contrast, Harris believes that secularism is more tolerant. He goes so far as to claim that religious moderation, which ironically he criticizes for being tolerant, is the 'product of *secular* knowledge and scriptural *ignorance*'.[10] Dawkins likewise, having emphasized the evils of religion, asserts 'I do not believe there is an atheist in the world who would bulldoze Mecca – or Chartres, York Minster or Notre Dame.'[11] Here we see examples of what historian John Coffey calls the *myth of secular tolerance*, the idea that 'tolerance comes naturally to the secular person, whilst intolerance comes naturally to the religious believer'.[12] Coffey argues that both aspects of the myth are mistaken, although here the focus will be his claim that secularists have often resorted to political intolerance through the use of state coercion.[13]

Coffey discusses the secular intolerance of the French Revolution, including 'the fierce campaign of de-Christianisation during the Reign of Terror', the Cultural Revolution in China and the Russian Revolution, which he claims:

> Ushered in a period of repression and martyrdom almost unprecedented in its scale. By 1939, not a single monastery or convent remained open out of a thousand or more with which the Soviet period began. The number of churches was reduced to barely a hundred, and thousands of clergy were arrested and liquidated.[14]

This clearly refutes Dawkins's claim about what atheists would or would not be likely to do. As we saw in chapter 2, Harris and Hitchens try to claim that totalitarianism is essentially a kind of religion and so atheists can distance themselves from it. In a not so subtle move, they blame religion for the terrible deeds perpetrated by atheists! Dawkins likewise tries to claim that Stalin's evil actions were not because of his atheism. Harris maintains that Enlightenment thought had no role to play in totalitarian regimes. But these views fail miserably to do justice to the motivation of such regimes. Coffey quotes John Gray, the Professor of European thought at the London School of Economics:

> The role of humanist thought in shaping the past century's worst regimes is easily demonstrable, but it is passed over, or denied, by those who harp on about the crimes of religion. Yet the mass murders of the 20th century were not perpetrated by some latter-day version of the Spanish Inquisition. They were done by atheist regimes in the service of Enlightenment ideas of progress. Stalin and Mao were not believers in original sin. Even Hitler, who despised Enlightenment values of equality and freedom, shared the Enlightenment faith that a new world could be created by human will. Each of these tyrants imagined that the human condition could be transformed through the use of science.[15]

The New Atheists have failed to take into account the role of Enlightenment ideas of progress that were central to such regimes or the fact that these regimes viewed the eradication of traditional religious belief as a necessary requirement for achieving that progress. I should add that I am not claiming that Hitler was an atheist or that Christianity was without blame in its response to Nazism. I am claiming, however, that the motivation behind such regimes was deeply secular in terms of the role of Enlightenment ideals and that they were certainly opposed to anything remotely like orthodox Christianity. As Coffey goes on to say:

> But there may also be distinctive features of the secularist worldview which foster intolerance. The secular myth of progress tends to create a triumphalist and intolerant eschatology. People who believe that the future is secular, and that only backward religions stand in the way of progress, face a strong temptation to give history a helping hand by aggressively clearing those roadblocks from the highway to human emancipation.[16]

In terms of the evidence relating to religion and evil the New Atheists have been quick to point out the evils carried out in the name of religion, but rather slower to point out the evils perpetrated by atheists. They have also been slower to point out the good carried out by religious people such as the role of Christians in the abolition of slavery, prison reform, the construction of hospitals and orphanages, relief organizations, founding of universities, contributions to science, and so on. It isn't that they don't mention any of these things, but when they do they tend to give the impression that the atheists carried out evil despite their atheism and that religious belief is often incidental to the good brought about by religious believers. Given the above discussion, Dawkins's claim that 'individual atheists may do evil things but they don't do evil things in the name of atheism' seems remarkably naive.[17]

The New Atheists have done a poor job in assessing all the relevant evidence and so have reached a biased and incorrect conclusion. However, I am certainly not claiming that the evidence supports the idea that atheism is the root of all evil and that religion is somehow without blame; that would clearly be just as preposterous a conclusion to reach. A more sensible conclusion is drawn by the Christian writer Tim Keller:

> We can only conclude that there is some violent impulse so deeply rooted in the human heart that it expresses itself regardless of what the beliefs of a particular society might be – whether socialist or capitalist, whether religious or irreligious, whether individualistic or hierarchical. Ultimately, then, the fact of violence and

warfare in a society is no necessary refutation of the prevailing beliefs of that
society.[18]

An interesting feature of this debate is that atheists as well as Christians
(and many other religious believers) can look at the evidence and make similar
judgments about the evils carried out in history. They may not agree in every
case, but by and large they agree about what constitutes evil. Furthermore,
both sides try to explain what is going wrong in cases where evil acts are
performed. If someone considers himself to be an atheist and yet murders
people, the New Atheists will tell us that this is incompatible with their brand
of atheism, perhaps because the person holds some beliefs that they consider
to be irrational. Similarly, when someone professes to be a Christian and yet
murders people, Christians will say that such actions are incompatible with
the teachings of Christ who commands us to 'love our enemies'. In response
to the New Atheists, many Christians will claim that the New Atheists have
no basis for distinguishing between right and wrong, while the New Atheists
will say that Christians have no such basis since the Bible does not provide
one. We shall now consider whether either of the two sides has a basis for
morality.

Atheism and morality

Given the importance of evolution in his belief system, it is not surprising
that Dawkins attempts to give an evolutionary explanation of morality. Many
people are inclined to think that without God there would be no such thing
as morality, but in offering an evolutionary explanation Dawkins hopes to
explain away the need for God in the context of morality just as he tried to use
evolution to explain away the need for God in biology.[19] At first glance, this
seems like a daunting task. After all, isn't evolution meant to be all about selfishness and survival of the fittest, while the weak are left to die? Well, things
aren't quite that simple. As Dawkins explains, there are various circumstances
in which altruistic behaviour could evolve. Dawkins discusses four types of
altruism, the simplest of which is kin altruism. Ants, for example, live in colo-
nies where worker ants are sterile and so do not pass on their genes directly,
but they contribute to the fitness of the colony as a whole.

Kin altruism, and the other kinds of altruism, are limited forms of altruism since they are restricted in scope. Dawkins argues that evolution could
have resulted in our ancestors being good to their own in-group, that is, their
own kin or those who could reciprocate such kindness. But what about the

goodness that humans often show to those who are not part of their in-group? Could evolution account for that? At this point, Dawkins claims that natural selection favours rules of thumb. An example of such a rule in a bird's brain would be to look after squawking things in its nest. Usually these would be its own offspring, but the rule would misfire if another baby bird got into the nest. That is, it would look after this baby bird even though it was not one of its kin and could not reciprocate such kindness. Dawkins then asks, 'Could it be that our Good Samaritan urges are misfirings, analogous to the misfiring of a reed warbler's parental instincts when it works itself to the bone for a young cuckoo?'[20] Dawkins refers to these misfirings as by-products of evolution or Darwinian mistakes, but, as we saw in chapter 7, he emphasizes that they are 'blessed, precious mistakes'.[21]

Let's assume all of this is biologically feasible. Does it explain morality? First of all, it is not clear how much evolution is explaining at all. What evolution accounts for is the limited kind of altruism that applies to the in-group but not the out-group. Dawkins rightly thinks that this limited altruism is not enough for morality, but *the problem is that it is the misfirings, not evolutionary processes such as natural selection, that account for altruism to the out-group*. Hence, if Dawkins's account works at all, something *accidental* to evolution is doing the explaining. But this is the least of Dawkins's problems. How do we decide what are 'blessed, precious mistakes' and what, by contrast, would be cursed, worthless mistakes? Dawkins points out that evolution can also account for xenophobic urges, but he presumably does not think that xenophobia is either blessed or precious. It is surely obvious that evolution does not make one good and the other bad. But then how does Dawkins decide which is which? It is certainly not on the basis of evolutionary theory.[22]

Just to emphasize this point, let's suppose that we did try to form our moral beliefs on the basis of what was good from the point of view of natural selection. What would we do if we were persuaded by Dawkins's account of altruistic behaviour to those outside our group? Since this is a misfiring from the point of view of natural selection, we should surely confine kindness to those inside our group. But this clearly makes no sense since the whole point was to try to account for kindness to those outside our group, which we all recognized to be good in the first place. Of course, Dawkins would agree that just because something has evolved does not make it right or wrong. In fact, he clearly thinks that in moral terms we have risen above our evolutionary past. On his website he writes:

> as a scientist I am a passionate Darwinian. But as a citizen and a human being, I want
> to construct a society which is about as un-Darwinian as we can make it. I approve of

looking after the poor (very un-Darwinian). I approve of universal medical care (very un-Darwinian).[23]

This presents two questions. Since this is his view, how has he managed to convince himself that he has given an evolutionary explanation of morality? Presumably, it is because he thinks evolution can explain the origin of certain types of moral *behaviour*. The problem is that evolution can at best account for the sorts of behaviour to which Dawkins refers, such as kindness to those outside our group, and the biological urges, instincts and tendencies behind the behaviour, but it cannot explain why such behaviour is good. In other words, it fails to explain what is moral about such behaviour and so leaves morality completely unexplained. A second question is, where then does he get his morality from? In chapter 7 of *The God Delusion* he refers to the *moral Zeitgeist* (spirit of the times) but this just seems like a term to conceal the fact that he has no answer to the question.

Harris identifies the problem with trying to find a basis for morality in biology:

> Fields like game theory and evolutionary biology, for instance, have some plausible stories to tell about the roots of what is generally called 'altruistic behavior' in the scientific literature, but we should not make too much of these stories. . . .
>
> To say that something is 'natural', or that it has conferred an adaptive advantage upon our species, is not to say that it is 'good'.[24]

The philosopher George Mavrodes makes a similar point by acknowledging that while an evolutionary explanation of moral feelings and beliefs can be given, it cannot account for actual moral obligations. He writes:

> I think that it is plausible (though I am not sure that it is correct) to suppose that everyone's having feelings of moral obligation might have survival value for a species such as Man, given of course that these feelings were attached to patterns of action that contributed to such survival . . . It is quite possible, it seems to me, for one to feel (or to believe) that he has a certain obligation without actually having it, and also vice versa. Now, beliefs and feelings will presumably have some effect upon actions, and this effect may possibly contribute to the survival of the species. But, so far as I can see, the addition of actual moral obligations to these moral beliefs and feelings will make no further contribution to action . . .[25]

And so he argues that moral obligations will 'not contribute to the survival of the species'.[26] He concludes that such an evolutionary approach 'cannot serve to explain the existence of moral obligations, unless one rejects [his] distinction and equates the obligations with the feelings'.

Take murder as an example. Suppose that it can be shown that there is a survival advantage to people believing (and feeling) that they are under an obligation not to murder. Although evolution accounts for the *belief* that we have an obligation in this case, it does not tell us whether we *actually* have such an obligation. Whether there really is an obligation is irrelevant from an evolutionary point of view since it is only our belief (and feeling) that influence our behaviour. So, an evolutionary approach fails to account for the existence of moral obligations.

Harris adopts a very different approach by attempting to base morality in happiness and suffering. He writes, 'To treat others ethically is to act out of concern for their happiness and suffering'.[27] He makes it clear that by happiness he does not mean pleasure, but a 'form of well-being that supersedes all others, indeed, that transcends the vagaries of experience itself'.[28] In his more recent book *The Moral Landscape* he explains his views on morality in much greater detail. There are two key components to his thesis. The first is the point already noted that morality is based on the notion of well-being. He claims that 'questions about values – about meaning, morality and life's larger purpose – are really questions about the well-being of conscious creatures'.[29] The second component is that well-being can be understood scientifically and so 'there *must* be a science of morality, whether or not we ever succeed in developing it: because the well-being of conscious creatures depends upon how the universe is, altogether'.[30] By the term *moral landscape* he refers to 'a space of real or potential outcomes whose peaks correspond to the heights of potential well-being and whose valleys represent the deepest possible suffering'.[31] His idea is that science will tell us more and more about this landscape, that is, about what courses of action are likely to result in peaks or valleys. In effect, science will tell us how to be moral.

It is extremely important to note that Harris is a moral realist, that is, 'in ethics, as in physics, there are truths waiting to be *discovered* – and thus we can be right or wrong in our beliefs about them'.[32] Another way of putting this is to say that moral truths are objectively true in the sense that their truth does not depend on whether anyone believes them to be true. This means that moral truth does not result from humans deciding what is true and it is not due to human consensus; even if consensus is important in helping to determine what is true, it does not make it true. As Harris puts it, 'It is quite conceivable that everyone might agree and yet be wrong.'[33] Obviously, I have no quibble with Harris on his claim that morality is objective in nature. Stalin and Hitler could not morally justify their ethics by appealing to a consensus.

As Harris is well aware, many of his fellow-atheists believe that his project of providing an objective account of morality based on science is doomed to failure. Indeed, part of his argument is with secular liberals who 'tend to imagine that no objective answers to moral questions exist'.[34] What are we to make of his account? Undoubtedly, science is relevant when it comes to addressing issues of well-being. For example, science can certainly inform us about what courses of action will tend to make us healthier and, while health is not all there is to well-being, it is certainly part of it. Furthermore, as science progresses we might expect it to provide more knowledge about how well-being can be achieved. Whether science is the *only* way to acquire such knowledge is more controversial. Theists will typically dispute Harris's claim that 'human well-being entirely depends on events in the world and on states of the human brain',[35] believing that there is a further dimension to well-being. But this is not an objection to Harris's attempt to develop an *atheistic* account of morality. Atheists might also object to the idea that science is the only source of knowledge about how to achieve well-being, but since Harris construes science very broadly to include all rational thought about empirical reality we shall not pursue this objection further.[36]

What about the notion of well-being itself? Various questions arise that might pose a problem for Harris. For example, how is well-being to be defined? He acknowledges that there is no precise definition, but notes that the same is true of the concept of health and that, like health, we can distinguish between clear cases where well-being exists and where it does not. Unless Harris clarifies what is included and what is excluded by 'well-being' he has not provided an account of any consequence. We can see this by asking the questions Harris leaves unanswered. Should I act to maximize well-being in my society even at the expense of my children's well-being? Or should I be prepared, in principle, to sacrifice my children's lives to maximize well-being? Does the individual human life have *intrinsic* value even when that human does not have well-being? Can society take away the well-being of minorities to promote the greater well-being of the majority? Because he does not answer these questions, Harris does not give an illuminating or useful account of morality. *Which is just to say, Harris has failed to explain morality.* He just seems to hold out the vague hope that, maybe, atheists can provide such an account in principle, if not in practice.

In the light of Harris's defence of torture,[37] we should note that Harris has less room for objective human rights than we might have expected. In fact, Harris does not believe that all human lives are equally valuable. He thinks that some people's lives have more value than his own because their deaths would result in greater suffering. Having said that, he nevertheless thinks that 'it also seems quite rational for us to collectively act *as though* all human lives were equally valuable'.[38] These points seem highly problematic, but it is not clear that they are central to his overall argument. An ironic consequence of his position seems to be that if belief in God could be shown to enhance well-being, then belief in God would seem to be a moral good irrespective of whether there is good evidence for God's existence! The irony is further enhanced by the fact that there is evidence that religious belief is beneficial to health, as Dennett points out, and some evidence that it might be beneficial in other ways too.[39]

Perhaps Harris can provide adequate answers to some of these questions, but the main problem with Harris's approach to morality is that it cannot account for moral obligations. Why am I *obligated* to put the well-being of other human beings ahead of my own? Granted, most humans would *prefer* a society with more happiness and health than suffering. But how do I get from that fact to a rule that insists that I set my own well-being aside when it conflicts with the well-being of others? Strangely, Harris does not see the failure to account for moral obligations as a problem at all. In fact, he sees no place for moral obligations. Describing the objection he writes, 'After all, in a world of physics and chemistry, how could things like moral obligations or values really exist? How could it be objectively true, for instance, that we *ought* to be kind to children?'[40] Ironically, Harris captures here precisely the problem with his account of morality since the notion of moral obligation is at the heart of the whole moral enterprise. Instead of answering the question, he rejects this notion of 'ought' since he finds it needlessly confusing, but it is far from clear what the problem with it is supposed to be.[41] He suggests an alternative way to think about the meaning of 'ought': 'to say that we *ought* to treat children with kindness seems identical to saying that everyone will tend to be better off if we do'.[42] The problem with this alternative definition is that it completely fails to capture exactly what 'ought' is intended to convey, that is, the obligatory nature of the action.

In *River out of Eden* Richard Dawkins states:

> In a universe of blind physical forces and genetic replication, some people are going to get hurt, other people are going to get lucky, and you won't find any rhyme or reason in it, or any justice. The universe that we observe has precisely the properties we should expect if there is, at bottom, no design, no purpose, no evil and no good, nothing but blind, pitiless indifference.[43]

If Dawkins is right, he shows why Harris's account of morality must fail, because the universe envisaged by the New Atheists cannot explain the moral value of human life. If there is no God and if we are the accidental result of an unplanned evolutionary process, what could possibly make it a fact that the well-being of the human race is morally significant? In the long run we are all dead. We shall pass into oblivion, and no one will regret or even note our passing. So why should we place any significance on the well-being of our species? We shall, of course, value practices that promote our own well being. We can play the morality 'game' as it suits our needs. But in Dawkins's universe I could rationally prefer a world with more suffering than well-being, if that world suits my own selfish goals.

Two points need to be made by way of clarification. First, I am not objecting to the existence of objective moral truths. I strongly endorse it, but the problem is that it is extremely difficult to see how Harris could explain these truths given his atheism. By contrast, if there is a God, there would be a moral dimension to reality that would provide a foundation for moral truths in a similar way to that in which the physical universe grounds truths in physics. Secondly, I do not wish to deny that there is a link between morality and well-being. My claim is rather that Harris has not provided any reason for believing that the enhancement of well-being should be equated with moral goodness and that this failure is due to his atheistic starting point. By contrast, I have good reason for believing that such a link exists, since even though I would not wish to *define* moral goodness in terms of well-being,[44] it is reasonable to believe that God would ensure that such a link does exist and so that the moral enterprise makes sense. More generally, I am neither claiming that atheists typically hold immoral beliefs nor that their behaviour is less moral than theists. For this reason, the efforts of the New Atheists to provide empirical evidence that atheists are no less moral (and perhaps more moral) than theists miss the point completely. My claim is that it is very difficult for atheists to provide a foundation for morality and so, ultimately, to provide a rational basis for why they *do* act morally.

There are, of course, other approaches that atheists might adopt to account for morality, so the argument presented above is certainly not exhaustive. Nevertheless, by examining the accounts of Dawkins and Harris, two general difficulties for an atheistic account of morality emerge. First, what is it that makes anything morally good or bad if atheism is true? Secondly, even if there are objective moral facts, that is, facts about what is morally good and bad, which are not just matters of human consensus, why would we have moral obligations? One approach would be to deny that there are objective moral facts and obligations, but this raises problems of its own and so is rejected by many atheists.[45]

God and morality

I have argued that providing a basis for morality presents problems for atheism, but how exactly is God supposed to help? The New Atheists are confident that there are conclusive reasons for thinking that God provides no help whatsoever and so, however morality is to be understood, there is no need to bring God into the picture. There are at least four main objections raised against the idea that God is relevant to morality, but as we shall see all four fail to come to terms with the fundamental issue. There are a number of ways in which God is relevant to morality and some of these will be explored in chapter 9, but in terms of whether morality points to the existence of God, the central issue is whether God provides a foundation for morality in a way that atheism cannot.

One objection is that there is no empirical evidence to suggest that religious believers are more moral than the non-religious. Dennett points out, 'The prison population in the United States shows Catholics, Protestants, Jews, Muslims, and others – including those with no religious affiliation – represented about as they are in the general population.'[46] In fact, he cites a study that supports the idea that atheists have the lowest divorce rate in the United States, and born-again Christians the highest. As we saw earlier, the New Atheists also have a point when they draw attention to a lot of evil that has been religiously motivated even though, as we also saw, they do not weigh up the evidence very carefully. Let's suppose that the New Atheists are right in claiming that in general religious believers do not behave more morally than non-believers. Does this mean that God is unnecessary for morality? Not at all. In claiming that atheism fails to provide a basis for morality, I am certainly not claiming that atheists are immoral or that they are morally inferior to Christians. After all, Christians believe that all humans are made in God's image and have a sense of right and wrong. As far as our current discussion is concerned, the central issue is not whether belief in God leads to better *behaviour*,[47] but whether God provides a foundation for morality.

A second objection is that there is no significant difference between atheists and believers in moral judgments made in the face of various moral dilemmas. Dawkins describes work by biologist Marc Hauser who posed hypothetical moral dilemmas to a range of subjects and found that their responses were largely independent of religious belief. Dawkins assumes that if our morality comes from religion, then religious believers and atheists should differ in their moral judgments. From the fact that there is no difference, he concludes that 'we do not need God in order to be good – or evil'.[48] Furthermore, he claims that it confirms the evolutionary roots of morality. His contention is that if our moral sense is rooted in our evolutionary past, we would expect to find universal attitudes to morality that are independent of geographical, cultural and religious differences, just as the research demonstrates.

There is, however, a serious problem with the conclusions Dawkins reaches. As noted above, Christians believe all humans are made in God's image and that our moral sense comes from God, and so would expect the kind of common attitudes Hauser found. More fundamentally, however, Dawkins is misconstruing the central issue about how God might be relevant to morality. It is not that we 'need God in order to be good – or evil', but that we need God for good and evil to exist in the first place. As we saw earlier, evolution can at best account for the origin of moral behaviour, altruism for example, but cannot determine whether such behaviour is morally good.

There is also an irony in the use to which Dawkins puts Hauser's work. The idea that God can provide a basis for morality makes sense only if morality is objective and is not merely something produced by humans. It is often claimed that if morality is objective in this sense and has a basis in God, then we would *expect* to find a common core to morality across cultures, but that in fact no such commonality exists. As we have seen, Hauser's work and Dawkins's argument based upon it go some way to *undermining this objection* to God as a foundation of morality.[49]

A third objection is based on a particular view about how God is relevant to morality. Dennett characterizes the viewpoint as follows:

Religion plays its most important role in supporting morality, many think, by giving people an unbeatable reason to do good: the promise of an infinite reward in heaven, and (depending on tastes) the threat of an infinite punishment in hell if they don't.[50]

He goes on to describe this as 'a demeaning view of human nature'. Dawkins also criticizes this role for God in morality, claiming that to do good only 'to gain God's approval and reward, or to avoid his disapproval and punishment' is not morality.[51] Alternatively, if you would do good anyway, then God is unnecessary for doing good. But again there are problems with this objection. As Dennett realizes, 'reward in heaven is not the only – and certainly not the best – inspirational theme in religious doctrine'.[52] He notes that a better motivation is that God is 'someone to emulate rather than fear'.[53] Once again, however, the main problem is that this objection misconstrues the central issue about God's relevance to morality. The point is not that God is necessary as a motivation for us to be good, but that without God there is no basis for any action to be good.

A final objection is that we don't get morality from the Bible. Dennett claims that 'the idea that religious authority grounds our moral judgments is useless in genuine ecumenical exploration'.[54] His point seems to be that if someone believes that a particular moral conviction is right just because it says so in the Bible and is not prepared to give any other reason for it, then such a person has nothing useful to say in persuading others. But just because appeals to the Bible do not help settle moral disagreements between believers and unbelievers, this would be a very weak reason indeed for rejecting the idea that 'religion is the foundation for morality'.[55] Dawkins, Harris and Hitchens take a somewhat different tack. Dawkins claims that basing morality on the Bible would 'encourage a system of morals which any civilized modern person, whether religious or not, would find – I can put it no more gently – obnoxious'.[56] It is very important to distinguish two points the New Atheists are trying to make. One is that the Bible cannot be divine revelation, for surely God would not do some of the things attributed to him or issue the sorts of commands found in the Bible and particularly in the Old Testament. On this matter, the New Atheists have a point that presents a challenge for Christianity and so we shall return to it in the next chapter. The second point is that given these difficulties with the Bible, it cannot provide a foundation for morality. Dawkins states that his purpose is to 'demonstrate that we (and that includes most religious people) as a matter of fact *don't* get our morals from scripture'.[57] Their idea is that wherever morality comes from it doesn't come from religion and so God cannot be the foundation of morality.

As with the previous objections to God's providing a foundation to morality, this one misses the point. Just because we cannot simply take every command found in the Bible and use this as the basis for morality, it does not follow that God is irrelevant to morality. Even if the New Atheists were correct (and they are not) that the Bible is so compromised morally that it has nothing of relevance to say to us from a moral point of view, it still would not follow that God is irrelevant to morality. The point is not that we can find out what is right and wrong only by reading the Bible, which is not a Christian viewpoint in any case, but that without God there is no basis for any action to be right or wrong.

At one point Dawkins seems to realize what the central issue is. He considers an imaginary apologist who argues as follows: 'If you don't believe in God, you don't believe in any absolute standards of morality . . . Only religion can ultimately provide your standards of good and evil.'[58] How does Dawkins respond to his imaginary apologist? First, he appeals to the philosopher Immanuel Kant. This presents a serious problem for an atheist, however, since as philosopher Paul Copan points out, 'Kant actually posits God, freedom, and immortality in order to make sense of morality; his is not a secular ethical system but one that requires God's existence.'[59] Dawkins seems to think that he can adopt the core ideas of Kant without Kant's belief in God, but consider the Kantian idea that we should never treat another human merely as a means to an end. Is Dawkins entitled to adopt an approach to morality that places so much value on humans? We can agree that humans are to be valued in this way, but why are they to be so valued? If, like Kant, we believe in God, then this makes sense, but if we are the accidental results of a purposeless process, as Dawkins believes, it is very difficult to see where this value comes from, as we discussed earlier. It seems clear that such a process could not create objective value. The New Atheists maintain that it is just obvious that humans are to be valued and, of course, they are right. But that is just the problem: humans are of value, but atheism lacks the resources to account for such value.

Anyway, it turns out that Dawkins is not overly impressed with Kant so he needs a different response, but at this point Dawkins manages to misunderstand his imaginary apologist! The idea was that only God could provide standards of right and wrong. By denying what he calls absolutism, which he takes to be the view that there are absolutes of right and wrong that make no reference to the consequences of actions, he thinks he has an adequate response. Suppose Dawkins is right that we can determine which actions are right and wrong by taking into account their consequences. If this approach is to work, some consequences such as Mill's 'greatest happiness for the greatest number' must be of greater value than other consequences. Once again, we must ask where such value comes from in an atheistic universe. Dawkins wants to focus on how we decide what is right and wrong, whereas the real problem for atheism is to account for how there can be any such thing as right and wrong in the first place.

Of course, one approach would be to reject the idea that there is any such thing as objective right and wrong, but this leads to other problems, as we saw earlier. One example of this relates to Dawkins's discussion about what he calls the moral Zeitgeist. His idea is that what we consider to be moral is constantly changing, but he clearly thinks that this change is progressive so that moral standards today are generally higher than they were in the past. Whatever one thinks of this idea, it seems to involve a clear commitment to an objective morality, for otherwise today's standards would not be *higher* but just *different* from those in the past. Similarly, it is difficult to see how the moral indignation of the New Atheists in their accounts of the evils of religion makes sense unless they accept an objective standard of right and wrong.

We have seen that the main objections of the New Atheists to the idea that God provides a foundation for morality all fail. Their objections are based on claims that believers are no more moral than non-believers, believers and non-believers making similar moral judgments, the role of religious rewards and punishments in morality, and the difficulties of blindly using the Bible to acquire moral rules. The problem is not so much that their claims are mistaken, but that they fail to address the central issue. In other words, they fail to address why it is that morality makes sense if there is a God, but does not make sense in the godless universe described by the New Atheists. If we are the result of an unguided and purposeless process in a universe where everything is to be understood in scientific and ultimately physical terms, how could such a process result in certain actions being right and others being wrong? Of course, it is conceivable that such a process has made us *think* that certain actions are right and others wrong, but that is a different matter from their actually *being* right and wrong. An objective notion of value with a basis in reality independent of whether humans believe such value to exist seems to have no place in such a universe. By contrast, if there is a God there is a basis in reality for certain actions being right and others wrong. This basis is to be found in the character of God. Why, for example, is murder wrong? Theists and atheists can agree that human life is valuable, but why is this the case? Because humans are made in the image of God and so are of value. Why do moral values such as love and justice exist? Because they are found in the character of God.[60]

The problem of evil

So far in this chapter we have considered the New Atheists' claim that belief in God leads to evil, their attempt to account for morality in purely natural terms and several objections they raise against the idea that God can provide a foundation for morality. In each case there are serious problems with their views. Indeed, we have seen that in terms of a foundation for morality just the opposite is true: God can provide a foundation, whereas moral values seem out of place in the purely physical universe of the New Atheists. There is, however, another way in which morality might be relevant to belief in God. It is the age-old question of the problem of evil: how can an all-powerful and perfectly good God permit evil and suffering to exist in the world?

Traditionally, this has been by far the most important objection to belief in God and so it is surprising that it is discussed so little by the New Atheists. Hitchens seems to think it is a good objection to belief in God, but devotes only a couple of paragraphs to it.[61] Dawkins mentions it, but doesn't take it very seriously. His reason is that the problem of evil is only an objection to a *good* God and so to avoid it he claims that one can 'postulate a nasty god'.[62] This is a rather odd response from Dawkins since his main target is not abstract conceptions of God, but revealed religions that do not generally express faith in a 'nasty god'. He also notes that some believers respond to evil and suffering as 'the price that has to be paid for free will in an orderly, lawful cosmos'.[63] He does, however, draw attention to the issue of cruelty and suffering in the history of life on Earth. We shall return to this point later.

Harris is not so cautious. He claims that the problem of evil is insurmountable.[64] In his *Letter to a Christian Nation*, he says, 'An atheist is a person who believes that the murder of a single little girl – even once in a million years – casts doubt upon the idea of a benevolent God.'[65] He then discusses the tragic loss of life in New Orleans due to Hurricane Katrina. He presents the challenge as follows:

> It is safe to say that almost every person living in New Orleans at the moment Hurricane Katrina struck shared your belief in an omnipotent, omniscient, and compassionate God. But what was God doing while Katrina laid waste to their city?[66]

The idea is that if God is omnipotent he would have been able to prevent the tragedy, and if he is compassionate he would have wanted to; but since he did not prevent it, then such a God must not exist.

There are two problems that the believer faces in giving a response. The first and most obvious one is that of showing that evil and suffering do not rule out belief in God. The other problem is that it seems somehow inappropriate even to try to answer the first problem. No matter what answer the believer gives, it is hardly likely to provide comfort to someone who has experienced terrible evil. And if the believer can explain how God can permit evil, would this not amount to saying that evil was not so bad after all? So before we go any further it is worth distinguishing between what is sometimes referred to as the intellectual problem of evil and the emotional problem of evil. A response to the intellectual problem tries to show that the existence of evil is compatible with God's existence, while a response to the emotional problem tries to provide comfort in the face of evil. Clearly, a response to the former might be inadequate as a response to the latter. It is also important to emphasize that the goal is not to explain away evil; no response should undermine the basic notion that evil exists, which provides the starting point for the problem of evil.

Does the existence of evil disprove the existence of an omnipotent and all-loving God? Perhaps surprisingly, it turns out that this age-old question has been answered and the answer (perhaps equally surprisingly) is 'no'. By updating what is called the *free will defence* to the problem of evil, philosopher Alvin

Plantinga has shown that the existence of evil does not disprove the existence of God.[67] He demonstrates that various arguments to disprove God's existence from evil simply do not work and then goes on to show that no such argument will work because God's existence is compatible with the existence of evil. The basic idea is as follows:

> God can create free creatures, but He can't *cause* or *determine* them to do only what is right. For if He does so, then they aren't significantly free after all; they do not do what is right *freely*. To create creatures capable of *moral good*, therefore, He must create creatures capable of moral evil; and He can't give these creatures the freedom to perform evil and at the same time prevent them from doing so.[68]

This, however, is not a limitation on God's omnipotence since God is not required to do things that are logically impossible, like make a round square or make a person who is a married bachelor or someone who is simultaneously an atheist and a believer in God. Nor is it a limitation on God's goodness since God in no way approves of his free creatures doing what is wrong, but the only way he could have prevented them from doing wrong would have been denying their freedom and hence their possibility of freely doing good.[69]

Most philosophers, whether theist or atheist, who have studied these arguments have concluded that the existence of evil does not *logically* disprove the existence of God.[70] But that is not the end of the matter. Perhaps the existence of evil does not completely rule out the existence of God, but doesn't the sheer amount of evil in the world count as evidence against God? And perhaps the free will approach is capable of accounting for at least some of the evil perpetrated by humans, but what about all the suffering due to natural disasters, sometimes called natural evil, such as Hurricane Katrina?

In attempting to respond to these kinds of questions, theists typically try to appeal to *greater goods*, which would outweigh, and so be reasons for God to permit, certain types of evil and suffering. We have already seen that free will might be one such greater good. A common reason given for the existence of natural evil is that it is an inevitable consequence of living in a world like ours; without plate tectonics and a climate system like that on Earth we would not be here, but these features of our planet also give rise to earthquakes and hurricanes. Our existence is seen as a greater good that outweighs natural evils without which we wouldn't exist. But there are problems with this approach since we might wonder whether such natural evils are really necessary and whether God could not have brought us into existence in some other way. Furthermore, it would still leave the question of why God permits earthquakes to take so many human lives; even if they are in some sense necessary for our existence, could God not intervene to prevent loss of life?

A more promising response comes into focus if we consider what kind of world we would live in if God intervened all the time to prevent suffering. Suppose that any time I did something that would cause me pain, such as putting my hand into a hot fire, God prevented me from feeling any pain and prevented any damage to my hand from occurring. And let's suppose that the same goes for everyone in any circumstances where they could come to harm. In such a world the consequences of our actions would be seriously curtailed as would our choices concerning whether to do good or evil since we could not inflict harm on anyone else. This would also apply if God did not need to intervene but had created us in such away that we could come to no harm and feel no pain. The philosopher Richard Swinburne argues along these lines, claiming that many natural evils are necessary if humans are 'to have the knowledge of how to bring about evil or prevent its occurrence, knowledge that they must have if they are to have a genuine choice between bringing about evil and bringing about good'.[71] So the greater good in this case is the acquiring of knowledge required for making a choice between good and evil.

Another greater good that can account for some evil and suffering is the existence of virtues such as courage, compassion, forgiveness and self-sacrifice, which could not exist in a world with no evil. This point also raises a question about what exactly is valuable in our lives. Most people realize that there is more to life than maximizing pleasure and minimizing pain. Indeed, we are inclined to think that people who think otherwise are not really living fulfilled lives since we know that most achievements of any significance require a great deal of perseverance and self-sacrifice. This point is particularly important from a Christian point of view, as expressed by philosophers J. P. Moreland and William Lane Craig:

> One reason that the problem of evil seems so intractable is that people tend naturally to assume that if God exists, then his purpose for human life is happiness in this world. . . . But on the Christian view this is false. . . . the goal of human life is not happiness per se, but the knowledge of God – which in the end will bring true and everlasting fulfillment. Many evils occur in life that may be utterly pointless with respect to the goal of human happiness; but they may not be pointless with respect to producing a deeper knowledge of God.[72]

The above points provide some greater goods that might provide reasons why God permits some of the evil and suffering in the world. Even so, there is much evil and suffering for which no greater good can be easily identified, evil that seems pointless. Perhaps in some cases evils that seem pointless later turn out to result in a greater good, but often we have no evidence that this is the case. If there really is pointless evil and suffering, this would seem to count against belief in God, but do pointless evil and suffering exist? Some atheists claim that there are pointless evils on the grounds that certain evils *seem* to be pointless. They claim that because there does not *seem* to be any reason for God to permit certain evils it is likely that there are *no* such reasons. But whether this is right depends on whether we would be in a position to know if God had reasons for permitting apparently pointless evils.

To draw on an illustration from an early chapter, if you look in my back garden you are in a good position to determine whether my pet elephant is in it, but not whether my pet ant is in it. Would we expect God's reasons for permitting apparently pointless evils to be obvious, like the elephant, or not at all obvious, like the ant? Since God, if he exists, would have much greater knowledge than us, the ant analogy seems more appropriate. God would know about potential repercussions of an evil act, perhaps in the distant future, of which we would have no knowledge.[73] In this context Christian belief in an afterlife would also be relevant since some evils that appear pointless when considered only in terms of this life might seem very different from an eternal perspective. Given our lack of knowledge of what such an afterlife would be like, this response is of limited value in trying to identify the reasons God has for permitting certain kinds of suffering, but it should make us hesitant about declaring that there can be no such reasons. Of course, the atheist will deny that there is an afterlife, but that is not the issue. The issue is whether Christians, believing what they do, should accept the atheist's claim that God could have no reason for permitting certain evils.

So far we have been considering evil and suffering in the context of human beings, but what about the suffering of animals? This raises additional problems since some of the responses that might be possible in the former case are not feasible in the latter. For example, the free will response is controversial enough when applied to humans without also trying to apply it to animals. Similarly, from a Christian point of view we cannot point to greater goods such as the knowledge of God, and few Christian theologians would be willing to appeal to an afterlife for animals.[74] Furthermore, the New Atheists argue that existence of suffering and death throughout the history of life is exactly what we would expect if life is the result of an unguided evolutionary process. Unless the theist can provide an adequate response, this suggests that such suffering and death counts as evidence against theism.[75]

How might the theist respond? There are some aspects of the earlier discussion that seem relevant for animals as well. Richard Swinburne claims that it 'is good that there be animals who show courage in the face of pain, to secure food and to find and rescue their mates and their young, and who show sympathetic concern for other animals'.[76] He argues that it is good that animals exhibit these characteristics even though they lack moral awareness and free will. He writes, 'God could have made a world in which animals got nothing but thrills out of life; but their life is richer for the complexity and difficulty of the tasks they face and the hardships to which they react appropriately.'[77] Swinburne presents a further argument based on the idea that the higher animals can acquire knowledge about the kinds of circumstances that result in their good or harm and then act upon that knowledge accordingly. He claims that it is good that the world contains creatures of this kind and also that suffering is necessary if they are to acquire knowledge in this way. The reason for this is that for such knowledge to be acquired there must be lawful consequences to actions. So, just as there is a justification for regularities in nature that result in human suffering, the same argument can be applied to animal suffering.

A potential difficulty concerns apparently pointless examples of animal suffering, where the suffering is intense and yet there is no plausible benefit to be gained. In the case of humans, it was possible to appeal to possible compensating goods in terms of the knowledge of God and an afterlife. The problem is that these goods are not available for animals. It is worth noting, however, that for an animal to suffer it must be conscious. It is difficult to say how far consciousness extends in the animal kingdom, but the issue of suffering is clearly most relevant for the higher animals. It seems clear that higher animals do experience pain, but it does not follow from this that animals' experiences of pain are equivalent to human experiences of pain in similar circumstances. For this reason, it is not clear that there are examples of intense animal suffering for which there could be no justification. Humans have a greater mental capacity than even the higher animals and so it certainly seems possible that animals' ability to experience pain, while very real, might be more limited than that of humans.

Looking at the problem from a different angle, we can consider the attitude of atheists to animal suffering. If atheists wish to argue that a good God would not permit the suffering of a gazelle predated upon by a lion, for example, consistency would seem to demand that they should seek to prevent such suffering where possible. Yet atheists do not think it is a moral failing on the part of humans to permit this kind of suffering rather than taking action, where possible, to prevent it. The reason for this cannot be because atheists think animal suffering is a matter of moral indifference. On the contrary, atheists and theists are generally in agreement that it is wrong for *humans to harm* animals unnecessarily. Whatever their reasoning, it is clear that the suffering of animals in the wild is not a matter of moral concern to most atheists. But if that is so, could God not have good reason to permit such suffering as well?[78]

Despite the various lines of response discussed so far, it could still be argued that evil and suffering provide evidence against the existence of God even if they do not disprove it. If this is correct, we would still need to weigh up all the evidence for and against the existence of God and, as we have seen in earlier chapters, there are various evidences that count strongly in favour of God's existence. So it is quite possible to hold that evil and suffering count against the existence of God to some extent, but that overall the evidence favours belief in God. Of particular relevance here are the arguments in early chapters concerning the existence of life and the existence of consciousness. It was argued that it is much more likely that life and consciousness would exist in a universe created by God than in a universe without God. Clearly, without life and consciousness there would be no suffering. So, on the one hand, the existence of suffering initially seems to count against God and yet, on the other, suffering cannot occur without life and consciousness, which count in favour of God. Ironically, this may well mean that suffering is much more likely to occur in a universe created by God.

There are also two reasons why taking evil as evidence against the existence of God is problematic. First, in so far as the arguments in early chapters give reason to believe in God, they provide reason for believing that apparently pointless evils are not pointless after all, since if there is reason to believe that God exists, there is reason to believe that there is no pointless evil. Secondly, as we saw earlier in this chapter, God provides a foundation for morality in a way that atheism cannot. But the problem of evil starts with the assumption that evil is an objective feature of reality, and so ironically the existence of evil makes sense only *if God does exist*. This raises a problem for taking evil as evidence against God's existence since, arguably, if there is no God the evidence would not exist since there would be no such thing as objective good and evil.

All of the discussion so far has focused on the intellectual problem of evil, but the problem of evil goes deeper. It is quite possible to look at all the arguments on both sides of the debate, reach the conclusion that perhaps the existence of evil is not as big a problem for belief in God as it first seems, and yet feel very dissatisfied. This is particularly so for those who have experienced terrible suffering. Someone in this position may well feel that if there is a God there would be plenty of reason to be angry with him and little reason to trust him. From a Christian point of view there is good reason to trust God in the face of evil and suffering even though we do not fully understand why he permits them to occur. This is because the God of Christianity is not one who stands at a distance passively observing human suffering, but he comes into the world as a man and experiences evil and suffering first hand. As Plantinga puts it:

> He was prepared to accept this suffering in order to overcome sin, and death, and the evils that afflict our world, and to confer on us a life more glorious than we can imagine. So we don't know why God permits evil; we do know, however, that he was prepared to suffer on our behalf, to accept suffering of which we can form no conception.[79]

By undergoing suffering, Christ not only identifies with us but suffers in order to defeat evil. Evil is clearly revealed as an enemy to be defeated and not merely a problem to be explained. The crucifixion shows us that God is concerned about our predicament and that he has not simply left us to our own devices. It also demonstrates that we have reason to trust God and to believe that he can bring good out of even the most evil situations. The atheist will, of course, deny that any of this is true, but once again the issue is whether Christianity has resources to address evil, and it seems clear that it does.[80]

Conclusion

It turns out that the New Atheists' claims concerning evil and belief in God are seriously flawed. They point to the many evils carried out in the name of religion, but while they are quite right to do so, they fail to deal with the issues adequately or to take all the evidence into account. In many cases the root of the problem lies elsewhere, although religion is often used as a label to demarcate different groups. It is also the case that much evil has been brought about by atheistic regimes, and claims that atheism was incidental in such cases do not stand up to scrutiny. Of course, this does not prove that atheism is false any more than evil carried out in the name of religion proves there is no God. In fact, the whole issue is really a red herring when it comes to assessing evidence for God's existence.

The New Atheists also attempt to explain morality either in evolutionary terms or in terms of well-being. Even if the former can give an account of the origins of our moral behaviour, it fails to give an account of morality itself since it provides no basis for saying whether such behaviour is good or evil. The latter account also fails and for similar reasons. No doubt, acting out of concern for the well-being of others is part of morality, but what resources do the New Atheists have to account for why acting in this way is good? If we are the result of a mindless, unguided process where events just happen and are neither good nor evil, why do we have moral obligations to act in certain ways but not in others? Harris will claim that it is just obvious that we should try to alleviate suffering and he is right, but the problem is that his atheism provides no foundation for moral obligations of this kind. In contrast to the New Atheists, I have argued that God can provide a basis for morality in a way that atheism cannot. They raise a number of objections to the idea that God is relevant to morality, but even though there is something to their points they fail to address the relevant issue.

We have also considered the very difficult question of the problem of evil. The traditional claim that the existence of evil disproves the existence of God is mistaken, but this still leaves the question of whether the evil and suffering in the world count as evidence against belief in God. I have argued that although the various lines of response do not provide a complete answer to the problem, they are sufficient to reject the claim that evil and suffering seriously undermine belief in God. We have also seen that morality provides us with another reason for belief in God. Christian beliefs about the life of Jesus Christ are also very relevant when considering the problem of evil, but these are based on the Bible, which the New Atheists reject as a source of reliable information. We shall turn to this topic in the next two chapters.

Notes

1. *GNG*, p. 280.
2. *TGD*, p. 1.
3. *TEF*, p. 45.
4. *TGD*, p. 21.
5. Ibid., p. 259, emphasis in original.
6. Ibid.
7. Ibid.
8. *TEF*, p. 13.
9. Ibid., p. 26.
10. Ibid., p. 21, emphasis in original.
11. *TGD*, p. 249.
12. John Coffey, 'The Myth of Secular Tolerance', *Cambridge Papers* 12 (2003), available at http://www.jubilee-centre.org/documents/Themythofsseculartolerance.htm (accessed 30 Sept. 2011).
13. He also claims that secularists have often resorted to polemical intolerance, which would cover much of the polemics of the New Atheists. In attacking the second

half of the myth, Coffey argues that the modern commitment to religious tolerance first emerged within the Christian tradition. He points to a theological basis for tolerance in the New Testament and particularly in the teaching of Jesus. Despite this theological basis, however, there has also been much intolerance in the history of Christianity. So I am not arguing that there is evidence to support the idea that tolerance comes naturally to Christians, or religious people more generally, but rather to challenge the idea that tolerance comes naturally to the secular person.

14. Coffey, 'Myth of Secular Tolerance', p. 3.

15. John Gray, 'The Myth of Secularism', *New Statesman*, 16 Dec. 2002, p. 70.

16. Coffey, 'Myth of Secular Tolerance', p. 3.

17. *TGD*, p. 278.

18. Timothy Keller, *The Reason for God* (London: Hodder & Stoughton, 2008), p. 56.

19. Although in chapter 6 I argued that he failed.

20. *TGD*, pp. 220–221.

21. Ibid., p. 221.

22. Note that this is just the same problem we saw in chapter 7 in our discussion of Dennett and Dawkins's by-product account of religion. Dawkins thinks that both religion and morality are evolutionary by-products, yet he considers religion to be irrational and morality rational. It is clearly something other than his evolutionary explanations that leads him to such different conclusions.

23. Richard Dawkins, 'Lying for Jesus', http://richarddawkins.net/article,2394,Lying-for-Jesus,Richard-Dawkins (accessed 1 Oct. 2009).

24. *TEF*, p. 185.

25. George Mavrodes, 'Religion and the Queerness of Morality', in W. L. Rowe and W. J. Wainwright (eds.), *Philosophy of Religion: Selected Readings*, 3rd ed. (Fort Worth, Tex.: Harcourt Brace, 1998), pp. 201–201. (First published in Robert Audi and William Wainwright [eds.], *Rationality, Religious Belief and Moral Commitment* [New York: Cornell University Press, 1986].)

26. Ibid., pp. 201–202.

27. *TEF*, p. 186.

28. Ibid., p. 205.

29. Sam Harris, *The Moral Landscape: How Science Can Determine Human Values* (London: Bantam, 2010), p. 1.

30. Ibid., p. 28, emphasis in original.

31. Ibid., p. 7.

32. *TEF*, p. 181, emphasis in original.

33. Ibid.

34. Harris, *Moral Landscape*, p. 5.

35. Ibid., p. 2.

36. See ibid., p. 195, n. 2.

37. *TEF*, pp. 192–199.

38. Harris, *Moral Landscape*, p. 199, emphasis in original.

39. *BTS*, pp. 272–277. For a detailed study of the effect of religious belief on health see Harold G. Koenig, *Medicine, Religion, and Health: Where Science and Spirituality Meet* (West Conshohocken, Pa.: Templeton Foundation, 2008). On other possible benefits of religious belief see Jonathan Haidt, 'Moral Psychology and the Misunderstanding of Religion', and replies from Sam Harris and others at http:// www.edge.org/3rd_culture/haidt07/haidt07_index.html (accessed 9 Aug. 2011).

40. Harris, *Moral Landscape*, p. 38, emphasis in original.

41. He also alleges, bizarrely, that moral obligation is a Judeo-Christian concept. This would surprise Hindus, Confucians, Buddhists and many others! As Alasdair MacIntyre makes clear in his *Short History of Ethics* (London: Routledge & Kegan Paul, 1967), ancient Greek city states helped form the Western concept of duty.

42. Harris, *Moral Landscape*, p. 38, emphasis in original.

43. Richard Dawkins, *River out of Eden: A Darwinian View of Life* (London: Phoenix, 1995), p. 133.

44. We must remember that Harris's goal is to *discover* moral truths, not to *redefine what we mean* by morality. This would take Harris back to the relativism he despises.

45. For a detailed discussion of these issues, see Paul Copan, 'God, Naturalism, and the Foundations of Morality', in R. B. Stewart (ed.), *The Future of Atheism* (London: SPCK, 2008), pp. 141–161.

46. *BTS*, p. 279.

47. The expression 'better behaviour' is ambiguous. As a Christian, I would want to say that becoming a follower of Christ, as opposed to merely assenting to Christian doctrines, does lead to an improvement in the believer's behaviour. It does not follow from this that in general there is better behaviour among Christians than atheists or followers of other religions. Of course, whether Christianity does lead to such an improvement is something that could, in principle, be assessed empirically.

48. *TGD*, p. 226.

49. For a more traditional defence of the idea that there is a common core to morality across culture see C. S. Lewis, *The Abolition of Man* (Glasgow: Fount Paperbacks, 1978), appendix.

50. *BTS*, p. 279.

51. *TGD*, p. 226. Now while Dennett and Dawkins have a point, this statement is surely too strong. It seems to imply that it is not moral to do good if anything is to be gained from it. This bears a striking resemblance to the Kantian idea that a truly moral act is one that is done solely for duty's sake, which is difficult to square with the idea that morality is grounded in biology, as Dawkins and Dennett maintain.

52. *BTS*, p. 283.

53. Ibid.

54. Ibid., p. 307.

55. Ibid. p. 277.

56. *TGD*, p. 237.

57. Ibid., p. 249, emphasis in original.

58. Ibid., p. 230.

59. Copan, 'God, Naturalism', pp. 150–151.

60. The Euthyphro dilemma is sometimes considered as a fatal objection to God as
    a foundation for morality. The idea, expressed by Plato, is that God's commands
    would either be arbitrary or else based on a standard independent of God and so
    in neither case would God provide a foundation for morality. But this seems to be
    a false dilemma since another option is that it is God's character that provides the
    basis for morality. See Copan, ibid., for further discussion.

61. *GNG*, p. 267–268.

62. *TGD*, p. 108.

63. Ibid.

64. *TEF*, p. 173.

65. Sam Harris, *Letter to a Christian Nation: A Challenge to Faith* (London: Bantam, 2007),
    p. 52.

66. Ibid., p. 52.

67. See Alvin Plantinga, *God, Freedom and Evil* (Grand Rapids: Eerdmans, 1974).

68. Ibid., p. 30, emphasis in original.

69. Plantinga's argument does not require that we *actually* possess free will in the sense
    he describes. His claim is that it is *possible* that we have free will in the sense required
    and this is enough to show that God's existence is compatible with evil. Whether we
    actually have free will and whether it is the explanation for evil is another matter.

70. The atheist philosopher William Rowe writes, 'Some philosophers have contended
    that the existence of evil is *logically inconsistent* with the existence of the theistic God.
    No one, I think, has succeeded in establishing such an extravagant claim. Indeed,
    granted incompatibilism, there is a fairly compelling argument for the view that
    the existence of evil is logically consistent with the existence of the theistic God'
    ('The Problem of Evil and Some Varieties of Atheism', in Rowe and Wainwright,
    Philosophy of Religion, p. 242, emphasis in original).

71. Richard Swinburne, *The Existence of God*, 2nd ed. (Oxford: Oxford University Press,
    2004), p. 245.

72. J. P. Moreland and William Lane Craig, *Philosophical Foundations of a Christian
    Worldview* (Downers Grove: IVP, 2003), p. 544.

73. See Alvin Plantinga, *Warranted Christian Belief* (Oxford: Oxford University Press,
    2000), pp. 458–499. Plantinga has an example very similar to the elephant–ant
    example.

74. This is not to rule out the possibility that there will be animals in the new creation.

75. One answer that Christians have given not only to the problem of animal suffering, but to the problem of evil in general, is that it is the result of the Fall. The Fall plays an important role in Christian theology and is certainly relevant to our discussion here since a lot of the suffering in the world is a result of human evil. This can be related to the free will response since free will may be the reason why God permits human evil. But there are several reasons for thinking that the Fall, central as it is to biblical theology, does not resolve all the philosophical problems associated with the existence of evil and suffering. First, there are certain kinds of suffering or pain that seem to be necessary for human (and animal) existence and so do not need to be explained as a consequence of the Fall. Secondly, the scientific consensus is that animal suffering predates human existence and so cannot be due to the Fall of humans. Thirdly, even if animal suffering did not predate human existence, there would still be a question as to why God would allow animals to suffer as a result of human wrongdoing and this is not addressed by simply appealing to the Fall. This is not to deny that the Fall had consequences for the natural world, including animals presumably, but it still leaves the moral question as to why God would allow animals to suffer because of human sinfulness. A similar problem arises for an evolutionary justification of animal suffering. If it is claimed that God allowed animal suffering because it was necessary for the evolution of humans, this raises the question of whether God needed to use such a process and why it was appropriate to let animals suffer as a means to bringing about the existence of humans.

76. Swinburne, *Existence of God*, p. 243.

77. Ibid., p. 245.

78. For an in-depth study on animal suffering see Michael J. Murray, *Nature Red in Tooth and Claw: Theism and the Problem of Animal Suffering* (Oxford: Oxford University Press, 2008).

79. Alvin Plantinga, 'Self-Profile', in J. E. Tomberlin and P. van Inwagen (eds.), *Alvin Plantinga*, Profiles 5 (Dordrecht: D. Reidel, 1985), p. 36 (quoted in Moreland and Craig, *Philosophical Foundations*).

80. Much more could be said about the problem of evil on both sides of the debate. A recent discussion between a leading Christian philosopher and atheist philosopher can be found in Alvin Plantinga and Michael Tooley, *Knowledge of God* (Oxford: Blackwell, 2008), pp. 70–183.

To believe in a God who created the universe is one thing, but to believe that God answers prayers or is the source of revelation in a holy book is quite another. Even if it is granted that there might be evidence for a deistic creator who got the universe up and running, could there be any rational basis for believing in a theistic God who takes an interest in the goings-on within the universe, including the lives of human beings? Of course, for most people who believe in God, it is not the mere existence of a remote being that is of interest, but the idea that God's existence has relevance for their lives. Just as this kind of belief holds more significance for religious believers, it also captures the interest of the New Atheists because it is precisely this kind of theistic belief that is of greatest concern to them.

Daniel Dennett makes it clear that his main goal in *Breaking the Spell* is not to evaluate the traditional arguments for or against the existence of God, but to study religion scientifically, where religions are understood to be 'social systems whose participants avow belief in a supernatural agent or agents whose approval is to be sought'.[1] He follows David Hume's distinction between *natural religion*, which is to be evaluated in terms of evidence and argument, and *revealed religion*, which he takes to be based on revelation rather than evidence. His focus is on studying revealed religions as natural phenomena so that 'we can come to understand how and why religions inspire such devotion, and figure out how we should deal with them in the twenty-first century'.[2] As we shall see later, there is no good reason to think that evidence is irrelevant to revelation, but clearly there is a difference between a revealed religion like Christianity and mere belief in a deity of some kind.

Richard Dawkins, Sam Harris and Christopher Hitchens also focus on revealed religions to a large extent. In *The End of Faith* Harris attacks faith in general, but most of his criticisms are targeted at Christianity and Islam with the former providing the focus for his later book *Letter to a Christian Nation*. Dawkins and Hitchens both make it clear that they are criticizing belief in any kind of deity, but again they reserve their severest attacks for revealed religions. Interestingly, they both admire some of the leading Founding Fathers of the United States such as Thomas Jefferson and Thomas Paine, who are generally considered to have been deists. The reason for this admiration is that both Jefferson and Paine were critical of the Bible and had a secular influence in politics. Such is Dawkins's contempt for the God of the Bible that at one point he almost comes across as sympathetic to deism, describing the deist God as

> an altogether grander being: worthy of his cosmic creation, loftily unconcerned with human affairs, sublimely aloof from our private thoughts and hopes, caring nothing for our messy sins or mumbled contritions. The deist God is a physicist to end all physics, the alpha and omega of mathematics, the apotheosis of designers; a hyper-engineer who set up the laws and constants of the universe, fine-tuned them with exquisite precision and foreknowledge, detonated what we would now call the hot big bang, retired and was never heard from again.[3]

However, lest we think that Dawkins is too sympathetic it should be noted that he is comparing the deist God with what he calls the 'Old Testament's psychotic delinquent'.[4] And, in any case, he claims, 'Unfortunately it is scarcely more likely that [the deist God] exists, or ever did. In any of its forms the God Hypothesis is unnecessary.'[5] Nevertheless, as noted in chapter 6 both Dawkins and Hitchens seem to think that deism might have been a feasible option before Darwin. Hitchens describes such a belief as 'a logical and rational one for its time'.[6]

In this chapter we shall investigate various objections to the idea of revealed religion that have been raised by the New Atheists. There are a number of general objections that need to be considered as well as specific objections to the Bible as divine revelation. Although some of the issues discussed here will be of a general nature and apply to any putative revelation, the main focus of this chapter and the next one will be on Christianity. In the next chapter we shall explore some evidence relating to the central claim of Christianity: the resurrection of Jesus. In this chapter, however, we shall start by considering some general issues about whether a revelation from God is even possible and, if so, whether we could recognize it as such. After that we shall look at some general issues regarding Christianity as a revelation and some specific issues relating to the Old Testament.

No God, no revelation

There is one very simple reason for rejecting the possibility of a revelation from God as ever having occurred: if there is no God, clearly there can be no revelation from God. Although this is an obvious point it is actually extremely important in how we approach the whole topic of revelation. Our views on the question of God's existence shape our attitudes to any evidence and arguments that might be offered in support of a revelation from God. If you are sure, for whatever reason, that there is no God, there probably isn't much point in reading the rest of this chapter. Why? Because if you are sure *there is no God*, then you are unlikely to be persuaded by any evidence or arguments that purport to show that a revelation *came from God*!

Alternatively, if you are sure there is a God, then such a revelation cannot be ruled out in principle. Of course, it does not mean that any and every claimed revelation from God must be accepted as authentic, but just that the evidence and arguments need to be considered on their merits. And the same applies if you are not sure about God's existence. If you consider God's existence to be somewhat plausible, perhaps based on the sorts of evidence and arguments presented in earlier chapters, then you cannot simply rule out the possibility of revelation in principle. Similar to the approach adopted in earlier chapters for God's existence, an appropriate strategy would be to say, 'If we suppose there is a God, how well would the evidence in question be explained on the supposition that a revelation from God had taken place?' Of course, this might be difficult if you think it unlikely that God exists, but the willingness to consider such a radically different viewpoint is necessary if a religion such as Christianity is to be taken seriously.

Arguably, the New Atheists' attitude to God's existence is partly responsible for their dismissal of revelation. They are convinced on other grounds that God does not exist and so do not need to take the possibility of a revelation from God seriously. Nevertheless, they do offer various objections to revelation and these must be considered on their merits, as they will be later in the chapter.

Reasons for a revelation

When considering the topic of revelation it is worth noting a distinction often made in Christian theology between *general* and *special* revelation. Theologian Millard Erickson defines the former as 'God's communication of himself to all persons at all times and in all places' and the latter as involving 'God's particular communications and manifestations of himself to particular persons at particular times, communications and manifestations which are available now only by consultation of certain sacred writings'.[7] The idea in general revelation is that various aspects of the universe point to God. Examples would include the order of the universe and the existence and nature of human beings as discussed in earlier chapters. The primary example of special revelation in the case of Christianity is God's revelation in Jesus Christ. Note that these two types of revelation are usually taken to be complementary so that special revelation builds upon, but does not contradict, the knowledge of God available from general revelation. In this chapter the focus is on special revelation, which for brevity will simply be referred to as 'revelation'.

The focus here will be on what is central to, and definitive of, the Christian revelation. This includes the central Christian beliefs about God and about the life, death and resurrection of Jesus Christ, whom Christians believe to be the incarnate Son of God who died for our sins. The idea of concentrating on central beliefs definitive of Christianity is consistent with the practice of the early church, in which there was widespread use of brief summaries of the Christian faith.[8] In fact, while this chapter deals with some objections to revelation in general and Christianity in particular, the main focus of the next chapter will be on Jesus and Christian claims about his resurrection. Again, this is consistent with the practice of the early Christians, whose message concentrated on the death and resurrection of Jesus, as can be seen in the book of Acts.

In taking this approach, the goal will not be to defend every part of the Bible, but rather to focus on the central claims of Christianity.[9] This is not to say that the Bible will be ignored either. Almost all of our information about Jesus is based on the Gospels and so they will be considered in the next chapter. Furthermore, given that Jesus considered Yahweh to be his Father, this means that we need to consider the claims of the New Atheists concerning the character of God in the Old Testament. For the primary focus to be on Jesus, however, seems to be appropriate from a Christian point of view. This can be seen by comparing Christianity and Islam in terms of revelation. Often the parallel is made between the Qur'ān and the Bible regarding their revelations, but this is to ignore the different roles of these books in their respective religions. Arguably, the appropriate parallel is not between the Qur'ān and the Bible, but between the Qur'ān and Jesus as the supreme revelation.[10]

If there is a God, would there be any reasons for him to provide a revelation to human beings? The philosopher Richard Swinburne claims, 'there are matters which it would be very good for us to know which are such that either we could not find them out for ourselves, or we have not previously proved persistent or honest enough with ourselves to do so'.[11] He then goes on to describe four reasons why God might be expected to provide a revelation. The first is so that we might know more about God. It is clear that the evidence and arguments for God's existence considered in early chapters, even if successful, provide only limited knowledge about what God is like. If we are to know more about God, he must reveal it to us in some way.

Swinburne's second reason for God to provide a revelation concerns the state of the world we live in. As he points out, 'if God made the world, it has proved to be (to some extent) a world of sin and suffering'.[12] He goes on to argue that God has reason to deal with this by becoming incarnate (taking on a human nature and human body), providing an atonement for our sins and identifying with our suffering. It is not obvious that we would have reason to believe in anything as specific as this in the absence of a revelation's claiming that it had actually happened. By reflecting on the state of our world it might be reasonable to think that God would address the situation in some way, but it is difficult to see how we could be any more precise than that.

The third and fourth reasons for revelation concern morality. The third is to provide encouragement to do what is good and avoid doing what is bad by providing rewards and punishments respectively, while the fourth is to provide us with moral information so that we know what is good or bad as the case may be. Concerning the third reason, Swinburne points out, 'Now of course the primary reason for doing good actions is intrinsic to them; the primary reason for feeding the poor is that it is good that people have enough to eat.'[13] However, he also draws attention to the fact that parents offer rewards and punishments to help children form their characters so that they naturally do good, and he argues that God may have reason to do this as well. Concerning the fourth reason, Swinburne is certainly not claiming that revelation is our only source of moral knowledge. He emphasizes that we have certain moral obligations whether or not they are commanded by God, to feed our own children for example. On the other hand, God is also able to issue commands that would not otherwise be obligatory for us. The injunction to pray for those who persecute us would presumably be an example of such a command (Matt. 5:44).

It is important to emphasize that such commands are not simply arbitrary commands. In fact, Swinburne's discussion as to why God would issue commands suggests a fifth reason for a revelation, which is implicit in his account. An important reason for God to issue commands would be to further his purposes for humanity, including transformation of our characters so that we become the kind of people God wants us to be. In order to achieve this it would be good for us to have knowledge about God's priorities and purposes for humanity. Of course, this would include knowledge about God (Swinburne's first reason), but it would also include knowledge about the universe, our place within it and our place in God's purposes. If we understood something of God's overall purposes, it would help us to understand why he commands us to live in a certain way.

An objection to these reasons for a revelation might be that Christianity has conditioned us to expect these features in a revelation. In response, it can be noted that with the exception of the second reason, which has been questioned, the other reasons given are quite general in nature. The first reason claims that we should expect a revelation to give us knowledge about God, but it does not suggest what the content of that knowledge should be. Furthermore, reasons three and four relate to morality and the fifth reason relates to the purpose for our existence, and so these reasons address concerns that are of fundamental importance to humans irrespective of their religion or culture.

Evaluating a revelation

The foregoing discussion has provided reasons why God might provide a revelation, but how would we go about evaluating whether a putative revelation came from God or not? The starting point would be to assess whether the revelation includes information relating to each of the reasons identified, but that would not take us very far. The problem is that someone who is sufficiently creative could simply come up with a story that satisfies this criterion and then claim it was a divine revelation. This raises the question as to what kind of revelation would be appropriate. Swinburne claims that although God might give private revelations to individuals, the reasons for a revelation relate to things that all humans would need to know about. Consequently, he argues, this would be a reason for expecting a revelation for which there would be public evidence. If so, this would give us the opportunity to investigate the putative revelation to evaluate whether it was genuine.

One consideration is the *external confirmation* of the revelation. The basic idea here is to determine whether the revelation is confirmed by other things we know or have good reason to believe. It might be doubted whether this is really feasible since the point of revelation is to tell us things we would *not* have known otherwise. However, this does not preclude the revelation from informing us about things we could know in other ways. Consider again the issue of moral information. If the revelation informs us of moral obligations which conflict with clear moral principles, that would present a problem, whereas if they agree with such principles, that provides some confirmation. If it is a public revelation, it will presumably tell us something about the historical and geographical context of that revelation, and so it might be possible to compare this with knowledge acquired in independent ways. One possibility here is that the revelation might provide us with information that can be tested in this way even though it could not have been when the revelation was originally claimed to have been given. An example of this might be the doctrine of creation *ex nihilo*, which asserts that the universe was created out of nothing, and which appears to receive confirmation from modern science.[14]

Another aspect to evaluating a revelation concerns *miracles*. If the revelation claims that one or more miracles occurred and if it is possible to evaluate such a claim, this could provide confirmation (or disconfirmation) that the revelation is genuine. Of course, the New Atheists are just as dismissive of miracles as they are of revelation in general. In fact, their contemptuous attitude towards miracles is a major factor in their negative approach to revelation. However, as we saw in chapter 3, the arguments for ruling out miracles in principle are very weak and so the only way to decide whether a miracle occurred is to consider the evidence and context in which it is claimed to have occurred.

When trying to evaluate evidence for a miracle, the context can be very important. If there is good evidence that an extremely unusual event occurred which cannot be explained scientifically, but there is no good reason to think that God (or some other supernatural agent) would have wanted to bring about such an event, it might be better just to consider it as an unexplained event. But if God would have had reason to bring it about and such an explanation accounts for the evidence much better than rival explanations, it is reasonable to infer that a miracle occurred. Is there any reason to think that God would ever perform miracles? It seems that there is. As a way of evaluating a revelation, *external confirmation* goes only so far. It can show that a putative revelation cannot be ruled out and that it might be quite plausible in certain respects. Clearly, public evidence would help in this regard, but if the revelation really was of importance for all humanity it would surely be a good thing for God to confirm it in some way. As Swinburne points out, 'The purported revelation needs to be delivered in a way that God alone can deliver it. It needs to come with God's authenticating signature.'[15] A miracle would certainly seem like an obvious way for God to achieve this.

Another way of evaluating a purported revelation is to assess its *theological value*. We have noted that we might expect God to provide a revelation to give valuable information about himself, and to bring about a moral transformation in its recipients. For philosopher Paul Moser, a key consideration in evaluating evidence for God is the character of the God in question. God is a title that signifies a being more worthy of worship than any other. Moser argues that this 'requires inherent (or self-contained) moral perfection, including moral righteousness, and such perfection in an agent demands, in turn, a perfectly loving character, including perfect love towards enemies'.[16]

Moser also emphasizes that we should expect evidence for God to be transformative in nature. He says:

> A God worthy of worship would not be in the business of just expanding our databases or simply giving us an informational plan of rescue from our troubles. Divine self-revelation . . . would seek to transform humans *motivationally*, toward perfect love and its required volitional cooperation with God.[17]

If so, we would expect that a purported revelation would issue a challenge to us. Rather than simply presenting information for us to evaluate, we would expect it to require a response from us. Moser describes how this changes the nature of the inquiry: 'What once seemed to be a merely intellectual inquiry would become morally and existentially loaded for us inquirers about God.'[18] Hence, we should expect a purported revelation to have a morally challenging component and a picture of God that makes God most worthy of worship.

These aspects (external confirmation, miracles and theological value) provide criteria for evaluating a revelation.[19] However, it is also important to emphasize a note of caution. Particularly in the case of external confirmation, we are evaluating the revelation on the basis of our beliefs about various matters and to some extent that is reasonable – what else could we do? But we must be careful here because there is a danger that we might exclude a revelation on the grounds that it does not match up with our preconceived notions. God would be allowed to speak to us only if he told us what we wanted to hear. And that would surely be an unreasonable constraint. There needs to be a willingness to consider things from a different point of view. Perhaps the revelation informs us that God has priorities for our lives which are very different from our current priorities (which of course seem reasonable to us). Nevertheless, it may be the case that once we understand the overall picture provided in the revelation, the priorities attributed to God are more reasonable than our current priorities.

General objections

The New Atheists raise a number of general objections to revelation. These include their disbelief in God in the first place and their rejection of miracles, which have already been considered in earlier chapters. They also claim that religion gives rise to violence, particularly because of the conflicting beliefs of different revealed religions, as discussed in the last chapter. But there are other objections as well. One of these is that the idea of a personal God, who takes an interest in the affairs of humans, is somehow a naive and demeaning conception of God. We saw earlier that Dawkins refers to the deistic God as a 'grander being' who is 'sublimely aloof from our private thoughts and hopes'. Elsewhere in the same book he says, 'The metaphorical or pantheistic God of the physicists is light years away from the interventionist, miracle-wreaking, thought-reading, sin-punishing, prayer-answering God of the Bible . . .'[20] But what exactly is objectionable about a God who takes an interest in human affairs? If there is a God who created us, why would it be so surprising to think that he would take an interest in what is going on, that he would have standards for how we should live our lives and be concerned about our failing to meet those standards? In fact, isn't this a greater conception of God? Of course, it might be claimed that it is wishful thinking to believe that God would take an interest in human affairs, but equally, if God exists it might be wishful-thinking to believe that he would not.

There is no reason to think that God's dealings with humanity, including listening to and answering prayers, must involve an ongoing sequence of miraculous interventions. So Dawkins's unreasonable antipathy to miracles does not explain his antagonism to a personal God. Another reason for his view might be based on the idea that belief in such a God can be easily explained away. For example, he thinks that the childhood phenomenon of the imaginary friend 'may be a good model for understanding theistic belief in adults' because of its consoling and counselling role.[21] The reasons for this thesis are extraordinarily weak, however. Part of the reason for taking such an idea seriously is that Dawkins seems to think of theistic belief in terms of voices that people hear inside their heads.[22] In fact, this kind of misconception of the nature of religious experience provides the basis for Dawkins's inept discussion of the argument for God's existence based on religious experience.[23]

Another general objection to revelation takes us back to the topic of faith and evidence, which was considered in chapter 2. Recall that the New Atheists consider faith to be belief without evidence. This raises its head in the context of revelation because they seem to think that revelation must simply be accepted on the basis of authority and that evidence or reasons would be irrelevant. Dawkins states the point clearly:

> The truth of the holy book is an axiom, not the end product of a process of reasoning. The book is true, and if the evidence seems to contradict it, it is the evidence that must be thrown out, not the book. By contrast, what I, as a scientist, believe (for example, evolution) I believe not because of reading a holy book but because I have studied the evidence.[24]

In the case of revelation, they seem to think the problem of faith is compounded by the fact that there are conflicting revelations. Hitchens gives expression to this concern as follows:

> Since all of these revelations, many of them hopelessly inconsistent, cannot by definition be simultaneously true, it must follow that some of them are false and illusory. It could also follow that only one of them is authentic, but in the first place this seems dubious and in the second place it appears to necessitate religious war in order to decide whose revelation is the true one.[25]

His point seems to be that evidence and reason cannot help to decide, so war is the only option. Harris also asserts that evidence and reason are of no value here:

> CONSIDER: every devout Muslim has the same reasons for being a Muslim that you have for being a Christian. And yet you do not find their reasons compelling. The Koran repeatedly declares that it is the perfect word of the creator of the universe. Muslims believe this as fully as you believe the Bible's account of itself.[26]

We have also seen that Dennett considers revealed religion to be based on revelation *rather* than evidence. Lest anyone try to invoke historical evidence to support revelation, he is quick to dismiss the possibility:

> The historical arguments are apparently satisfying to those who accept them, but they simply cannot be introduced into a serious investigation, since they are manifestly question-begging. (If this is not obvious to you, ask whether the *Book of Mormon* [1829] or the founding document of Scientology, L. Ron Hubbard's book *Dianetics*

[1950], should be taken as irrefutable evidence for the propositions it contains. No
text can be conceded the status of 'gospel truth' without foreclosing all rational
inquiry.)[27]

Note Dennett's comment 'should be taken as irrefutable evidence for the
propositions it contains'. Dennett seems to have in mind the sort of argument which claims that the propositions in the Bible must be true because the
Bible is God's word and God would not lie. Clearly, such an argument would
be ridiculous since, as he points out, it is 'manifestly question-begging'. Does
he really think that this is the only kind of argument that can be offered in
support of a revelation? It seems he does, because the quoted passage ends
his single paragraph on historical arguments in a section entitled 'Does God
exist?' But this is just plain false. Swinburne's book *Revelation*, to which we
have been referring, is a sustained argument for the truth of the Christian
revelation. Even if one disagrees with Swinburne, it is obvious that he is not
proposing the kind of argument to which Dennett refers – a book would
hardly have been required for that!

Is it really the case that there is no evidence to distinguish the Gospels
in the New Testament from *The Book of Mormon* or *Dianetics*? Consider, for
example, the historical context. The Gospels are set in a first-century Jewish
context that has been studied extensively by historians and the information
about people, places and political and religious practices described in the
Gospels is consistent with what is known from other sources.[28] Of course,
this does not come close to proving that the Gospels are divine revelation, but
it is part of the external confirmation that can be used to evaluate a putative
revelation. By contrast, *The Book of Mormon* claims to record God's dealings
with the ancient peoples of the Americas over a period of a couple of thousand years. It turns out that these peoples were descended from Jews who
migrated at different times. In particular, two large nations, the Nephites and
Lamanites, were descended from a group of Jews who left Jerusalem about
600 BC. It is claimed that native Americans are descended from the Lamanites.
Does Dennett think there is evidence for this? Of course, Mormons will
claim that there is evidence, but does Dennett think that these claims stand up
to scrutiny in the way in which historical research confirms the first-century
context of the Gospels?[29]

The point is that revelation need not simply be accepted on the basis of
authority or blind faith. The previous section of this chapter set out a strategy
for how evidence and reason can be used to evaluate a revelation. The New
Atheists are correct, however, to point out inconsistencies between different
putative revelations. If central Christian claims about the person of Jesus – his

divine nature and resurrection from the dead – are true, then religions that deny these claims are not.[30]

Another objection to revelation concerns the contents of a revelation. Hitchens and Harris both think that a revelation from God should consider detailed scientific information. Here is what Hitchens has to say:

> Here again one sees the gigantic man-made fallacy that informs our 'Genesis' story. How can it be proven in one paragraph that this book was written by ignorant men and not by any god? Because man is given 'dominion' over all beasts, fowl and fish. But no dinosaurs or plesiosaurs or pterodactyls are specified, because the authors did not know of their existence, let alone of their supposedly special and immediate creation.[31]

In similar vein, Harris claims:

> A book written by an omniscient being could contain a chapter on mathematics that after two thousand years of continuous use, would still be the richest source of mathematical insight humanity has ever known. . . . Why doesn't the Bible say anything about electricity, or about DNA, or about the actual age and size of the universe? What about a cure for cancer?[32]

These claims betray a horrendous misconception about the whole point of revelation. It is often said that the Bible is not a scientific textbook, but this is never intended as a criticism of the Bible. It was argued in chapter 3 that belief in God provides a basis for science, but the point is that God has given *us* the ability to do science. The point of revelation is not for God to impress us with his knowledge but, at least in part, to call us and transform us. Of course, there are other things we would like to know and that it would be good to know, but in most cases God expects us to pursue such knowledge ourselves.

And besides, how exactly is the fact that Genesis does not mention pterodactyls supposed to show that it is not divine revelation? Hitchens seems to be claiming that it shows that Genesis was written by ignorant men and so it is not of divine origin. But the Bible *was* written by ignorant men. That is not in dispute; Christians have never claimed otherwise. What Christians claim is that men who were ignorant of many things, including dinosaurs, electricity and DNA, were inspired by God in their writing of the Bible. To assess that claim we need to consider the evaluation strategy considered earlier.

The general objections to revelation considered here do not seem at all persuasive, but other specific objections have been raised against Christianity by the New Atheists. Some of these will be considered in the rest of this chapter and the next.

External confirmation

How does Christianity fit with other things we know? A key respect in which Christianity is open to external confirmation or disconfirmation is due to its historical nature. It is not just that the revelation was given in a historical context, but that the truth or falsity of Christianity depends on historical events in a very fundamental way. In particular, it depends on the life, death and resurrection of Jesus. In Buddhism the events of the life of the Buddha are not so critical, because it is his teaching that is important, and the validity or otherwise of his teaching does not depend on the details about his life. Islam is a much more historical religion, but it also does not depend on historical events in the same critical way. Of course, the events of Muhammad's life are very important for Muslims, but the central claims of Islam are based on the revelations given to him, not the events of his life. By contrast, if Jesus is not who Christians claim him to be and if he did not rise from the dead, then orthodox Christianity is false.[33] It is not just Jesus' teaching, but Jesus himself, on which Christianity depends. Of course, this point does not show that either Buddhism or Islam is false, but it does indicate that Christianity is much more amenable to confirmation or disconfirmation on the basis of historical knowledge. We shall return to this topic in the next chapter when we consider some of the central claims of Christianity.

This is not the only way in which Christianity can be compared with other things we know. Arguably, the Christian understanding of the human condition makes a lot of sense. While humans might have more in common with other creatures than we might previously have thought, it is clear that we have remarkable capabilities which distinguish us from the rest of the animal kingdom. In fact, this seems to be presupposed in much research in areas such as cognitive science, which try to determine how the human mind works. And besides, Christian doctrine affirms our common status with the animals as fellow-creatures; it just claims there is something unique about us as well.

Similarly, the Christian belief that something is wrong with the world fits with our experience. When we consider the terrible suffering and injustices brought about by humans, it is obvious that there is a serious problem with the world. Of course, from an atheistic perspective we might expect such things. As Dawkins points out, in a world of purely physical forces there does not seem to be any basis for thinking that there is 'any rhyme or reason in it, or any justice' or indeed anything other than 'blind, pitiless indifference'.[34] But that's just the problem with such a perspective because most people, including Dawkins himself, have a deeply ingrained belief that there is something fundamentally wrong and unjust about many of the things that go on in the world. This belief seems much more in keeping with the Christian view that that there really is a rhyme and reason to it all and that there really is justice, but that things are not the way they are supposed to be.[35]

A similar point applies at the level of the individual as well. For example, we are all aware of moral standards we fail to meet. C. S. Lewis draws attention to two points in this regard in his book *Mere Christianity*:

> First, that human beings, all over the earth, have this curious idea that they ought to behave in a certain way, and cannot really get rid of it. Secondly, that they do not in fact behave in that way. They know the Law of Nature; they break it. These two facts are the foundation of all clear thinking about ourselves and the universe we live in.[36]

In a similar way the moral philosopher John Hare refers to a *moral gap* between the moral demands placed upon us and our natural capacities to meet those demands.[37] We are unable to meet the demands of morality for a variety of reasons, particularly our inability to be impartial since we have a tendency to put ourselves first. This leads to moral failure and a sense of guilt. Hare outlines several strategies for dealing with this sense of guilt.[38] One strategy is to exaggerate our sense of what we can achieve so as to meet the demands of morality. According to this strategy, ignorance is the problem and more knowledge, particularly awareness of the effects of our actions on others, would enable us to meet the demands of morality. There is no doubt that if we want to be moral such knowledge can help us, but surely the twentieth century has taught us that people can have perfect knowledge of the harm produced by their actions and persist in terrible atrocities nevertheless.

Another strategy is to reduce the demands of morality so that we are able to meet them. This strategy can involve denying the need for impartiality in morality or restricting our obligations in various ways so that, for example, we have obligations only to those who are close to us. Hitchens seems to adopt an approach similar to this second strategy when he says:

> The order to 'love thy neighbour' is mild and yet stern: a reminder of one's duty to others. The order to 'love thy neighbour *as thyself*' is too extreme and too strenuous to be obeyed, as is the hard-to-interpret instruction to love others 'as I have loved you.' Humans are not so constituted as to care for others as much as themselves: the thing simply cannot be done . . .[39]

His point is that the impartiality required in Jesus' command is too demand-ing and so it should be replaced with something more manageable. Moral demands must be restricted to demands that are within our reach. As G. K. Chesterton once wrote, 'The Christian ideal has not been tried and found wanting; it has been found difficult; and left untried.'[40] Hitchens is also criti-cal of the Old Testament commandment not to covet and Jesus' claim that anyone who looks at a woman lustfully has committed adultery in his heart on the grounds that such teaching attempts 'to place impossible restraints on human initiative'.[41] Jesus' point, however, is that our moral failings go much deeper than wrong actions; they are the result of a much more fundamen-tal problem at the level of our desires and motivations.[42] If we wish to be truly moral, we must surely face up to the full demands of morality rather than reducing the demands so that we can meet them. There is no point in a student who is struggling with mathematics setting himself an easy test that he knows he can pass. He would just be deluding himself and his approach would not help him to reach the required standard. No, if he is to have any chance, he must start by realizing that he is failing to meet the standard.

It is extremely important to emphasize that Hare's claim is that the moral gap is not just an artefact of Christian morality, but follows from the nature of morality in general. It also seems to be true to our own experience as Lewis pointed out. Of course, the existence of the moral gap does not prove the truth of Christian revelation, but it fits remarkably well with the Christian viewpoint and so to that extent provides external confirmation of it.

But where does this leave us? If morality places demands upon us that we are unable to meet, isn't that a depressing conclusion? Well, yes it is, just as it is depressing for the mathematics student to realize that he is failing to meet the required standard. As Hare argues, however, what Christianity teaches is that we are unable to meet the required standard *on our own*, but that God comes to our assistance in order to bridge the gap. From a Christian point of view, our problem is not just that we fail in some of our moral obliga-tions, but that we have wronged God, not least by turning away from him and going our own way. In doing so, we have cut ourselves off from the very source of goodness and so are no longer able to meet God's standards. In order for the problem to be addressed, we need to be forgiven and recon-ciled to God so that we can begin a new kind of life where God enables us to live according to his standards. Not that we actually reach God's standards in this life. It is the beginning of a process in which God transforms us. The Christian notion of the atonement is central at this point since it is the death and resurrection of Jesus that makes this reconciliation and new life possible.

Neither Hitchens nor Dawkins likes the idea of an atonement. Dawkins writes:

> I have described the atonement, the central doctrine of Christianity, as vicious,
> sado-masochistic and repellent. We should also dismiss it as barking mad, but for its
> ubiquitous familiarity which has dulled our objectivity. If God wanted to forgive sins,
> why not just forgive them, without having himself tortured and executed in payment
> . . .[43]

Setting aside Dawkins's overblown rhetoric, his central objection is that an atonement was unnecessary because God could just have forgiven us; but is that really the case? In his discussion of forgiveness, Hare discusses the roles of both the offender and the victim. Reconciliation between the two parties requires the offender to *make good* the offence, which typically involves some form of reparation, and the victim to forgive the offender.[44] In this case forgiveness and making good the offence go together. According to an alternative understanding of forgiveness, there is no requirement that the offence be made good. But in this latter case a paradox arises: either forgiveness involves condoning the offence since the offence is not made good or, if the offence is made good, there is justice but no longer any forgiveness. Hare's point is that the paradox is due to a mistaken notion of forgiveness, one that does not require the making good of the offence. And it is precisely this notion of forgiveness that Dawkins seems to have accepted uncritically. Hare distinguishes between 'forgiving a debt' and 'forgiving a person':

> To forgive a debt is to relinquish it, or deliberately not to exact it. To forgive a person
> may not be, however, to forgive that person's debt in that sense. It may be, rather,
> to accept the payment of the debt that the person has made. . . . by distinguishing
> between forgiveness of debts and persons, we can say both that our debt was paid
> and that God forgives us as persons.[45]

The problem is that to 'just forgive' as Dawkins suggests would be to condone the wrong that has been done. It fails to do justice to the seriousness of the wrongdoing and so forgiveness would come at the expense of justice. As Hare says, 'Taking seriously the wrong that offenders do means taking seriously the value of the people that the offenders wrong.'[46] And this is why 'God's demanding reparation for our wrongdoing is a good thing because it takes seriously not only the offender, but the offender's victim.'[47] In other words, it takes seriously not just us as the offenders, but also the value of the victim of our wrongdoing, God.

Hitchens and Dawkins also raise an objection to the idea of Jesus' making reparation (or paying the price or taking the punishment) on our behalf. If there is reparation to be made, should it not be the wrongdoers themselves who make it rather than an innocent party? In most cases it should be the wrongdoer who makes reparation, but what if the nature of the offence is such that the wrongdoer is unable to do so? Is there any way in which reparation can be made by someone other than the wrongdoer? Hare discusses several scenarios where this is possible, including one where a child does something horrible to a dinner guest. The parents may be responsible for the way in which they have brought the child up, but in addition to this they are 'part of a unit (the family) which is together discredited by the actions of one member'.[48] In such a case it is appropriate for the parents (and siblings) to apologize and make reparation as required on behalf of the child. Similarly, in the case of our offence against God we are unable to make reparation. In fact, we are incapable of simply changing our ways to live a life that meets God's standards because of the moral gap, never mind making reparation for our past wrongdoing. But in Christianity Jesus identifies with us and makes reparation by living a perfect life and dying for us. This is acceptable to God and provides the basis for our forgiveness if we are willing to identify with Jesus and the reparation he has provided.[49]

It is a gross understatement to say that a lot has been written on the subject of the atonement in Christian theology and the account provided here certainly does not do justice to the topic. But unless the account here (or something like it) can be shown to be incoherent, it is sufficient to refute the accusations of Dawkins and Hitchens. As we have seen, Christianity identifies a fundamental problem with humanity as a whole, which also applies to each of us as individuals, in a way that fits very well with our experience. The Christian account of the atonement addresses this problem by treating it with the utmost seriousness and yet offering a way in which a loving God can reconcile us to himself while not ignoring the demands of justice.

Morality and the Bible

There is no doubt that Christianity has had a profound influence on the values and legal systems of Western culture, but the New Atheists have raised a lot of objections to the Bible from a moral perspective. In the last chapter we considered some objections; one of them being that we can know right from wrong without needing to appeal to the Bible. The main problem with the points raised was that they failed to address the relevant issue about an adequate foundation for morality. However, they base other objections on specific issues addressed within the Bible itself. These include the character of God, particularly in the Old Testament, and biblical views on war, women, homosexuality, hell, slavery, the atonement and legal and penal matters. Clearly, it would be impossible to deal with all of these topics here,[50] but before focusing on specific issues relating to the Old Testament it is worth making a few more general comments.

It is important to distinguish between two kinds of objections raised by the New Atheists on these topics. The most obvious kind of objection is that they take the Bible to be advocating *beliefs* which they consider to be morally unacceptable. The other kind of objection is that holding these beliefs results in *practices* which they consider to be morally unacceptable. Dawkins is particularly good at finding examples to illustrate the latter. On the topic of hell, he refers to the Hell Houses of Pastor Keenan Roberts that are designed to terrify children;[51] on the topic of homosexuality, he refers to Pastor Fred Phelps of Westboro Baptist Church and his 'God Hates Fags' campaigns;[52] on the topic of abortion, he refers to the Reverend Paul Hill who murdered a doctor to prevent him from carrying out abortions.[53]

Now, of course, Dawkins is quite right that these cases are all morally unacceptable. Ironically, however, the extreme nature of these cases actually undermines Dawkins's case because orthodox Christians who hold *beliefs* that Dawkins finds morally unacceptable will nevertheless agree with him that the *practices* in these three cases are morally unacceptable. This is particularly clear from the abortion example since it is obvious that Paul Hill's horrendous crime does not tell us whether abortion is morally acceptable or not. In fact, in a footnote Dawkins provides another example that makes the point. He refers to animal liberationists who threaten violence against scientists, but again such violence, whether threatened or actual, does not help us decide whether the use of animals in medical research is morally acceptable or not.

Admittedly, not all Dawkins's examples are as extreme as the three cited above and it must also be acknowledged that there are legitimate questions here. Orthodox Christians will rightly reject Hell Houses, but where is the line to be drawn between what is acceptable and what is not when it comes to teaching children? Similar questions can be asked about Christian opposition to homosexuality or abortion. Granting that the approaches of Phelps and Hill are unacceptable, what are acceptable ways of giving expression to views on these issues? An easy answer would be to say that there are no acceptable ways of expressing such views, but that is not a plausible answer in a liberal democracy where communities with conflicting views have to live side by side. In fact, this is the whole *point* of a liberal democracy! No one religion or comprehensive world view should be privileged, including atheism.[54] It must also be noted that it is not just Christians who need to ask these kinds of questions. Irrespective of the acceptability or otherwise of their *beliefs*, what are acceptable *practices* for gay rights campaigners, animal rights activists, environmentalist campaigners or anti-capitalism demonstrators? Or, for that matter, atheists campaigning against the evils of religion?

A more fundamental objection is that the Bible advocates *beliefs* that are morally unacceptable. Here we shall consider a central objection to the Bible raised by the New Atheists concerning the character of God and the nature of morality found in the Old Testament. Dennett expresses concern about the character of God revealed there: 'Part of what makes Jehovah such a fascinating participant in stories of the Old Testament is His kinglike jealousy and pride, and His great appetite for praise and sacrifices. But we have moved beyond this God (haven't we?).'[55] According to Harris, the Bible requires that we must 'stone people to death for heresy, adultery, homosexuality, working on the Sabbath, worshipping graven images, practicing sorcery, and a wide variety of other imaginary crimes'.[56] Both Dawkins and Hitchens devote lengthy sections to cataloguing moral problems with the Old Testament.[57] Hitchens claims that the Bible contains 'a warrant for trafficking in humans, for ethnic cleansing, for slavery, for bride-price, and for indiscriminate massacre',[58] and he also refers to the 'horrors and cruelties and madnesses of the Old Testament'.[59] Referring to the conquest of Canaan, Dawkins says, 'The ethnic cleansing begun in the time of Moses is brought to bloody fruition in the book of Joshua, a text remarkable for the bloodthirsty massacres it records and the xenophobic relish with which it does so.'[60]

Clearly, the New Atheists are not impressed with the Old Testament! And these are only a flavour of the concerns they raise. So what is the Old Testament like? Is the picture one gets from the New Atheists a fair portrayal? The answer to this is very definitely 'no'. Without wishing to diminish the significance of the issues they raise, it must be pointed out that their coverage of the Old Testament is highly selective. From reading their material, one would not realize that the Old Testament continually emphasizes God's concern for the poor, orphans, widows and foreigners. Deuteronomy, for example, tells us that God 'defends the cause of the fatherless and the widow, and loves the alien' (Deut. 10:18) and the people are commanded 'to be openhanded towards your brothers and towards the poor and needy in your land' (Deut. 15:11). They are commanded not to deny justice to the poor (Exod. 23:6) and later on the prophet Amos takes Israel to task for its failure in this regard (Amos 2:7). God is portrayed as loving, just and merciful. He is 'gracious and compassionate, slow to anger and abounding in love, and he relents from sending calamity' (Joel 2:13). It is also clear from the prophets that God's priority is not to be found in mere rule-keeping and sacrifices; he desires 'mercy, not sacrifice' (Hos. 6:6) and requires his people to 'act justly and to love mercy and to walk humbly with your God' (Mic. 6:8). It is important to emphasize that these are not just a few isolated, unrepresentative passages, but are themes found throughout the Old Testament as a little reading will confirm. Of course, these points do not fully answer the issues raised by the New Atheists, but they do help to provide a much more balanced picture.

In an article entitled 'Is Yahweh a Moral Monster?' the Christian philosopher Paul Copan responds to the issues raised by the New Atheists by exploring the relevant texts in their ancient Near Eastern context and within the broader framework of the biblical canon.[61] It would be impossible to do justice here to all the different examples raised by the New Atheists or to Copan's response, but it is worth drawing attention to some of his points. One of the most obvious is that just because something is described in the Bible does not mean it is thereby being approved. Copan argues that when the New Atheists draw attention to the failings of key figures such as Abraham or Moses as recorded in the Bible, they are missing the point of the text. They are not being portrayed as moral examples but as a 'mixed moral bag'. He also points out that many Old Testament stories are intended to present *negative* role models, a conclusion based on the texts themselves as well as New Testament reflection upon them.

A central dimension of Copan's response is that Old Testament texts need to be considered within their original ancient Near Eastern context rather than from a twenty-first century perspective. He claims that

> we should not view the [Old Testament] as offering an ideal ethic for all cultures
> across the ages. Rather than attempt to morally justify all aspects of the Sinaitic
> legal code, we can affirm that God begins with an ancient people who have imbibed
> dehumanizing customs and social structures from their [ancient Near East] context.[62]

Rather than bringing about a complete overhaul, he claims that God changes things in 'incremental humanizing steps' and so there is a distinction between the *ideal* and the *actual*, between God's high standards and the reality of dealing with a 'sinful, stubborn people' in their ancient environment. Again, he argues that this conclusion is based on the Bible itself. He discusses developments within the Old Testament and emphasizes Jesus' teaching about divorce, which indicates that the Mosaic Law 'tolerated morally inferior conditions because of the *hardness of human hearts*'.[63] Indeed, he also draws attention to the 'planned obsolescence' of the Mosaic Law to make way for a new covenant, which is anticipated in the Old Testament and ultimately fulfilled in Jesus Christ. The point is not that the Law was bad, but that it paved the way for something better. As such, the Law is not God's final word. This certainly undermines the claims of Harris, who seems to think that anyone who takes the Bible seriously ought to be committed to implementing all aspects of the Mosaic Law. Ironically, taking the Bible seriously shows us that this is not the case at all.

The focal point of the New Atheists' concerns about the Old Testament is the conquest of Canaan. What are we to make of God's people taking the Promised Land, destroying cities and killing their inhabitants in the process? Isn't this a clear example of the morally unacceptable nature of the Bible? Needless to say, many Christians find these accounts deeply disturbing and struggle to try to make sense of them. The events in question are not portrayed as negative examples and they seem to require an explanation that goes beyond God's toleration of morally inferior conditions. Rather than trying to find a single, simple answer the starting point should be to consider the context of the events and to try to see how they might fit in with an overall biblical picture.

A relevant point is addressed by Copan, who asks, 'if God exists, does he have any prerogatives over human life?', and he answers, 'If God is the author of life, he is not obligated to give us seventy or eighty years of life.'[64] Swinburne expresses the same point: 'if there is a God, our life for each of us is a gift from God, a temporary gift; and in the course of time he takes the gift back – sometimes after only a few years, sometimes after eighty years'.[65] This point certainly does not provide a solution to the problem, but it still might be relevant as part of the overall picture. Also, it must be stressed that this does not mean that we can attribute anything we like to God without impugning his character, but it does mean that we should not *assume* that God has the same obligations as us.

Furthermore, the Bible portrays the events in question as God's judgment on the Canaanites because of their evil behaviour, including child sacrifice and temple prostitution associated with fertility cults. It seems reasonable to believe that one reason for God to end human life would indeed be judgment for evil behaviour. Perhaps one lesson we can glean from these texts is that God's judgment cannot be made aesthetically pleasing; it comes at a terrible cost and takes a terrible toll. This need not be in conflict with God's also being merciful and compassionate. As noted earlier, the Old Testament portrays God as being 'slow to anger' and one who 'relents from sending calamity'. Of relevance to the present context is the fact that God informs Abraham that his descendants would not return to the land until the fourth generation because 'the sin of the Amorites has not yet reached its full measure' (Gen. 15:16). The point is that God is portrayed as patient in his judgment, waiting until it is fully deserved. Furthermore, as Copan points out, in God's judgment of Sodom, he agreed to spare the city if even ten innocent people could be found. They couldn't, but even then God did spare Lot and his family before he judged the city and, as Dawkins notes, Lot is hardly a good moral role model. Similarly, early in the book of Joshua we are introduced to Rahab, who is spared from God's judgment on Jericho. As Old Testament scholar Christopher Wright points out, the prominence of the story of Rahab is intended to convey God's willingness to spare those who would change their ways.[66]

These points go some way in helping to set the biblical context, but there seem to be two reasons why they are inadequate to account for the killing of the Canaanites. First, while it can be accepted that God can take human life, an objection might be raised on the grounds that he commands other humans (i.e. the Israelites) to do so in this case. A second objection concerns the death of non-combatants, especially children. A response to the first of these objections is that if God has the right to execute judgment on human beings, it is difficult to see why he could not command humans to do so on his behalf.[67] Of course, it is wrong for one human to take the life of another unless it is morally justified, a point clearly taught in the Bible and enshrined in the sixth commandment. This means, as Copan points out, that the Israelites would not have been justified in taking the lives of Canaanites in the absence of God's command to do so. However, if God had good reason to take their lives because of their evil behaviour, then the Israelite action would have been justified given God's command.

This might raise further questions. Did God really command them to attack the Canaanites? Didn't they just *claim* that God commanded them to justify their actions? But these questions miss the point, which is to determine whether the biblical account *as it stands* is morally acceptable. *According to the biblical account*, God did command them for morally justifiable reasons, in which case their taking of Canaanite lives would be justified. This might give rise to a further concern that accepting this conclusion would be equivalent to accepting a present-day regime's claim that in taking the lives of others they are obeying God's command. But this is certainly not the case. These are unique texts, describing unique events. The commands are limited to a particular time and place and cannot be used to justify such actions in the modern world.

The argument is not that taking life is justified simply because *it is claimed* that God commanded it, only that if God really did command such a thing, it would have been justified. This is a subtle distinction, but it is of vital importance. Whether such a claim can be accepted in the case of the Bible depends on the overall case for accepting the truth of Christianity. It must also be emphasized that from a Christian point of view there would be every reason *not* to accept any such claim today. In fact, such a command would imply that the New Testament is false, that Jesus has not fulfilled Israel's destiny, and that the ethics of the kingdom of God are no longer operative. The Israelites were selected to play a particular role for a particular period of time and with the coming of Christ there is no longer any grouping of people who are supposed to play that role.

What about the death of non-combatants, particularly children? Although the ultimate justification for the killing of the Canaanites is God's judgment because of their evil behaviour, there is no suggestion here that God was judging the children. So what kind of response might be provided? Part of Copan's response here is a just war analogy. He claims that a cause such as defeating Hitler can be morally justified even if innocent civilians might be killed.[68] In this case there would need to be good reason to believe that the death of non-combatants was necessary to prevent even greater loss of life or to bring about some other greater good that would have justified their deaths. Hence, such a reason would need to be present in the case of the innocent Canaanites, but the problem is that it is not clear exactly what that reason would be. However, an all-knowing God would know what the consequences of various actions would be, including the consequences for the survival of the Jewish people and so for the coming of the Messiah.

Furthermore, given the context of God's judgment on a people who had become morally depraved and that God has no obligation to give anyone a long life, perhaps it is possible to make some sort of case along these lines. Also, death is not the end of our existence from a Christian point of view. Hence, it is possible for God to provide a kind of compensation in an afterlife. Such compensation would not justify taking life any more than the action of one human causing another to suffer can be justified by providing compensation, but if God had reason to take life on other grounds, such compensation should be considered *as part of the overall picture*. Still, a lot of questions could be raised about this kind of response so we shall explore another approach.

The evidence provided by the texts themselves is of greatest importance. We must look closely at what the Bible actually claims happened and not make lazy assumptions about its meaning. According to the texts, did God command the complete destruction of the Canaanites and did the Israelites carry out a genocide? If we look at some passages it would seem so. Consider the fate of the city of Debir: 'They took the city, its king and its villages, and put them to the sword. Everyone in it they totally destroyed. They left no survivors' (Josh. 10:39). We are also told that 'Joshua took the entire land, just as the LORD had directed Moses . . . Then the land had rest from war' (Josh. 11:23). However, things are not quite as straightforward as they seem. Just two chapters later (Josh. 13) we find areas in this territory that have not been taken over at all.[69] For these reasons Copan and others have drawn attention to the rhetorical use of hyperbolic language in some of the claims in the book of Joshua. This point is clearly expressed by Christopher Wright:

> But this must have been intended as rhetorical exaggeration, for the book of Judges (whose final editor was undoubtedly aware of these accounts in Joshua) sees no contradiction in telling us that the process of subduing the inhabitants of the land was far from completed and went on for considerable time, and that many of the original nations continued to live alongside the Israelites.[70]

In fact, in the first chapter of Judges we find the Israelites attacking Debir again. In his extensive study *On the Reliability of the Old Testament* Egyptologist Kenneth Kitchen is particularly critical of those who have misread Joshua and then declared it to be in conflict with the book of Judges. He says:

> It is the careless reading of such verses as these, without a careful and close reading of the narratives proper, that has encouraged Old Testament scholars to read into the entire book *a whole myth of their own making*, to the effect that the book of Joshua presents a sweeping, total conquest and *occupation* of Canaan by Joshua, which can then be falsely pitted against the narratives in Judges.[71]

Kitchen emphasizes the limited and strategic nature of the accounts in the book of Joshua, albeit described in hyperbolic language. He points to the defeat of two minor centres soon after the Israelites' entry into Canaan followed by attacks on a small number of towns in the south and north of Canaan. He stresses that the text of Joshua is very clear that these 'campaigns were essentially *disabling raids*; they were not territorial conquests with instant Hebrew occupation'.[72] The nature of the campaign raises a question mark about the extent to which non-combatants would have died. Consider the cases of Jericho and Ai, which according to the text were burned by the Israelites. Kitchen points to evidence that both were small towns and it has also been argued that the evidence suggests they may have been military forts rather than towns.[73] If so, this would certainly be consistent with the strategic nature of the campaign and would make it unlikely that many non-combatants lived there.[74]

It must be emphasized that Kitchen, Copan and Wright appeal to the use of rhetoric not because they wish to reject what the Bible says, but precisely because they are taking what the Bible says seriously. Furthermore, they are not saying that the rhetorical claims are asserting falsehoods. Wright puts it like this:

> So when we are reading some of the more graphic descriptions, either of what was commanded to be done or of what was recorded as accomplished, we need to allow for this rhetorical element. This is not to accuse the biblical writers of falsehood, but to recognise the literary conventions of writing about warfare.[75]

Kitchen also notes that this type of rhetoric was a regular feature of military reports in the second and first millennia BC and cites examples including Mesha king of Moab, who about 840/830 BC boasted that 'Israel has utterly perished for always', which Kitchen notes was 'a rather premature judgment at that date, by over a century!'[76]

Although there are other difficult passages in the Old Testament, the conquest of Canaan has been considered here because it is generally thought to be one of the most problematic issues where the morality of the Bible is concerned. Perhaps the most important point to note is that both textual evidence from the Old Testament itself and archaeological evidence confirm that no total conquest took place and so claims that a genocide took place are completely unfounded. In terms of other ethical issues raised by the text, some possible lines of response have been explored. In particular, the rhetorical nature of some aspects of the biblical account has been explored. While a rhetorical analysis does not remove all the morally problematic aspects of the texts, it does suggest that these problems may not be as pressing as a superficial reading would suggest.

One thing to note is that for someone who thinks it very unlikely that God exists or who thinks there are no good reasons for considering the Bible to be a revelation from God it would be very easy to dismiss these texts. For such a person, the arguments considered above are unlikely to have much impact. But the real question is whether these texts provide good enough grounds for ruling out the truth of Christianity. The answer to this seems to be 'no'. Few Christians will be entirely satisfied by the arguments considered above either, but perhaps they hint at possible explanations. And besides, we need to be careful about what exactly could be established on the basis of these difficulties. Even if there were no acceptable explanations, this would not provide any reason to reject belief in God or the resurrection of Jesus.

How do Christians typically respond when the New Atheists or others challenge the character of God based on some of these Old Testament texts, essentially claiming that God has done something that would be morally unacceptable for him to do? A common response is to claim that there is indeed an apparent problem but that there must be some kind of explanation for it, even if it is not known what that explanation is. The reason for taking this approach is that Christians think they have good reason to believe in and trust God. This seems reasonable since it is exactly the approach we take when a human, whom we know and trust implicitly, stands accused of something completely out of character. Atheists, by contrast, respond to the same texts in a very different way since they think there is no reason to trust God and so no reason to assume that there must be some explanation. In other words, the differing world views of theists and atheists shape how they respond to these texts.

This seems to be borne out by a recent conference on these Old Testament texts held at the University of Notre Dame in the US. It brought together a high-profile list of philosophers, both atheists and Christians, to discuss these topics. An atheist philosopher, Evan Fales, presented a case along similar lines to the New Atheists, while a Christian philosopher, Nicholas Wolterstorff, offered a detailed account of the use of rhetoric in the book of Joshua along similar lines to that sketched earlier. Overall, it seemed clear that while there was diversity among the Christians about the right way to think about these issues and how successful the various proposals were, the atheist contributors could see no reason to think that there must be some benign explanation to these difficult texts. Given their different world views it was not obvious that either Fales or Wolterstorff were being irrational in how they approached the topic.

Another Christian philosopher, Eleonore Stump, offered a different kind of explanation from Wolterstorff.[77] Although I shall not go into details about her argument, the basic idea was that at least some of the problematic texts play an important role in a larger narrative in which God's primary aim is to form a people for union with himself, a people who are just, good and loving. When considering some of these texts, it might seem that there are only two options: deny the truth of the account concerning God's commands or else accept the account as true, but give up deeply entrenched moral intuitions. Stump offers a third way: accept the account as true, but see it in the context of the larger narrative. I shall not try to defend her particular account here, but I want to draw on a story she told to emphasize the impact that different perspectives can have.

The gist of the story is that there is a being called Max who lives on another planet on which all the inhabitants are in extremely good health and never die. Max comes into contact with a human who shows him a video of various events in a hospital on Earth. Max is horrified. The video shows footage of people in terrible pain and a surgeon commanding his staff to cut patients open with a knife. Never having come across anything like this before, Max naturally assumes that the purpose of the hospital is to torture people. He is horrified that anyone would consider the surgeon to be a good man who is trying to help others. From Max's point of view there are only two possible options: either we reject the idea that the surgeon is good, or, if we want to claim that he is good, we must radically change our view as to what is morally acceptable to include torture. But we know that Max is mistaken since there is another explanation. We are aware of a larger narrative that makes a third option possible.

What about God as portrayed in the Old Testament? Must we conclude that the God portrayed there is not good, or, if we wish to maintain that he is good, must we radically change our views as to what is morally acceptable? At most we have prima facie evidence against the goodness of the God of Israel. However, we also have evidence in favour of God's goodness that cannot be swept under the carpet, and a closer examination of the texts reveals that they are not as problematic as they first appear. Given these considerations and the limitations of our knowledge, it is entirely possible that further information could remove the tension between the texts that describe the war on the Canaanites and the texts that command mercy. This being the case the orthodox Christian can retain belief in the inspiration of these texts.

Conclusion

In this chapter I have attempted to show that the possibility of a revelation from God cannot be dismissed easily and should be taken seriously. Of course, anyone who is already convinced that there is no God is unlikely to be persuaded that God has provided a revelation. But in the absence of such an atheistic starting point there is no convincing reason to exclude the possibility of a revelation. Indeed, in so far as there is reason to believe in God, there is also some reason to expect a revelation. Furthermore, various criteria (external confirmation, miracles and theological value) can be used to evaluate a putative revelation to determine whether it is genuine. The New Atheists have offered a number of general objections to the possibility of a revelation, but these seem to be very weak indeed.

A more specific objection, however, is that the Bible approves of many things that are morally unacceptable, particularly in the Old Testament. While the New Atheists paint an unrepresentative picture of the Old Testament and overstate the objections, there are nevertheless passages that are genuinely troubling and difficult for Christians. No completely satisfactory response to these issues has been provided, but various ideas have been considered which provide possible (or partial) answers. It certainly seems that these concerns are insufficient to rule out the truth of Christianity. Our attitude to these concerns will to a large extent be shaped by our overall attitude towards Christianity. In particular, what we make of the central claims of Christianity will be of crucial importance and so in the next chapter we shall consider the external confirmation of the Gospels and the question of miracles in the context of the resurrection.

Notes

1. *BTS*, p. 9.
2. Ibid., p. 28.
3. *TGD*, p. 38.
4. Ibid.
5. Ibid., p. 46.
6. *GNG*, p. 65.
7. Millard J. Erickson, *Christian Theology* (Grand Rapids: Baker, 1995), pp. 153–154.
8. Known as the 'rule of faith'. It was used by many leading Christian figures, including Irenaeus and Tertullian who discussed it at length and saw it as summarizing the central claims of Scripture. See Andreas J. Köstenberger and Michael J. Kruger, *The Heresy of Orthodoxy* (Wheaton, Ill.: Crossway, 2010).
9. This does not mean that detailed defences of the Bible are inappropriate. It seems to me that Jesus took a high view of the truthfulness of the Old Testament. It is also important to note that it is quite possible to adopt an evangelical approach to the Bible while taking the historical evidence very seriously. See, for example, K. A. Kitchen, *On the Reliability of the Old Testament* (Grand Rapids: Eerdmans, 2003); and Craig L. Blomberg, *The Historical Reliability of the Gospels*, 2nd ed. (Leicester: Apollos, 2007).
10. See, for example, David Fergusson, *Faith and its Critics: A Conversation* (Oxford: Oxford University Press, 2009), p. 170.
11. Richard Swinburne, *Revelation: From Metaphor to Analogy*, 2nd ed. (Oxford: Oxford University Press, 2007), p. 80.
12. Ibid., p. 81.
13. Ibid., p. 84.
14. This use of evidence relating to the beginning of the universe is different from that in chapter 4. There the point was to provide support for the claim that the universe had a beginning, which in turn was used as the basis for an argument for a creator. This applies irrespective of whether such a creation is part of a putative revelation.

For a defence of the claim that the doctrine of creation *ex nihilo* is revealed in the Bible, see Paul Copan and William Lane Craig, *Creation out of Nothing: A Biblical, Philosophical, and Scientific Exploration* (Leicester: Apollos; Grand Rapids: Baker Academic, 2004).

15. Swinburne, *Revelation*, p. 112.

16. Paul K. Moser, *The Evidence for God* (New York: Cambridge University Press, 2010), p. 23. Moser is not writing about revelation as such, but many of his arguments are relevant to evaluating a purported revelation.

17. Ibid., p. 26, emphasis in original.

18. Ibid., p. 31.

19. Another factor might be the internal consistency and coherence of the revelation. Consistency and coherence on their own would not be very significant since a work of fiction can be both consistent and coherent. There would be a problem if a revelation was inconsistent, but the central claims of the Christian message seem to be both consistent and coherent. Some have claimed that certain Christian doctrines such as the Trinity and incarnation are incoherent, but while there is no doubt that such doctrines are difficult to understand, there does not appear to be any convincing reason to think that they are inconsistent or incoherent. See, for example, J. P. Moreland and William Lane Craig, *Philosophical Foundations for a Christian Worldview* (Downers Grove: IVP, 2003); Richard Swinburne, *The Christian God* (Oxford: Clarendon, 1994).

20. *TGD*, p. 19.

21. Ibid., p. 349.

22. Ibid., pp. 350–351.

23. Ibid., pp. 87–92. For a defence of the argument from religious experience, see Richard Swinburne, *The Existence of God*, 2nd ed. (Oxford: Oxford University Press, 2004), pp. 293–327.

24. *TGD*, p. 282. In this passage Dawkins is discussing fundamentalism, but his discussion suggests that he intends it to apply to anyone who takes revelation seriously, which may well be what Dawkins means by 'fundamentalist'.

25. *GNG*, pp. 97–98.

26. Sam Harris, *Letter to a Christian Nation: A Challenge to Faith* (London: Bantam, 2007), p. 6.

27. *BTS*, pp. 240–241.

28. More on this in the next chapter.

29. See James Herrick, *The Making of the New Spirituality: The Eclipse of the Western Religious Tradition* (Downers Grove: IVP, 2003), pp. 185–191.

30. Of course, this does not mean that the truth of Christianity entails that *everything* about other religions is false.

31. *GNG*, p. 90.

32. Harris, *Letter to a Christian Nation*, pp. 60–61.

33. As noted in chapter 1, I assume an orthodox viewpoint throughout. For a comparison with a liberal view see David L. Edwards and John R. W. Stott, *Essentials: A Liberal–Evangelical Dialogue* (London: Hodder & Stoughton, 1988), which includes dialogue on some of the topics considered here.

34. Richard Dawkins, *River out of Eden: A Darwinian View of Life* (London: Phoenix, 1995), p. 133.

35. Within Christianity this is understood in terms of human rebellion against God as captured by the doctrine of the Fall. This does not mean that all suffering results from human sinfulness. See chapter 8 for further discussion.

36. C. S. Lewis, *Mere Christianity* (London: Fontana, 1955), p. 6.

37. John Hare, *The Moral Gap* (Oxford: Oxford University Press, 1997).

38. Ibid., pp. 99–169.

39. *GNG*, p. 213, emphasis in original.

40. G. K. Chesterton, *What's Wrong with the World* (New York: Dodd, Mead, 1910), p. 38.

41. *GNG*, pp. 212–213.

42. See, for example, Mark 7:20–23.

43. *TGD*, p. 253. See also *GNG*, pp. 208–210.

44. Hare follows Swinburne in identifying repentance (which at least involves internal admission of guilt by the offender), apology, reparation (removal of the harm caused by the offence) and penance (a token of sincerity that goes beyond reparation) as the components involved in making good the offence, although not all are necessary in every case. See Hare, *Moral Gap*, pp. 226–227; and Richard Swinburne, *Responsibility and Atonement* (Oxford: Oxford University Press, 1989), p. 25.

45. Hare, *Moral Gap*, p. 229.

46. Ibid., p. 248.

47. Ibid., p. 247. Because reparation has to be exacted, Hare considers it to be punishment. In fact, Hare is defending a version of the view of the atonement known as 'penal substitution'. Swinburne, whose account is very similar to Hare's in many respects, does not consider his account to be a version of penal substitution. The main reason for this is that Swinburne thinks that Christ's suffering and death were not a punishment because he underwent it voluntarily, but, as Hare points out, this does not seem sufficient to deny that it was punishment.

48. Ibid., p. 251.

49. Hare discusses this in terms of the biblical idea of being incorporated 'in Christ' (ibid., pp. 248–256).

50. See, for example, Brian J. Dodd, *The Problem with Paul* (Downers Grove: IVP, 1996); Christopher Ash, *Marriage: Sex in the Service of God* (Leicester: IVP, 2003); Jonathan

Kvanvig, 'Resurrection, Heaven, and Hell', in Charles Taliaferro and Paul Draper (eds.), *A Companion to Philosophy of Religion*, 2nd ed. (Boston: Routledge, 2010), pp. 630–639.

51. *TGD*, pp. 319–320.

52. Ibid., pp. 290–291.

53. Ibid., pp. 294–297.

54. See, for example, Robert Audi and Nicholas Wolterstorff, *Religion in the Public Square: The Place of Religious Convictions in Political Debate* (Lanham, Md.: Rowman & Littlefield, 1997).

55. *BTS*, p. 265.

56. Harris, *Letter to a Christian Nation*, p. 8.

57. *TGD*, pp. 237–250; *GNG*, pp. 97–107.

58. *GNG*, p. 102.

59. Ibid., p. 103.

60. *TGD*, p. 247.

61. Paul Copan, 'Is Yahweh a Moral Monster?', *Philosophia Christi* 10 (2008), pp. 9–37.

62. Ibid., p. 16.

63. Ibid., p. 28.

64. Ibid., p. 25.

65. Swinburne, *Revelation*, p. 91.

66. Christopher J. H. Wright, *The God I Don't Understand: Reflections on Tough Questions of Faith* (Grand Rapids: Zondervan, 2008), p. 101.

67. It could be argued that it would morally corrupt or psychologically damage those carrying it out, but this very much depends on the people involved. Since it seems that this kind of warfare was common at the time, it is not clear that it would have had much effect beyond what would have been expected by any kind of military combat.

68. Sam Harris agrees that such 'collateral damage' is morally acceptable (*TEF*, pp. 192–203). In fact, he goes much further and argues that torture would be acceptable in any circumstances in which collateral damage would be acceptable.

69. This is also apparent from Josh. 23.

70. Wright, *God I Don't Understand*, p. 88.

71. Kitchen, *Reliability of the Old Testament*, pp. 173–174, emphasis in original.

72. Ibid., p. 162, emphasis in original.

73. Richard S. Hess, 'War in the Hebrew Bible', in Richard S. Hess and E. A. Martens (eds.), *War in the Bible and Terrorism in the Twenty-first Century* (Winona Lake, Ind.: Eisenbrauns, 2008), pp. 29–30.

74. Those reading the texts in ancient times would have been better able than we are to differentiate between the rhetoric of Joshua and the strategic campaign described in Judges.

75. Ibid., p. 88. Copan argues that appealing to rhetoric in the case of what Israel was commanded to do by God resolves a further tension in the text. See Paul Copan, *Is God a Moral Monster? Making Sense of the Old Testament God* (Grand Rapids: Baker, 2011), p. 173.

76. Kitchen, *Reliability of the Old Testament*, p. 174.

77. The articles by Fales, Wolterstorff and Stump can be found in M. Bergmann, M. J. Murray and M. C. Rea (eds.), *Divine Evil? The Moral Character of the God of Abraham* (Oxford: Oxford University Press, 2011). In fact, Stump focuses on the killing of the Amalekites in 1 Sam. 15 rather than the Canaanites.

In a letter to Christians in Corinth the apostle Paul wrote that 'if Christ has not been raised [from the dead], our preaching is useless and so is your faith' (1 Cor. 15:14). The New Atheists would no doubt concur. The truth of the historic Christian faith depends on the actual occurrence of certain events. As far as the New Atheists are concerned this is just the problem, because the events in question never happened. They are not alone in their conclusion. For over two hundred years Jesus of Nazareth has been the subject of much historical investigation in what is known as the 'Quest for the historical Jesus'. The goal in this quest has been to find out what can be known about Jesus on historical grounds and not simply on the basis of taking the Gospels at face value. For much of the quest the conclusions reached have been sceptical in nature. In particular, it was claimed that we could know very little about Jesus and that there was no historical case for key Christian beliefs about Jesus, especially the resurrection; the 'Jesus of history' could not be equated with the 'Christ of faith'. Historic Christianity was no longer tenable. Or so it was argued.

The New Atheists assert these sceptical conclusions with confidence. If they are to be believed, we can know virtually nothing about Jesus and can be certain that there was no resurrection and that none of the other miracles occurred either. They claim that the Gospels were written long after the events, are generally unreliable, borrow from ancient myths, were selected over rival accounts without justification, and have been corrupted since they were originally written. If that is not bad enough, Dawkins and Hitchens even raise a question mark over whether Jesus existed at all. Not surprisingly, their thesis here fits in very well with their views on faith and reason more generally: faith has come into conflict with reason (here in the form of historical scholarship) and it should now be clear to any rational person that faith has come off worst.

One thing that the New Atheists fail to tell us, however, is that scholarship on the historical Jesus has become much less sceptical in recent decades. On the basis of the evidence available, many have reached the conclusion that we can know quite a lot about the historical Jesus. While few scholars of the historical Jesus treat the Gospels as faultless historical records, nearly all would be horrified at the claims of the New Atheists. It is worth noting that some leading researchers in this field have argued that the evidence points to a Jesus of history quite compatible with orthodox Christian belief. Indeed, various authors have mounted a very serious case for the resurrection on historical grounds. We shall pursue some of these issues in this chapter, addressing some of the issues raised by the New Atheists along the way, and finish up by focusing on the resurrection.

The historical Jesus

What can be known about Jesus on the basis of historical evidence? For most of the twentieth century the consensus among scholars working on the historical study of Jesus was that very little could be known. Rudolf Bultmann, one of the leading scholars in this field of study in the first half of the twentieth century, summed up the views of many when he wrote, 'I do indeed think that we can know almost nothing concerning the life and personality of Jesus.'[1] With the advent of what has become known as the 'third quest' for the historical Jesus, since about 1980, the consensus about what can be known on the basis of the evidence has shifted considerably.[2] So much so that E. P. Sanders, one of the leading scholars in this field in the second half of the twentieth century, claimed that a significant amount could be known about Jesus on the basis of the evidence. In his book *The Historical Figure of Jesus*, where his stated aim is 'to lay out, as clearly as possible, what we can know, using the standard methods of historical research',[3] he contends that there 'are no substantial doubts about the general course of Jesus' life' and goes on to catalogue a list of statements about Jesus' life that are 'almost beyond dispute'. These include that he was born about 4 BC, spent his childhood and early adult years in Nazareth, was baptized by John the Baptist, called disciples, taught in the towns, villages and countryside of Galilee, preached 'the kingdom of God', went to Jerusalem for the Passover in about AD 30, created a disturbance in the temple, had a final meal with his disciples, was arrested and interrogated by Jewish authorities (specifically the high priest), and was executed on the orders of the Roman prefect, Pontius Pilate. He adds some 'equally secure facts about the aftermath of Jesus' life' and also notes that a 'list of everything that we know about Jesus would be appreciably longer'.[4] It is important to emphasize that Sanders does not hold these beliefs on the basis of an uncritical acceptance of the Gospels as historical truth. And it should also be noted that he does not arrive at orthodox Christian conclusions, but his work illustrates how dramatically things have changed since Bultmann.

In the light of this consider Dawkins's claim that it is 'possible to mount a serious, though not widely supported, historical case that Jesus never lived at all',[5] and Hitchens's reference to the 'highly questionable existence of Jesus',[6] even though neither actually denies the existence of Jesus. What is going on here? How could they question the existence of Jesus, when an expert in this field of study like Sanders claims we can know a lot about him? Not even someone as sceptical about the historical evidence as Bultmann ever claimed that the very existence of Jesus was in question. But how can we know anything about Jesus, even that he existed? What evidence is there?

Even though Jesus did not have any political power and lived in a remote part of the Roman Empire, there are a number of ancient sources outside the New Testament that refer to him. One is found in the *Annals* of the Roman historian Tacitus in the context of his discussion of Nero's persecution of Christians in Rome. He refers to Christus having 'suffered the extreme penalty during the reign of Tiberius at the hands of one of our procurators, Pontius Pilatus', which is in complete correspondence with the Gospels.[7] Jesus is also mentioned twice in the *Antiquities of the Jews* by Josephus, a first-century Jewish historian. One of these is a reference to the death of James, 'the brother of Jesus, who was called Christ'.[8] Another is a much-debated passage that appears to be generally regarded as reliable in referring to Jesus and his crucifixion even though it contains Christian interpolations as well.[9] There are also references to the practices of early Christians in ancient letters, including one by Pliny the Younger, which refers to the early worship of Jesus.[10] The Jewish Talmud refers to Jesus as a false teacher who was put to death on the eve of the Passover and who practised sorcery, which seems to confirm the belief that he performed miracles.[11] Interestingly, all of these sources are non-Christian and indeed anti-Christian in some cases. There are also other ancient sources outside the New Testament that contain information about

Jesus, including early Christian documents such as a letter by Clement of Rome.[12]

While it is clear that the New Testament is not the only source of information about Jesus, it is certainly true that almost all of what can be known about Jesus is based on the documents within it, especially the Gospels. And, of course, the New Testament material should not be excluded. A historian could hardly be expected to accept uncritically everything reported in the New Testament documents, but it would clearly be inappropriate to go to the other extreme and reject them as historical sources altogether unless, of course, there were good reasons for doing so. A much more reasonable assumption would be that the evidence should be assessed just as it would in any other historical case.[13] In particular, ancient documents that refer to Jesus should be treated on their historical merit, open to the same kinds of scrutiny as other ancient documents. This being the case, it would be unreasonable simply to exclude the New Testament documents from the picture, or only to accept what they say when it can be corroborated from other sources. If this approach were taken with other ancient documents, we would have almost no historical knowledge at all.

Within the New Testament, letters that pre-date the Gospels, such as those written by the apostle Paul, contain information about Jesus and there is evidence that some of these letters contain early creeds that date back earlier still and contain some of the earliest information about Jesus.[14] Before dealing with some of the New Atheists' concerns about the Gospels, however, it is worth noting that even the most sceptical scholars think the Gospels provide at least some information about the historical Jesus. The claim that Jesus might not have existed is not even on their radar.[15]

The gospel truth

Despite their claims noted above, Dawkins and Hitchens seem to accept that Jesus existed as a historical figure. However, in general the New Atheists' attitudes towards the Gospels suggest that, like Bultmann, they would claim that very little can be known about the life of Jesus. Dawkins, for example, claims:

> Although Jesus probably existed, reputable biblical scholars do not in general regard the New Testament (and obviously not the Old Testament) as a reliable record of what actually happened in history. . . . The only difference between *The Da Vinci Code* and the gospels is that the gospels are ancient fiction while *The Da Vinci Code* is modern fiction.[16]

Dawkins's evaluation of the situation seems little better than wishful thinking, however, and is certainly not based on an attempt to assess what biblical scholars in general believe. For example, in addition to referring to a couple of biblical scholars who do take a very sceptical view, his case against Scripture is based on the claims of Tom Flynn, the editor of *Free Inquiry* magazine, A. N. Wilson and G. A. Wells (who wrote a book questioning the existence of Jesus), none of whom are biblical scholars. It is also worth noting that Wilson has since revoked his atheism in favour of Christianity.[17]

Now, of course, the impression should not be given that most biblical scholars have reached orthodox Christian conclusions on the basis of the evidence. Had Dawkins claimed that they do not regard the New Testament as a *completely* reliable record he would certainly have been correct. But as noted earlier, the vast majority of biblical scholars believe, on the basis of historical considerations, that the Gospels provide us with at least a reasonable amount of reliable information about the life of Jesus. Consider, for example, a group of North American biblical scholars known as the Jesus Seminar, who adopt a highly sceptical stance on these issues and have been heavily criticized by other scholars on historical grounds.[18] Yet even they believe that about 18% of the sayings attributed to Jesus in the Gospels were actually spoken by him. And the reason they have been so controversial is because other scholars think they are much too sceptical in their treatment of the evidence. Dawkins's claim that the Gospels can simply be dismissed as 'ancient fiction' is itself a fiction if the views of experts in this area are to be taken seriously.

But, of course, truth is not established by majority vote. So even if the New Atheists overstate the scepticism of biblical scholarship, we cannot conclude from this that their own scepticism is unjustified. We must ask then on what grounds they adopt this highly sceptical stance despite the much more positive assessment of the evidence in recent scholarship. As we shall see, the grounds for this scepticism are very flimsy indeed. In responding to the New Atheists it is important to emphasize that my goal is not to argue for the complete reliability of the Gospels or to demonstrate that they are a revelation from God,[19] but to argue that they should be taken seriously as historical sources that provide us with sufficient information to obtain a reliable picture of Jesus. For Christians the Gospels are more than just historical sources and can be rationally accepted as revelation, but it is not necessary to demonstrate this in order to evaluate the central claims of Christianity.

One objection to the four Gospels as reliable sources of historical information is based on the claim that they were included in the New Testament canon at the expense of alternative accounts, which were suppressed because they were in conflict with the views of those who had risen to power in the church. Referring to the documents found at Nag Hammadi in Egypt in 1945, which include the *Gospel of Thomas*, the *Gospel of Philip* and the *Gospel of Mary*, Hitchens says, 'These scrolls were of the same period and provenance as many of the subsequently canonical and "authorized" Gospels . . . They include the "Gospels" or narratives of marginal but significant figures in the accepted "New" Testament . . .'[20] Although Dennett does not discuss the matter, he quotes the theologian Elaine Pagels from her book *The Gnostic Gospels*:

> We now begin to see that what we call Christianity . . . actually represents only a small selection of specific sources, chosen from among dozens of others. Who made that selection, and for what reasons? Why were these other writings excluded and banned as 'heresy'? What made them so dangerous?[21]

Dawkins also claims:

> The four gospels that made it into the official canon were chosen, more or less arbitrarily, out of a larger sample of at least a dozen . . . The gospels that didn't make it were omitted by those ecclesiastics perhaps because they included stories that were even more embarrassingly implausible than those in the four canonical ones. . . .
> there is no more and no less reason to believe the four canonical gospels. All have the status of legends . . .[22]

Ironically, given their emphasis on the importance of evidence, the New Atheists have uncritically adopted some of the most extreme views on the Gospels instead of taking the best evidence and scholarship into account. Consider the dating of the Gospels and the Gnostic texts.[23] Although it is extremely difficult to date any of these documents precisely, there seems to be an almost complete consensus that the four canonical Gospels were written in the first century, with Mark written in the 60s, Matthew and Luke in the 70s and John in the 90s.[24] By contrast, the Gnostic gospels are generally dated much later with, for example, the *Gospel of Mary* usually dated to the second half of the second century.[25] Despite the names associated with them, we can be confident that they were not written by significant figures in the New Testament as Hitchens claims. There appears to have been more debate about the dating of the *Gospel of Thomas*, which is considered by the Jesus Seminar to be on a par with the canonical Gospels, but again the consensus is that it is a middle or late second-century document.

Dawkins's claim that the selection process for the canon was more or less arbitrary displays a complete disregard for the relevant evidence. Although the final list of twenty-seven books that constitute the New Testament was not finalized until much later, most of the canon was established by the end of the second century. The Muratorian canon, which dates to this period, consisted of twenty-one or twenty-two of the New Testament books, including the four Gospels. New Testament scholars Carson and Moo identify the three primary criteria for deciding whether a document should be included in the canon: (1) its conformity with established Christian belief, (2) that it was written by apostles or their associates, and (3) that it had been in widespread and continuous acceptance and use by churches everywhere.[26] The four Gospels satisfied all three criteria and there never seems to have been any doubt that they should be included among the authoritative books. The same cannot be said for the Gnostic gospels. Indeed, given the second of the three criteria, the Gnostic gospels were never serious candidates.[27] There is also a significant contrast between these texts and the canonical Gospels in terms of content, but we shall return to this point later.

It is worth quoting one of the leading researchers in historical study of Jesus on this topic, John Meier:

> For better or worse, in our quest for the historical Jesus, we are largely confined to the canonical Gospels; the genuine 'corpus' is infuriating in its restrictions. For the historian it is a galling limitation. But to call upon the Gospel of Peter or the Gospel of Thomas to supplement our Four Gospels is to broaden out our pool of sources from the difficult to the incredible.[28]

Meier can hardly be accused of simply accepting what the four Gospels say uncritically. Why he thinks being confined to the four Gospels is such a limitation is far from clear; ancient historians would give anything to have similar resources to draw on for other historical figures. But whatever his reasoning, these are the only Gospels we have. It is interesting that while Dawkins thinks the Gospels, like Dan Brown's book *The Da Vinci Code*, are works of fiction, his views on the inclusion of the Gospels in the canon are practically identical to those found in Dan Brown's book and seriously at odds with the vast majority of scholarly opinion.

Chinese whispers

A second objection raised by the New Atheists concerns how the Gospels came to be in their current form. Hitchens remarks that 'just like the Old Testament, the "New" one is also a work of crude carpentry, hammered together long after its purported events' and then goes on to quote

H. L. Mencken, who claimed that most of the New Testament documents 'show unmistakable signs of having been tampered with'. Hitchens considers this conclusion to be irrefutable and to 'have been borne out by later scholarship'.[29] He also claims that many of the sayings and teachings of Jesus are 'hearsay upon hearsay upon hearsay'.[30] Dawkins asserts that the Gospels 'were written long after the death of Jesus' and adds that they 'were then copied and recopied, through many different "Chinese Whispers generations" . . . by fallible scribes who, in any case, had their own religious agendas'.[31]

It is important to distinguish between two issues here. First, there is the claim that the Gospels have been corrupted in the process of transmission down through the centuries so that the Gospels we have today do not correspond to the originals. Secondly, there is the claim that the original Gospels were written too long after the death of Jesus to be reliable. On the first point, even though there is an intuitive plausibility to Dawkins's Chinese whispers analogy, there is precious little evidence to back it up and plenty that counts against it. It's not that no errors occurred in the copying process. They did, but by cross-checking various copies it is possible to see where errors have been made. By way of analogy, consider a schoolteacher writing a sentence on the board for young children to copy and suppose all of the children make one or two minor errors, an incorrect letter or two. It would be likely in such a scenario that no two copies would be identical. Now suppose we wish to determine the original sentence, but only have the children's copies to go on. Would it be possible? Yes, since by cross-checking their copies we would see where they had gone wrong. Similarly, textual scholars examine numerous manuscripts of the New Testament to examine the variations between them. And, of course, the more there are the better the prospects for identifying problems. In the case of the New Testament they have a lot of manuscripts to deal with; somewhere in the region of 5,700 Greek manuscripts as well as many translated into other languages, including over 10,000 in Latin.[32] In terms of such manuscript evidence, no other ancient manuscript comes close. Homer comes in second with about 2,500 extant manuscripts, but a figure of about 20 is more typical in most cases.

In the vast majority of cases the textual variants are inconsequential and have little or no effect on the meaning. The New Testament scholar Craig Blomberg claims that 'overall, 97–99% of the [New Testament] can be reconstructed beyond any reasonable doubt, and no Christian doctrine is founded solely or even primarily on textually disputed passages'.[33] Both Hitchens and Dawkins draw attention to the work of another New Testament scholar, Bart Ehrman, emphasizing his rejection of what they describe as fundamentalist Christianity on the basis of some of these issues as documented in his book

Misquoting Jesus.[34] Hitchens focuses on two variants in the New Testament that
are discussed by Ehrman, the story of the woman accused of adultery in John
7:53 – 8:11 and the ending of Mark's Gospel (Mark 16:9–20).[35] Several brief
points must be noted, however. First, these two variants are by far the longest
variants in the New Testament. Secondly, they have been known about for a
long time. And, thirdly, most modern translations of the Bible note that they
are not found in the earliest manuscripts. It is difficult to see why this would
undermine the credibility of the New Testament as a whole. Ironically, these
variants can help illustrate that the New Testament *has not been* seriously corrupted because they are the exceptions that prove the rule. As a result of
textual criticism we know where there is some dispute about the text and,
more importantly, where there is no dispute (i.e. almost all of it).

Of course, there is more to Ehrman's case than the points mentioned
by Hitchens. It might be thought that if all his arguments were taken into
account, the case against the Gospels would be compelling. After all, if
someone as formerly conservative as Ehrman has given up his faith, doesn't
this show that taking historical and textual issues seriously inevitably leads to
the conclusion that the Gospels are unreliable? To see that this is not the case,
we need look no further than Ehrman's colleague Bruce Metzger, who is one
of the world's leading authorities on the textual study of the Bible and under
whom Ehrman studied at Princeton Theological Seminary. Metzger's study of
textual variants has not resulted in any loss of confidence in the reliability of
the Gospels. Quite the reverse in fact. Metzger holds to orthodox Christian
beliefs and considers the case for the reliability of the Gospels to be extremely
convincing.[36] Why would Ehrman give up his faith as a result of textual considerations when Metzger is convinced that the textual evidence supports his
faith? Another New Testament scholar, Craig Evans, has some interesting
suggestions. Considering the kinds of objections Ehrman raises about the
Bible, he suggests that Ehrman may have placed too much emphasis on the
doctrine of inerrancy. Evans refers to a 'brittle fundamentalism' that takes
the attitude 'Show me one mistake in the Bible and I will throw out the whole
thing.' He emphasizes that

> The truth of the Christian message hinges not on the inerrancy of Scripture or on
> our ability to harmonize the four Gospels but on the resurrection of Jesus. And the
> historical reliability of the Gospels does not hinge on the inerrancy of Scripture or
> on proof that no mistake of any kind can be detected in them.[37]

Whether or not Evans is right about Ehrman, these points seem to apply to
the New Atheists. By pointing out what they consider to be inconsistencies,

they seem to think that the Gospels can be easily dismissed as historically unreliable.[38] In an article on the resurrection, Timothy and Lydia McGrew draw attention to eighteenth-century opponents of Christianity who used this tactic to 'point to various discrepancies, real or imagined, in the telling of the same story and to conclude that the texts contradict each other and therefore are untrustworthy at best and worthless at worst'. They claim that minor discrepancies in the Gospel accounts such as Peter's denial of Christ or the resurrection narratives

> have afforded sceptics a pretext for discounting the narratives tout court, and some earnest defenders of the gospels have played into their hands by insisting that every detail is reported with minute accuracy, even if this forces one to the conclusion that Peter denied Christ six or twelve times rather than three.[39]

They go on to illustrate that reports in secular history 'always display selection and emphasis and not infrequently contradict each other outright', and yet 'this fact does not destroy or even significantly undermine their credibility regarding the main events they report'. Furthermore, they point out that in law 'it has long been recognized that minor discrepancies among witnesses do not invalidate their testimony – indeed, they provide an argument against collusion'.[40]

Let's now consider the second issue arising from Hitchens and Dawkins's claims relating to the production of the Gospels, that they are unreliable because they were written long after the events they describe. We have seen that there are serious objections to the idea that something akin to Chinese whispers has resulted in substantial corruption of the Gospels in their transmission down through the centuries. However, could it be that the Chinese whispers analogy applies not to the transmission of the Gospels but to their production in the first place? The idea is that whatever actually took place in the life of Jesus, stories about him were told and retold many times before the Gospels were written down. With these retellings the stories were embellished so much that they became legends. As Dawkins puts it, they 'have the status of legends, as factually dubious as the stories of King Arthur and his knights of the Round Table'.[41]

Views along these lines were very popular in the first half of the twentieth century and were the basis for the sceptical position of Bultmann and others, but there are now known to be very serious problems with this position. One of the most important factors concerns the date of authorship of the Gospels. In the past, some scholars believed the Gospels were written much later than was actually the case, particularly John's Gospel, which was sometimes given dates after AD 150. Had that been the case, it might have made this kind of legendary development possible, but now there is a consensus that John was written in the first century. One of the reasons for this earlier date is due to the discovery of a small fragment of John 18, referred to as papyrus 52, which has been dated to about AD 130, while other considerations push the date earlier still.[42] And as we saw earlier, the other Gospels are earlier than John.

These dates are very significant for two reasons. First, the length of time between when the document was written and the date of the earliest manuscript evidence is much shorter in the case of the Gospels than it is for many other ancient documents. The writings of the historian Tacitus, for example, are based on just a handful of manuscripts from the ninth century, even though he wrote in the early second century – a gap of seven hundred years. By contrast, the Gospels are based on numerous manuscripts, some of which date to the second century, with the earliest only about forty years after the date of writing.[43] Secondly, the date between the events described and the date of writing is shorter in the case of the Gospels than in many ancient histories and biographies. Craig Blomberg points out that the two relatively reliable biographers of Alexander the Great wrote more than four hundred years after his death and yet it was only in subsequent writings that more fictitious stories developed.[44]

Still, even if there was not enough time for legends to develop to the extent Dawkins suggests, how reliable are the Gospels if they were written between AD 60 and 100 when the events they describe took place about AD 30? Again, for Bultmann and others the answer was that they are not reliable at all. The idea was that the Gospels were based on short units that pre-dated them and were transmitted orally. These oral traditions were supposedly shaped or even created by the early church to address the issues with which the Christian community was dealing at the time. It was claimed that there were no mechanisms in place to ensure stability in the community's transmission of the traditions and as a consequence both the traditions and the Gospels on which they depend are unreliable as history. There are now known to be serious objections to this approach,[45] however, not least the fact discussed above that the time between the life of Jesus and the Gospels is not nearly as long as had been thought.

A particular objection concerns the idea that the traditions would be subject to greater modification and development over time, an idea that is assumed in the Chinese whispers analogy. Leading scholars in historical Jesus research N. T. Wright and James Dunn have argued that an alternative model for transmission of early Christian traditions proposed by another

New Testament scholar, Kenneth Bailey, is much more plausible.[46] Roughly, Bailey's idea, which is based on observation of oral tradition in the Middle East, is that the transmission process can preserve the traditions even when there is no formal structure in place such as recognized teachers. In the telling of stories or reciting of poetry, the community itself preserves these traditions since someone who makes a mistake will be corrected by other members of the community. Complete correctness is required in the case of poetry, but for stories some flexibility is allowed although the key features are fixed, and so the essential nature of the story cannot change.[47] Dunn draws attention to the fact that each retelling of a story is not a development of the previous retelling, but simply a retelling of the story itself. This means that the story does not develop from one retelling to the next, to the next, and so on, until it becomes unrecognizable. In other words, it is nothing like Chinese whispers.

Interestingly, Dennett discusses similar ways in which traditions can be preserved, particularly through public rituals. He draws attention to the 'majority rule' strategy as a way of ensuring copy fidelity and notes:

> It can be seen at work in any oral tradition, religious or secular, in which people act in unison – praying or singing or dancing, for instance. Not everybody will remember the words or the melody or the next step, but most will, and those who are out of step will quickly correct themselves to join the throng, preserving the traditions much more reliably than any of them could do on their own.[48]

Dennett's scenario as well as the model advocated by Wright and Dunn are based on a community's ability to preserve traditions without the need for more formal structures. In the case of the Gospels, however, biblical scholar Richard Bauckham argues that more formal structures *were* in place to further enhance the preservation of the oral traditions.[49] In particular, he draws attention to the formal process of receiving and passing on traditions referred to in Paul's writings (e.g. in 1 Cor. 15:3), the role of memorization, which would have been enhanced by Jesus' use of parables and aphorisms, the likely use of written accounts preceding the Gospels to aid memory, and, most significantly, the important role of eyewitnesses in preserving the traditions. Bauckham presents a detailed case for the claim that eyewitnesses played a key role, including the following: the use of names in the Gospels; the twelve disciples as official eyewitnesses; the use of a literary device in Mark, Luke and John that he argues points to the role of eyewitnesses; the importance of eyewitnesses in Paul's account of the resurrection appearances as well as in other early accounts, including Peter's speeches in the book of Acts; and the availability of eyewitnesses in the time prior to the writing of the Gospels, particularly in the Jerusalem church. He also argues that the early Christians were concerned to preserve the history of Jesus because, in effect, their salvation depended upon it. Furthermore, drawing on psychological studies relating to the factors that enhance the reliability of memory, Bauckham argues that the kind of events recorded in the Gospel narratives are such that we would expect them to be remembered correctly by eyewitnesses.[50]

A further response to the objection of Dawkins and Hitchens is based on external confirmation from archaeology. For example, there is plenty of evidence that Luke, who wrote both the Gospel of Luke and the book of Acts, is reliable as a writer of history. Numerous facts about people, titles of local officials, geography, religious practices, and so on have been confirmed independently.[51] The Roman historian A. N. Sherwin-White wrote, 'For Acts the confirmation of historicity is overwhelming. Any attempt to reject its basic historicity even in matters of detail must now appear absurd.'[52] There is likewise external confirmation of various people, places and practices described in the Gospels, not least in the Gospel of John, which had often been dismissed as a historical source. For example, excavations carried out under the ruin of an ancient church discovered in 1888 appear to have identified the pool of Bethesda, including its porticoes, mentioned in John 5:2, while excavations in 2004 appear to have identified the pool of Siloam mentioned in John 9:7.[53]

In an interesting study, Richard Bauckham compared the names of people in the Gospels with those obtained from other ancient sources. He found a close correspondence between the relative frequencies of names found in the Gospels and Palestinian Jewish sources of the period more generally, but no such correspondence with Jewish names from outside Palestine. His claim is that such a correspondence 'would be difficult to explain as the result of random invention of names within Palestinian Jewish Christianity and impossible to explain as the result of such invention outside Jewish Palestine'. He adds, 'All the evidence indicates the general authenticity of the personal names in the Gospels.'[54]

It is certainly true that the external confirmation noted above does not prove the truth of everything contained within the Gospels, but it does show that the Gospels are set in a real historical context and that, in so far as we are able to cross-check with other sources of information, there is a high degree of general reliability. Taking into account the evidence of the earliness of the Gospels and of their being historical in genre and based upon eyewitness testimony can give us confidence that the accounts in the Gospels accurately reflect what was *claimed* by the disciples themselves. The fact that they made these claims about Jesus then stands in need of explanation.

Based on the evidence there is good reason to take the Gospels seriously as sources of historical information and so they cannot be easily dismissed. By contrast, what can be easily dismissed is Dawkins's absurd claim that 'all the essential features of the Jesus legend . . . are borrowed – every last one of them – from other religions already in existence in the Mediterranean and Near East region'.[55] The primary reason why these alleged parallels between Christianity and the Mystery Religions are not taken seriously, even by scholars who reject the central claims of Christianity, is very straightforward. In contrast to Christianity, which has a very definite link with history, the Mystery Religions were based on the annual cycle of birth and death in nature and not on specific historical claims. Other objections to Dawkins's claim are that when scrutinized more closely the differences are far more striking than the parallels, which are not nearly as strong as they superficially appear to be, and that in so far as there has been any borrowing it has been the Mystery Religions borrowing from Christianity and not vice versa.[56]

No matter how much the New Atheists might like to think otherwise, there is no disputing the fact that the Gospels provide us with historical information about Jesus. But even if this is granted, it still might be claimed that there is no reason to accept the central tenets of Christianity concerning the person of Jesus. In particular, the Gospels tell us not only about the teaching of Jesus, but about miracles he performed and that he rose from the dead. Surely there is no reason to take belief in the resurrection seriously. Or is there?

Resurrection: the facts

There is no doubting the importance of the resurrection to Christianity. It is emphasized in letters of the apostle Paul, as highlighted at the start of this chapter, and as the New Testament scholar N. T. Wright has pointed out, 'There is no form of early Christianity known to us that does not affirm that after Jesus' shameful death God raised him to life again.'[57] Given its importance to Christianity, it is surprising that the New Atheists do not say more about it. Of course, their overall attitude to miracles[58] makes it clear that they consider belief in the resurrection to be irrational, so perhaps they simply think that it does not warrant serious discussion. Hitchens, however, makes the following comment:

> Having no reliable or consistent witness, in anything like the time period needed to certify such an extraordinary claim, we are finally entitled to say that we have a right, if not an obligation, to respect ourselves enough to disbelieve the whole thing.[59]

Is it really the case that there is no basis for belief in the resurrection? It is difficult to see how Hitchens reaches such a confident conclusion since he makes little attempt to deal with the topic in any detail. Just as the New Atheists' dismissal of the Gospels comes at a time when experts in this area of research have become much less sceptical based on the evidence available, so Hitchens's scepticism about the resurrection comes at a time when very detailed arguments for it are being proposed. Consider N. T. Wright's *The Resurrection of the Son of God* and Richard Swinburne's *The Resurrection of God Incarnate*, as well as scholarly works by William Lane Craig and Timothy and Lydia McGrew.[60] Whatever one makes of the orthodox conclusions reached by these authors, their arguments should at least be taken seriously. The discussion that follows will draw on their arguments to some extent.

It is worth pausing for a moment to ask whether the whole enterprise may be futile. There may be three reasons for thinking this. Some would maintain that both those who claim we should not believe in the resurrection because the evidence is against it and those who claim just the opposite are mistaken since belief in the resurrection is simply a matter of faith. This view presupposes that faith and evidence must be kept separate and is not the view of faith adopted in this book.[61] Even if one were to adopt this view, it would still leave the question as to what the person without such faith should do: should she simply disbelieve the resurrection? Of course, there is more to faith than assessing evidence, but it is difficult to see why there is anything inappropriate about considering the evidence.

A related view is that while there is no objection to assessing evidence, no conclusion will ever be reached by such an approach; it will just lead to a stalemate between the believer and unbeliever. But this seems much too sceptical. It certainly must be recognized that the evidence is never assessed in the absence of other beliefs, not least belief in the existence or non-existence of God. It still seems clear, however, that the evidence might point in one direction or the other. Indeed, this fits the approach of this book whereby different pieces of evidence can help us make an overall assessment about belief in God and the Christian faith. A third attitude is that there is no point considering the evidence because it is always irrational to believe in a miracle, but this point has been dealt with in chapter 3. It seems that the only way to proceed is to consider the evidence.

What evidence? As we have seen in the case of God's existence, a lot depends on what we count as appropriate evidence. If the New Atheists are looking for something akin to a scientific experiment to provide evidence, this would seem unreasonable for several reasons. First, many beliefs we hold in everyday life are not based on this kind of experimental evidence even though they may well be based on evidence nonetheless. Secondly, beliefs about history are rarely based on this kind of evidence and so, if we were to adopt this approach, we would have almost no historical knowledge. Thirdly, much of science itself, especially scientific claims about the past, cannot be based on experimental 'proof'. As throughout the book, the approach here will be to consider relevant evidence to see how it can best be accounted for. If the evidence is better accounted for by the hypothesis that the resurrection occurred than it is by rival hypotheses, it will count as evidence in favour of the resurrection. It should be noted that the resurrection will be understood in the traditional sense of a physical resurrection and not in a purely spiritual sense of the term that did not involve the resurrection of Jesus' body.[62]

There are a number of well-supported facts surrounding Jesus' death and the events which followed that are in some way relevant to the resurrection. These include:

1. Jesus was put to death by crucifixion.
2. His body was buried in a tomb.
3. The tomb was found to be empty a few days later.
4. The discovery of the empty tomb was made by a group of women followers of Jesus.
5. The disciples were not expecting Jesus to be resurrected.
6. Multiple appearances took place in which many people who had known Jesus well believed they had seen him alive again.
7. Paul, who initially persecuted the early Christians, became a follower of Jesus as a result of believing he had seen the risen Jesus.
8. James, the brother of Jesus, who was not a follower of Jesus before the crucifixion became a follower afterwards. He also became a leader in the church in Jerusalem and was put to death for his faith.
9. The Christian movement started in Jerusalem, where Jesus had been crucified, shortly after the crucifixion.
10. The message of the early Christians focused on the death and resurrection of Jesus.
11. The early Christians met on the first day of the week.
12. The early Christian church had a highly exalted view of Jesus.
13. The early Christians were willing to die for their faith.
14. The Jews had various ways of envisaging life after death, but the early Christians claimed that Jesus had been resurrected, which was supposed to happen to the righteous at the end of history, not to the Messiah in the middle of history.

15. Later Jewish apologetic, which claimed that the disciples stole the body, agreed that the tomb was identifiable and empty.
16. The early church grew in a Hellenistic context that would have been hostile to the idea of bodily resurrection.

The first and most obvious question to ask is whether these events can really be considered to be well-supported facts. It is extremely important to emphasize that the authors considered here are basing their arguments on *historical* grounds. Of course, many of the facts above are found in the Gospels, but the authors in question (Wright, Swinburne, Craig and the McGrews) are certainly not claiming that just because something is in the Gospels it must be true. Their starting point is to treat the Gospels and other ancient documents as texts that can be mined for historical information.[63]

It is not possible to go into all the evidence for these facts here, but it is worth looking at a couple of central ones: that the tomb was empty (3) and the appearances (6). Starting with the latter, it should first be emphasized that the claim is that people *believed* they had seen Jesus alive again. It would clearly be begging the question to claim that they had *actually* seen him alive again. A key source for this information is found in the writings of Paul in a passage at the start of 1 Corinthians 15. Based on the formal terms used for receiving and passing on a tradition, as well as the structure and language used in the text, this passage is known to contain a very early Christian creed. Indeed, there are very good reasons to date this creed to within several years of the crucifixion,[64] a view held by many critical scholars.[65] N. T. Wright claims that it was 'probably formulated within the first two or three years after Easter itself' and adds, 'We are here in touch with the earliest Christian tradition.'[66] The creed states that Jesus had been buried, was raised to life on the third day and that he appeared to Peter and to the twelve disciples. Paul goes on to say that Jesus appeared to more than five hundred people at one time as well as to James, to all the apostles and to Paul himself. It is also important to note that Paul was in a position to know whether the people in question believed they had seen Jesus alive. He certainly knew Peter, James and the other apostles and his comment concerning the five hundred, that 'most of whom are still living, though some have fallen asleep' (1 Cor. 15:6), is very interesting. As Wright puts it, Paul gives

the strong implication – they could be interrogated for their own accounts of what they saw and knew. The whole thrust of the paragraph is about evidence, about eyewitnesses being called, about something that actually happened for which eyewitnesses could and would vouch.[67]

The point is that in the creed we have a very early source of information about what the early Christians believed and eyewitness testimony (both Paul's and those referred to in the creed) to have seen Jesus alive after his crucifixion. It is clear from this source alone that belief in the resurrection and claims concerning the appearances are not legends that developed much later, but historical facts dating back to within a few years of the crucifixion.

Paul's account is not the only ancient source for resurrection appearances, however. The Gospels of Matthew, Luke and John also contain accounts where people believed they had seen the risen Jesus.[68] In the case of the appearance to the twelve disciples quoted by Paul, there are independent accounts provided by Luke and John confirming this to be the case. Such independent confirmation adds to its historical credibility. Furthermore, as discussed earlier, there are no grounds for thinking that the Gospel accounts were subject to legendary development. To see this, we can compare the Gospel accounts of the resurrection appearances with some of the non-canonical gospels, which are much later and display considerable legendary development in places. For example, in the account of the resurrection in the *Gospel of Peter*, the stone roles away by itself, the guards, the centurion and the elders all see two angels and the risen Christ, whose heads reach up to heaven, coming out of the tomb, and there is a talking cross into the bargain. The Gospel accounts are very mundane in comparison. In Luke's account, for example, Jesus has to convince the disciples that he is not a ghost.

A further consideration concerns both the appearances and the empty tomb: the testimony of the women. According to all four Gospels, it was women who first discovered the empty tomb. Furthermore, in Matthew and John it is women (only Mary Magdalene is mentioned in John's case) who are the first to see the risen Jesus. It is well known that women were not considered to be reliable witnesses on serious matters,[69] and so, had the stories been invented, it would have been of much greater apologetic value to have Peter or John discover the empty tomb. But it seems clear the Gospel writers did not feel free to change the story in this way, much less to invent a story with direct witnesses of Jesus leaving the tomb, as in the *Gospel of Peter*. By far the best explanation of the role of the women is that the Gospel writers are telling the truth: it was the women who first discovered the empty tomb and first claimed to have seen Jesus alive again.

Again, there are various other lines of evidence that provide additional support for the claim that the tomb was empty. William Lane Craig discusses such evidence, including detailed evidence to show that the burial occurred in the first place; that the empty tomb is implied by the creed quoted by Paul;

that the account in Mark is based on very early source material; the use of the expression 'the first day of the week' proves that the account in Mark (16:2) is very old; that Mark's account is simple and lacks legendary development; independent accounts in Luke and John of an investigation of the empty tomb by disciples; that it would have been impossible for the disciples to proclaim the resurrection in Jerusalem had the tomb not been empty; that the earliest Jewish propaganda against the Christians presupposes the empty tomb; and that Jesus' tomb was not venerated as a shrine.[70] Both Richard Swinburne and N. T. Wright draw attention to the significance of the fact that the early Christians met on the first day of the week to break bread.[71] Given the importance of the sabbath within Judaism, this focus on Sunday is in need of explanation. Wright claims that by far the best explanation is that 'all the early Christians believed that something had *happened* on that first Sunday morning'.[72]

Perhaps the most prominent writer to deny the historicity of the empty tomb is the historical Jesus scholar John Dominic Crossan. Crossan thinks that, instead of being buried in a tomb, the body of Jesus was buried in a common grave in the same way as the bodies of others who were crucified.[73] The problem is that this seems to ignore the specific information relating to Jesus' case. In particular, his approach does not seem to do justice to the creed from 1 Corinthians, which affirms the burial, or the claim in the Gospels that the body of Jesus was buried in the tomb of Joseph of Arimathea. On the latter, he thinks that this story does not make any sense because Joseph was supposedly a member of the Jewish Sanhedrin, who unanimously condemned Jesus to death. For reasons along these lines, he thinks that Mark invented the story.

But it is difficult to see why the story of Joseph of Arimathea is such a problem. Luke states that he had not consented to the decision of the Sanhedrin, while Matthew and John claim he was a disciple of Jesus. Furthermore, as Craig points out, it is surely 'unlikely that early Christian believers would invent an individual, give him a fictional name and nearby town of origin, and place that fictional character on the historical council of the Sanhedrin, whose members were well known'.[74] Given how easy it would have been to disprove such a story had it been false, the best explanation for its inclusion is that it is true. Moreover, according to the Gospels, a group of women witnessed the burial, which is very unlikely to have been made up for the reason stated earlier concerning the status of women. Finally, all four Gospels mention the burial by Joseph of Arimathea, which provides additional confirmation. The McGrews' assessment, that Crossan offers a 'profoundly inadequate set of reasons to abandon an inconvenient section of a primary source – or, in this case, four primary sources',[75] seems entirely justified.

It is worth emphasizing that many scholars who are not Christians never-theless agree on the basic facts. The classical scholar Michael Grant, who does not believe in the resurrection, says concerning the empty tomb:

> Even if the historian chooses to regard the youthful apparition as extra-historical, he
> cannot justifiably deny the empty tomb. True, this discovery, as so often, is described
> differently by the various Gospels – as critical pagans early pointed out. But if we
> apply the same sort of criteria that we would apply to other ancient literary sources,
> then the evidence is firm and plausible enough to necessitate the conclusion that the
> Tomb was empty.[76]

The Jewish historian Geza Vermes, who like Grant does not believe in the resurrection, notes:

> The closest approach to first-hand evidence is the testimony of several trustworthy
> men who assert that Jesus appeared to them – to the Twelve, to all the apostles,
> and to over five hundred brethren, in addition to the leaders of the Church, Peter
> and James. It is their collective conviction of having seen their dead teacher alive,
> combined with the initial discovery of the empty tomb, that provides the substance
> for faith in Jesus' rising from the dead.[77]

For good measure, he goes on to refer to 'one disconcerting fact: namely that the women who set out to pay their last respects to Jesus found to their consternation, not a body, but an empty tomb'.[78] Although the empty tomb is well supported by the evidence, the historical case for the resurrection appearances is even stronger. In a very insightful survey of views on the res-urrection by critical scholars the philosopher Gary Habermas comments that while there is disagreement on the nature of the experiences, 'it is still crucial that the nearly unanimous consent of critical scholars is that, in some sense, the early followers of Jesus thought that they had seen the risen Jesus'.[79] In fact, he notes that 'virtually every critical scholar recognizes this fact, or some-thing very similar' and that it 'is very difficult to find denials of it'.[80] He also provides a long list of references where sceptical scholars, including Crossan, affirm the historicity of these experiences.

Much more could be said about these two historical facts and the others as well. The books and articles referred to above provide a good starting point for looking into this subject in more detail. The main point, however, is that there is considerable agreement on the core historical facts.

Resurrection: foolishness, wisdom and the cross

Before going on to look at the explanation for the facts, it is worth looking in a bit more detail at several other facts. While there is no doubt that the empty tomb and appearances are of central importance in any case for the resurrection, other facts are also highly relevant. Consider the following comment by Dawkins:

> It is, when you think about it, remarkable that a religion should adopt an instrument of torture and execution as its sacred symbol, often worn around the neck. Lenny Bruce rightly quipped that 'If Jesus had been killed twenty years ago, Catholic school children would be wearing little electric chairs around their necks instead of crosses.'[81]

Dawkins is quite right: it is remarkable. Worship of someone who had been crucified might seem like madness today, but even more so in the first century. Here Dawkins is engaging, whether unwittingly or not, in the ancient practice of mocking Christian belief in a crucified Messiah. Paul draws attention to this in a letter to the Corinthian church where he describes the Christian Gospel with its focus on the cross as 'a stumbling-block to Jews and foolishness to Gentiles' (1 Cor. 1:23).

As theologian Derek Tidball points out, the idea of a crucified Messiah would not have come within a million miles of Jewish expectations, especially when such a person would have been considered to be under God's curse. He recalls how a Jewish friend, many of whose family had died in Auschwitz, told him that for a Jew to boast about the cross would be like boasting about a gas chamber. He also explains that the Roman use of crucifixion 'combined pain with indignity, and torture with humiliation, to maximum effect' and notes that it was an embarrassment to polite Roman society, quoting Cicero that 'the very word "cross" should be far removed not only from the person of a Roman citizen but from his thoughts, his eyes and his ears'.[82] A particularly graphical example of this is the Alexamenos graffito, which is a Roman inscription probably dating to the first century. It mocks Christian worship by depicting a young man worshipping Jesus, who is on a cross and is represented with the head of a donkey.[83] As for the Greeks with their focus on wisdom, a religion based on God as the ultimate source of reason was acceptable, but one based on a crucified man was utter foolishness.

This is the context in which the early Christians found themselves as they proclaimed their message, which was considered to be an absurdity by the Greeks, an embarrassment to Romans and a scandal to Jews. It must be remembered that the message of the cross was not just a non-essential part of their message, but was what it was all about. Furthermore, when we take into account fact 12, that the early Christians had a very exalted view of who Jesus was, which again appears to be well established on historical grounds,[84] and when we recall that the first Christians were Jews and that Jews worshipped only God, an obvious question arises: why did the early Christians proclaim such a message? And how did Christianity take root in an environment that was so hostile to its beliefs?

Even if we had no evidence for an empty tomb or for resurrection appearances these facts alone are in need of explanation. It would be difficult enough to explain how a group of devout Jews could worship a human being, but that they did so knowing he had been crucified by the Romans seems inconceivable unless they had some very good reason for it. No general appeal to how religions start seems convincing. If we use the language of memes, the memes central to Christianity were not well adapted to survive in the first-century environment in which they took root. As Tidball puts it:

> If the powerful gods of Greece and Rome died, as some of them did, they died heroic deaths which added to their mystique and majesty. They would never have succumbed to such a humiliating form of death as this. To claim, as Christians did and do, that one who died like a slave was now not only Saviour, but exalted to be the Lord of the whole creation, was patent nonsense.[85]

Unless, of course, the early Christians had some very convincing reason to believe in the resurrection. If so, the evidence would start to make sense.

Resurrection: explaining the facts

So far the focus has been on the facts, but now we must ask how these facts can best be explained. We shall consider some attempts to explain them in purely natural terms to start with.

Clearly, not all of these facts can be considered as providing independent evidence for the resurrection. Fact 13, for instance, does not provide direct evidence for the resurrection since the mere fact that Christians were willing to die does not tell us whether their beliefs about the resurrection were true. It is obviously possible to be sincere but mistaken. However, fact 13 is still very important because it counts as strong evidence that the disciples sincerely *believed* that Jesus had risen from the dead and so hypotheses involving deliberate deceit on the part of the disciples are generally considered to be non-starters. To die for a mistaken belief is one thing, to die for something known to be a lie is quite another. And as the McGrews point out, it is not just that they were willing to die for a belief or ideology, but that they were willing to die in attestation of an empirical fact. E. P. Sanders's assessment of conspiracy theories is clear:

> I do not regard deliberate fraud as a worthwhile explanation. Many of the people [who claimed to have seen the risen Jesus] were to spend the rest of their lives proclaiming that they had seen the risen Lord, and several of them would die for their cause. Moreover, a calculated deception should have produced greater unanimity [in the Gospel accounts].[86]

The whole idea of such a deception is psychologically implausible. It is worth adding that there was nothing to be gained by it; indeed, persecution and possible death could easily have been predicted. And in the light of the persecution that did occur they would have had every opportunity to give up. Furthermore, given the discussion in the last section, they could not have thought that it was likely to convince many people.

Another attempt to explain the evidence in natural terms that is even less convincing is the idea that Jesus did not actually die. The idea that Jesus might somehow have survived crucifixion and gone on to persuade his disciples that he had risen from the dead is not taken seriously for a number of reasons. First, given the Romans' expertise in crucifixion and the horrific nature of crucifixion itself, it is virtually impossible that Jesus would have survived. Also, according to the Gospel accounts Jesus first received a brutal flogging, which would have imposed severe injuries, and Jesus was also pierced by a spear to ensure that he was dead. Denying these accounts would amount to combining the apparent death theory with a deliberate deceit, which we have already seen is implausible. Secondly, even if he had somehow survived, it is unlikely that he would have been able to escape from the tomb given the extent of his wounds. Thirdly, had this somehow happened, he certainly could not have convinced his disciples he had been raised from the dead. A nineteenth-century historical Jesus scholar, David Strauss, who denied the resurrection, famously wrote:

> It is impossible that a being who had stolen half-dead out of the sepulchre,
> who crept about weak and ill, wanting medical treatment, who required
> bandaging, strengthening, and indulgence, and who still at last yielded to his
> sufferings, could have given the impression that he was a Conqueror over death
> and the grave, the Prince of Life, an impression which lay at the bottom of their
> future ministry.[87]

Fourthly, it would seem to require Jesus to have been involved in a deliberate deceit himself, but this is completely in conflict with everything we know
about Jesus. Craig emphasizes that 'no contemporary scholar would support
such a theory; it has been dead for over a hundred years'.[88]

Another naturalistic approach argues that although various people did
indeed have an experience of seeing Jesus alive again as the Gospels and Paul
testify, what they saw was in their minds. We can distinguish between two different types of explanation here. The first approach is to attribute the appearances to visions. The problem is that visions would not have resulted in the
disciples claiming that a resurrection had taken place. As Wright points out,
claiming to have had a vision would be one way to interpret an experience of
having seen someone who had died. He also remarks that 'such visions meant
precisely, as people in the ancient and modern worlds have discovered, that
the person was dead, not that they were alive'.[89] Attributing the appearances
to visions would also fail to account for the physical nature of the resurrection accounts.[90] Furthermore, it would also fail to account for other evidence,
particularly the empty tomb, and so would need to be combined with another
explanation.

The second approach is to attribute the appearances to hallucinations,
which are different from visions because people having them genuinely
mistake the experience as a physical encounter. This approach also faces
serious objections, some of which represent further problems for the vision
theory too. Timothy and Lydia McGrew state four objections. First, the disciples were not expecting a resurrection and so were not in a psychological
state that rendered them susceptible to a hallucination of this kind. There
was no basis for expecting such a resurrection within Judaism and, in fact,
the Gospels portray the disciples as sceptical about reports that others had
seen Jesus. Secondly, hallucinations would have to be invoked for more than a
dozen people simultaneously, but a collective hallucination is highly implausible, especially given the level of detail in some of the resurrection accounts.[91]
Thirdly, the hallucinations would have to be not only parallel but also inte-
grated to account for scenarios where the disciples were interacting with each
other as well as with Jesus. Fourthly, hallucinations would have to be invoked
repeatedly over a period of more than a month. Finally, as with visions, this
approach would not account for other evidence such as the empty tomb and
so would need to be combined with another explanation.

Various other purely natural explanations have been proposed, but none
seems even remotely convincing.[92] So what about the resurrection as an
explanation? How does it fare? The various authors who have argued for
the resurrection have structured the arguments in slightly different ways. For

example, of the facts identified earlier, Swinburne focuses on 3, 6 and 11, Wright on 3, 6 and 13, Craig on 3, 6 and facts such as 10–13 relating to the origin of the Christian faith, while the McGrews go about it in a different way by concentrating on the testimony of the women, the disciples and Paul.[93] But they are all agreed that the resurrection hypothesis is by far the best explanation of the evidence. It seems clear that the resurrection hypothesis accounts for all the facts very easily: the empty tomb, the appearances, the transformation of the disciples, the conversion of sceptics like James and Paul, and the origins of Christianity are exactly the kinds of things we would expect if Jesus rose from the dead. By contrast, the naturalistic hypotheses do not do nearly so well. Some fail to explain any evidence, and even if others can account for some of the evidence, they leave other evidence unaccounted for. So even to the extent that such hypotheses explain any of the evidence, they do not *explain away* the evidence for the resurrection. Since the facts are so well accounted for by the resurrection hypothesis and so poorly by the rival hypotheses, the evidence confirms the resurrection hypothesis very strongly indeed.

But the resurrection is a supernatural explanation and for this reason it might be argued that it is not a good explanation after all. According to this viewpoint, no matter how poor the naturalistic explanations are, they are always to be preferred to a supernatural explanation. Here we must distinguish two factors: first, how well an explanation accounts for the evidence; secondly, how probable it is in the first place, before the evidence is taken into account. It seems clear that on the first point the resurrection hypothesis easily beats rival accounts, but what about the second point? Isn't the resurrection hypothesis very improbable? Let's grant for the moment, before the evidence is taken into account, that it is indeed very improbable. Is this a serious problem for the resurrection hypothesis? No, as we saw in the general discussion on miracles in chapter 3, something can be very *improbable* before the evidence is taken into account, but very *probable* afterwards. The illustration of winning the lottery was discussed in chapters 3 and 6. When my friend Tom bought a lottery ticket it was highly improbable that he would win, but once I obtained evidence (such as Tom's appearance in the media, etc.) that is much better accounted for by the fact that he won, it becomes highly probable that he did in fact win. Arguably, exactly the same applies in the case of the resurrection.

Perhaps it could be claimed that the resurrection is so incredibly improbable to begin with that the evidence is insufficient to make it probable. This seems to be the kind of objection to miracles underlying the New Atheists' views. Three responses can be made to this. First, it must be stressed that someone who takes this view is not entitled to claim that there is therefore no evidence for the resurrection. Quite the contrary, even for such a person the evidence confirms the resurrection, making it much more probable than it would otherwise be. Secondly, since the evidence is judged to be insufficient, the obvious question is, *why* is it judged to be insufficient? If the facts considered earlier are insufficient, how much more evidence, and of what kind, is required? Often the claim that there is insufficient evidence turns out to be little more than a thinly veiled philosophical commitment to reject the supernatural, as we saw in David Hume's case in chapter 3.

Thirdly, why is the resurrection judged to be so incredibly improbable before the evidence is taken into account? If the hypothesis was that Jesus rose from the dead by natural means, that would indeed be very improbable; but instead it is that God raised Jesus from the dead. And as the apostle Paul said a long time ago, 'Why should any of you consider it incredible that God raises the dead?' (Acts 26:8). Of course, someone might argue that it is very improbable because he thinks it is unlikely there is a God in the first place. But merely thinking that God's existence was unlikely would not be sufficient to rule out the resurrection any more than thinking that Tom's winning the lottery was unlikely would be sufficient to deny that he had done so once the evidence was taken into account. The onus would be on the atheist not only to show that God's existence was unlikely, but so incredibly unlikely that the resurrection could be ruled out. As we saw in chapter 6, Dawkins's attempt to establish an extremely low probability for God's existence fails miserably.[94]

A further objection might be that even if there is a God, the resurrection would still be highly improbable. After all, God does not generally raise people from the dead, so why would he raise Jesus from the dead? Richard Swinburne argues that the resurrection is 'God's signature on his life and death – as accepting his sacrifice and authenticating his teaching.'[95] If Jesus was the Son of God who died for the salvation of humankind, then there would be very good reason for God to raise him from the dead. It would authenticate these claims and provide a basis for taking the message to others. It would also be very appropriate given the nature of salvation, which involved new life, defeat of death and a future resurrection. Jesus' resurrection would be the beginning of God's new creation.[96] How does all of this relate to the objection? It is certainly true that God would be extremely unlikely to raise a given person from the dead, but it does not follow that this would be true in the case of Jesus as well. Given the uniqueness of Jesus in terms of the life he lived, his teaching, the claims he made and his death, there is no good reason to believe it would be highly improbable. And recall that this is before the evidence is taken into account.[97] If it is not too improbable before the evidence is considered, the discussion earlier suggests that it will be highly probable once the evidence is factored in.

We saw in chapter 3 that there were no good reasons for simply ruling out miracles in principle and that the only way to decide whether one has occurred is to consider the evidence. Now that we have considered the evidence in one particular case, it seems clear that there are a number of well-established facts which strongly confirm the claim that at least one miracle has occurred: that God raised Jesus from the dead.

Conclusion

This chapter and the preceding one have considered the topic of revelation from a Christian point of view. The New Atheists claim that belief in the central tenets of Christianity must be based on simply taking on faith (by which they mean belief without evidence) what it says in the Bible and that there is no way of independently confirming such beliefs. Indeed, they think that if such beliefs are scrutinized they will easily be shown to be false. But this is simply not the case. It might have been thought that belief in the resurrection of Jesus from the dead would have been one of the Christian beliefs that was least amenable to evidential considerations and yet, as we have seen, there are a number of well-supported facts, generally accepted by historians, that are relevant. In trying to account for these facts naturalistic explanations do not seem up to the task. By contrast, the facts are very well accounted for by the resurrection hypothesis. If the New Atheists really wanted to form their beliefs on the basis of the evidence, it is far from clear why they would not take the evidence for the resurrection more seriously. The problem is not a lack of evidence, but a philosophical stance on miracles that is inconsistent with their demand for evidence and in any case is flawed, as we saw in chapter 3.

Notes

1. R. Bultmann, *Jesus and the Word* (New York: Scribner's, 1934), p. 14 (quoted in Ben Witherington III, *The Jesus Quest: The Third Search for the Jew of Nazareth*, 2nd ed. [Downers Grove: IVP, 1997], p. 281, n. 5).

2. For an overview of the third quest see Witherington, *Jesus Quest*.

3. E. P. Sanders, *The Historical Figure of Jesus* (London: Allen Lane, 1993), p. 5.

4. Ibid., pp. 10–11.

5. *TGD*, p. 97.

6. *GNG*, p. 114.

7. Cornelius Tacitus, *The Annals* 15.44, tr. Alfred John Church and William Jackson Brodribb, available at http://www.sacred-texts.com/cla/tac/index.htm (accessed 18 Nov. 2011).

8. Flavius Josephus, *Antiquities of the Jews* 20.9.1, tr. William Whiston, available at http://www.sacred-texts.com/jud/josephus/index.htm (accessed 18 Nov. 2011).

9. Ibid. 18.3.3.

10. Pliny the Younger, *Epistles* 10.96, available at http://www.vroma.org/~hwalker/Pliny/PlinyNumbers.html (accessed 18 Nov. 2011).

11. Babylonian Talmud, Sanhedrin 43a, tr. Jacob Shachter and H. Freedman, available at http://www.come-and-hear.com/sanhedrin/index.html (accessed 18 Nov. 2011).

12. See, for example, Darrell L. Bock, *Studying the Historical Jesus: A Guide to Sources and Methods* (Leicester: Apollos; Grand Rapids: Baker Academic, 2002), pp. 45–63; Gary R. Habermas, *The Verdict of History* (Eastbourne: Monarch, 1988), pp. 91–180.

13. As noted earlier, research in this area is not as sceptical as in the past, but extremely sceptical approaches are still present. As many authors have pointed out, this is particularly true with the methodology of the Jesus Seminar. Historical Jesus scholar Ben Witherington comments, 'Yet another methodological problem is the apparent presumption of many members of the seminar that Jesus' sayings *must* be regarded as inauthentic unless they can be proved to be authentic. This is assumed to be *the* critical view. But in reality it is a perspective steeped in negative bias, not a neutral or open stance' (*Jesus Quest*, p. 47, emphasis in original).

14. Habermas, *Verdict of History*, pp. 125–143.

15. For a rebuttal of the particular case against the existence of Jesus to which Dawkins refers, see ibid., pp. 33–39.

16. *TGD*, p. 97.

17. See his article in the *New Statesman*, 6 April, 2009, pp. 24–26.

18. See, for example, Witherington, *Jesus Quest*, pp. 42–57.

19. See, for example, Craig L. Blomberg, *The Historical Reliability of the Gospels*, 2nd ed. (Leicester: Apollos, 2007).

20. *GNG*, p. 112.

21. Quoted in *BTS*, p. 167.

22. *TGD*, p. 95–96.

23. Not all of the gospels that the New Atheists have in mind are Gnostic in character and there is debate as to which are and which are not. Here they will be referred to as Gnostic since those considered in the text probably do fall into that category.

24. And these are conservative estimates. Some scholars would assign dates as early as the 50s for some of the Gospels.

25. The dates quoted here are those considered to be widely accepted by the historical Jesus scholar Craig A. Evans in his book *Fabricating Jesus: How Modern Scholars Distort the Gospels* (Nottingham: IVP, 2007). Further references can be found in his book.

26. D. A. Carson and D. J. Moo, *An Introduction to the New Testament*, 2nd ed. (Leicester: Apollos, 2005), pp. 736–737. See also Bruce M. Metzger, *The Canon of the New Testament: Its Origin, Development and Significance* (Oxford: Clarendon, 1987).

27. For further discussion see J. Ed Komoszewski, M. James Sawyer and Daniel B. Wallace, *Reinventing Jesus: How Contemporary Sceptics Miss the Real Jesus and Mislead Popular Culture* (Grand Rapids: Kregel, 2006), pt. 3.

28. Quoted in Evans, *Fabricating Jesus*, p. 60.

29. *GNG*, p. 110.

30. Ibid., p. 120.

31. *TGD*, p. 93.

32. These figures are taken from Komoszewski, Sawyer and Wallace, *Reinventing Jesus*, p. 71.

33. In his contribution to William Lane Craig, *Reasonable Faith*, 2nd ed. (Wheaton, Ill.: Crossway, 1994), p. 194.

34. Bart D. Ehrman, *Misquoting Jesus: The Story Behind Who Changed the Bible and Why* (San Francisco: HarperSanFrancisco, 2005).

35. *GNG*, pp. 120–122, p. 142.

36. See, for example, the interview with Metzger about the New Testament manuscripts in Lee Strobel, *The Case for Christ* (Grand Rapids: Zondervan, 1998), pp. 70–94.

37. Evans, *Fabricating Jesus*, p. 31. His point is not that inerrancy is false, but just that it should not be made central to Christian faith.

38. See Dawkins's comments particularly about the birth narratives (*TGD*, pp. 93–95), Hitchens on the same topic (*GNG*, pp. 114–115) and his charge of inconsistency (*GNG*, p. 122, p. 143), and Harris's claims about contradictions (*TEF*, p. 85, and *Letter to a Christian Nation* [London: Bantam, 2007], pp. 58–59).

39. Timothy and Lydia McGrew, 'The Argument from Miracles: A Cumulative Case for the Resurrection of Jesus of Nazareth', in William Lane Craig and J. P. Moreland (eds.), *Blackwell Companion to Natural Theology* (Chichester: Wiley-Blackwell, 2009), p. 598.

40. Ibid.

41. *TGD*, p. 96.

42. See, for example, F. F. Bruce, *The New Testament Documents: Are They Reliable?*, 6th ed. (Leicester: IVP; Grand Rapids: Eerdmans, 1981). In fact, the main question about the dating of John's Gospel seems to be whether it should be dated *earlier* than the 90s. See, for example, the discussion in Carson and Moo, *Introduction to the New Testament*, pp. 264–267.

43. See Bruce, *New Testament Documents*, pp. 10–20.

44. See Craig, *Reasonable Faith*, p. 207.

45. For discussion of various criticisms of this approach see James D. G. Dunn, *Jesus Remembered* (Grand Rapids: Eerdmans, 2003); and Richard Bauckham, *Jesus and the Eyewitnesses: The Gospels as Eyewitness Testimony* (Grand Rapids: Eerdmans, 2006).

46. Dunn, *Jesus Remembered*, pp. 205–210; N. T. Wright, *Jesus and the Victory of God* (London: SPCK, 1996), pp. 133–137.

47. This certainly seems to fit with what we find in the Gospels. In many instances, accounts of the same event in different Gospels agree on the key points even though they are not identical.

48. *BTS*, p. 147.

49. Bauckham, *Jesus and the Eyewitnesses*, pp. 264–289.

50. Ibid., pp. 319–357.

51. See, for example, Bruce, *New Testament Documents*, pp. 80–92; and Colin J. Hemer, *The Book of Acts in the Setting of Hellenistic History* (Tübingen: Mohr, 1989).

52. A. N. Sherwin-White, *Roman Society and Roman Law in the New Testament* (Oxford: Clarendon, 1963), p. 189.

53. See Urban C. von Wahde, 'Archaeology and John's Gospel', in J. H. Charlesworth (ed.), *Jesus and Archaeology* (Grand Rapids: Eerdmans, 2006), pp. 523–586.

54. Bauckham, *Jesus and the Eyewitnesses*, p. 84.

55. *TGD*, p. 94. See also *GNG*, pp. 22–23.

56. For detailed discussion of this topic see Komoszewski, Sawyer and Wallace, *Reinventing Jesus*, pp. 219–258.

57. N. T. Wright, 'Christian Origins and the Resurrection of Jesus: The Resurrection of Jesus as a Historical Problem', *Sewanee Theological Review* 41.2 (1998), pp. 107–123.

58. As discussed in chapter 3.

59. *GNG*, p. 143.

60. N. T. Wright, *The Resurrection of the Son of God* (London: SPCK, 2003); Richard Swinburne, *The Resurrection of God Incarnate* (Oxford: Oxford University Press, 2003); William Lane Craig, *Assessing the New Testament Evidence for the Historicity of the Resurrection of Jesus* (Lewiston, N. Y.: Edwin Mellen, 2002); McGrew and McGrew, 'Argument from Miracles'. See also Craig's more popular work *The Son Rises: Historical Evidence for the Resurrection of Jesus* (Chicago: Moody, 1981). For another detailed study see Michael R. Licona, *The Resurrection of Jesus: A New Historiographical Approach* (Downers Grove: IVP Academic; Leicester: Apollos, 2010).

61. See chapter 2 for more discussion.

62. N. T. Wright shows in great detail that this was indeed the understanding of 'resurrection' in early Christianity.

63. That is not to say that they believe the Gospels to be nothing more than ancient documents to be mined for historical information. They probably hold differing

views on the status of the Gospels as divine revelation and what implications that
might have in terms of the truthfulness of the Gospels, but whatever their views on
these matters, they do not form part of their arguments for the resurrection.

64. See, for example, Bauckham, *Jesus and the Eyewitnesses*, pp. 264–269; and Habermas,
     Verdict of History, pp. 130–134.

65. See Gary R. Habermas, 'Resurrection Research from 1975 to the Present: What
     Are the Critical Scholars Saying?', *Journal for the Study of the Historical Jesus* 3.2 (2005),
     pp. 135–153.

66. Wright, *Resurrection*, p. 319.

67. Ibid., p. 325.

68. As discussed earlier, it seems clear that Mark 16:9–20, which includes appearances,
     was not the original ending of Mark's Gospel.

69. See Wright, *Resurrection*, pp. 607–608, and references therein.

70. Craig, *Son Rises*, pp. 45–90.

71. Swinburne, *Resurrection*, pp. 163–170; Wright, *Resurrection*, pp. 579–580. The
     significance of this point appears to go back to the seventeenth-century Irish
     Anglican Charles Leslie, *A Short and Easy Method with the Deists* (London: F. C.
     and J. Rivington, 1815; first published 1697).

72. Wright, *Resurrection*, p. 580, emphasis in original.

73. John Dominic Crossan, *Who Killed Jesus? Exposing the Roots of Anti-Semitism in the
     Gospel Story of the Death of Jesus* (San Francisco: HarperSanFrancisco, 1995).

74. Craig, *Son Rises*, p. 53.

75. McGrew and McGrew, 'Argument from Miracles', p. 606.

76. Michael Grant, *Jesus* (London: Phoenix, 1999), p. 176.

77. Geza Vermes, *Jesus the Jew: A Historian's Reading of the Gospels* (London: Collins, 1973),
     p. 41.

78. Ibid.

79. Habermas, 'Resurrection Research', p. 151. The consensus on the empty tomb is
     not quite so strong, but he notes that 75% of critical scholars consider it a historical
     fact.

80. Ibid., p. 151. Of course, the real reason for believing this is not the scholarly
     consensus, but rather the evidence on which this consensus is based, which includes,
     for example, the fact that there are accounts in multiple early sources and that it is
     documented in the early creed quoted by Paul in 1 Cor. 15.

81. *TGD*, p. 251.

82. Derek Tidball, *The Message of the Cross* (Leicester: IVP, 2001), p. 203.

83. See http://www.ntresources.com/alex_graffito.htm (accessed 10 Sept. 2011).

84. See Larry W. Hurtado, *Lord Jesus Christ: Devotion to Jesus in Earliest Christianity* (Grand
     Rapids: Eerdmans, 2003); and Wright, *Resurrection*, pp. 563–578.

85. Tidball, *Message of the Cross*, p. 203.

86. Sanders, *Historical Figure of Jesus*, p. 280.

87. David F. Strauss, *A New Life of Jesus*, 2nd ed. (London: Williams & Norgate, 1879), vol. 1, p. 412 (quoted in Craig, *Son Rises*, p. 39).

88. Ibid., p. 40.

89. Wright, *Resurrection*, pp. 690–691.

90. If the Gospels falsely portray the appearances as physical events when they were in fact visions, this would itself require explanation since it is not obvious why they would want to do this. Indeed, since the Gospels were written within the lifetime of the disciples, it would seem to require deceit on their part, which as we have seen is implausible.

91. The level of detail in the accounts is closely linked to their physical nature as noted in the previous footnote.

92. See, for example, Swinburne, *Resurrection*, pp. 174–186. The works by Wright, Craig and the McGrews cited earlier also deal with various naturalistic hypotheses.

93. This is not to say that other facts play no role in these accounts. For example, Wright's argument is in two steps: first, facts 3 and 6 are needed to account for the origins of Christianity (including facts such as 9–12); secondly, the resurrection is the best explanation of facts 3 and 6.

94. And it does so for the same kinds of reasons we are discussing here.

95. Swinburne, *Resurrection*, p. 197.

96. See Wright, *Resurrection*, p. 712.

97. Swinburne draws attention to the striking coincidence that the only prophet for whom there is significant evidence that he satisfied the requirements that he was God incarnate is also the only prophet about whom there is significant evidence for a resurrection having taken place. See *Resurrection*, pp. 202–203.

In January 2009 the Atheist Bus Campaign took to the streets of Britain with the message 'There's Probably No God. Now Stop Worrying and Enjoy Your Life'. The campaign received financial and moral support from Richard Dawkins and captured the ethos of the New Atheism more generally. The atheists behind the campaign did not want their message confined to academic journals or even books. It was too important for that and needed to be brought to the streets where it could have a wider impact.

Ironically, their attitude is very similar to that of the religious believers they criticize and the similarity does not end there. A bit like a church in decline, wishing to get its message out, but not quite knowing how to do it, they end up trivializing their message and probably embarrassing their supporters in the process. As we have seen in early chapters, a key feature of the New Atheism is that its message should have an impact. It is not merely about presenting rational arguments, but making a difference in the world by changing people's minds and attitudes. According to the New Atheists, religious belief is not only mistaken, but irrational and, worse still, dangerous. The stakes are high and something must be done.

The bus campaign advertisement had two components to it: the first about the non-existence of God and the second about the implications of this for how we should live our lives. Most of this book has concentrated on the first component by responding to the New Atheists' objections to belief in God and to Christian belief. Despite the fact that I have disagreed with most of the main claims of the New Atheists, there have also been some areas of agreement. For example, I think they are right to emphasize the importance of truth, to view the question of God's existence and the claims of Christianity as factual matters rather than as metaphors for something else, and to believe that evidence is relevant to these topics. My objection to the New Atheism is not that it takes truth, rational thinking and evidence seriously, but that it does not take them seriously enough.

In this final chapter we turn our attention to the second component, that is, the implications of the New Atheism for the meaning and purpose of our lives. Here too I agree with them that the question of God's existence is extremely important. Many people have no interest in whether God exists or not; it is of no practical importance to them and has no impact on their lives. Now, of course, neither the New Atheists nor I think that non-belief or belief should be coerced, but we do agree that it has important implications. For the New Atheists, belief in God is significant because it is irrational and dangerous. I too think that it is significant, but for a very different reason.

Meaning and purpose in the New Atheism

In his discussion of whether religion gives meaning to life, Dennett claims that many religious believers 'would say that without their religion their lives would be meaningless'.[1] He says that it is initially tempting just to take them at their word, but then rightly points out that there are serious questions to be asked. For example:

> Can just *any* religion give lives their meaning, in a way that we should honor and respect? What about people who fall into the clutches of cult leaders, or who are duped into giving their life savings to religious con artists? Do their lives still have meaning even though their particular 'religion' is a fraud?[2]

It is important here to distinguish between a subjective and objective meaning to life. To say that there is an objective meaning to life is to say that there really is a meaning to life and that it is independent of whether anyone believes it to have such a meaning.[3] By contrast, to say that there is just a subjective meaning to life is to deny that there is an objective meaning and to say instead that individuals can decide what makes life meaningful for them. If a religion is a fraud, then it does not provide an objective basis for meaning even though its followers believe that it does.[4] Meaning and truth are in conflict in such a case, but if Christianity is true, as I have argued it is, then no such conflict arises.

Dennett objects to the idea that religious belief can provide meaning on the grounds that it leads to intolerance and violence. He says, 'In the adult world of religion, people are dying and killing, with the moderates cowed into silence by the intransigence of the radicals in their own faiths.'[5] He adds, 'If *this* is the precious meaning our lives are vouchsafed thanks to our allegiance to one religion or another, it is not such a bargain, in my opinion.'[6] The attitude Dennett has in mind here is one which says that religion *in general* is not to be criticized because it can give a subjective sense of meaning to people's lives. On that point Dennett's assessment seems right since it is difficult to see why any belief system, whether religious or not, should be immune from criticism just because some people derive significance from it.

One problem with Dennett's discussion is that he does not really engage with the question of an objective meaning to life. This becomes clear when he talks about 'moderates who revere the tradition they were raised in, simply because it is *their* tradition' and then claims, 'This is like allegiance to a sports team, and it, too, can give meaning to life – if not taken too seriously.'[7] After describing his support for the Red Sox he says, 'This is a kind of love, but not the rabid love that leads people to lie, and torture, and kill.'[8] As we saw in chapter 8, this kind of blanket criticism of all types of religious belief is unwarranted and so cannot be used to rule out the idea that objective meaning is to be found in a faith such as Christianity, whose adherents are enjoined to love their enemies.

In referring to a sports team's giving meaning to life, perhaps Dennett is just poking fun at what he calls 'moderates' who are not sure whether they believe their religion is true at all, but it is still very misleading. The reason for this is that the question of the meaning of life is hardly a trivial matter because it concerns whether there is any real significance to our existence and is closely related to whether there is a purpose for our existence, what kind of lives we ought to live, the value of human life, and so on. And assuming Dennett is not recommending that atheists should address these kinds of issues by reference to their favourite sports teams, it leaves the question as to where meaning is to be found if there is no God.

Dawkins attempts to provide at least a partial answer to this question in the final chapter of *The God Delusion*, where he discusses consolation and inspiration. He distinguishes two kinds of consolation: a direct physical consolation and consolation based on a new fact or new way of looking at things. In both cases, he acknowledges that belief in God may well provide consolation, but points out that 'false beliefs can be every bit as consoling as true ones, right

up to the moment of disillusionment'.[9] This is correct, but in his discussion
of consolation Dawkins seems to have in mind a subjective feeling of consolation or comfort in the face of difficult circumstances, whether there is any
basis for it or not. For example, Dawkins finds consolation in a passage from
Bertrand Russell, which commences, 'I believe that when I die I shall rot, and
nothing of my ego will survive.' The reason for this is that he sees it as facing
up to reality, 'standing up and facing into the strong keen wind of understanding'.[10] Many will find these views deeply disturbing rather than consoling,
but if it is all about a subjective feeling of consolation, then this is not an
objection to the fact that Dawkins finds it consoling.

So perhaps Dawkins is right that some atheists will be able to find the kind
of consolation he is talking about, but in approaching the topic in this way
he completely fails to do justice to the real questions about the meaning and
purpose of life. For example, does Dawkins's atheism provide an objective
purpose for our existence? To this question, the answer is clearly 'no'. As
Dawkins made clear in his book *The Blind Watchmaker*, we are the accidental
by-products of the unguided, unplanned process of natural selection, which
is the blind watchmaker that has 'no purpose in view'.[11] In fact, he says that
'living organisms exist for the benefit of DNA rather than the other way
around'.[12] This, it seems, is the reason for our existence. Elsewhere he has
written:

> Nature is not cruel, only pitilessly indifferent. This is one of the hardest lessons
> for humans to learn. We cannot admit that things might be neither good nor evil,
> neither cruel nor kind, but simply callous – indifferent to all suffering, lacking all
> purpose.[13]

So from an objective point of view, it is clear that Dawkins's atheism has no
room for either purpose or value, even if we have subjective feelings or attitudes about such things.

The subjective nature of Dawkins's discussion becomes more obvious
when he turns his attention from consolation to inspiration. He writes, 'This
is a matter of taste or private judgment, which has the slightly unfortunate
effect that the method of argument I must employ is rhetoric rather than
logic.'[14] His rhetoric is extremely good and those of us who have had the
privilege of working in science and many who have not will agree with him
that science has given us astonishing and inspiring insights into what the
world is like. Hitchens makes a similar appeal to science. After reassuring us
that atheists 'do not wish to deprive humanity of its wonders or consolations',
he writes:

If you will devote a little time to studying the staggering photographs taken by the Hubble telescope, you will be scrutinizing things that are far more awesome and mysterious and beautiful – and more chaotic and overwhelming and forbidding – than any creation or 'end of days' story.[15]

Harris makes the same point:

This universe is shot through with mystery. The very fact of its being, and of our own, is a mystery absolute, and the only miracle worthy of the name. . . . No personal God need be worshipped for us to live in awe at the beauty and immensity of creation.[16]

But while Dawkins, Hitchens and Harris are quite right to highlight the remarkable understanding science has given us, this does nothing to address the issues of meaning, purpose and value.[17] Despite their impressive rhetoric – which incidentally is almost religious in nature with its emphasis on awe, mystery and beauty – if they are right, we are cosmic accidents, the unplanned result of unguided processes. The French biologist and Nobel Prize-winner Jacques Monod expressed the idea clearly: 'man knows at last that he is alone in the universe's unfeeling immensity, out of which he emerged only by chance'.[18]

Life without God

If we really are the accidental by-products of natural processes, then there is no ultimate purpose to our existence. This does not mean that we cannot have a purpose of any kind. Clearly, we can set certain goals for ourselves in life and this might give us a subjective sense of purpose, but this is very different from there being a higher and objective purpose to our existence. It might be claimed that we can commit ourselves to some good cause such as alleviating human suffering and that this would at least provide objectivity since it is not an arbitrary purpose but is based on doing something beneficial. Essentially, the idea is that meaning and purpose can be found by doing something morally good.

The problem with this strategy is that it will provide objective meaning and purpose only if the morality on which it is based is objective in nature and, as we saw in chapter 8, the New Atheists have failed to provide an adequate foundation for objective morality. There are objective facts about how to alleviate human suffering and enhance well-being, but despite Harris's efforts, the New Atheists provide no reason to think that such actions are morally good if atheism is true. Now, of course, it *is* good to alleviate human suffering, but this presupposes the value of human life and it is very difficult to account for such value in the kind of universe envisaged by the New Atheists where we are the accidental by-product of an unguided evolutionary process.

If there is no objective purpose to our existence and no objective basis to morality, it is difficult to see how there can be any objective meaning or significance to our lives. Obviously, humans can achieve great things, but if the New Atheists are right, what objective significance is there? We would assume that someone who found a cure for a serious disease would have achieved something extremely significant, but if there is no basis for the value of human life, it would have no objective value and so no objective significance.[19] And this is all compounded by the fact that eventually humanity (and life as a whole) will die out no matter what we achieve and so ultimately the outcome is the same irrespective of what we do with our lives. It is difficult to see any ultimate significance to human existence if humanity comes into existence accidentally, lasts for a short time in the lifetime of the universe and then becomes extinct. And, of course, what is true for humanity as a whole is also true for us as individuals: whatever we do with our brief lives, our fate is death and then we 'shall rot', as Russell put it.[20]

Apparently, Dawkins is not too concerned about death. 'Being dead', he writes, 'will be no different from being unborn – I shall be just as I was in the time of William the Conqueror or the dinosaurs or the trilobites. There is nothing to fear in that.'[21] Both Dawkins and Hitchens express admiration for people like Thomas Jefferson, Thomas Paine and David Hume who seem to have had no fear of death despite not believing in an afterlife.[22] Again, there is both a subjective and an objective aspect to this. As we saw earlier, in discussing consolation Dawkins's focus is largely on the subjective aspect. Perhaps some atheists will find consolation in Dawkins's remarks to enable them to face death without fear, but no doubt others will not find them very helpful at all. The real issue is whether death, and our subsequent non-existence if atheism is true, has any implications for whether there is an objective basis for the meaning and significance of our lives. Harris certainly thinks so. He writes:

> Not only are you bound to die and leave this world; you are bound to leave it in such a precipitate fashion that the present significance of anything – your relationships, your plans for the future, your hobbies, your possessions – will appear to have been totally illusory. While all such things, when projected across an indefinite future, seem to be acquisitions of a kind, death proves that they are nothing of the sort. When the stopper on this life is pulled by an unseen hand, there will have been, in the final reckoning, no acquisition of anything at all.[23]

In fact, Harris claims that 'the fact of death is intolerable to us'.[24] As we shall see shortly, he thinks that faith is just a means of escaping from this fact, but considers it to be a fact nevertheless. In the light of this, where does Harris think meaning and significance are to be found? Surprisingly, he thinks the answer is found in human experiences that

> can be appropriately described as 'spiritual' or 'mystical' – experiences of the
> meaningfulness, selflessness, and heightened emotion that surpass our narrow
> identities as 'selves' and escape our current understanding of the mind and brain.[25]

He adopts an Eastern approach to spirituality, which he distinguishes from religion because he claims that there are empirical reasons for accepting an Eastern approach and no reasons for accepting the claims of any religion. He places a lot of emphasis on meditation, a practice which he thinks can enable us to see that the self is an illusion.[26] He is not denying that consciousness exists, but appears to be saying that there is a single consciousness and that we are not really 'separate from the rest of the universe'.[27] Rather less surprisingly, the other New Atheists have little time for this sort of thing and Hitchens is just as scathing in his criticisms of Eastern as of Western spirituality.[28]

Does Harris's spirituality provide an objective basis for meaning? There are a number of problems with his account. First, it still provides no ultimate purpose for our existence. Harris presumably believes we are the accidental by-products of unguided processes. Secondly, as we saw in chapter 8, Harris's view fails to provide an adequate foundation for an objective morality. Thirdly, he contrasts *analysing* the world in terms of concepts (which he calls 'science') with *experiencing* the world without concepts (which he calls 'mysticism').[29] The problem is that it is difficult to see here how an experience on its own could have the resources to provide objective meaning. Such experiences may well be enjoyable and even transformative, as Harris claims, but that would at best account for a subjective sense of meaning. Finally, to the extent that Harris can address any of these issues, it appears to require a move well beyond the straightforward atheism of his fellow New Atheists.

It is not just theists who have claimed that atheism provides no objective basis for meaning, purpose and value. In his book *God and the New Atheism*, theologian John Haught contrasts what he calls the *soft-core atheism* of the New Atheists with the *hard-core atheism* of Nietzsche, Camus and Sartre. According to hard-core atheism, denying the existence of God leads to nihilism, the view that life is meaningless and that nothing is really of value. Haught claims that the New Atheists are being inconsistent in not following their atheism through to its logical conclusion. His point is that they basically want to get rid of religion, but that otherwise they want life to go on more or less as normal. By contrast, he claims that the hard-core atheists would have been nauseated by this attitude because they 'understood that if we are truly sincere in our atheism the whole web of meanings and values that had clustered around the idea of God in Western culture has to go down the drain along with its organizing center'.[30] He even claims that

> Atheism at the least possible expense to the mediocrity of Western culture is not atheism at all . . . the new atheism, when measured against the stringent demands of a truly thoroughgoing unbelief, would be exposed as different only superficially from the traditional theism it wants to replace.[31]

It is the views of the hard-core atheists that philosopher William Lane Craig has in mind when he writes:

> Modern man thought that when he had gotten rid of God, he had freed himself from all that repressed and stifled him. Instead, he discovered that in killing God, he had only succeeded in orphaning himself.
> For if there is no God, then man's life becomes absurd.[32]

The New Atheists certainly provide no objective basis for meaning and purpose in life. Dawkins writes that 'our life is as meaningful, as full and as wonderful as we choose to make it. And we can make if very wonderful indeed.'[33] The problem is that he is clearly talking about a *subjective* meaning we can give to our lives, but this is not in question. The real question for the New Atheists is whether there is an objective meaning. Later he adds, 'If the demise of God will leave a gap, different people will fill it in different ways. My way includes a good dose of science, the honest and systematic endeavour to find out the truth about the real world.'[34] Again, the subjective nature of his viewpoint is clear. If theists and hard-core atheists, who believe that the demise of God does leave a gap, are right, it cannot be filled by science because science, wonderful as it is, is incapable of providing a basis for meaning, purpose or value.

Life with God

The New Atheists have a response to the idea that their atheism renders life meaningless: perhaps religious belief is an attempt to escape the unpalatable truth that life *is* meaningless. Harris and Hitchens both claim that religious faith is a way of dealing with our fear of death. Harris writes, 'Clearly, the fact of death is intolerable to us, and faith is little more than the shadow cast by our hope for a better life beyond the grave.'[35] Dawkins expresses the idea in more general terms:

> There must be a God, the argument goes, because, if there were not, life would be empty, pointless, futile, a desert of meaninglessness and insignificance. How can it be necessary to point out that the logic falls at the first fence? Maybe life *is* empty.[36]

My intention, however, is not to argue that there must be a God because otherwise life would be meaningless. Dawkins is right that from a logical point of view one could just as easily come to the conclusion that life is meaningless. That is exactly the conclusion reached by the hard-core atheists. My point is rather that the stakes are extremely high when we consider the question of God's existence. It cannot be a purely intellectual matter, but has consequences for our lives: for where we find meaning, for what we consider to be worthwhile, and for whether there is any purpose to our existence or not. As C. S. Lewis put it, 'Christianity is a statement which, if false, is of *no* importance, and, if true, of infinite importance. The one thing it cannot be is moderately important.'[37]

What are we to do if we conclude that God's existence is unlikely, but also conclude that without God life is meaningless? One option would be to grant that life is meaningless from an objective point of view, but note that there are plenty of things that make life subjectively satisfying. If that is all there is to life, however, it is difficult to see what the problem is with someone who just opts for a life of selfishness with the attitude 'let us eat and drink for tomorrow we die'.

Another option might be to *pretend* that life is meaningful and live as if real values exist. But as the philosopher J. P. Moreland points out, this would be to 'live one's life in a self-induced delusion . . . Life would be a placebo effect.'[38] Is it possible to live a life consistent with the belief that everything is meaningless? In other words, is it possible to be a truly consistent nihilist? Haught thinks it isn't. He points out that the hard-core atheists failed to live out their atheism consistently. In their case the problem was that there was a conflict between what they believed to be true and living a meaningful life. In such a scenario something has to give. It seems to me that a problem for the New Atheists is that they are in such a scenario even though they may not realize it. Consider again Dawkins's remarks about facing up to reality no matter how depressing it might seem:

There is more than just grandeur in this view of life, bleak and cold though it can
seem from under the security blanket of ignorance. There is a deep refreshment to be
had from standing up and facing straight into the strong keen wind of understanding:
Yeats's 'Winds that blow through the starry ways'.[39]

This is not so much a basis for meaning as an acceptance of the fact that
there is none. What Dawkins finds refreshing is the challenge of facing up
to the fact that there is no meaning. But if that is the case, then like the hard-
core atheists, he confronts a conflict between living a meaningful life and yet
believing that there is no objective basis for it.

By contrast, if Christian theism is true, then no such conflict exists. As
argued in chapter 8, the existence of God provides an objective basis for
moral values since they can be grounded in the very character of God himself.
There is a purpose for our existence, which is to know God, the very source
of goodness and love, and to live in accordance with his will, which has many
dimensions, including our responsibilities to other people. Our lives have significance because we have been made in the image of God and so we are not
the accidental by-products of unguided natural processes. This significance
extends to all areas of our lives since God calls us to respond to him and live
according to his purposes for us. This means that the choices we make about
what we do with our lives, how we spend our time, how we treat people and
what we value, to give just some examples, are truly and objectively significant.
They also have eternal significance since there is life after death. This eternal
dimension is extremely important because it means that there is a basis for
hope even in seemingly hopeless situations, including in the face of death. All
of this stands in stark contrast to the New Atheism, according to which there
is no purpose for our existence, no reason to think that our lives have objective meaning and even the subjective meaning we can find in life comes to an
inevitable end in death.

Many atheists will agree that Christian theism has all the resources needed
to give our lives meaning, or, rather, it would have if only it were true. If it
seems too good to be true, they will claim that this is because it isn't true.
Some will claim that it is just wishful thinking to believe that it is; but far from
being wishful thinking, I have been arguing throughout the book that there
are strong reasons for believing that Christian theism is in fact true. As well as
considering various objections raised by the New Atheists, we have considered
evidence for Christian theism. In chapters 4 and 5 we considered the existence
of the universe, the beginning of the universe, the order expressed in the laws
of nature, the fine-tuning of the physical constants and the existence of conscious minds as evidence for theism. The idea was that each of these features

of the universe is explained much better by theism than by atheism, and so they constitute strong evidence in favour of theism. In chapter 6, we evaluated Dawkins's claim to have shown that God almost certainly does not exist, but we saw that his argument fails for multiple reasons.

The relevance of morality for belief in God was discussed in chapter 8. I argued that the existence of God provides a much better foundation for morality than do atheistic accounts such as that proposed by Harris, and so morality provides a further reason for theism. We also looked at the problem of evil in chapter 8. This is without doubt the main objection to theism, but we saw that various responses can be offered and that even if evil counts against theism to some extent, there are reasons to believe that the *overall* case for theism, based on all the evidence, is good.

In addition to evidence for theism we also investigated the case for the central claims of Christianity. In particular, in chapter 10 we looked at evidence relating to the life, death and resurrection of Jesus of Nazareth. The New Atheists have made no attempt to deal with any of the material on this topic seriously and have adopted a position of extreme, unfounded scepticism towards the historical evidence for Jesus. In reality, the evidence relating to Jesus is much stronger than the New Atheists realize, and this includes evidence relevant to assessing the case for the resurrection. We saw that this evidence is much better explained by the resurrection hypothesis than by naturalistic explanations, and so it counts strongly in favour of the resurrection.

The New Atheists would be very dismissive of any such claim about a miracle, but arguably that is because they are already convinced that there is no God; it is certainly not because of their evaluation of the evidence in this case. However, if there is no convincing reason to reject theism, the evidence for the resurrection should be taken seriously. Indeed, since there is good evidence for theism, this makes the case for the resurrection even stronger. Overall, I have argued that there is a strong case not just for theism, but for Christian theism.

In conclusion, it must be emphasized that there is a difference between believing Christian theism to be true and being a Christian since the latter requires a response to God. It is only the latter that enables true meaning in life to be found. This is where faith comes into the picture. As pointed out in chapter 2, faith is not believing something without evidence, but consists in trusting God. We saw in chapter 9 that there is a moral gap between how we ought to live and how we actually live. But God has bridged the gap through the life, death and resurrection of his Son and by trusting in what he has done we can enter into the kind of life God calls us to, which is the very purpose of our existence. Since there are good reasons to believe that Christian theism is true, there is no conflict between truth on the one hand and meaning and purpose on the other. We can know the truth and the truth will set us free (John 8:32).

Notes

1. *BTS*, p. 286.
2. Ibid., emphasis in original.
3. We came across the same idea in chapter 8 when discussing objective morality.
4. Of course, it might still give its followers a subjective sense of meaning.
5. *BTS*, p. 291.
6. Ibid., emphasis in original.
7. Ibid., emphasis in original.
8. Ibid., p. 292.
9. *TGD*, p. 355.
10. Ibid.
11. Richard Dawkins, *The Blind Watchmaker* (London: Penguin, 1986), p. 21.
12. Ibid., p. 126.
13. Richard Dawkins, *River out of Eden: A Darwinian View of Life* (London: Phoenix, 1995), p. 112.
14. *TGD*, pp. 360–361.
15. *GNG*, p. 8.
16. *TEF*, p. 227.
17. In focusing on meaning, purpose and value, I am following William Lane Craig, *Reasonable Faith: Christian Truth and Apologetics*, 3rd ed. (Wheaton, Ill.: Crossway, 2008), pp. 65–90.
18. Jacques Monod, *Chance and Necessity*, tr. Austryn Wainhouse (London: Penguin, 1997), p. 180.
19. Would it not have an objective significance for all the people who benefit? The problem here is that if there is no basis for the value of human life, it would have only a subjective significance for each person.
20. For further discussion on these points, see for example Craig, *Reasonable Faith*, pp. 65–90; and J. P. Moreland, *Scaling the Secular City: A Defence of Christianity* (Grand Rapids: Baker, 1987), pp. 105–132.
21. *TGD*, p. 357.
22. *TGD*, p. 354; *GNG*, pp. 268–269.
23. *TEF*, p. 37.
24. Ibid., p. 39.
25. Ibid., pp. 39–40.

26. Ibid., pp. 217–220.
27. Ibid., p. 40.
28. *GNG*, pp. 195–204.
29. *TEF*, p. 221.
30. John Haught, *God and the New Atheism: A Critical Response to Dawkins, Harris and Hitchens* (Louisville, Ky.: Westminster John Knox, 2008), p. 22.
31. Ibid., p. 21.
32. Craig, *Reasonable Faith*, p. 71.
33. *TGD*, p. 360.
34. Ibid., p. 361.
35. *TEF*, p. 39. See also *GNG*, p. 103.
36. *TGD*, p. 360, emphasis in original.
37. C. S. Lewis, 'Christian Apologetics', in *Timeless at Heart* (London: Fount, 1987), p. 28, emphasis in original.
38. Moreland, *Scaling the Secular City*, p. 121.
39. *TGD*, p. 355.

INDEX OF NAMES

INDEX OF SUBJECTS